Meaning, Mortality, and Choice

MEANING, MORTALITY, AND CHOICE

The Social Psychology of Existential Concerns

Edited by Phillip R. Shaver and Mario Mikulincer

American Psychological Association • Washington, DC

Published by
American Psychological Association
750 First Street, NE
Washington, DC 20002
www.apa.org

To order
APA Order Department
P.O. Box 92984
Washington, DC 20090-2984
Tel: (800) 374-2721; Direct: (202) 336-5510
Fax: (202) 336-5502; TDD/TTY: (202) 336-6123
Online: www.apa.org/pubs/books
E-mail: order@apa.org

In the U.K., Europe, Africa, and the Middle East, copies may be ordered from
American Psychological Association
3 Henrietta Street
Covent Garden, London
WC2E 8LU England

Typeset in Goudy by Circle Graphics, Inc., Columbia, MD

Printer: Edwards Brothers, Inc., Ann Arbor, MI
Cover Designer: Mercury Publishing Services, Inc., Rockville, MD
Cover Art: Edward Hopper (American, 1882–1967), Automat, 1927, oil on canvas; 36 × 28⅛ in. (91.4 × 71.4 cm.), Des Moines Art Center Permanent Collections; Purchased with funds from the Edmundson Art Foundation, Inc., 1958.2

The opinions and statements published are the responsibility of the authors, and such opinions and statements do not necessarily represent the policies of the American Psychological Association.

Library of Congress Cataloging-in-Publication Data

Meaning, mortality, and choice : the social psychology of existential concerns / edited by Phillip R. Shaver and Mario Mikulincer.
    p. cm.
  Includes bibliographical references and index.
  ISBN 978-1-4338-1155-5 (alk. paper) — ISBN 1-4338-1155-3 (alk. paper) 1. Existential psychology. I. Shaver, Phillip R. II. Mikulincer, Mario.
  BF204.5.M43 2012
  150.19'2—dc23
                            2012001149

British Library Cataloguing-in-Publication Data
A CIP record is available from the British Library.

Printed in the United States of America
First Edition

DOI: 10.1037/13748-000

THE HERZLIYA SERIES ON PERSONALITY
AND SOCIAL PSYCHOLOGY

Mario Mikulincer and Phillip R. Shaver, Series Editors

Series Titles

Prosocial Motives, Emotions, and Behavior: The Better Angels of Our Nature
   Edited by Mario Mikulincer and Phillip R. Shaver

Human Aggression and Violence: Causes, Manifestations, and Consequences
   Edited by Phillip R. Shaver and Mario Mikulincer

The Social Psychology of Morality: Exploring the Causes of Good and Evil
   Edited by Mario Mikulincer and Phillip R. Shaver

Meaning, Mortality, and Choice: The Social Psychology of Existential Concerns
   Edited by Phillip R. Shaver and Mario Mikulincer

CONTENTS

CONTRIBUTORS

Jamie Arndt, PhD, Department of Psychological Sciences, University of Missouri, Columbia

Avi Assor, PhD, School of Education, Ben-Gurion University, Beer-Sheva, Israel

Noa Bigman, MA, Department of Psychology, The Hebrew University of Jerusalem, Jerusalem, Israel

Edward L. Deci, PhD, Department of Clinical and Social Sciences in Psychology, University of Rochester, Rochester, NY

Donald Edmondson, PhD, Columbia University Medical Center, New York, NY

Lisa Firestone, PhD, The Glendon Association, Santa Barbara, CA

Robert W. Firestone, PhD, The Glendon Association, Santa Barbara, CA

Michele Gelfand, PhD, Department of Psychology, University of Maryland, College Park

Jamie L. Goldenberg, PhD, Department of Psychology, University of South Florida, Tampa

Jeff Greenberg, PhD, Department of Psychology, University of Arizona, Tucson

Rohan Gunaratna, PhD, Nanyang Technological University, Singapore

Gilad Hirschberger, PhD, School of Psychology, Interdisciplinary Center (IDC) Herzliya, Herzliya, Israel

Thomas E. Joiner Jr., PhD, Department of Psychology, Florida State University, Tallahassee

Yaniv Kanat-Maymon, PhD, School of Psychology, Interdisciplinary Center (IDC) Herzliya, Herzliya, Israel

Rachel Kaplan Milgram, PhD candidate, School of Philosophy, Tel Aviv University, Tel Aviv, Israel

Lucas A. Keefer, MA, Department of Psychology, University of Kansas, Lawrence

Pelin Kesebir, PhD, Department of Psychology, University of Colorado at Colorado Springs

Laura A. King, PhD, Department of Psychology, University of Missouri, Columbia

Arie W. Kruglanski, PhD, Department of Psychology, University of Maryland, College Park

Mark J. Landau, PhD, Department of Psychology, University of Kansas, Lawrence

Nicole Legate, MA, Department of Clinical and Social Sciences in Psychology, University of Rochester, Rochester, NY

Nava Levit Binnun, PhD, School of Psychology, Interdisciplinary Center (IDC) Herzliya, Herzliya, Israel

Mario Mikulincer, PhD, School of Psychology, Interdisciplinary Center (IDC) Herzliya, Herzliya, Israel

Christopher P. Niemiec, PhD, Department of Clinical and Social Sciences in Psychology, University of Rochester, Rochester, NY

Crystal L. Park, PhD, Department of Psychology, University of Connecticut, Storrs

Tom Pyszczynski, PhD, Department of Psychology, University of Colorado at Colorado Springs

Jacob Raz, PhD, Department of East Asian Studies, Tel Aviv University, Tel Aviv, Israel

Abira Reizer, PhD, Department of Psychology, Ariel University Center of Samaria, Ariel, Israel

Guy Roth, PhD, School of Education, Ben-Gurion University, Beer-Sheva, Israel

Zachary K. Rothschild, MA, Department of Psychology, University of Kansas, Lawrence

Richard M. Ryan, PhD, Department of Clinical and Social Sciences in Psychology, University of Rochester, Rochester, NY

Kirk J. Schneider, PhD, Saybrook University and The Existential–Humanistic Institute, San Francisco, CA

Barry Schwartz, PhD, Department of Psychology, Swarthmore College, Swarthmore, PA

Dan Shaham, MA, Department of Psychology, Bar-Ilan University, Ramat Gan, Israel

Phillip R. Shaver, PhD, Department of Psychology, University of California, Davis

Caroline Silva, BA, Department of Psychology, Florida State University, Tallahassee

Sheldon Solomon, PhD, Department of Psychology, Skidmore College, Saratoga Springs, NY

Daniel Sullivan, MA, Department of Psychology, University of Kansas, Lawrence

Orit Taubman – Ben-Ari, PhD, School of Social Work, Bar-Ilan University, Ramat Gan, Israel

Kipling D. Williams, PhD, Department of Psychological Sciences, Purdue University, West Lafayette, IN

Iftah Yovel, PhD, Department of Psychology, The Hebrew University of Jerusalem, Jerusalem, Israel

PREFACE

Why are human beings so afraid of death? How does our awareness of mortality affect our goals, attitudes, defenses, and behavior? How do we make sense of a life plagued by threats, change, confusion, and doubt? How do we retain confidence in our freedom and autonomy in the face of growing evidence that every thought and move is programmed or constrained by layers of causality, from neurons to cultures? How desirable are freedom and autonomy, in any case, when modern life offers so many—perhaps too many—options, products, pursuits, and lifestyles? What is a healthy balance between social entanglements and social isolation? Such questions weigh heavily on contemporary human beings, causing some to despair and a considerable number to use drugs, illegal or legally prescribed, to blunt the misery. A few even decide to end their lives.

These are basic human questions and issues concerning mortality, meaning, choice, and social engagement. They have bothered people for eons, as indicated by ancient poetry, dramas, artworks, and rituals. In modern times, they have spawned existential philosophies (e.g., those of Nietzsche, Heidegger, and Sartre) and related personality theories and approaches to psychotherapy (e.g., Biswanger, Boss, Fromm, Horney, Rank, Yalom). Within the contemporary field of personality and social psychology, existential concerns have received considerable attention and have inspired generative theories (e.g., terror management theory, self-determination theory, aspects of attachment theory, Buddhist psychology, positive psychology). These theoretical ventures have generated a large and still growing body of creative research.

In the first three volumes of the Herzliya Series on Personality and Social Psychology, we focused, first, on prosocial motives, emotions, and behavior; then on aggression, violence, and their effects; and most recently on morality ("good and evil"). In this, the fourth volume, we deepen our analysis of human behavior by examining ways in which people deal with four key existential concerns: mortality, meaning, freedom, and social isolation. We are especially interested in how people's ways of coping with these concerns are affected by internal psychological and external social and cultural forces, and how effective coping strategies can be encouraged by parents, therapists, and social institutions.

This volume contains 22 chapters organized around the four existential concerns. The first four sections, one on each concern, are devoted to state-of-the-art personality and social theories and research. The fifth section addresses ways of personally understanding and coping with existential threats.

The chapter authors, all acknowledged experts in their fields, generously agreed to come to Herzliya and deliver lectures in the 2011 Herzliya Symposium on Personality and Social Psychology, participate in hours of discussion of the lectures, and then return home and prepare chapters based on the lectures and discussions. The meeting was cohosted by the two of us, and we worked with the chapter authors to make the resulting book as accessible, coherent, and readable as possible, so it would be suitable for researchers and application-oriented professionals as well as university classes and the educated public. The book provides a highly readable and up-to-date review of new social–psychological and clinical approaches to issues in existential psychology. It includes chapters on death anxiety; the threat of meaninglessness; the challenges of freedom, autonomy, and choice; the pain of social rejection and isolation; ways in which people cope with these concerns; the harmful consequences of certain coping strategies; and therapeutic practices that promote effective coping.

We are grateful to everyone who made the preparation of this book enjoyable and successful. We thank all of the chapter authors—an amazing group of scholars and admirable human beings who care about both their sciences and the betterment of human existence. We especially wish to thank Professor Uriel Reichmann, president of the Interdisciplinary Center Herzliya, who provided financial and staff support for an annual series of conferences on personality and social psychology. We thank the staff of the Interdisciplinary Center Herzliya—Keren Mifano, Tammy Berger, Shulli Sardes, and Tsachi Ein-Dor—who handled all of the arrangements for the conference, dealt effectively with the many on-site details, and coped masterfully with the inevitable glitches and emergencies. We would also like to thank Maureen Adams, senior acquisitions editor at American Psychological Association (APA) Books, for seeing the value of this book and the series in which it appears and for being a generous, thoughtful, and supportive friend during this book's preparation. Finally, we express our appreciation to the members of the APA Books team, particularly Elizabeth Brace, Tyler Aune, Erin O'Brien, and Ron Teeter, and to an anonymous academic reviewer who made many helpful suggestions.

Phillip R. Shaver, PhD
University of California, Davis

Mario Mikulincer, PhD
Interdisciplinary Center, Herzliya, Israel

Meaning, Mortality, and Choice

INTRODUCTION

PHILLIP R. SHAVER AND MARIO MIKULINCER

In a classic book on existential psychotherapy, Irvin Yalom (1980) described four key "givens of existence": the problem of death and finitude, the threat of meaninglessness, the challenge of freedom, and the pain of existential isolation. Given everyone's personal familiarity with these issues in the 21st century, one might expect them to occupy center stage in personality, social, and clinical psychology. In fact, however, the field of social and personality psychology has concerned itself mainly with smaller issues and phenomena—attributions, attitudes, prejudice, self-esteem, conformity, cognitive consistency—derived from intuition and informal observation rather than a larger theoretical framework. And although clinical psychology has always included existential and humanistic strains, as indicated in Yalom's book, the research base of clinical psychology has come primarily from major trends in academic psychology, such as psychodynamic personality theories, behavioristic theories of learning, and research on basic cognitive processes, such as perception and memory.

Fortunately, in recent years several theories and associated research methods have been devised by social–personality psychologists to tackle larger existential concerns and to place ad hoc constructs such as self-esteem into larger conceptual frameworks: terror management theory (TMT; Greenberg, Chapter 1, this volume), self-determination theory (Ryan, Legate, Niemiec, & Deci, Chapter 12, this volume), and attachment theory (Shaver & Mikulincer, Chapter 16, this volume). To date, these theories have rarely been included in a single conversation or published anthology, and their connections with contemporary approaches to psychotherapy are only beginning to be considered. The present volume is intended to provide resources for a broader psychology of human concerns that links social, personality, developmental, and clinical psychology.

THE HISTORICAL CONTEXT OF RESEARCH ON EXISTENTIAL CONCERNS

When one begins to tackle the larger problems of human existence, one is necessarily confronted with the amorphous body of writing loosely organized under the heading *existential philosophy* or *existentialism*. The term *existentialism* was embraced in the 1940s and 1950s by the philosopher Jean-Paul Sartre and his French associates (e.g., de Beauvoir, Merleau-Ponty, Camus). It was based in part on German writings by Karl Jaspers, Martin Heidegger, and Martin Buber, although Heidegger explicitly rejected the claim that he was an existentialist. Eventually, as philosophers and literary scholars attempted to characterize and systematically evaluate existentialism (e.g., Blackham, 1983; Camus, 1991; Wartenberg, 2008), it was seen to have earlier roots in the 19th century writings of Kierkegaard, Nietzsche, Dostoevsky, Ibsen, and Kafka, among others, and to have influenced not only philosophy but also theology (in the writings of Bultmann, Tillich, Barth, and others), psychology (e.g., Binswanger, Boss, Rank, Frankl, May, Laing, Yalom), and anthropology (Becker).

With the benefit of hindsight, we can see that existentialism was partly a reaction to threats to personal religious beliefs and experiences and to traditional cultures posed by rationalist philosophies such as Hegel's, by mechanistic-seeming science, and by large-scale industrialization, the rise of large cities and bureaucracies, and the increasing scale, mechanization, and brutality of warfare. Religious conceptions of the meaning of life were challenged, for example, by Darwin's theory of evolution and the first mechanistic conceptions of the body and mind. Large-scale mechanized wars challenged Europeans' sense that individual lives had meaning and sacred value. Existentialist writings in philosophy, literature, and psychology were attempts both to characterize the subjective experience (phenomenology) of individuals attempting to find meaning and make choices in a potentially meaningless world, and to propose attitudes, values, and strategies for coping with the new threats to human significance. The emphasis in philosophical discussions of ethics and morality changed from what religious traditions had said was right and wrong according to God to concepts such as authenticity, courage, choice, and "bad faith" (the existentialists' equivalent of sin). Writers such as Camus (1991) tried to make a case against committing suicide even if life's struggles were similar to the mythic Sisyphus's rolling a huge rock up a hill and watching it roll back down, time after time.

The effect of philosophical existentialism on psychology has been to encourage various phenomenological, humanistic, and nonmechanistic alternatives to therapies based on basic scientific theories that, implicitly at least, characterize human beings as biochemical machines programmed by social forces. Just as existentialism itself was a challenge to rationalist and mechanistic themes in previous philosophical traditions, existential psychotherapy has often been viewed as a challenge to mainstream clinical theories based on concepts such as mental "illness," distorted cognitive "structures," and dysfunctional neurochemical processes.

The present volume takes up the challenge of tackling existential themes and concerns with scientific methods. We and the other chapter authors acknowledge the importance of the concerns highlighted by existential philosophers and psychologists: mortality, meaninglessness, freedom of choice, and the pain of existential isolation (creating a life that is ultimately one's own responsibility). We disagree with many past existentialist writers who thought that facing existential conundrums required a rejection of scientific methods. We propose to look mortality, meaning, choice, and individual responsibility directly in the face and attempt to understand them more fully by applying contemporary scientific and clinical methods.

OVERVIEW OF THE VOLUME

Our goal in hosting a conference on contemporary scientific approaches to existential concerns was to provide an opportunity for lively discussion among major proponents of theories, research programs, and psychotherapies related to concerns with mortality, meaning, choice, and social isolation. The book is organized around these four existential challenges. The first section includes six chapters on the problem of death and the ways in which people cope with death anxiety. The second section includes five chapters on finding meaning in life, and the effects of different meaning-making strategies on psychological functioning and social behavior. The third section includes four chapters on the challenges of freedom and choice, highlighting the human capacity to act autonomously, the potential constraints on freedom imposed by the nature of the brain and sociocultural forces, and the modern problem of having too many options among which to choose. The fourth section includes three chapters on the pain of social isolation and the ways in which relational closeness can buffer a person against frightening existential concerns. The fifth section includes three chapters describing therapeutic approaches for dealing with the threats and challenges of the givens of existence. In the final chapter, Sheldon Solomon, one of the originators of TMT, a now well-researched theory of coping with mortality, provides an integrative overview of the conference on which the book is based and on the preceding chapters in the book.

Anxiety Concerning Finitude and Death

The first section of the book is devoted to psychological reactions to finitude and death. In Chapter 1, Jeff Greenberg presents the most recent version of TMT. According to TMT, (a) human beings' awareness of their mortality—a unique anomaly in the animal kingdom—creates an ever-present threat of experiencing terror, and (b) this threat is countered by attempts to maintain self-esteem within the framework of a cultural worldview. People remain fairly secure as long as they have faith in their worldview and are functioning successfully within it. In his chapter, Greenberg explains the origin and roots of TMT in Ernest Becker's (1973) book *The Denial of Death*, and he summarizes TMT's main hypotheses, recent elaborations, and main empirical findings. He includes a discussion of recent research on brain activation patterns associated with terror management and of the theory's implications for emotional disorders, aging, supernatural fantasies, and the desire for fame.

In Chapter 2, Mario Mikulincer and Phillip R. Shaver deal further with the question of why, exactly, death is so terrifying. We review theory and research concerning the meanings people assign to their mortality and the strategies they use to manage death concerns. We then argue that helplessness is an important feature of death and dying that adds to its fearsomeness. Death awareness arouses strong fears of helplessness and powerlessness, and when terror management defenses against death awareness fail or are weak, the threat of utter helplessness is part of what arouses terror. We present new research showing that feelings of helplessness and helplessness-related behavioral deficits arise when terror management mechanisms (e.g., cultural worldviews, self-esteem, close relationships) are interfered with.

In Chapter 3, Jamie Arndt explains, in terms of TMT, why people need self-esteem, and he reviews research showing that self-esteem is a means by which people protect themselves from awareness of their mortality. Arndt also reviews recent research showing that terror-management processes sometimes result in paradoxically risky behavior that actually makes death more likely. The chapter concludes by identifying issues ripe for further research on the intersection of self-esteem with other forms of existential defense, such as close relationships and adherence to cultural worldviews.

In Chapter 4, Tom Pyszczynski and Pelin Kesebir discuss the terror management functions served by religion, ethnicity, and political ideologies, showing how they relate to each other and explaining the role they play in war and other lethal conflicts. The authors show how culture, ideology, morality, and religion are affected by awareness of mortality, and they review recent research showing how reminders of death alter a person's cultural, moral, religious, and ideological convictions. Pyszczynski and Kesebir also rebut recent attempts to attribute terror-management effects on cultural worldviews to alternative threats, such as meaningless and uncertainty. They argue, and present data showing, that death awareness is a unique motivational force that affects reliance on culture, ideology, and religion.

In Chapter 5, Jamie L. Goldenberg presents a terror management analysis of people's attitudes toward their animal nature, as reflected in their bodies and physical sensations. Goldenberg's central thesis is that human beings are caught in a perpetual struggle between (a) the need to deny their mortality and (b) reminders that they are flesh-and-blood creatures with animalistic needs and desires, a fact that indicates they are mortal, like any other animal. Goldenberg argues that when mortality concerns are salient, people distance themselves from the physicality of their bodies by concealing their more creaturely aspects or by imbuing the physical body with symbolic significance. She reviews research testing these hypotheses and shedding light on the effects of death awareness on attitudes toward the body, discomfort with bodily functions (e.g., eating, sex), the condemnation and objectification of women's bodies, compliance with recommendations for maintaining good health, and belief in a life hereafter. This chapter exemplifies the creative value of organizing research around a powerful theory of existential concerns.

In the last chapter (Chapter 6) of the first section, all of which deals with the problem of death, Gilad Hirschberger and Dan Shaham analyze people's ambivalent attitudes toward stability and change (i.e., resistance to change vs. the sense of stagnation and decay one feels when change is absent) from a terror management perspective. They propose that both change and permanence can be experienced as existential threats. Whereas change and the progression of time remind one of life's emptying hourglass, permanence may be equally threatening because an absence of progress and rejuvenation may erode a person's conviction that mortality is being transcended. The authors explain how change can be both an existential threat and a possible remedy for the threat. They present new research examining the association between the prospect of change in three different domains (vocational, interpersonal, and political) and death-related concerns, and discuss how a terror management perspective on change may help people deal with aging and the various social and political challenges confronting modern societies.

The Threat of Meaninglessness

The second section of the book is devoted to the threat of meaninglessness and the ways in which people find meaning in their daily experiences and significance in their lives. In the first chapter of this section (Chapter 7), Laura A. King shows that meaning is often directly "sensed" despite the supposed shadow of death hanging over every human being. In contrasting social–cognitive approaches to meaning, which view it as a product of effortful, intentional cognitive processes (meaning making) often initiated by a struggle or a search following traumatic events, King presents a very different approach to meaning inspired by William James's (1890) concept of a nonsensory "fringe" of consciousness. From this perspective, meaning is a ubiquitous aspect of human experience that emerges from intuitive processes and is detected through metacognitive experiences, mental heuristics, and feelings. King presents fascinating evidence that meaning is everywhere, widely available, and routinely accessed in an effortless fashion because it is inherent in human experience. Further, she discusses the contribution of this perspective to understanding what the broader sense of meaning in life may be and how meaning can be reinstated after one's expectations have been violated by traumatic events.

In Chapter 8, Crystal L. Park and Donald Edmonson consider a particular—and nearly universal—form of meaning: the one provided by religious beliefs. The authors consider an existential function of religion (meaning restoration) that is somewhat different from the terror management function described by Pyszczynski and Kesebir in Chapter 4. Religion is clearly a path for finding meaning in life and especially for restoring meaning following traumatic events (accidents, illnesses, twists of fortune, and the loss of loved ones). The authors review research on the issue of meaning restoration through religion and raise questions for further research regarding religion as a source of meaning.

In the next chapter (Chapter 9), Orit Taubman – Ben-Ari moves away from traumatic events, existential threats, and defensive processes of meaning restoration in a further analysis of the meaning-making process. She argues that certain positive life events, such as becoming a parent or grandparent, contribute to a person's sense of meaning, perhaps for biological reasons as important as fear of death. In her view, these life transitions provide a natural opportunity to intuitively sense the meaning that emerges from the situation itself (using King's concept of meaning sensing) and to experience personal growth. Taubman – Ben-Ari reviews a recent series of studies examining the possibility of psychological growth in the wake of the transitions to parenthood and grandparenthood and identifies some of the internal and external resources that contribute to this experience.

Whereas Chapters 7 through 9 focus on positive aspects of meaning making and imply that people who experience meaning in life are well-adjusted and happy, Chapters 10 and 11 raise a red flag concerning a one-sided, overly optimistic construal of meaning making and identify two social perils that can arise during the search for meaning and significance. In Chapter 10, Mark J. Landau and coauthors explain how the search for meaning can sometimes foster scapegoating and the creation of enemies. They propose that having enemies and scapegoats allows people to attribute negative outcomes to a comprehensible and controllable source, thus adding to the sense that life is meaningful. The authors review recent studies showing that induced threats of meaninglessness increase the likelihood of treating other people as enemies or scapegoats; moreover, offering a visible enemy or scapegoat to one's perceptions of calamities leads to a restoration of the sense of meaning.

In Chapter 11, Arie W. Kruglanski and coauthors propose that the threat of meaninglessness sometimes activates a defensive, maladaptive search for meaning that can culminate in acts of political terrorism, including suicide bombing. According to this analysis, when individual methods of attaining or maintaining meaning seem insufficient, a collectivistic shift may take place in which individuals fervently embrace group causes. When a group perceives itself to be in a deadly conflict with its enemies, serving the group's causes (in the interest of bolstering meaning and significance) may require considerable personal sacrifices from individuals, including martyrdom, which bestows a grand sense of personal significance. The authors review survey research and experimental evidence suggesting that personal loss of significance leads to the adoption of group causes, that the adoption of group causes reduces one's sense of meaninglessness, and that in countries where an ideology is accessible that calls for sacrifice in defense of the group, adoption of collectivistic causes is associated with support for killing members of an enemy group or society.

The Challenge of Freedom

The third section of the volume deals with the challenge of freedom, the psychological benefits of autonomous motivation, the external and internal constraints on autonomy, and the problems that freedom of choice can paradoxically create. In Chapter 12, Richard M. Ryan and coauthors summarize self-determination theory and consider evidence related to this theory that highlights people's ability to act autonomously in accord with integrated values, and to be mindful of, and able to resist, habitual ways of acting. The authors also summarize a large body of findings showing that with a sense of autonomy, people are more successful at attaining both personal and collective goals, more prosocial and connected to others, less defensive, and more vital and alive. Of course, the authors do not deny that autonomy is challenged by outside and internal forces (a key issue in classical existential philosophy), but the limitations of a deterministic perspective become clearer when one focuses on human capacities for self-awareness, choice, and integrity. This chapter in particular shows how a far-reaching scientific approach to existential concerns can support, rather than challenge, a humanistic sense of freedom and autonomy.

In Chapter 13, Yaniv Kanat-Maymon and coauthors build on self-determination theory and analyze ways in which social contexts can interfere with desirable autonomy. They focus especially on the use of conditional positive and negative regard in the socialization of children and the treatment of adult relationship partners, which can inhibit autonomy and erode well-being. The authors review recent studies showing that both forms of conditional regard—positive as well as negative—have harmful effects on autonomous motivation, academic achievement, psychological well-being, and relationship quality.

In Chapter 14, Nava Levit Binnun and coauthors continue the analysis of potential constraints on one's sense of freedom and potential ways to remove these constraints. They move to the level of sensory and basic cognitive processing and show that mindfulness practices rooted in Buddhism can remove sensory and cognitive constraints and facilitate autonomous behavior. They apply insights from occupational therapy as well as Buddhist psychology, showing how differences in the "tuning" of sensory systems constrain one's choices and decisions. They use insights from neuroscience to explain how mindfulness practices may increase one's actual and perceived personal freedom and remove constraints on personal choices.

In closing this section, Barry Schwartz (Chapter 15) warns against a one-sided, positive view of choice and freedom, which was more or less assumed in the other three chapters in this section. Schwartz reviews research showing that when people have too many options, they become paralyzed and disappointed rather than liberated. Thus, although choice is a necessary part of freedom, it is not sufficient for a positive sense of freedom. Too many options, in too many life domains, can turn people into passive "pickers" rather than active "choosers," and the proliferation of options can erode a person's sense of self-definition and turn the task of self-definition over to local culture. Schwartz reviews research findings concerning possible mechanisms by which choice overload drives a wedge between choice and freedom, so that more of the former results in less of the latter. Schwartz also discusses the kinds of constraints that enable people to reconnect choice with freedom and autonomy.

The Pain of Social Isolation

In opening the fourth section of the book, Phillip R. Shaver and Mario Mikulincer present a theoretical analysis derived from attachment theory suggesting that the provision of a sense of safety and security in close relationships not only eases worries about rejection and isolation but also allows people to experience an authentic sense of continuity, coherence, meaning, and autonomy. In other words, security, anchored in loving relationships, mitigates the existential concerns reviewed elsewhere in this volume. On the basis of an extensive review of empirical research, the authors show that worries about finitude, isolation, meaninglessness, and lack of freedom automatically activate desires for proximity to intimates, and the availability of a loving and supportive external or internalized attachment figure (e.g., parent, lover, sibling, therapist, or religious figure) buffers a person effectively against the four core existential threats explored by other chapter authors. This is a scientific conclusion that flies in the face of Sartre's famous claim in his play *No Exit* that "hell is other people" because their views place constraints on one's ability to define oneself.

In Chapter 17, Kipling D. Williams analyzes the pain of social exclusion and ostracism in terms of his temporal need–threat model. For the purposes of this book, he focuses especially on research pertinent to feelings of meaninglessness, research that shows that being ostracized, even in brief and seemingly minor ways, elicits temporary feelings of invisibility along with a painful sense of having no worth, purpose, or meaning. This research also shows that, unlike other aversive interpersonal behaviors, ostracism can uniquely threaten existential needs related to being recognized as existing and being worthy of attention. Links between ostracism and vulnerability to group influence and aggression are also discussed. Williams's penetrating analysis and creative research suggests that "hell is other people" mainly when those people exclude one from joint meaningful relationships and activities.

In closing this section, Thomas E. Joiner Jr. and Caroline Silva (Chapter 18) eloquently illustrate how the pain of existential isolation can sometimes lead to suicide. Their interpersonal-psychological theory of suicidal behavior highlights three factors that characterize individuals most at risk of suicide: feeling that one is a burden on loved ones; feeling isolated; and, perhaps most chillingly, having learned to tolerate pain and injury. The authors present convincing evidence that their theory is compatible with diverse evidence from clinical anecdotes, history, literary fiction, popular culture, anthropology, epidemiology, genetics, and neurobiology: facts concerning suicide rates of men and women; White and African American men; anorexics, athletes, prostitutes, and physicians; and members of cults, sports fans, and citizens of nations in crisis.

Overcoming Existential Threats and Challenges

The final section of the book focuses on therapeutic approaches that help people cope with existential concerns and reduce defensiveness, psychological stagnation, violence, and psychopathology. In Chapter 19, Kirk J. Schneider, coauthor of a recent book on existential psychotherapy (Schneider & Krug, 2009), presents a clinical case that illustrates this approach and, in the process, shows how social psychological findings reviewed throughout this volume can transform existential threats into opportunities for personal growth. Schneider specifically focuses on the sense of "groundlessness" that is purported to underlie death anxiety and the ability to stay present with one's most turbulent fears and find meaning, even awe, in life. His case example penetrates below the surface of many of the laboratory studies reviewed by the other authors and shows how courage, imagination, and communication within a therapeutic relationship can allow a person to remain open and fully present even in the face of frightening, but also beautiful, experiences and insights.

In Chapter 20, Robert W. and Lisa Firestone discuss separation theory and voice therapy, perspectives that integrate psychoanalytic and existential systems of thought. Separation theory explains how early trauma leads to defense and how early defenses are reinforced as a developing child becomes aware of his or her mortality. Voice therapy helps clients identify and free themselves from "fantasy bonds" and destructive "critical voices" rooted in past dysfunctional attachment relationships. Whereas the fantasy bond, an illusion of connection with another person, is the primary defense against both interpersonal and existential pain, the critical inner voice can be conceptualized as a secondary line of defense. This chapter shows how a person's vitality and zest for life can be sapped by internalizing experiences in relationships that undermine autonomy and self-esteem. In that way, the chapter adds to social psychological studies reviewed in previous chapters dealing with meaning, autonomy, conditional regard, the potential for corrective experiences, and personal growth.

In the last chapter of this section, Iftah Yovel and Noa Bigman (Chapter 21) focus on acceptance and commitment therapy (ACT), an evidence-based treatment for unwanted subjective experiences (e.g., existential anxiety). This form of therapy does not aim to directly modify the form, content, or frequency of unwanted feelings, cognitions, urges, or physical sensations. Instead, it focuses on changing the context in which these internal events occur (e.g., when they need to be controlled, explained, or acted on), often by encouraging mindful acceptance of unwanted experiences. (The chapter dovetails nicely with others in the volume that include emphases on autonomy and Buddhist psychology.) Yovel and Bigman view ACT as a means of choosing and enacting core values without being preoccupied with negative concerns and fantasies. The authors review other theoretical perspectives consistent with unique aspects of ACT, contrasting ACT with other cognitive behavioral approaches, and they describe recent laboratory research that examines specific interventions and treatment processes.

CONCLUSION

As can be gleaned from these thumbnail sketches of the first 21 chapters, this unusual volume covers a broad array of fascinating theories and bodies of research concerning Yalom's (1980) four major givens of existence: meaning, mortality, freedom, and connectedness. It reveals how people often mount defenses against threats raised by the "givens," how they can choose more or less destructive and crippling coping strategies, and how certain kinds of therapy can promote constructive coping and greater personal growth. The book incorporates knowledge coined from qualitative and quantitative research methodologies, and it is truly interdisciplinary in its attempt to integrate social psychology, personality, and clinical psychology.

As discussed in Sheldon Solomon's final commentary on the preceding chapters (Chapter 22), the book is both realistic—not minimizing existential threats and concerns—and hopeful. It is realistic because the authors courageously recognize that fears and vulnerabilities, defenses, narrow-mindedness, interpersonal and intergroup aggression and violence, emotional pain, psychopathological responses, and even suicide are pervasive and are unlikely to be eliminated by any kind of superficial "happy talk." They are inherent and inevitable parts of human existence, and it behooves psychology to recognize and understand them. The book is also hopeful in showing that freedom and autonomy are possible (contrary to simplistic versions of scientific determinism); that meaning is available; that some ways of coping with mortality are more constructive, personally and interpersonally, than others; that there are therapies and personal practices, as well as ordinary good relationships, to help us appreciate and enjoy life while contributing substantially to others' lives, despite our mortality and what Nietzsche famously called "the death of God" (1882/2009), which he mistakenly thought would lead to solipsism.

The chapter authors, who do not always agree with each other but are willing to engage in friendly and constructive dialogue, have provided a great service to readers by writing clearly and compellingly about their areas of expertise and cross-referencing their chapters to help readers pursue useful connections. (Many of them have written excellent books, which they cite in their chapters, spelling out their approaches in greater detail.) The present volume offers a stimulating and encouraging vision of human existence and the ways in which social and clinical research can contribute to becoming what the humanistic psychologist Carl Rogers (1961) called a *fully functioning person* and what Ludwig Binswanger (1958), one of the early existential psychotherapists, called *living an authentic life*. We hope this book makes a seminal contribution to establishing what might seem to be an oxymoron, existentialist science.

REFERENCES

Becker, E. (1973). *The denial of death*. New York, NY: Free Press.

Binswanger, L. (1958). The existential analysis school of thought. In R. May, E. Angel, & H. F. Ellenberg (Eds.), *Existence* (pp. 191–213). New York, NY: Basic Books.

Blackham, H. J. (1983). *Six existentialist thinkers*. London, England: Routledge.

Camus, A. (1991). *The myth of Sisyphus and other essays*. New York, NY: Vintage.

James, W. (1890). *Principles of psychology*. London, England: Macmillan.

Nietzsche, F. (2009). *The gay science* (*The joyful wisdom*; T. Common, Trans.). Lawrence, KS: Digireads.com. (Original work published 1882)

Rogers, C. R. (1961). *On becoming a person*. Boston, MA: Houghton Mifflin.

Schneider, K. J., & Krug, O. T. (2009). *Existential–humanistic therapy*. Washington, DC: American Psychological Association.

Wartenberg, T. E. (2008). *Existentialism*. Oxford, England: Oneworld.

Yalom, I. (1980). *Existential psychotherapy*. New York, NY: Basic Books.

I

THE PROBLEM OF FINITUDE

1

TERROR MANAGEMENT THEORY: FROM GENESIS TO REVELATIONS

JEFF GREENBERG

Humans live by existential illusions. These fictions about existence help us cope with the big five existential concerns: death, identity, meaning, social isolation, and freedom (Pyszczynski, Greenberg, Koole, & Solomon, 2010). They allow us to feel as though we are significant and enduring beings in a meaningful world, even though science tells us we are just material organisms with a brief life span in an indifferent universe and members of a species that will likely eventually become extinct. Death is inevitable. Our identities and meanings are cultural constructions that don't amount to a hill of beans in the context of billions of years of time and the vast enormity of space. Our most cherished relationships are inherently limited; we can never know the inner life of another person or reliably expect someone else to put our interests above their own. We strive for freedom while we are all imprisoned by our cultural upbringing and largely dependent on following others' rules for survival. If we have too much freedom, it causes us anxiety and stress, and we often don't know what to do with it.

Theory and research on these topics, dubbed *experimental existential psychology* (XXP; Greenberg, Koole, & Pyszczynski, 2004; Pyszczynski et al., 2010), is covered in many of the chapters in this volume. In the present chapter, I focus on my least favorite existential problem, which also happens to be the one that generated the first large-scale program of XXP research: Death. Terror management theory (TMT) has directly focused on how people cope with this problem and has generated a wide range of novel hypotheses that have been supported by over 400 studies conducted in over 15 countries. Obviously, I will not be reviewing all of this work in this brief chapter, nor is that needed, because broad and focused reviews have been provided in a variety of recent chapters, such as Greenberg, Landau, and Arndt (in press) and Greenberg, Solomon, and Arndt (2008), and in *The Worm at the Core* (Solomon, Greenberg, & Pyszczynski, in press). Here, I concisely summarize the basic findings and some recent developments, and consider the broad contributions of TMT so far.

ORIGIN AND ROOTS OF TERROR MANAGEMENT THEORY

As social psychology graduate students at the University of Kansas from 1978–1981, Sheldon Solomon, Tom Pyszczynski, and I found ourselves amused but dissatisfied with the prevailing view of humans as dispassionate, albeit imperfect, information processors. It simply did not ring true with respect to our families and peer groups or from our knowledge of history or the understanding of humans gleaned from our favorite novelists, poets, philosophers, and filmmakers.

We began discussing two well-established propensities that seemed to us central aspects of human social behavior: the inability of people from different cultures to peacefully coexist and the proneness for people to go to great lengths to protect their self-esteem. It occurred to us that we needed to understand why people were so defensive of their cultural beliefs, ingroups, and positive self-image. But surveying the existing literature in social psychology, we saw no clues as to what people are trying to accomplish in their daily lives or how the basic motivations underlying their actions lead to the intergroup biases and egotism so well-documented in social psychology experiments. Thus, we became determined to seek answers outside our own discipline.

After a few years of searching, we stumbled on an interdisciplinary Pulitzer Prize–winning book by cultural anthropologist Ernest Becker. That book, *The Denial of Death* (Becker, 1973), in conjunction with Becker's earlier *The Birth and Death of Meaning* (Becker, 1962/1971) and later *Escape from Evil* (Becker, 1975), provided the answers we were looking for and became the primary basis of TMT. These books also revealed the rich tradition of existential psychoanalytic thought that Becker built on, a tradition that can be traced to figures such as Sigmund Freud, Otto Rank, Gregory Zilboorg, Harry Stack Sullivan, and Robert Jay Lifton. Our elaboration of TMT owes much to these figures, along with Becker, our training in social psychology, and to sociologists George Herbert Mead and Erving Goffman.

TERROR MANAGEMENT THEORY: THE BASIC THEORY AND HYPOTHESES AND KEY ELABORATIONS

All humans are biologically predisposed to want to continue living, and at the same time we are smart enough to realize that we are going to die and that it could happen at virtually any time for a wide variety of reasons. Given this existential predicament, how do we humans function without being perpetually anxious? According to TMT, we do so by viewing ourselves as enduring beings living in a permanent, meaningful world full of symbols instead of as mere material animals in an indifferent universe fated only to cease existing on death.

From birth on, we are socialized into a worldview that tells us we are significant beings in a meaningful world. We have souls and possible after-lives, and we are part of lasting entities such as nations and family lines. We have identities that will live on past our physical deaths in the seemingly permanent marks we have made on the world: children, memorials, artistic creations, accomplishments in business and science, and so forth. Thus, we function with our deepest anxiety under wraps as long as we believe we are enduring, significant contributors to a meaningful, permanent world. When we are not simply seeking survival or pleasurable experiences, we spend much of our time buttressing our claims of legacy within the symbolic reality we psychologically inhabit. When this view of ourselves and the world is threatened, we experience anxiety and defend against such threats by reasserting our own value and that of our groups, and strengthening our faith in the meaningful world in which we believe.

Many TMT studies converge on three primary points that support the theory. The first is known as the *mortality salience* (MS) hypothesis. If worldviews and self-worth protect people from anxiety regarding mortality, then reminders of your mortal nature should instigate efforts to bolster the value of yourself and your groups (self-esteem striving), and faith in an orderly, stable view of the world and one's self (for reviews, see Greenberg et al., in press, and Greenberg et al., 2008). For example, regarding self-esteem striving, MS leads people who base their self-worth on driving ability to drive more boldly. One common consequence of the need to bolster faith in one's worldview is to derogate and lash out at people and ideas that call the validity of your beliefs into question (worldview defense). Thus, people who identify with a certain nation become more negative in their reactions to someone who criticizes that nation.

A fundamental terror management function of worldviews is to provide an orderly, structured, and sensible view of reality and oneself that allows for the possibility of being a significant contributor to a meaningful existence. Thus, MS should motivate people to want their cognitions to fit together, for people and events to be consistent, for the world to be just, for art to be meaningful, and for the self to seem to be an enduring entity, linked from past to present to future. A wide range of fairly recent studies have supported these notions, especially for people relatively high in need for structure in their lives (see Greenberg et al., in press).

The methods used to induce MS, or what is more precisely heightened death-thought accessibility, warrant brief consideration. The first and most commonly used MS induction involves asking participants to respond to two prompts. First, they are asked to describe the emotions that thinking about their own death arouses in them. Second, they are asked what they think will happen to them as they are dying and once they are dead. Interestingly, so far, content analyses have not found any evidence that what the individual specifically writes in response to these death-focused prompts affects his or her reactions to the induction. The control condition for this induction has consisted of either writing about a neutral topic or, more commonly, an unpleasant, potentially anxiety-provoking topic not directly connected to death. Controls have included thinking of dental pain, intense pain, unpredictable bouts of severe pain, an upcoming exam, failure, public speaking, general anxieties, worries after college, feelings of uncertainty, temporal discontinuity, meaninglessness, unexpected events, expectancy violations, social exclusion, and being paralyzed. In the majority of studies, MS has shown different effects than the salience of these other potentially aversive topics.

In addition, many other methods of increasing the accessibility of death-related thoughts have been employed (e.g., accident footage; proximity to a funeral home; word puzzles with death words imbedded; writing one sentence about death, health or risk warnings; images or reminders of terrorism or destruction), and these other methods have yielded converging support for TMT hypotheses. For example, studies have found that subliminal priming with the word *dead* intensified American subjects' negative reactions to an anti-American author relative to subliminally priming with the word *pain* or *fail* (Pyszczynski, Greenberg, & Solomon, 1999).

The second hypothesis supported by substantial evidence is that stably high or temporarily raised self-esteem and bolstered faith in one's worldview allow people to function with minimal anxiety and defensiveness. The first set of studies demonstrated this by showing that if self-esteem was boosted by false feedback, people were able to endure normally anxiety-provoking images of death and threats of electric shock with no self-reported or physiological signs of increased anxiety (see Greenberg et al., in press). Additional evidence has shown that affirming important values eliminates worldview defense after MS and that, following MS, the opportunity to display pro-American bias reduced the accessibility of death-related thoughts back to baseline levels. Arndt (Chapter 3, this volume) covers this line of work in detail.

The third central hypothesis is that threats to terror management resources will increase the accessibility of death-related thought. Studies have shown that threats to one's self-worth, threats to the belief that we humans are more than just animals, threats to cherished beliefs (e.g., the righteousness of one's nation), and threats to cherished close relationships all bring thoughts of death closer to mind. In one interesting example, Landau et al. (2004) found that learning that the victim of a brutal knife attack was a really good person led to higher death-thought accessibility if the victim was portrayed in a positive rather than a negative way. Landau et al. argued that this was because something bad happening to a good person threatens belief in a just world. There are now over 90 TMT studies that have measured the accessibility of death-related thought, a literature recently reviewed by Hayes, Schimel, Arndt, and Faucher (2010).

TMT research also led to a dual-defense model, which posits that people respond to reminders of death with two distinct sets of defenses. The seminal set of studies that inspired this refinement was reported by Greenberg, Pyszczynski, Solomon, Simon, and Breus (1994); the model was fully articulated in Pyszczynski et al. (1999) and is elaborated by the Arndt chapter in this volume (Chapter 3). The first set of proximal defenses is designed to remove death-related thoughts from consciousness and consists of efforts to distract oneself from such thoughts and convince oneself that death is far off (e.g., "I am healthy and will start exercising more regularly"). When death-related thought is not in focal attention but is hovering on the fringes of consciousness, people engage distal symbolic defenses to shore up their sense of significance and faith in their meaningful view of the world. Thus, the processes activated by conscious death thought flow from proximal to distal defenses.

Mikulincer, Florian, and Hirschberger (2003; see also Hart, Shaver, & Goldenberg, 2005) suggested another possible refinement of the theory, that there may be a third independent component of terror management: secure attachment provided by close relationships (see Chapter 16, this volume). However, I am not convinced that the theory needs revision to accommodate a special role for close relationships. Although these researchers have gathered evidence consistent with this tripartite view, close relationships clearly buttress faith in one's worldview and bolster one's self-esteem (see, e.g., Kosloff, Greenberg, Sullivan, & Weise, 2010). Furthermore, theoretically, the anxiety-buffering function of faith in the worldview and self-worth develop in childhood out of the security-providing function of the parents' love and protection (see, e.g., Becker, 1962/1971; Solomon et al., in press). It is therefore unclear to me why, if such attachments were sufficient for terror management, faith in a symbolic worldview and one's sense of value within that worldview would be so sorely needed—the love of one's parents and close others would be sufficient.

TMT posits that such love is not enough because as children develop, they become aware of the limitations of parents and other individuals for protection from the ultimate threat of mortality. Thus, the basis of protection has to broaden to more potent modes of death transcendence such as spiritual beliefs, great accomplishments, and identification with lasting entities such as the nation, science, or nature. Does this mean that close relationships have no anxiety-buffering function besides as a basis for worldview and self-worth validation? No, loved ones can be of value as proximal defenses by increasing a sense of safety, and may also buffer anxiety through a relatively primitive connection between physical and emotional closeness and felt security. However, I would view these latter effects not as a symbolic mode of handling the problem of death, but as something that reduces anxiety the way popular pharmacological interventions such as Valium and Xanax, and even more widely used recreational drugs such as alcohol and opiates, and perhaps mindfulness (Niemiec et al., 2010) and meditative states, do. One could argue either that any form of blocking or reducing anxiety is terror management, in which case drug use and hugging loved ones should be included, or that the term should be reserved for symbolic bases of feeling that one will transcend mortality in some way; it may just be a matter of personal preference or perceived scientific clarity or utility.

SOME RECENT DIRECTIONS IN TERROR MANAGEMENT THEORY RESEARCH

The TMT literature includes five well-developed research programs that are covered in other chapters in this book: Arndt (Chapter 3), Goldenberg (Chapter 5), Hirschberger and Shaham (Chapter 6), Pyszczynski and Kesebir (Chapter 4), and Shaver and Mikulincer (Chapter 16). In the remainder of this chapter, I focus on providing brief updates regarding just a subset of other recent developments in terror management research.

Brain Processes Associated with Terror Management

A social neuroscience approach to terror management is still in its early stages. Ideally, I would suggest that terror management involves high-level thoughts produced by the prefrontal cortex that generate a path toward amygdala activation, which sparks other high-level thoughts buttressing faith in one's worldview and a sense of personal significance, which then deactivates the potentiation of processes in the amygdala that generate fear, dread, or terror. Some initial evidence consistent with this sequence of processes was provided by the only functional magnetic resonance imaging TMT study to date. Quirin et al. (in press) showed that answering questions about death was associated with increased activation of the right amygdala, left rostral anterior cingulate cortex, and right caudate nucleus. The first two structures seem to play a role in anxiety responses, whereas the caudate nucleus has been suggested to be an indicator of stereotypic thinking as well as love-oriented emotions.

The three other studies to date on the parts of the brain activated by death-related thought do not directly pertain to my hypothesized sequence of processes, but they do inform us about certain aspects of how brain processes contribute to the effects of MS. Henry, Bartholow, and Arndt (2010) measured event-related potentials (ERPs) as (White) participants viewed pictures of Black or White faces after being reminded of death (vs. control). This study found that MS increased amplitude of the N2 component of the ERP to pictures of angry White faces and latency of the P3 component. These findings suggest that when faced with reminders of death, people may be especially sensitive to threats to the ingroup.

A recent study of Americans by Kosloff, Greenberg, Allen, and Martens (2011) using EEG showed that MS shifted people toward greater activation of the right prefrontal cortex. In addition, this study showed that for people prone to eyeblink startle responses, extent of right hemispheric shift was associated with larger eyeblink responses to anti-American images but not other negative images. This study suggests that MS activates the hemisphere of the brain associated with anxiety and withdrawal motivation, a finding opposite research suggesting a left-hemisphere shift in response to concerns with uncertainty (McGregor, Nash, Mann, & Phills, 2010). This may make sense in that uncertainty may motivate approach-oriented proactive responses, whereas MS activates defensive ones.

In a final TMT neuroscience study, Kosloff, Greenberg, and Allen (2011) examined whether MS-induced self-esteem striving behavior is implemented through neurocognitive performance monitoring systems. During a task framed as diagnostic of self-esteem-relevant attributes, participants received subliminal death or control primes while response-locked event-related brain potentials were recorded. Results showed that death-primed (vs. control) participants exhibited heightened neural reactivity to self-esteem-relevant performance miscues, as indexed by larger amplitude of the error-related negativity (ERN). Larger ERN due to MS predicted intensified behavioral efforts to improve self-esteem-relevant task performance; and in the MS condition, such behavioral compensation correlated with attenuations in death-thought accessibility. These initial findings suggest that unique defensive and anxiety-related brain processes are instigated by death-related thought.

Managing Terror Through Assimilation to One's Worldview

TMT theorists proposed that people historically have used four strategies to defuse the threat posed by those who espouse alternative worldviews: derogation, assimilation, accommodation, and annihilation. Many studies have supported the first and last of these defenses by showing that MS increases negativity toward people who implicitly or explicitly challenge the validity of one's own culture's worldview (see Solomon et al., in press; see also Chapter 4, this volume).

Research has also shown that MS can contribute to aggression and even a desire to annihilate such different others. McGregor et al. (1998) showed that MS increased allocation of painfully hot salsa to critics of the participants' political views. Pyszczynski, Abdollahi, et al. (2006) showed that MS intensified support among Iranians for lethal violence directed at Americans, and similarly intensified support among conservative Americans for lethal violence directed against potentially threatening groups. Hayes, Schimel, and Williams (2008) showed that, after MS, reading about Muslims being killed reduced death-thought accessibility in Canadians.

The two other proposed defenses against worldview threat have not garnered much attention. Accommodation involves incorporating aspects of alternative worldviews into one's own in a manner that does not threaten core values of one's worldview. Research has yet to examine this defense. However, Kosloff, Cesario, and Martens (2011) studied MS-induced assimilation. Assimilation involves attempting to convert people with alternative worldviews to abandon their views and adopt one's own. Missionary activity and efforts to spread ideologies such as secular democratic capitalism and communism are real-life examples.

In their first study, Kosloff, Cesario, and Martens (2011) had Christians and non-Christians think about mortality or a control topic and then had them read about either a successful or an unsuccessful conversion of a Hindu person to Christianity. MS generally increased death-thought accessibility in the non-Christians. It also increased death-thought accessibility in Christians who read about the failed conversion. However, the death-thought accessibility of Christians who read about the successful conversion was as low as that of participants in the non-MS control condition.

In a second study, after an MS manipulation, Christians engaged in an advice-giving task after they read two passages supposedly written by another student, one of which revealed the target's attitudes toward religion. One condition conveyed that the target was a staunch atheist, whereas the other portrayed the target as an atheist open to alternatives. The Christian participants then wrote advice to that person, believing that the advice would be returned to the target and the effect of it on the target would be tracked over the next semester. After giving advice, participants privately rated their attitudes about the target. Content analysis of the advice given found that MS increased advising the target to consider giving belief in God a try but only if the target seemed open to persuasion. The liking measure showed that MS led to more liking of the potentially receptive target and less liking of the nonreceptive target.

A third study showed that after an MS induction, proevolution participants exposed to a target who was a strong advocate of creationism showed high death-thought accessibility, but if such participants were given an opportunity to communicate their preference for evolution to the creationist, their death-thought accessibility was as low as in a non-MS condition. This suggests that assimilation efforts may reduce death-related concerns. Furthermore, in the MS condition, the evolutionists made especially strong efforts to convince the creationist target to abandon his or her own beliefs and adopt their own. This line of work reveals one motivation for persuading others and has the potential to broaden our understanding of important forms of terror management.

Terror Management and the Allure of Stardom

The notion that one could attain symbolic immortality—having one's identity live forever—dates back at least to the ancient Greeks. Thus, one way to cope with concerns about mortality seems to be to seek fame and reinforce the possibility of symbolic immortality through fame. In the age of YouTube, mass media celebrity-watching such as on TMZ, reality television, and a de-emphasis in many cultures on traditional religious modes of immortality striving, it seems likely this form of terror management is becoming more and more popular. Thousands of young women move to Los Angeles every year seeking acting fame. Many other folks around the world try for fame through singing or through enduring horrendous challenges for shows such as *American Idol* and *Survivor*. Other people, perhaps less convinced of their own capacity to become famous, seek to connect themselves to the famous.

The most unfortunate version of this fame seeking may manifest itself through committing heinous acts. Individuals repeatedly feeling humiliated and insignificant have killed to become immortal. John David Chapman admitted that this was one of his motives for assassinating John Lennon. Seung-Hui Cho, the Virginia Tech killer, provided perhaps the most compelling example of this horrid form of fame seeking. After killing two people on the campus, he left the campus to mail a video to NBC in which he proclaimed he was like Jesus and would be immortalized for standing up for the meek by committing the largest-scale school shooting in history. He then returned to the campus to complete his mission.

Consistent with a terror management analysis of fame seeking in its many forms, Greenberg, Kosloff, Solomon, Cohen, and Landau (2010) found that MS, relative to the salience of intense pain, temporal discontinuity, general uncertainty, and meaninglessness, led to a postdelay increased self-reported desire for fame, interest in having a star named for oneself, and liking for an abstract painting if it was attributed to a celebrity. Additional research will explore phenomena such as the potential terror management value of negative fame (notoriety), responses to celebrities who have fallen from grace, and reactions to those who advocate alternative worldviews. We also hope to explore Internet behavior directed toward gossiping about and connecting to celebrities.

Terror Management and Supernatural Fantasy

In addition to gravitating toward real-life superstars, people also seem to be drawn to deities and fictional superheroes, a phenomenon dating back as long as recorded history and, in the case of superheroes, at least to Hercules. The impulse to become famous and to admire those with special powers may be the same: to try to feel larger than life, so special as to be exempt from the normal limitations of mortal life. You can do this either by connecting with those who seem larger than life or fantasizing being so yourself. Celebrity is one way to feel this, and we have seen how MS draws people to that. Wealth is another way, and research shows that MS does increase the desire for wealth and status (Solomon et al., in press).

Defying the laws of nature may be another way. Many of the most popular movies and best-selling books of all time involve characters with special powers: the "Force" utilized by Luke Skywalker; the amazing powers of Superman and Spiderman, the X-Men, Harry Potter and the vampires and werewolves of Twilight; or the technology-aided superfeats of Iron Man. It is interesting that most admired superheroes have the power of flight in one form or other. In addition, fantasies of human flight are extremely common across cultures and are often linked to attainment of immortality. This led Cohen et al. (2010) to posit that fantasies of flight may serve a special terror management function by giving people a sense that they can transcend the human physical limitation due to gravity, and if that, why not mortality as well, like an immortal state of a disembodied soul ascending to heaven? In their first study, MS led participants to express greater desire to fly. A second study replicated this effect and showed that it did not extend to other supernatural feats such as walking through walls or reading minds. This suggests that flight fantasies may have a unique role in ameliorating concerns with mortality.

Consistent with this possibility, two subsequent studies showed that after MS, participants who engaged in flight fantasy did not subsequently show the typical increased worldview defense found in a nonflying fantasy condition (Cohen et al., 2010). A final study showed that flight fantasy, but not other pleasurable or empowering fantasies, decreased death-thought accessibility after MS, and this effect was mediated by a feeling of freedom from bodily limits. These findings help explain the popularity of flight fantasies and raise the possibility that other forms of fantasy may also mitigate the need for terror management defenses.

Terror Management, Anxiety Disorders, and Dissociation in Response to Trauma

Strachan et al. (2007) suggested that anxiety disorders sometimes result from a focalization of fear of mortality onto smaller, more manageable potential threats of either death or onto constructs such as self-worth, which protect people from their fear of mortality. In support of this idea, Strachan et al. demonstrated that MS decreases self-controlled exposure to images of spiders among spider phobics, increases time washing one's hands among persons high in obsessive compulsiveness, and increases social avoidance among persons high in social phobia.

Other psychological difficulties result directly from traumas, which most often involve the threat of death and, often, threats to people's anxiety-buffering worldview. A common disorder resulting from trauma is post-traumatic stress disorder (PTSD), and one response to trauma that seems to predict subsequent development of PTSD is dissociation in response to the trauma. In support of a role for mortality concerns in dissociative responses to trauma, Kosloff et al. (2006) found that MS increased retrospective reports among New Yorkers of dissociation and anxiety sensitivity in response to the 9/11 terrorist attacks. In a recent follow-up study, Kosloff, Greenberg, Solomon, Cohen, and Gershuny (2011) found that MS also increased dissociation, anxiety sensitivity, and the accessibility of death-related thought in direct response to an impactful video of the events of 9/11.

In complementary research assessing Iranian earthquake survivors, Abdollahi, Pyszczynski, Maxfield, and Lusyszczynska (in press) found following an earthquake in Iran, that high dissociators failed to exhibit normal defensive responses to MS but later were prone to developing PTSD. This work suggests that people who dissociate from traumas do not engage in normal terror management in response to subsequent reminders of mortality but instead develop PTSD. Those who do not dissociate in response to trauma seem to react to death reminders with normal terror management defenses.

Given that dissociation to trauma has long-term negative consequences, how could this response be reduced? Perhaps strengthening faith in one's worldview might reduce the need to dissociate when faced with traumatic experiences. Charismatic political figures serve this bolstering function, and MS has been shown to increase preference for them if the worldview they espouse is consistent with one's own (Greenberg et al., in press). Thus, before the 2008 American presidential election, Kosloff, Greenberg, Solomon, et al. (2011) tested whether watching an inspiring speech by a worldview-consistent political candidate would reduce dissociation in response to the 9/11 video. Obama supporters, McCain supporters, and undecided voters watched inspiring excerpts of a speech by either Obama or McCain. After the video, participants rated how inspiring it was and then watched the 9/11 film and completed a dissociation measure. Obama supporters and undecided voters dissociated least if they watched the Obama speech prior to the disturbing video. McCain supporters dissociated least if they watched the McCain speech before the video. In addition, the more inspired the participant was by the speech she or he watched, the less the person dissociated in response to the 9/11 video. Consistent with this finding, a prior study (Simon, Arndt, Greenberg, Solomon, & Pyszczynski, 1998) showed that after MS, an opportunity to defend the American worldview increased perceived meaning in life in depressed Americans.

Taken together, this work shows that mortality concerns contribute to symptoms associated with various psychological disorders and that strengthening terror management resources can ameliorate these symptoms. This suggests that, in line with the theorizing of Becker (1973), further research into the role of mortality concerns in psychological disorders and in approaches to treatment may be in order.

Terror Management in Older People

Traumas bring people close to death, but so does the natural process of aging. Maxfield et al. (2007) recently spearheaded research examining how elderly people respond to MS. Older people are probabilistically closer to death and more likely to have experienced life-threatening illness and the death of members of their social network. This suggests a number of plausible questions regarding how they might react differently to MS than young and middle-aged adults. Is mortality so salient to them that our inductions would have no effect? Is it such an imminent issue for them that they would respond even more strongly? Is there a process by which as people get older they more effectively come to terms with their mortality and hence react less defensively?

We do not have definitive answers to these questions yet, but using American samples, we have found some interesting ways in which elderly people respond differently to MS than younger samples. First, they seem to respond more strongly to incidental exposure to death-related words than to the classic MS induction, suggesting that perhaps they are so used to blatant reminders of death that they are more likely to be affected by more subtle reminders. In three studies, we found that in a control condition elderly samples were harsher toward moral transgressors than were young adults and just as harsh as young adults toward a critic of the United States (Maxfield et al., 2007). However, in these three studies we found that MS had opposite effects for elderly and young adult samples. As usual, MS led the young adults to be more negative toward moral transgressors and critics of their culture. However, MS actually led older adults to become more lenient toward moral transgressors and more tolerant of a critic of the United States.

Our samples in these studies tended to be healthy, high-functioning older adults, people who had endured a lot but were still doing well. Therefore, we thought that this startling contrast may have occurred because, when confronted with mortality, well-functioning elderly people draw on a broader perspective on life and a more benevolent perspective on imperfections and differences among us humans. Thus, we hypothesized that the MS-leniency effect would be found in elderly people who exhibit effective executive functioning, whereas the usual MS-punitive effect would occur in older adults relatively poor in executive functioning.

Thus, in a follow-up study we first tested a broadly recruited elderly sample and a college student sample on executive functioning using a combination of three well-established cognitive tasks. Participants were then led to think of their own mortality and asked how much a set of hypothetical moral transgressors should be punished. MS led the young adults to be more punitive regardless of their level of executive functioning. However, as predicted, the MS responses of the older adults depended on their executive functioning. Those functioning well became more lenient after MS. However, those older people low in executive functioning became more punitive after MS, mirroring the general effect for the young adults. These findings suggest the hopeful notion that as people get older, they get more benevolent in response to reminders of their mortality, as long as they are functioning at a high cognitive level. Of course, more research is needed to fully understand why and how this happens.

More Constructive Forms of Terror Management?

The research on older adults' responses to MS raises the possibility that the potential terror of death can be managed in more benign ways than most terror management research implies. A number of other recent lines of research explore ways besides graceful aging that might lead to such constructive approaches. First, evidence suggests that people low in personal need for structure and in authoritarianism may embrace worldviews that encourage more open, tolerant ways of coping with mortality (e.g., Vess, Routledge, Landau, & Arndt, 2009). Evidence also suggests that creative thinking and deeper, more elaborate contemplation of death may encourage more constructive and open-minded reactions to reminders of death (see, e.g., Cozzolino, 2006; Greenberg et al., in press; Janoff-Bulman & Yopyk, 2004). At present, my colleagues and I are exploring how different ways of consciously construing one's own death may affect the extent to which death-related thoughts contribute to defensive versus growth-oriented responses. For example, could viewing death as an integral part of life lead to more openness and tolerance than viewing death as the opposite of life?

TERROR MANAGEMENT AND OTHER PSYCHOLOGICAL MOTIVES

I am going to touch on this topic only briefly, because it has been covered extensively elsewhere (e.g., Pyszczynski, Greenberg, Solomon, & Maxfield, 2006; Pyszczynski et al., 2010) and is also discussed in this volume by Solomon (Chapter 22), Mikulincer and Shaver (Chapter 2), and Pyszczynski and Kesebir (Chapter 4). TMT was originally developed to explain basic psychological propensities for self-esteem and negative reactions to different others. It also helps explain a variety of other human propensities ranging from aggression, conformity, and obedience, to political leanings and religiosity, to prosocial behavior and romantic love. However, we have always acknowledged that terror management is not the only psychological motive and that it is rarely, if ever, the only concern affecting a particular thought or action. It is not that any particular human behavior can be fully explained as terror management, but that terror management plays a role in many, if not most, aspects of human behavior. Similarly, not all psychological threats can be reduced to the problem of death. Although issues of uncertain beliefs and meaning, identity and social relationships, often arouse terror management concerns, they can be troubling for other reasons as well. People like some certainties and meanings and dislike others, depending on their implications. Just as such concerns cannot be reduced solely to serving terror management, the concern with mortality cannot be reduced to some broader, vague concern such as uncertainty and meaning. Death is a unique threat because so many of our biological systems are oriented toward averting it, and yet it is the only inevitable future event; further, death is the ultimate threat to all human desires as the potential end of control, social connections, meaning, competence, growth, cognition, and so forth. The need for denial of death cannot be denied.

THE CONTRIBUTIONS OF TERROR MANAGEMENT THEORY

At the risk of immodesty, I will conclude with a brief consideration of how TMT has contributed to scientific knowledge so far. In one sense, the major contribution has been to systematize the analysis of human motivation developed by Becker (1971, 1973) and his predecessors and to provide ways to assess it empirically, ways that have strongly supported and refined the analysis. The theory was the first to ask what function self-esteem serves and provided the first and, to me, only compelling explanation for why people are so driven to establish and defend their sense of self-worth and honor. The theory clarifies that self-esteem buffers anxiety and is dependent on meeting the standards of value prescribed by the worldview to which one subscribes.

The theory also established a basic psychological function of culture: to provide a meaningful view of reality that offers the possibility of transcending death through both literal and symbolic bases of immortality. Furthermore, the theory provides a central explanation of prejudice and why cultures have such a difficult time peacefully coexisting. Because each culture's worldview is so central to its members' psychological security, the mere existence of people who subscribe to alternative worldviews is psychologically threatening and must be defended against. Thus, the theory explains why people are so prone to derogating, trying to convert, and even attacking people who hold beliefs different from their own.

When Sheldon, Tom, and I were first confronted with ideas we systematized into TMT over 25 years ago, we were convinced we were on to something true and important. However, since that time, we have been perpetually surprised by how generative the theory has been in terms of the range of testable hypotheses and areas of application it has inspired. Aside from the topics touched on in this chapter, the theory has generated research pertinent to such areas as stereotyping, legal and medical decision making, risk taking, consumer behavior, communication, language use, journalism, literary and film criticism, politics, human ambivalence regarding sex, animal–human relations, environmentalism, reactions to the handicapped, parenting, close relationships, health-relevant behaviors, creativity, anxiety disorders, depression, attitudes toward women, the functions of art, and robotics.

Most generally, I think that TMT and its associated research programs have helped the science of psychology mature. Our first presentation of TMT back in 1984, titled "The Psychopathology of Social Psychology," started with the brash observation that social psychology had become an acultural, ahistorical, atheoretical, and virtually autistic field focused narrowly on explaining lab findings by splitting hairs as finely as possible rather than on explaining human social behavior out in the world. In retrospect, this was probably not the best way to persuade our social psychology audiences of the value of the subsequent theory we laid out for them. However, I do believe that our efforts, in conjunction with other coincident developments, have helped the field broaden its conceptual scope in four important ways.

First, TMT helped pry open the door for a return to broad theoretical thinking, something that was shunned in academic psychology as part of the backlash against psychoanalysis. Second, it has contributed to evidence showing that the basic motivations that drive human behavior lie outside of consciousness. Third, TMT has increased understanding of the central role of cultural worldviews in psychological functioning. This helps to explain, among many other things, why it is so hard to forcefully convert other cultures to one's own worldview—for example, to change "hearts and minds" in places such as Iraq and Afghanistan. Fourth, the work has injected existential thought into psychology. This provided a major impetus to the development of the subdiscipline of experimental existential psychology that is central to this edited volume. Issues such as death, identity, freedom, meaning systems, political ideology, and religion, once considered outside the bounds of scientific inquiry in mainstream psychology, are now of central interest to scientists throughout the world, as we shall see over the course of this volume.

REFERENCES

Abdollahi, A., Pyszczynski, T., Maxfield, M., & Lusyszczynska, A. (in press). Posttraumatic stress reactions as a disruption in anxiety-buffer functioning: Dissociation and responses to mortality salience as predictors of severity of post-traumatic symptoms. *Psychological Trauma: Theory, Research, Practice, and Policy*.

Becker, E. (1971). *The birth and death of meaning: An interdisciplinary perspective on the problem of man* (2nd ed.). New York, NY: Free Press. (Original work published 1962)

Becker, E. (1973). *The denial of death*. New York, NY: Free Press.

Becker, E. (1975). *Escape from evil*. New York, NY: Free Press.

Cohen, F., Sullivan, D., Solomon, S., Greenberg, J., & Ogilvie, D. (2010). Finding everland: Flight fantasies and the desire to transcend mortality. *Journal of Experimental Social Psychology, 47*, 88–102. doi:10.1016/j.jesp.2010.08.013

Cozzolino, P. J. (2006). Death, contemplation, growth, and defense: Converging evidence of a dual-existential system? *Psychological Inquiry, 17,* 278–287. doi:10.1080/10478400701366944

Greenberg, J., Koole, S., & Pyszczynski, T. (Eds.). (2004). *Handbook of experimental existential psychology.* New York, NY: Guilford Press.

Greenberg, J., Kosloff, S., Solomon, S., Cohen, F., & Landau, M. J. (2010). Toward understanding the fame game: The effect of mortality salience on the appeal of fame. *Self and Identity, 9,* 1–18. doi:10.1080/15298860802391546

Greenberg, J., Landau, M. J., & Arndt, J. (in press). Mortal cognition: Viewing self and the world from the precipice. In D. Carlston (Ed.), *Handbook of social cognition.* Oxford, England: Oxford University Press.

Greenberg, J., Pyszczynski, T., Solomon, S., Simon, L., & Breus, M. (1994). Role of consciousness and accessibility of death-related thoughts in mortality salience effects. *Journal of Personality and Social Psychology, 67,* 627–637. doi:10.1037/0022-3514.67.4.627

Greenberg, J., Solomon, S., & Arndt, J. (2008). A uniquely human motivation: Terror management. In J. Shah & W. Gardner (Eds.), *Handbook of motivation science* (pp. 114–134). New York, NY: Guilford Press.

Hart, J., Shaver, P. R., & Goldenberg, J. L. (2005). Attachment, self-esteem, worldviews, and terror management: Evidence for a tripartite security system. *Journal of Personality and Social Psychology, 88,* 999–1013. doi:10.1037/0022-3514.88.6.999

Hayes, J., Schimel, J., Arndt, J., & Faucher, E. H. (2010). A theoretical and empirical review of the death-thought accessibility concept in terror management research. *Psychological Bulletin, 136,* 699–739. doi:10.1037/a0020524

Hayes, J., Schimel, J., & Williams, T. J. (2008). Fighting death with death: The buffering effects of learning that worldview violators have died. *Psychological Science, 19,* 501–507. doi:10.1111/j.1467-9280.2008.02115.x

Henry, E. A., Bartholow, B. D., & Arndt, J. (2010). Death on the brain: Effects of mortality salience on the neural correlates of race bias. *Social Cognitive and Affective Neuroscience, 5,* 77–87. doi:10.1093/scan/nsp041

Janoff-Bulman, R., & Yopyk, D. J. (2004). Random outcomes and valued commitments: Existential dilemmas and the paradox of meaning. In J. Greenberg, S. L. Koole, & T. Pyszczynski (Eds.), *Handbook of experimental existential psychology* (pp. 122–140). New York, NY: Guilford Press.

Kosloff, S., Cesario, J., & Martens, A. (2011). *Resistance is futile: Mortality salience increases efforts to assimilate others to one's own worldview.* Unpublished manuscript.

Kosloff, S., Greenberg, J., & Allen, J. J. B. (2011). *Terror-related negativity: Mortality salience heightens neural indices of conflict monitoring and behavioral compensations during a self-esteem relevant task.* Unpublished manuscript.

Kosloff, S., Greenberg, J., Allen, J. J. B., & Martens, A. (2011). *Mortality salience heightens neural and autonomic indices of withdrawal from symbolic threat.* Unpublished manuscript.

Kosloff, S., Greenberg, J., Solomon, S., Cohen, F., & Gershuny, B. (2011). *Fatal distraction II: Further exploring the role of death-related concerns in dissociative responses to cultural trauma.* Unpublished manuscript.

Kosloff, S., Greenberg, J., Sullivan, D., & Weise, D. (2010). Of trophies and pillars: Exploring the terror management functions of short-term and long-term relationship partners. *Personality and Social Psychology Bulletin, 36,* 1037–1051. doi:10.1177/0146167210374602

Kosloff, S., Solomon, S., Greenberg, J., Cohen, F., Gershuny, B., Routledge, C., & Pyszczynski, T. (2006). Fatal distraction: The impact of mortality salience on dissociative responses to 9/11 and subsequent anxiety sensitivity. *Basic and Applied Social Psychology, 28,* 349–356. doi:10.1207/s15324834basp2804_8

Landau, M. J., Johns, M., Greenberg, J., Pyszczynski, T., Solomon, S., & Martens, A. (2004). A function of form: Terror management and structuring of the social world. *Journal of Personality and Social Psychology, 87,* 190–210. doi:10.1037/0022-3514.87.2.190

Maxfield, M., Pyszczynski, T., Kluck, B., Cox, C., Greenberg, J., Solomon, S., & Weise, D. (2007). Age-related differences in responses to thoughts of one's own death: Mortality salience and judgments of moral transgressors. *Psychology and Aging, 22,* 341–353. doi:10.1037/0882-7974.22.2.341

McGregor, H. A., Lieberman, J. D., Solomon, S., Greenberg, J., Arndt, J., Simon, L., & Pyszczynski, T. (1998). Terror management and aggression: Evidence that mortality salience motivates aggression against worldview threatening others. *Journal of Personality and Social Psychology, 74,* 590–605. doi:10.1037/0022-3514.74.3.590

McGregor, I., Nash, K. A., Mann, N., & Phills, C. (2010). Anxious uncertainty and reactive approach motivation (RAM). *Journal of Personality and Social Psychology, 99,* 133–147. doi:10.1037/a0019701

Mikulincer, M., Florian, V., & Hirschberger, G. (2003). The existential function of close relationships: Introducing death into the science of love. *Personality and Social Psychology Review, 7,* 20–40. doi:10.1207/S15327957PSPR0701_2

Niemiec, C. P., Brown, K. W., Kashdan, T. B., Cozzolino, P. J., Breen, W. E., Levesque-Bristol, C., & Ryan, R. M. (2010). Being present in the face of existential threat: The role of trait mindfulness in reducing defensive responses to mortality salience. *Journal of Personality and Social Psychology, 99,* 344–365. doi:10.1037/a0019388

Pyszczynski, T., Abdollahi, A., Solomon, S., Greenberg, J., Cohen, F., & Weise, D. (2006). Mortality salience, martyrdom, and military might: The Great Satan versus the Axis of Evil. *Personality and Social Psychology Bulletin, 32,* 525–537. doi:10.1177/0146167205282157

Pyszczynski, T., Greenberg, J., Koole, S., & Solomon, S. (2010). Experimental existential psychology: Coping with the facts of life. In S. Fiske, D. Gilbert, & G. Lindzey (Eds.), *Handbook of social psychology* (Vol. 2, pp. 724–760). London, England: Wiley.

Pyszczynski, T., Greenberg, J., & Solomon, S. (1999). A dual-process model of defense against conscious and unconscious death-related thoughts: An extension of terror management theory. *Psychological Review, 106,* 835–845. doi:10.1037/0033-295X.106.4.835

Pyszczynski, T., Greenberg, J., Solomon, S., & Maxfield, M. (2006). On the unique psychological import of the human awareness of mortality: Themes and variations. *Psychological Inquiry, 17,* 328–356. doi:10.1080/10478400701369542

Quirin, M., Loktyushin, A., Arndt, J., Kustermann, E., Lo, Y., Kuhl, J., & Eggert, L.D. (in press). Existential neuroscience: A functional magnetic resonance imaging investigation of neural responses to reminders of one's mortality. *Social Cognitive and Affective Neuroscience.*

Simon, L., Arndt, J., Greenberg, J., Solomon, S., & Pyszczynski, T. (1998). Terror management and meaning: Evidence that the opportunity to defend the worldview in response to mortality salience increases the meaningfulness of life in the mildly depressed. *Journal of Personality, 66,* 359–382. doi:10.1111/1467-6494.00016

Solomon, S., Greenberg, J., & Pyszczynski, T. (in press). *The worm at the core: On the role of death in life.* New York, NY: Random House.

Strachan, E., Schimel, J., Arndt, J., Williams, T., Solomon, S., Pyszczynski, T., & Greenberg, J. (2007). Terror mismanagement: Evidence that mortality salience exacerbates phobic and compulsive behaviors. *Personality and Social Psychology Bulletin, 33,* 1137–1151. doi:10.1177/0146167207303018

Vess, M., Routledge, C., Landau, M.J., & Arndt, J. (2009). The dynamics of death and meaning: The effects of death-relevant cognitions and personal need for structure on perceptions of meaning in life. *Journal of Personality and Social Psychology, 97,* 728–744. doi:10.1037/a0016417

2

HELPLESSNESS: A HIDDEN LIABILITY ASSOCIATED WITH FAILED DEFENSES AGAINST AWARENESS OF DEATH

MARIO MIKULINCER AND PHILLIP R. SHAVER

Death anxiety and the defenses people use to keep it at bay have fascinated psychologists for decades, and two lines of research and theory have developed as a result. One line, which emerged from studies of death anxiety per se, focuses mainly on measuring the fear of death and discovering how personality variables, cultural factors, and context affect its intensity (e.g., Kastenbaum, 2000). The other line of work, which arose within experimental social psychology, focuses on the ways in which people manage the "terror" aroused by awareness of one's mortality (e.g., Solomon, Greenberg, & Pyszczynski, 1991; see also Chapter 1, this volume). Research along both lines reveals that the fear of death and the defenses against it are complex.

In this chapter, we consider a somewhat neglected theme in research on death awareness and death anxiety: Why, exactly, is death is so terrifying? The assumption has been that contemplating the end of one's existence—the ultimate form of "lights out"—is reason enough for terror. However, we suspect that an additional cause of the terror is extreme helplessness. Awareness of mortality arouses fears of helplessness and powerlessness, a primitive cause of fear from infancy onward, and when defenses against death awareness fail or are weak, the threat of utter helplessness may be part of what elevates fear.

We begin this chapter with a review of research on the meanings people assign to their mortality and the strategies they use to manage death concerns. We then present a case for believing that helplessness is an aspect of death that adds to its fearsomeness and that when terror management mechanisms are interfered with or fail, the threat of helplessness becomes measurable. We then briefly describe three new experimental studies we conducted to explore the possibility that helplessness arises when terror management defenses are interfered with.

COGNITIVE AND MOTIVATIONAL ASPECTS OF THE FEAR OF DEATH

In this section, we review theory and research on the cognitive and motivational aspects of the fear of personal death. We first consider the various meanings people assign to their own death. We then address the various action tendencies that the fear of personal death can elicit.

Meanings of Death Anxiety

Confronting one's finitude is known to be a primal source of existential anxiety (Bakan, 1971). Early studies of the fear of death were based on a fairly simplistic, unidimensional conceptualization of this fear (see Kastenbaum, 2000, for a review). Although these studies often relied on self-report scales that tapped diverse worries about death and nonexistence (e.g., concern over loss of bodily integrity, fear of a painful death), a single score was computed for each study participant by averaging ratings of all the scale items (e.g., Kastenbaum, 2000). As a result, early studies failed to reveal the diverse concerns and worries that underlie most people's fear of death.

Other researchers began to develop multidimensional conceptualizations of fear of death and proposed that a variety of personal concerns contribute to this fear and that different meanings can be ascribed to mortality (e.g., Hoelter, 1979; Murphy, 1959). For example, Murphy (1959) suggested seven interpretations a person might give to death, representing different reasons for fearing it: fear of death as the end of life, fear of losing consciousness, fear of loneliness, fear of the unknown, fear of retribution, fear of the consequences of one's death for loved ones, and fear of failure. Hoelter (1979) also proposed that mortality awareness elicits a variety of concerns: (a) concerns about decay, isolation, and decomposition of the body; (b) concerns about failing to accomplish important life tasks; (c) worries about the psychologically painful consequences of one's death for family and friends; and (d) worries about the mystery surrounding what, if anything, happens after death.

Following in this line of research, Florian and his colleagues (Florian & Kravetz, 1983; Florian, Kravetz, & Frankel, 1984) content-analyzed the multidimensional conceptualizations of fear of death and the existing self-report scales designed to measure it. These researchers then integrated the different approaches in a single theoretical model and designed a comprehensive, multidimensional self-report scale to operationalize the constructs in the model. They proposed a tridimensional model of fear of death and suggested that people can attach a variety of intrapersonal, interpersonal, and transpersonal meanings to death. *Intrapersonal meanings* include concerns related to the consequences of death for one's own mind and body, such as worries about the decay and decomposition of the body, worries about failure to accomplish important life goals, and worries about missing out on meaningful personal experiences. *Interpersonal meanings* include concerns related to the psychologically painful effects of death on one's relationship partners, such as worries about the cessation of one's marriage, worries about one's inability to care for family and friends, and worries about losing one's social identity and being forgotten. *Transpersonal meanings* include concerns related to the hereafter, such as fear of punishment in the hereafter and worries about what will happen to one's mind, or spirit, after death (e.g., as it wends its way through the Buddhist *Bardo,* or transition, state).

On the basis of their tridimensional conceptualization of fear of death, Florian and Kravetz (1983) constructed a 31-item self-report questionnaire, the Fear of Personal Death (FPD) scale, to assess the various meanings people attach to their future demise. Each of the items relates to a specific reason for being afraid of death, and participants rate each one on a 7-point scale to indicate the extent to which they agree with it. Factor analysis of the scale (Florian & Kravetz, 1983) revealed that the 31 items form six factors reflecting intrapersonal, interpersonal, and transpersonal concerns related to death. Two factors are concerned with intrapersonal meanings of death: fear of lost self-fulfillment (e.g., "Death frightens me because my life will not have been properly used") and fear of self-annihilation (e.g., "I am afraid of death because of the decomposition of my body"). Two other factors concern the interpersonal meanings of finitude: fear of loss of social identity (e.g., "Death frightens me because my absence may not be much regretted by others") and fear of consequences of the death for family and friends (e.g., "I'm afraid of my death because my family will still need me when I'm gone"). The two final factors capture transpersonal meanings of death: fear of the transcendental consequences of death (e.g., "Death frightens me because of the uncertainty of any sort of existence after death") and fear of punishment in the hereafter (e.g., "I am afraid of death because of the expected punishment in the next world"). This six-factor structure has been replicated in many studies of respondents from different ethnic and religious groups (e.g., Florian & Snowden, 1989).

In a related study, Mikulincer, Florian, and Tolmacz (1990) found that one's *attachment orientation*—the systematic pattern of relational expectations, emotions, and behaviors that results from a particular history of interactions with close relationship partners (see Chapter 16, this volume)—is also associated with the meanings a person attaches to his or her mortality. In particular, the two dimensions of attachment insecurity—anxiety and avoidance—are associated with the interpersonal and transpersonal dimensions of the fear of death. *Attachment anxiety* (chronic worries about rejection and abandonment and negative representations of oneself as insufficiently lovable and likely to be rejected or abandoned) was associated with more intense concerns about the consequences of death for one's social identity. *Attachment-related avoidance* (preference for emotional distance from relationship partners, negative mental representations of others, and striving to be self-reliant) was associated with more intense transcendental fear of the unknown nature of the hereafter.

According to Mikulincer et al. (1990), these findings imply that people tend to be afraid of death for the same reasons they are distressed while alive (e.g., rejection, loss of self-control). People scoring high on attachment anxiety tend to magnify worries about rejection, separation, and others' availability (Mikulincer & Shaver, 2007), hence tending to exaggerate concerns about being unloved, abandoned, and forgotten after death. People scoring high on avoidance vigorously try to cope with life's adversities in a self-reliant manner, thereby not needing to depend on others (Mikulincer & Shaver, 2007). This defensive emphasis on extreme self-reliance may exacerbate concerns about the uncertain and unknown aspects of death because they threaten an avoidant person's sense of control and mastery.

The Motivational Force of Mortality Awareness

Fear of death, like any other emotion, has an action-tendency component that motivates people to take a specific course of action in response to fear arousal (Frijda, 1986). In 1991, a group of eminent social psychologists (Solomon et al., 1991) formulated a theory (terror management theory, or TMT) delineating this action tendency and the cognitive and behavioral maneuvers people use to manage death concerns. As reviewed by Greenberg (Chapter 1, this volume), death awareness tends to activate three main defenses: (a) adhering to a cultural worldview, (b) enhancing one's self-esteem, and (c) fostering connectedness and a sense of attachment security. Individuals who adhere to a cultural worldview enjoy the solace of understanding how the world was created, what the meaning and purpose of life are, and what happens after death (see Chapter 4, this volume). People with high self-esteem feel they are good exemplars of their culture, and they enjoy the protection from mortality concerns that the culture offers (see Chapter 3). People who maintain satisfactory close relationships enjoy a sense of attachment security, which strengthens their resilience in dealing with existential concerns, soothes anxieties and worries (because of feeling comforted by available others), and facilitates restoration of emotional balance (see Chapter 16).

In a series of experimental studies, Florian and Mikulincer (1997) attempted to integrate knowledge concerning the components of fear of death with studies of its motivational force. They hypothesized that activating defenses following a mortality salience induction depends on (a) a person's predominant death-related concerns (intrapersonal, interpersonal, transpersonal), (b) the specific concerns elicited by the death reminder, and (c) the specific death-related concerns that are buffered by the defenses. In other words, mortality salience should activate a person's defenses when it increases awareness of a particular person's predominant death-related concerns and when the defense buffers that predominant fear. When death reminders increase death-related concerns that do not characterize a person, or the defense does not buffer the predominant death-related concern, death reminders should not activate that particular defense.

Florian and Mikulincer (1997) designed a complex experiment in which they examined a previously observed cultural worldview defense: negative reactions to social transgressors (Rosenblatt, Greenberg, Solomon, Pyszczynski, & Lyon, 1989). Participants completed the FPD scale assessing intrapersonal and interpersonal fears of death. They were then randomly divided into three experimental conditions in which (a) intrapersonal death-related concerns, (b) interpersonal death-related concerns, or (c) a neutral theme (control condition) was made salient. Following a distracting task, participants were presented with a series of 20 cultural transgressions and rated the severity of each of these transgressions and the severity of the punishment the transgressors should receive. Ten of the transgressions were described as having either intrapersonal consequences for the body and the victim's sense of self, and the remaining 10 transgressions were described as having interpersonal consequences for the victim's social identity and family.

Mortality salience produced higher social-transgression severity ratings and more severe punishments for transgressors than the control condition only when (a) people who were predominantly afraid of the intrapersonal consequences of death were exposed to a reminder of this specific fear and were asked to judge transgressions that had direct personal effects on the victim's body and self and (b) people who were predominantly afraid of the interpersonal consequences of death were exposed to a reminder of this specific fear and were asked to judge transgressions that had direct interpersonal repercussions for the victim's social identity and family. That is, cultural worldview defenses seemed to be activated mainly when there was a fit between the particular death-related concern that was made salient, the aspect of death that a person feared most, and the type of transgression to be punished.

The findings of existing research, although quite interesting, leave unanswered the basic question of what accounts for death's terror-inducing power. As mentioned earlier, we—perhaps because our studies are rooted in attachment theory, a theory that focused initially on the incredible helplessness and dependency of human infants and the vulnerability of people of all ages to uncontrollable natural and human-caused forces—suspect that part of the power of death as an instigator of fear is that it implies one's ultimate helplessness. If this intuition is correct, people should be especially concerned with the threat of helplessness when the three defenses against death awareness are not activated or are activated ineffectively.

HELPLESSNESS LIES AT THE HEART
OF CONCERNS ABOUT DEATH

What is so terrifying about death? Theorists have thought that death is anxiety provoking because it blocks the accomplishment of important life goals, forces an abrupt and lasting separation from loved ones, and arouses uncertainty about what will happen to one's mind or essence in the hereafter. We suspect that these worries are closely associated with another fundamental threat: helplessness. According to Seligman (1975), a sense of helplessness follows one's recognition that no action can change the occurrence of important life events; in other words, we humans are sometimes powerless to alter fate. Although we may take preventive actions to delay or "cheat" death (e.g., by engaging in physical exercise, taking needed medicines, cultivating healthy habits), we cannot avoid death and cannot know or control when or how we will die. Maybe we will suffer a heart attack in 10 years, or maybe we will be swept away by a tsunami tomorrow.

We believe that the sense of helplessness is entwined with all of the reasons that Florian and Kravetz (1983) included in their multidimensional model of the meanings of death. It is natural to feel helpless and powerless when recognizing that one cannot prevent the decay and decomposition of one's dead body (although people try to postpone this fate by purchasing expensive caskets and burial vaults); one cannot do much to accomplish life goals that death interrupts; one cannot help family and friends, except indirectly (with insurance policies), in times of need; one cannot avert separation from loved ones after death; and one cannot prevent the gradual erasure of one's image in the minds of people who live on and then die, as one historical epoch morphs into another. Of course, many people battle against these various uncontrollable consequences of death. They may prepare a will that ensures their mummification, divvy out money to friends and relatives, donate money for statues or buildings with their name on them, or invest effort in creative or scientific works whose effects reverberate after they die. We view these efforts as defenses against the sense of helplessness that thinking about death arouses.

Helplessness is also a natural feeling that accompanies thinking about the unknown nature of death and our lack of control over it. Although religious texts tell us how to behave to avoid punishment in the hereafter, and the Tibetan Book of the Dead prepares us for what will happen in the Bardo (the eerie transition from one life to another), these are fragile cultural constructions that provide an illusion of control to assuage the core feelings of helplessness. They do not leave many people feeling fully or comfortably in charge of their demise.

The three defenses proposed by TMT are also ultimately aimed at providing an illusion of control to soften fear of helplessness and powerlessness and keep it out of awareness. As studied extensively in the past several decades, a sense of helplessness is one of the psychological factors that underlie despair and depression; apathy, passivity, and disengagement from life; lack of resilience in the face of life's struggles and obstacles; and poor performance in a variety of life tasks (see Mikulincer, 1994, for a review). In other words, the feeling of helplessness that arises in awareness when we are reminded of our biological finitude may be part of what interferes profoundly with peace of mind, impairs adaptive functioning, and prevents successful engagement in daily tasks. People therefore need positive illusions of control, power, mastery, efficacy, and worth in order to banish the sense of helplessness from awareness. These are the positive illusions that symbolic defenses create when mortality is made salient and feelings of helplessness and powerlessness threaten to surface in consciousness.

By adhering to predominant cultural worldviews or behaving according to the standards and norms prescribed by their culture whenever death reminders intrude, people can feel somewhat protected by their seemingly powerful culture. Likewise, by seeking proximity to loved ones and eliciting their support, care, and attention, one can feel somewhat protected by them in times of need. In both cases, a symbolic institution (e.g., culture, nation, race, community, group) or what Bowlby (1979) called a "stronger and wiser caregiver" (p. 129), can provide a sense of safety and security that temporarily counteracts the sense of helplessness and powerlessness implied by ultimate personal extinction. Just as a child attributes omnipotence to his or her parents, adults imbue their culture with strength, power, order, meaning, and value, which in turn offers positive illusions of control and mastery to a helpless person. By internalizing and identifying with parental and cultural images, people incorporate into themselves the sense of control and strength associated with these images (Mikulincer & Shaver, 2004; see also Chapter 11, this volume), thereby quelling intimations of helplessness. Moreover, both culture and loving caregivers are sources of personal value and self-worth (Bowlby, 1973, 1988; Solomon et al., 1991) that help people maintain an illusion of control and power to counter feelings of vulnerability and helplessness.

To date, most terror management studies have focused on the activation of symbolic defenses following death reminders and the effects that these defenses have on the accessibility of death-related thoughts (see Chapter 1, this volume). This body of knowledge, although enlightening, does not provide much information about the hypothesized role that helplessness and powerlessness may play in the experience and management of death concerns.

To begin to examine this role, we wanted to consider cases in which symbolic defenses fail to accomplish their protective goal. In our view, this malfunction of the defenses should go beyond increasing the accessibility of death-related thoughts and activate a sense of helplessness and its associated emotions (e.g., demoralization, depression) and tendency to interfere with task performance. These affective and behavioral manifestations of helplessness are not necessarily evident following death reminders, because terror management defenses may be quickly activated and suppress not only thoughts of death but also the sense of helplessness we believe is associated with it. Feelings of helplessness emerge only when defenses against death awareness fail, leaving a person defenseless against the awareness of biological finitude.

In a recent study, Pyszczynski and Kesebir (2011) began to inquire about the psychological consequences of defense disruption. In an attempt to understand the origins of posttraumatic stress disorder (PTSD) following traumatic experiences, Pyszczynski and Kesebir proposed anxiety buffer disruption theory. They argued that traumatic events can undermine one's ability to maintain important aspects of one's cultural worldview (cf. Janoff-Bulman's, 1992, shattered assumptions theory of trauma), erode one's sense of self-worth, and arouse feelings of loneliness and insecurity. As a result, terror management defenses cannot provide a sense of safety in a frightening world, and this breakdown of defenses leads people to experience overwhelming anxiety and PTSD symptoms. In support of this view, four studies conducted in different cultures, relating to different kinds of trauma, revealed that people suffering from PTSD failed to activate defenses following death reminders. Although Pyszczynski and Kesebir did not directly measure helplessness in their studies, a sense of helplessness is one of the major symptoms of people who have been exposed to trauma (see Solomon, 1993, for a review).

Another recent study, this one conducted by Routledge et al. (2010), explored the psychological effects of disrupting one kind of terror management defense, self-esteem enhancement. In a series of eight studies, Routledge et al. measured or manipulated participants' self-esteem and found that when self-esteem does not accomplish its protective goal (in the case of dispositional or experimentally induced low self-esteem), death reminders have an array of negative emotional, cognitive, and behavioral consequences. For example, death reminders decreased feelings of vitality, decreased people's sense that life has meaning, interfered with exploratory activities, and increased negative affectivity and social withdrawal in participants who had dispositional or experimentally induced low self-esteem but not in participants with high self-esteem. Although Routledge et al. did not assess feelings of helplessness, we consider lack of vitality, weak engagement in life, and heightened depression, anxiety, and social withdrawal, which they did measure, to be emotional and motivational derivatives of helplessness.

These recent studies encouraged us to take the additional step of assessing feelings of helplessness and consequent performance deficits following death reminders and the disruption of terror management defenses, either cultural worldview adherence, self-esteem enhancement, or seeking closeness and relatedness to other people. We conducted three experimental studies to test the hypothesis that helplessness would emerge into awareness and impair functioning when people were reminded of their finitude and could not rely on terror management defenses for preventing the realization that they are helpless and powerless in relation to their fundamental existential condition.

Mortality Salience, Cultural Worldview Threat, and Helplessness

In Study 1, we examined the hypothesis that death reminders would lead to a state of helplessness, indicated by both feelings and behavior, when people could not validate their cultural worldview. According to TMT, cultural worldview validation is a symbolic defense that assists people in keeping death concerns at bay (see Chapters 1 and 4, this volume). In fact, several studies have found that a threat to this validation process increases the accessibility of death-related thoughts (see Hayes, Schimel, Arndt, & Faucher, 2010, for a recent review). Therefore, if the intrusion of death-related thoughts into awareness is marked by the emergence of a sense of helplessness, a worldview threat following death reminders might automatically lead to feelings of helplessness and powerlessness.

We suggest that when cultural worldview validation following death reminders is blocked by internal forces (e.g., chronic lack of identification with one's culture) or external forces (e.g., messages about the moral deficiencies of one's culture), people are left defenseless, and a sense of helplessness arises. This collapse may be associated with an implicit or explicit realization that culture cannot provide a sense of power and invulnerability, which may lead to feelings of despair and observable deficits in task performance (which Seligman, 1975, called *learned-helplessness deficits*).

In Study 1, we manipulated mortality salience (yes, no) and a threat to cultural worldviews (yes, no) and assessed participants' performance on a subsequent task and feelings of helplessness. Eighty Israeli undergraduate students (51 women and 29 men) were invited individually to a laboratory experiment, completed a battery of questionnaires, and were randomly assigned to a mortality salience or physical pain condition. In the mortality salience condition, they received the following instruction and question: "Please briefly describe the emotions that the thought of your own death arouses in you" and "What do you think happens to you as you physically die and once you are physically dead?" Participants in the physical pain condition were given similar items, replacing references to death with "experiencing intense dental pain."

Immediately following this manipulation, participants read a one-page essay and were randomly assigned to either a worldview threat condition or a neutral condition. In the worldview threat condition, participants received an anti-Israeli essay consisting of statements that were highly critical of Israel, focusing on economic and ethnic inequities, fundamentalism, militarism, and lack of sympathy for foreigners. In the neutral condition, participants received a neutral essay about Israel.

All participants then completed the Remote Associates Test (RAT; Mednick, 1962), which measures creative problem solving. Participants were asked to generate a word that formed a compound with each of three other words (e.g., *common* is the correct response to *sense, courtesy, place*). Participants were given 1 minute to provide an answer to each item, and we counted the number of correct responses a participant generated. Following this task, participants received a list of 15 emotions and were asked to rate the extent to which they experienced each of them during the experiment; five of them were helplessness-related feelings (helplessness, despair, depression, powerlessness, and hopelessness). We computed a total helplessness score for each participant by averaging the five item scores.

A two-way analysis of variance (ANOVA) with mortality salience and worldview as the independent variables revealed significant interactions predicting task performance, $F(1, 76) = 3.73$, $p < .05$, and helplessness-related feelings, $F(1, 76) = 4.02$, $p < .05$. As can be seen in Table 2.1, simple main effects tests indicated that participants who were exposed to the mortality salience and worldview threat manipulations performed significantly worse on the RAT and reported more intense feelings of helplessness than participants in the other three conditions, $Fs > 6.47$, $ps < .01$. No significant difference was found between the other three conditions. Because helplessness feelings

TABLE 2.1

Means and Standard Deviations for Task Performance and Helplessness Feelings According to Mortality Salience and Threat to Terror Management Defenses in Each of the Three Studies

	Mortality salience condition		Control (dental pain) condition	
	Threat	No threat	Threat	No threat
Study 1				
Task performance M	3.75	5.90	5.55	6.05
SD	1.94	1.75	1.88	2.06
Helplessness M	3.63	2.77	2.91	2.92
SD	0.79	1.11	0.99	0.97
Study 2				
Task performance M	3.66	5.80	5.40	5.07
SD	1.84	2.21	2.16	2.21
Helplessness M	3.86	2.14	2.48	2.41
SD	0.81	0.89	0.87	0.79
Study 3				
Task performance M	3.33	5.38	5.20	5.40
SD	1.68	1.31	1.61	1.68
Helplessness M	3.95	2.48	2.45	2.77
SD	0.62	0.88	0.86	0.99

Note. The threat condition included cultural worldview threat in Study 1, self-esteem threat in Study 2, and attachment-related threat in Study 3.

were reported following RAT performance, group differences in these feelings might have reflected variations in task performance rather than effects of mortality salience and worldview threat. We therefore recomputed the two-way ANOVA for helplessness feelings while statistically controlling for task performance. There was still a significant interaction between mortality salience and worldview threat predicting helplessness feelings, $F(1, 75) = 3.94$, $p < .05$. Overall, the findings support our hypotheses and show that reminding people of their mortality and making it difficult for them to rely on cultural worldview validation has affective and behavioral effects indicating helplessness.

Mortality Salience, Self-Esteem Threat, and Helplessness

In Study 2, we examined the hypothesis that affective and behavioral manifestations of helplessness would follow death reminders when people could not bolster their self-worth. According to TMT, self-esteem is an anxiety buffer that pushes death anxiety out of awareness (see Chapter 3, this volume). Indeed, there is evidence that self-esteem threats tend to increase the accessibility of death-related thoughts (see Hayes et al., 2010, for a review). Therefore, if a sense of helplessness is associated closely with our primal fear of death, a self-esteem threat following death reminders should automatically lead to feelings of helplessness and powerlessness. We propose that when self-validation processes are disrupted by either internal forces (e.g., depression proneness) or external forces (e.g., messages that highlight personal deficiencies), people are left defenseless and a sense of helplessness arises in awareness.

To examine this hypothesis, we manipulated mortality salience (yes, no) and a self-related threat (yes, no) and assessed participants' performance on a subsequent task and feelings of helplessness. Sixty Israeli undergraduate students (41 women and 19 men) were individually invited to a laboratory experiment in which they received the same general instructions and manipulation of mortality salience or dental pain as in Study 1.

Immediately following the mortality salience manipulation, we manipulated self-esteem threat by highlighting aspects of participants' undesired or feared selves (Ogilvie, Cohen, & Solomon, 2008). Half of the participants were randomly assigned to the self-esteem threat condition and were asked to respond to two open-ended probes: "Describe what it is like when you are at your worst" and "Write down as specifically as you can what happens to you when you are at your worst." These questions were based on Ogilvie et al.'s (2008) manipulation. The remaining participants were asked to think about an acquaintance and responded to similar questions about this acquaintance (e.g., "Describe what it is like when this person is at his or her worst"). All of the participants then completed the RAT and the emotions scale used in Study 1.

A two-way ANOVA with mortality salience and self-esteem threat as the independent variables revealed significant interactions predicting task performance, $F(1, 56) = 5.11$, $p < .05$, and helplessness feelings, $F(1, 56) = 14.40$, $p < .01$. As can be seen in Table 2.1, simple main effects tests indicated that participants who were exposed to the mortality salience manipulation and thought about their undesired or feared self performed worse and reported more intense feelings of helplessness than participants in the other three conditions, $Fs > 5.59$, $ps < .05$. No significant differences were found among the other three conditions. Controlling for task performance, as in Study 1, did not eliminate the significant interaction between mortality salience and self-esteem threat, $F(1, 55) = 13.65$, $p < .01$. In line with predictions, reminding people of their mortality and interfering with a self-promoting defense resulted in affective and behavioral indications of helplessness.

Mortality Salience, Attachment-Related Threat, and Helplessness

In Study 3, we examined the hypothesis that affective and behavioral manifestations of helplessness would follow death awareness when people's attachment security was threatened by reminders of separation or rejection. Mikulincer, Florian, and Hirschberger (2003) argued that attachment security acts as a natural anxiety buffer that helps people defend against death concerns. Supporting this idea, Mikulincer, Florian, Birnbaum, and Malishkevich (2002) found that having participants contemplate separation from a romantic partner reduced attachment security and increased the accessibility of death-related thoughts. If a sense of helplessness underlies or is closely associated with the fear of death, threats of rejection, separation, or loss following death reminders should automatically arouse feelings of helplessness and powerlessness. We propose that when proximity seeking is inhibited by either internal forces (e.g., dispositional attachment insecurities) or external forces (e.g., threats of separation), people are left defenseless in the face of mortality concerns, and a troubling sense of helplessness arises.

To examine this hypothesis, we manipulated mortality salience (yes, no) and separation threat (yes, no) and assessed task performance and reported feelings of helplessness. Sixty Israeli undergraduate students (34 women and 26 men) were invited to a laboratory experiment in which they received the same instructions and manipulations of mortality salience or dental pain used in Studies 1 and 2.

Immediately following the mortality salience manipulation, we manipulated attachment-related threat by asking participants to think about a painful separation (see Mikulincer et al., 2002, for a similar manipulation). Half of the participants were randomly assigned to the separation-threat condition and asked to respond to two open-ended probes: (a) "Describe the thoughts that unwanted separation from a romantic partner arouses in you" and (b) "How do you feel about this situation?" The remaining participants were assigned to a control condition and received written instructions asking them to imagine a TV program they usually watched and to complete the two open-ended probes about watching that program. All of the participants then completed the RAT and the emotions scale used in Studies 1 and 2.

A two-way ANOVA with mortality salience and attachment threat as the independent variables revealed significant interactions for both task performance, $F(1, 56) = 5.22$, $p < .01$, and feelings of helplessness, $F(1, 56) = 16.69$, $p < .01$. As can be seen in Table 2.1, simple main effects tests indicated that participants who were exposed to mortality salience and thought about an unwanted separation from a romantic partner performed worse on the RAT and felt more helpless than participants in the other three conditions, $Fs > 9.66$, $ps < .01$. No significant difference was found between the other three conditions. In addition, a two-way ANOVA for helplessness feelings, controlling statistically for task performance, still yielded a significant interaction between mortality salience and attachment threat, $F(1, 55) = 18.68$, $p < .01$. These findings indicate that reminding people of their mortality and preventing them from gaining a sense of attachment security produce affective and behavioral manifestations of helplessness.

CONCLUDING REMARKS

The investigation of death anxiety has revealed the complexity of people's conceptions of death and its meaning. The investigation of defenses against death anxiety has revealed at least three kinds of defenses: aligning oneself with a cultural worldview that provides meaning and possibilities to contribute to something much larger than oneself, working to maintain high self-esteem in relation to the standards of one's culture, and becoming involved in comforting, supportive close relationships. One of the most frightening aspects of imagining one's own death is the anticipated helplessness associated with it: Ultimately, no one can avoid death, know when or how it will occur, or be certain of what, if anything, comes after physical death. From infancy on, human beings are terrified of helplessness and lack of power to influence painful experiences. Although infants are blissfully unaware of death, they are familiar with uncontrollable hunger, pain, and caregiver delays in restoring a sense of safety and security. As they learn about death, one of the most difficult aspects of thinking calmly about it is its uncontrollability. Religions and philosophies have been designed to help people view death (and in many cases, life after death) as at least somewhat controllable. However, there are likely to be moments when everyone, no matter how religious or stoic, realizes that they are whistling in the dark when it comes to controlling death.

Research on helplessness has shown how closely it is related to terror and, if not managed effectively, to depression, despair, and PTSD. To the extent that unmanageable thoughts of death arise in the mind, it seems likely that a dread of helplessness is part of the reaction. We have shown here, in three preliminary experiments, that feelings of helplessness and disrupted cognitive performance occur when the three main kinds of death-terror-management mechanisms are interfered with. Further research is needed to determine (a) whether death awareness arouses explicit or implicit thoughts of helplessness (this could be studied either with open-ended questions to tap conscious thoughts about helplessness or with implicit measures such as lexical decision tasks or Stroop tasks; see Mikulincer, Gillath, & Shaver, 2002, for examples of these methods in studies of implicit attachment-related processes); (b) whether manipulating helplessness just before manipulating mortality salience heightens the use of terror management defenses; and (c) whether suggestions of ways to control some of the helplessness aspects of mortality and its aftermath (e.g., meditation techniques that reduce the need to control experiences, spiritual practices within a particular religion that are claimed to make a satisfying life after death more likely) reduce the need to defend against awareness of physical death (see Chapters 8 and 14, this volume). Such studies might suggest new ways, or new uses for old ways, to reduce symptoms of psychopathology (see Chapters 19, 20, and 21, this volume), and they might lead to a more elaborated TMT that takes helplessness more fully into account.

REFERENCES

Bakan, D. (1971). *Disease, pain, and sacrifice: Toward a psychology of suffering.* Boston, MA: Beacon Press.

Bowlby, J. (1973). *Attachment and loss: Vol. 2. Separation: Anxiety and anger.* New York, NY: Basic Books.

Bowlby, J. (1979). *The making and breaking of affectional bonds.* London, England: Tavistock.

Bowlby, J. (1982). *Attachment and loss: Vol. 1. Attachment* (2nd ed.). New York, NY: Basic Books.

Bowlby, J. (1988). *A secure base: Clinical applications of attachment theory.* London, England: Routledge.

Florian, V., & Kravetz, S. (1983). Fear of personal death: Attribution, structure, and relation to religious belief. *Journal of Personality and Social Psychology, 44,* 600–607. doi:10.1037/0022-3514.44.3.600

Florian, V., Kravetz, S., & Frankel, J. (1984). Aspects of fear of personal death, levels of awareness, and religious commitment. *Journal of Research in Personality, 18,* 289–304. doi:10.1016/0092-6566(84)90014-X

Florian, V., & Mikulincer, M. (1997). Fear of death and the judgment of social transgressions: A multidimensional test of terror management theory. *Journal of Personality and Social Psychology, 73,* 369–380. doi:10.1037/0022-3514.73.2.369

Florian, V., & Snowden, L. (1989). Fear of personal death and positive life regard: A study of different ethnic and religious-affiliated American college students. *Journal of Cross-Cultural Psychology, 20,* 64–79. doi:10.1177/0022022189201004

Frijda, N. H. (1986). *The emotions.* New York, NY: Cambridge University Press.

Hayes, J., Schimel, J., Arndt, J., & Faucher, E. (2010). A theoretical and empirical review of the death-thought accessibility concept in terror management research. *Psychological Bulletin, 136,* 699–739. doi:10.1037/a0020524

Hoelter, J. W. (1979). Multidimensional treatment of fear of death. *Journal of Consulting and Clinical Psychology, 47,* 996–999. doi:10.1037/0022-006X.47.5.996

Janoff-Bulman, R. (1992). *Shattered assumptions: Towards a new psychology of trauma.* New York, NY: Free Press.

Kastenbaum, R. (2000). *The psychology of death* (3rd ed.). New York, NY: Springer.

Mednick, S. A. (1962). The associative basis of the creative process. *Psychological Review, 69,* 220–232. doi:10.1037/h0048850

Mikulincer, M. (1994). *Human learned helplessness.* New York, NY: Plenum Press.

Mikulincer, M., Florian, V., Birnbaum, G., & Malishkevich, S. (2002). The death-anxiety buffering function of close relationships: Exploring the effects of separation reminders on death-thought accessibility. *Personality and Social Psychology Bulletin, 28,* 287–299. doi:10.1177/0146167202286001

Mikulincer, M., Florian, V., & Hirschberger, G. (2003). The existential function of close relationships: Introducing death into the science of love. *Personality and Social Psychology Review, 7,* 20–40. doi:10.1207/S15327957PSPR0701_2

Mikulincer, M., Florian, V., & Tolmacz, R. (1990). Attachment styles and fear of personal death: A case study of affect regulation. *Journal of Personality and Social Psychology, 58,* 273–280. doi:10.1037/0022-3514.58.2.273

Mikulincer, M., Gillath, O., & Shaver, P. R. (2002). Activation of the attachment system in adulthood: Threat-related primes increase the accessibility of mental representations of attachment figures. *Journal of Personality and Social Psychology, 83,* 881–895. doi:10.1037//0022-3514.83.4.881

Mikulincer, M., & Shaver, P. R. (2004). Security-based self-representations in adulthood: Contents and processes. In W. S. Rholes & J. A. Simpson (Eds.), *Adult attachment: Theory, research, and clinical implications* (pp. 159–195). New York, NY: Guilford Press.

Mikulincer, M., & Shaver, P. R. (2007). *Attachment in adulthood: Structure, dynamics, and change.* New York, NY: Guilford Press.

Murphy, C. (1959). Discussion. In H. Feifel (Ed.), *The meaning of death* (pp. 129–138). New York, NY: McGraw-Hill.

Ogilvie, D., Cohen, F., & Solomon, S. (2008). The undesired self: Deadly connotations. *Journal of Research in Personality, 42,* 564–576. doi:10.1016/j.jrp.2007.07.012

Pyszczynski, T., & Kesebir, P. (2011). Anxiety buffer disruption theory: A terror management account of posttraumatic stress disorder. *Anxiety, Stress, and Coping, 24,* 3–26. doi:10.1080/10615806.2010.517524

Rosenblatt, A., Greenberg, J., Solomon, S., Pyszczynski, T., & Lyon, D. (1989). Evidence for terror management theory: I. The effects of mortality salience on reactions to those who violate or uphold cultural values. *Journal of Personality and Social Psychology, 57,* 681–690. doi:10.1037/0022-3514.57.4.681

Routledge, C., Ostafin, B., Juhl, J., Sedikides, C., Cathey, C., & Liao, J. (2010). Adjusting to death: The effects of mortality salience and self-esteem on psychological well-being, growth motivation, and maladaptive behavior. *Journal of Personality and Social Psychology, 99,* 897–916. doi:10.1037/a0021431

Seligman, M. E. P. (1975). *Helplessness: On depression, development, and death.* New York, NY: Freeman.

Solomon, S., Greenberg, J., & Pyszczynski, T. (1991). A terror management theory of social behavior: The psychological functions of self-esteem and cultural worldviews. In L. Berkowitz (Ed.), *Advances in experimental social psychology* (Vol. 24, pp. 93–159). New York, NY: Academic Press.

Solomon, Z. (1993). *Combat stress reactions: The enduring toll of war.* New York, NY: Plenum Press.

3

A SIGNIFICANT CONTRIBUTOR TO A MEANINGFUL CULTURAL DRAMA: TERROR MANAGEMENT RESEARCH ON THE FUNCTIONS AND IMPLICATIONS OF SELF-ESTEEM

JAMIE ARNDT

Growing up, I had an older brother who used to run around the house singing, "I want to be special!" At the time, I did what most any little brother would do: I made fun of him. I did not appreciate what Ernest Becker (1971) illuminated in his book *The Birth and Death of Meaning,* a few years earlier: My brother's exclaimed wish to be special might have gone to the heart of the human existential condition. One of Becker's most important contributions to our understanding of what it means to be human was to ask and answer the question, Why do people need to feel like they matter, like they are *some*body and not just *any*body? In short, why do people need self-esteem?

The question of why people so desperately need to feel good about themselves, though often assumed in psychological research to be a central motivational force in human social behavior, was largely neglected until Becker's analysis was given empirical direction in the following decade with terror management theory (TMT; Greenberg, Pyszczynski, & Solomon, 1986). In the now 20-plus years since TMT was proposed, there have been various assessments, elaborations, and refinements of the theory's empirical foundation (e.g., Pyszczynski, Greenberg, Solomon, Arndt, & Schimel, 2004; see also Chapter 1, this volume). We have learned a great deal, although, to be sure, there is still much to be understood. The goals of this chapter are to convey some of what we have learned; to illustrate some of the insight it affords into one particular area of daily life, that of health decisions; and finally, to provide a forecast of where the field may be going in its effort to understand the intersection of self-esteem and other ways of managing existential fear.

TERROR MANAGEMENT THEORY'S DEVELOPMENTAL ANALYSIS OF SELF-ESTEEM

Given the chapter in this volume by Greenberg (Chapter 1), there is little to be gained by rehashing the basics of the terror management analysis, and we can directly address the development of the self-esteem motive. Working from Becker's (1971) insights, TMT's core answer to the question of why people need self-esteem is that it helps to protect them from anxiety that would otherwise render life unlivable.

TMT builds on Becker (1971, 1973) and a range of other theorists (e.g., Bowlby, 1969; Rank, 1929/1978; see also Chapter 1, this volume) to propose that a deep association between a sense of value and protection from anxiety begins early in life, given human children's profound immaturity at birth. Given children's inability to procure even the basic sustenance necessary for survival, let alone to protect themselves, they are totally dependent on their caregivers. When sensing that he or she is alone and uncared for, an infant experiences anxiety and seeks parental contact, if not affection, to signal that needs will be met, thus reducing anxiety.

This generally works well enough until, with the child's continued development, the soothing balm of parental contact becomes conditional. No longer is simple existence sufficient to garner continual parental affection. At a certain point, the parent tries to teach the child to act in particular ways, and in order to earn the same sense of security from caregivers, the child must alter his or her behavior in accord with standards of value espoused by the parents. With age and development, these standards increasingly take on a symbolic form, reflecting the values and norms of society (e.g., "We don't pick our nose at the dinner table"). When the child eschews these parental standards (and digs full-force and in full view for that tough-to-reach nostril nugget), he or she experiences, at the least, an absence of the overt affection that renders secure functioning possible. Thus, failing to meet standards of value leads to anxiety. However, when the child meets these standards and does what Mom and Dad are trying to teach, affection is restored or expressed, and anxiety subsides. Thus begins the connection between living up to standards of value and the abatement of anxiety.

Two critical developments add considerable nuance to this process. First, the child begins to traffic in temporal, abstract, and—critically—self-reflective thought. Although there are tremendous self-regulatory upsides to these sophisticated cognitive capabilities, there is a potent downside as well. No longer is anxiety experienced only in the face of immediate threat but now also in a threat that has yet to occur. In particular, people develop an awareness of the inevitability of death. As the authors of the previous chapters have explained, given a biological proclivity for survival that humans share with other living organisms, TMT posits that the dawning awareness that death is always potentially imminent and ultimately inevitable engenders a uniquely human capacity for experiencing potentially debilitating terror.

Such debilitating anxiety would render goal-directed functioning difficult if not impossible. The maturing child must therefore develop ways of managing that fear. This is when the second critical development comes into play. As the child begins to realize that the parents cannot provide omnipotent protection from death and vulnerability, the security blanket transfers from parental standards of value to those derived from the culture into which the child is being socialized. He or she attends school, joins clubs and teams, watches movies and television, and so forth, all of which contribute to a broad cultural worldview conveying what it means to be a valuable person. As people develop, the worldview continues to prescribe routes and roles, internalized to varying degrees, by which one can feel valuable (and thus garner psychological security): being a good student, gang member, spouse or parent, scientist, Catholic, or Democrat. The more one meets and exceeds these standards of value, the more one can make one's mark on the world as defined by one's worldview, and ultimately, the more secure one's qualification for either a literal (e.g., ascendance to Heaven) or symbolic (e.g., a legacy, a book on library shelves, an inscribed park bench) form of death transcendence.

Thus, for TMT, self-esteem is a culturally based construction that consists of viewing oneself as living up to specific contingencies of value (Crocker & Wolfe, 2001) that are derived from the culture at large but are integrated into a unique, individualized blueprint by each person. As Goldenberg (Chapter 5, this volume) articulates, these routes toward self-significance offer ways to take one's individual existence and elevate it above that of a mere defecating and copulating animal with which one would otherwise share a mortal fate. The problem of mortality is solved in part by meeting the contingencies that embed human beings in an enduring symbolic reality transcending the biological reality of death.

Two important implications follow from this analysis, although there is not space here to fully delve into them. First, because these standards of value are embedded in a larger belief system, or cultural worldview, there is considerable variability across cultures in the contingencies toward which an individual strives to feel valuable (Pyszczynski, Greenberg, Solomon, Arndt, & Schimel, 2004; Sedikides, Gaertner, & Toguchi, 2003). Second, there are also many self-esteem-affording roles within a culture. In the following sections, I touch on research that highlights a few of the many ways an individual can try to feel valuable and thereby manage mortality awareness. However, a critical question for evaluating "cultural health," as it were, is the extent to which members of a culture truly have access to the primary routes of value that the culture prescribes and whether the behaviors that follow from these prescriptions lead to action and decisions that ultimately benefit the individual, society, and future generations.

CORE TERROR MANAGEMENT THEORY RESEARCH ON A CRITICAL PSYCHOLOGICAL FUNCTION OF SELF-ESTEEM

According to TMT, the self-esteem motive emerges, in part, as a primary form of psychological protection, or defense, against existential anxieties ultimately tethered to the awareness of death. This gives rise to a number of specific hypotheses that have been assessed over the years. Because this research has been extensively reviewed elsewhere (e.g., Pyszczynski et al., 2004), I only briefly cover some of the early evidence for this proposition and then turn to work that is more recent.

Self-Esteem Buffers Anxiety

The first, and most basic hypothesis, is that self-esteem should serve as a buffer against anxiety. This was one starting point of TMT research and was the hypothesis first tested by Greenberg and colleagues (1992, 1993) in a series of studies that measured or manipulated self-esteem and then assessed anxiety or anxiety-related defensiveness, such as denying vulnerability to a short life expectancy, in response to various threats. This work showed that dispositionally high or experimentally elevated self-esteem is associated with lower levels of anxiety (measured through self-reports or physiologically) in response to such threats as gory accident footage and the prospect of painful electric shock. Further, dispositionally high or experimentally elevated self-esteem eliminated participants' tendency to deny vulnerability to a short life expectancy. Taken together with correlational links between self-esteem and anxiety, this work helped to establish the basic anxiety-buffering function of self-esteem.

Self-Esteem Reduces Mortality Salience Effects

Of course, as Greenberg explained in Chapter 1 of this volume, one of the core hypotheses of TMT is that to the extent that cultural beliefs protect an individual from the awareness of death, reminders of death (i.e., mortality salience [MS]) should intensify identification with those beliefs, leading people to approve more those who support their worldview and approve less those who threaten it. Yet, if self-esteem offers protection from the awareness of death, then high levels of self-esteem should render people less in need of engaging these worldview defenses. Harmon-Jones et al. (1997) reported a series of studies in accord with this hypothesis, and more recently Schmeichel et al. (2009) offered evidence suggesting that the ability of self-esteem to protect against the effects of death awareness on worldview defense stems primarily from implicit (or nonconscious) self-esteem rather than explicit self-esteem. Although space precludes a deeper consideration of the implications of these findings, it merits noting that the potential distinction in existential security between implicit and explicit self-esteem represents an exciting direction for future research.

It also appears that the protective capacities of self-esteem are broader than just attenuating fervent defense of one's worldview. Routledge et al. (2010) recently explored an idea at the heart of the TMT analysis but that had surprisingly escaped empirical scrutiny; that is, that the nonconscious awareness of death would have an adverse effect on psychological functioning. Across eight studies, they found that death-related cognition that was outside of focal attention, either measured or manipulated, decreased reports of satisfaction with life, subjective vitality, meaning in life, and open-minded exploration, and increased reports of negative affect, state anxiety, and social avoidance. Critically, however, this was the case only for individuals with low, but not high, self-esteem.

Mortality Salience Influences Self-Esteem Striving

Although a majority of terror management research has focused on how death-related thoughts increase defenses that bolster an individual's cultural worldview, TMT more broadly explains how people obtain a sense of security, or symbolic value, when faced with existential anxieties. The guiding hypothesis is that if self-esteem assuages the threat of death by conveying that one is living up to culturally derived standards of value, then reminders of one's mortality should increase both self-esteem striving and self-esteem defense. Put simply, the awareness of death should lead people to do (or at least to believe they are doing) that which fits into their understanding of what a valuable or significant person does.

There are dozens of such findings in the literature, covering a variety of self-esteem contingencies and self-esteem maintenance strategies (e.g., self-serving attributions; Mikulincer & Florian, 2002). As examples, among those who derive self-esteem from engaging in "green" (proenvironmental) behavior, reminders of death increase intentions to engage in such behavior (Vess & Arndt, 2008), and among those who derive self-esteem from risky driving, MS actually increases risky driving in a simulator (Taubman – Ben-Ari, Florian, & Mikulincer, 1999). Illustrating the variability of how cultural standards funnel the trajectory of responses to awareness of death, Kashima, Halloran, Yuki, and Kashima (2004) found that individuals with low self-esteem in Japan responded to MS by becoming less individualistic, whereas Australian participants with low self-esteem responded to MS by becoming more individualistic. Such examples convey how awareness of death can motivate behavior that promises to impart to an individual a sense of their value and worth within their own cultural framework.

Threatening Self-Esteem Increases Death-Thought Accessibility

What about looking at the connection between self-esteem and awareness of mortality from the other direction? Most of the studies described thus far have examined how self-esteem mitigates or alters the effects of death reminders. Yet, if self-esteem helps to insulate individuals from the awareness of death, then threats to self-esteem should increase the cognitive accessibility of death-related thought. Here, *accessibility* refers to how close to consciousness a particular theme is; in this case, how much people may be thinking about death even if they are not aware of doing so.

Following research showing that compromising faith in the worldview increases such death-thought accessibility (Hayes, Schimel, Arndt, & Faucher, 2010), a number of studies have examined just this idea. Ogilvie, Cohen, and Solomon (2008), for example, found that having participants recall when they felt they were at their worst and thus failed to meet standards of value (i.e., their *undesired self*) increased the accessibility of death-related thoughts. Hayes, Schimel, and Williams (2008), rather than having participants imagine past failures, experimentally manipulated a failure experience to threaten self-worth. Whether it was giving participants who were invested in the belief that they were intelligent some information suggesting that their intelligence was below average or informing them that their personality was ill-suited for their career aspirations or rigging a public speaking task so as to create expectations of failure, these different forms of self-esteem threat provoked increased levels of death-thought accessibility relative to conditions that did not threaten self-esteem. Moreover, these effects were specific to death-related cognition and were not the result of a general increase in the accessibility of negative constructs. Finally, providing participants with the opportunity to affirm and thus fortify their self-worth eliminated the increase in death-related thought following self-esteem threat.

In sum, the basic buffering function of self-esteem has been examined and confirmed in a variety of different ways. One of the generative aspects of the TMT framework is that it facilitates insights into different domains of human social behavior, from consumer decision making to legal decisions, to health behavior, to understanding facets of psychopathology. The following section focuses on health behavior to illustrate how transporting the analysis to a more applied domain allows for further insights into the nature and operation of self-esteem as an existential resource. In particular, research on health behavior allows us to highlight the connection between self-esteem and specifically nonconscious thoughts of death, the malleability of bases of self-worth when in need of existential protection, and the influence of different types of self-esteem in managing existential fear.

ILLUSTRATING THE POWER (AND NUANCES) OF THE SELF-ESTEEM MOTIVE: HEALTH DECISION MAKING

A casual inspection of the social world reveals that people make a variety of health-related decisions, from exercising and scheduling screening exams to smoking and suntanning, that can either benefit or harm their physical health. Over the years, we have learned that such decisions often reflect not only concerns with health but also more distal, and heuristically processed, implications for the self more broadly and its value specifically (e.g., Jackson & Aiken, 2006; Leary, Tchividjian, & Kraxberger, 1994; Wakefield, Flay, Nichter, & Giovino, 2003). However, what has largely been missing is an understanding of when self-esteem motives are likely to exert an especially potent influence and when they take a backseat to more rationally (or at least pseudo-rationally) oriented health motives.

The terror management health model (TMHM; Arndt & Goldenberg, 2011; Goldenberg & Arndt, 2008) has been proposed to offer just these kinds of insights. As might be expected from what I have covered thus far, the model portrays death-related cognition as a critical catalyst in engaging the influence of self-esteem motives in health decisions. Given the functional analysis of self-esteem—which views it as a protective shield against the awareness of death—it is perhaps not surprising that the health context, with its central association to death-related concerns (e.g., Arndt, Cook, Goldenberg, & Cox, 2007), would be a particularly apt domain in which to observe the influence of terror-management processes.

Implicating the Connection Between Nonconscious Thoughts of Death and Self-Esteem Striving

Building from the dual process model of terror management (Pyszczynski, Greenberg, & Solomon, 1999), the TMHM suggests that it is specifically nonconscious thoughts of death that are most likely to activate self-esteem motives in the context of health decisions. In the course of examining this proposition, a number of findings speak to the specific connection between nonconscious thoughts of death and motives for self-enhancement.

The gist is that when people are consciously thinking about death, health decisions are guided in part by the goal of removing such thoughts from focal awareness. This can be accomplished in a variety of ways. In many cases, this can involve behavior (or intentions) that facilitate health, such as when, in the face of conscious thoughts of death, people increase their intentions to exercise (Arndt, Schimel, & Goldenberg, 2003). Yet, because the underlying goal is to remove death thoughts from consciousness, people can also do so through threat-avoidance responses (e.g., Greenberg Arndt, Simon, Pyszczynski, & Solomon, 2000). They can try to forget about it, distract themselves, or push the problem of death far into the future. Whether an individual responds with behavioral health or threat avoidance tactics as a means of ridding death thoughts from consciousness appears to depend on factors that pertain to an individual's (or a response's) ability to effectively manage the health situation and its implications for fatality (e.g., response efficacy, health optimism; Arndt, Routledge, & Goldenberg, 2006; Cooper, Goldenberg, & Arndt, 2010).

Motives for self-esteem, and the contingencies on which they are based, take a backseat when people are faced with conscious death-related thoughts. That is, when thoughts of death are conscious, people make decisions irrespective of the relevance of the behavior to their self-esteem. In contrast, as noted earlier, when death thoughts are activated but are outside conscious attention, people engage in distal defenses that are oriented toward perceptions of personal significance and symbolic worldview beliefs. Although TMHM research has examined a few different ways in which this may be accomplished, given the present focus of this chapter, I specifically consider work implicating self-esteem contingencies.

In health contexts, for example, immediately after explicit reminders of death, when thoughts of mortality are conscious, participants increase their sun protection and exercise intentions across the board (i.e., without moderation by self-esteem contingencies; Arndt et al., 2003; Routledge, Arndt, & Goldenberg, 2004). However, a different picture emerges when thoughts of death are allowed to fade from focal awareness (i.e., there is a delay following the mortality reminder). Here, people who reported basing their self-esteem on fitness respond with increased exercise intentions, and people whose self-esteem is contingent on being tanned actually report increased tanning intentions. As with suntanning, these effects occur both with "healthy" and "unhealthy" behavior. Indeed, when confronted with graphic cigarette warning labels that conjure up thoughts of death, people who smoke for self-esteem-related reasons report decreased intentions to quit smoking (Hansen, Winzeler, & Topolinski, 2010).

Knowing when self-esteem-oriented motives are relevant in turn allows us to predict when certain types of messages are likely to persuasively encourage a desired behavior. Consider celebrity endorsement. Celebrities are compelling figures in part because of their embodiment of the cultural ideals of what it means to be a desirable or valuable person. As such, we might expect celebrity endorsements to exert a more potent influence on decision preferences when thoughts of death are active but outside of focal awareness (see Chapter 1, this volume).

To explore this idea, McCabe, Vail, Arndt, and Goldenberg (2011) engaged participants in a consumer marketing study in which they indicated how much they would pay for a brand of bottled water. The water was advertised with an endorsement by popular celebrity actor Jennifer Aniston or by a medical doctor, and participants made their price estimates immediately after being reminded of mortality (vs. control) or after a delay when such thoughts had faded from conscious attention. When thoughts of death were conscious, participants were willing to pay more for water that was endorsed by a medical doctor. However, when participants were reminded of death but then distracted, they were willing to pay more for water endorsed by Jennifer Aniston. A second study conceptually replicated this pattern but instead found that the same endorsements also influenced how much water participants actually consumed when the respective bottles were presented in what they were told was a taste test. Not only is this relevant to strategies for communicating effectively about health, it also provides insights into the connection between self-esteem motives and nonconscious thoughts of death, as well as a convergent perspective on the appeal of celebrities and fame for terror management (see Chapter 1, this volume).

On the Existential Malleability of Self-Esteem Standards

An additional implication of this work is that standards of self-esteem exist within the context of cultural meanings and societal prescriptions for value. Thus, when individuals are provided with information concerning the societal value of particular standards (e.g., for appearance) in the context of activated, nonconscious mortality awareness, people's health decisions should reflect efforts to attain these standards. This imparts a certain amount of culturally infused malleability to the standards of value that people will pursue to manage existential fear.

This hypothesis has been supported in a number of health domains. In the context of tanning decisions, exposing participants to a picture of an attractive tanned woman (Routledge et al., 2004) or a fashion article titled "Bronze is Beautiful" (Cox et al., 2009), in combination with mortality reminders and a delay, increased suntanning intentions. Conversely, exposing participants to a fashion article touting an increasing societal consensus that "pale is pretty" led to decreased intentions to tan under the same conditions (Arndt et al., 2009), suggesting an augmentation of the appeal of the appearance standard, and also led beach patrons in South Florida to request sample lotions with higher sun protection factors (Cox et al., 2009). These findings inform us about the malleability of self-esteem standards in the context of using self-enhancement to manage existential fear. When the norms of society change, so too can the ways in which individuals try to feel valuable (Jonas et al., 2008).

Types of Self-Esteem Contingencies

When people make "health" decisions in the face of accessible thoughts of death, they often rely on their contingencies of self-esteem as a road map of how to respond. However, to continue the metaphor, different people use different maps. That is, global differences in how a person derives self-esteem matter, and in the present context they moderate health responses to accessible thoughts of death.

One distinction focuses on whether individuals base their self-esteem on extrinsic standards (i.e., more conditional acceptance from others as compared with an intrinsic, or internalized, sense of self-acceptance; Schimel, Arndt, Pyszczynski, & Greenberg, 2001). Arndt et al. (2009) reasoned that such extrinsically oriented individuals would be more susceptible to bend with the socially articulated breeze after thoughts of death had been activated and then had receded from focal awareness, and that this susceptibility would color their health-relevant responses toward whatever was advocated by the social context. Such effects have been observed in tanning, smoking, and exercise domains. For example, people who base their self-esteem on extrinsic standards responded to MS with increased interest in tanning (presumably because tanned skin is considered socially attractive) but were also more influenced by the situational primes touting or undermining the attractiveness of tanned skin. Thus, people can be pushed toward either healthy or unhealthy trajectories based on the salient standards of value and their attentiveness to such externally defined standards. Indeed, when individuals who smoke for extrinsic reasons were reminded of mortality and exposed to an antismoking commercial with negative peer group reactions to smoking, they reported stronger intentions to quit smoking.

One of the emerging ideas is that exposure to the self-esteem-relevant prime increases the associated self-esteem contingency (e.g., of being tanned), which in turn guides responses to accessible death-related thoughts. Arndt et al. (2009) tested this hypothesis in the context of fitness. The situational prime involved exposing participants to a positive example of people who exercise (i.e., a "prototype"; Ouellette, Hessling, Gibbons, Reis-Bergan, & Gerrard, 2005) or a negative example of people who do not exercise, both subsequent to participants being reminded of and then distracted from death-related thought. Uniquely among those participants who had been exposed to MS and the positive exercise prototype, as extrinsic self-esteem increased, so too did the relevance of exercising to self-esteem. Thus, one of the mechanisms by which death-related cognition exerts its influence on behavior is by elevating the importance of a self-esteem contingency to which the individual may be especially sensitive.

UNDERSTANDING THE ROLE OF SELF-ESTEEM IN THE LANDSCAPE OF EXISTENTIAL DEFENSE

The health-oriented research reviewed in the previous section showcases one context in which self-esteem motivations are at work. However, as other chapters in this volume elaborate, the awareness of death motivates a variety of responses beyond self-esteem striving. Two of the more widely studied are defending cultural beliefs and investing in close relationships (see Chapters 4 and 16, this volume). In thinking about where TMT research on self-esteem might head next, it seems that one of the more interesting issues is the intersection between self-esteem and these other forms of existential defense (Hart, Shaver, & Goldenberg, 2005). There are emerging lines of work that speak to such issues, and in the sections that follow I discuss examples that focus on the connection between self-esteem and close relationships, and self-esteem and worldview maintenance.

Self-Esteem and Close Relationships

Extensive research pioneered by Mikulincer and colleagues showed that people use close relationships as a way of protecting themselves from the awareness of death (see Mikulincer, Florian, & Hirschberger, 2003, for a review). Among other findings, MS instigates close relationship striving, and secure close relationships function in part to hold the accessibility of death-related cognition at bay. What is less clear is the role that self-esteem motives play in such existentially motivated interpersonal connections.

We know from prior research that awareness of mortality can lead to differential effects on broader group identification, depending on the implications of that identification for one's ability to derive self-worth. I will not focus on this work except to note that after MS, although people may at times prefer a proximal affiliation over upholding their beliefs (Wisman & Koole, 2003), they also opt to identify with groups (e.g., ethnic, gender, university) that enable them to feel good about themselves, and dis-identify from groups that do not (e.g., Arndt, Greenberg, Schimel, Pyszczynski, & Solomon, 2002; Dechesne, Greenberg, Arndt, & Schimel, 2000).

Certainly, close relationships provide solace independent of their implications for self-worth, but people may also maintain close relationships because of the self-validation they provide (Crocker & Wolfe, 2001; Murray, Holmes, & Griffin, 2000). In a scene from Alan Arkin's film *Little Murders* (Brodsky, 1971), Patsy prefaces her marriage proposal to Alfred by saying, "I love the man I want to mold you into." Her statement reflects the notion that close relationships can help us maintain our own valued identity. We want people to be the persons who will serve our own psychological goals. And as we know from studies by Florian, Mikulincer, and Hirschberger (2001), people's desire to validate their identity may be driven in part by their cognizance of their mortality.

Recently, Cox and Arndt (in press) conducted a line of studies to examine the possibility that people use close relationships for the existentially motivated maintenance of perceived regard; that is, having others view them positively. Two studies showed that when reminded of mortality, people are more likely to exaggerate how positively their romantic partners see them, which Murray et al. (2000) showed is a means of bolstering self-worth and also bolstering relational security. A third study showed that when reminded of death, the more people saw their partners as a source of perceived regard and the more committed they reported being to the relationship. People hope to stick with close others who make them feel good about themselves. An additional pair of studies indicated that these effects are most pronounced for people who base their self-esteem on relationships (those high in relationship self-esteem contingencies).

Of course, people have a variety of different relationships, and for certain individuals certain relationships may be more useful in bolstering self-esteem. In previous research, Cox et al. (2008) measured attachment anxiety and avoidance, manipulated MS, and then presented participants with a purported "cell phone calling plan" in which they could allocate minutes to different relationships. After being reminded of mortality, securely attached individuals (those low on attachment anxiety and avoidance) allocated significantly more minutes to their romantic partners, whereas anxiously attached participants allocated significantly more minutes to their parents. Such desires for contact, it seems, may reflect self-esteem-bolstering motivation. Cox and Arndt (in press) also found that after being reminded of death, anxious individuals exaggerated how positively their parents saw them, whereas secure individuals exaggerated how positively their romantic partners saw them.

Whereas certain individuals may be more prone to using (certain) relationships for self-esteem-enhancing purposes in light of mortality awareness, different relationship stages can be conducive to different terror management goals. Kosloff, Greenberg, Sullivan, and Weise (2010) explored how short-term dating relationships afford a potent opportunity for self-esteem enhancement, whereby the relationship partner can become a trophy attesting to one's own value. Long-term relationships, in contrast, may often provide an opportunity to erect a pillar supporting one's meaningful worldview. Three studies were in accord with this possibility, and thus not only provided further insight into nuances of the intersection between close relationship striving and self-esteem but also introduced interesting issues about the interface between self-esteem and worldview defense.

Self-Esteem Defense and Worldview Maintenance

The title of this chapter is paraphrasing Becker (1971), who wrote that "one critical function of culture is to . . . provide the individual with the conviction that he is *an object of primary value in a world of meaningful action*" (p. 79, emphasis in original). This raises a question: Is it more important that one be a significant contributor or that the drama be meaningful? Clearly, the answer depends on a host of factors, and in the majority of situations the two go hand in hand. However, sometimes they do not. The Kosloff et al. (2010) studies suggest that, at least at the beginning of a relationship, self-esteem motives may trump those for worldview validation. Is this necessarily or even often the case? In many cases, it seems that the worldview must be maintained for the individual to have value within that worldview, and thus the former may often be the more fundamental source of existential fortitude. Indeed, if the values on which one's self-esteem is predicated are undermined, then the anxiety-buffering qualities of the resultant self-esteem would be similarly compromised.

Arndt and Greenberg (1999) initially explored this idea, showing that self-esteem-boosting personality feedback attenuated MS-induced worldview defense, unless the domain of the worldview that was under attack was the basis for the self-esteem boosting feedback. This suggests that self-esteem may be only as effective as the worldview on which it is based. Extending this line of thought, Landau, Greenberg, and Sullivan (2009) were more directly interested in the question of how people respond when routes to self-esteem and worldview maintenance collide. One way in which this collision manifests, they reasoned, occurs when self-enhancing on a particular dimension means outperforming a revered other who lends stability to the worldview. They constructed scenarios in which self-enhancement would demand putting oneself above the revered other, thus undermining the worldview. Maintaining the worldview, however, would mean downplaying one's performance, thus sacrificing the opportunity for self-enhancement. Across a series of studies, Landau et al. found support for the former pattern. Thus, participants reminded of their mortality were more likely to rate themselves especially highly on valued dimensions, unless doing so meant outperforming their parent or an admired cultural icon. Such findings converge to suggest that although self-esteem is a vital cog in the engine that manages fears about death, it is often if not generally predicated on first maintaining faith in the worldview.

Clearly, there is much more to be understood about how people manage existential insecurity and with which defenses they prefer to do so. What is especially exciting about some of the recent research is that it begins to explore such options, rather than simply presenting participants with one given outcome to which they can respond. As Greenberg (Chapter 1, this volume) and Pyszczynksi and Kesebir (Chapter 4) briefly describe, we are starting to see research on the possibility of managing terror in ways that bear less negative consequences for different others and potentially foster more socially and individually healthy outcomes (see Vail et al., 2011). This certainly represents one of the more hopeful and encouraging directions for further research.

CODA

In the *Birth and Death of Meaning*, Becker (1971) suggested that if you want to truly understand someone, you need to ask how that person thinks of himself or herself as a hero. In other words, what is the avenue along which the person endeavors to feel valuable? I have always found that thought quite comforting because it can be seen as offering a kind of bridge to others, both those similar and those seemingly quite different. It suggests that all people are on a parallel quest, trying to endure the all-too-often hardship of life and their awareness of inevitable death to feel that they count, they matter. There is comfort in being in the same, albeit inevitably sinking, ship. Perhaps, then, I should have asked my brother: In what way would you like to be special?

REFERENCES

Arndt, J., Cook, A., Goldenberg, J.L., & Cox, C. (2007). Cancer and the threat of death: The cognitive dynamics of death thought suppression and its impact on behavioral health intentions. *Journal of Personality and Social Psychology, 92,* 12–29. doi:10.1037/0022-3514.92.1.12

Arndt, J., Cox, C.R., Vess, M., Goldenberg, J.L., Cohen, F., & Routledge, C. (2009). Blowing in the (social) wind: Implications of extrinsic esteem contingencies for terror management and health. *Journal of Personality and Social Psychology, 96,* 1191–1205. doi:10.1037/a0015182

Arndt, J., & Goldenberg, J.L. (2011). When self-enhancement is in the driver's seat: Using the terror management health model to understand health behavior. In C. Sedikides & M. Alicke (Eds.), *The handbook of self-enhancement and self-protection* (pp. 380–398). New York, NY: Guilford Press.

Arndt, J., & Greenberg, J. (1999). The effects of a self-esteem boost and mortality salience on responses to boost relevant and irrelevant worldview threats. *Personality and Social Psychology Bulletin, 25,* 1331–1341. doi:10.1177/0146167299259001

Arndt, J., Greenberg, J., Schimel, J., Pyszczynski, T., & Solomon, S. (2002). To belong or not to belong, that is the question: Terror management and identification with gender and ethnicity. *Journal of Personality and Social Psychology, 83,* 26–43. doi:10.1037/0022-3514.83.1.26

Arndt, J., Routledge, C., & Goldenberg, J.L. (2006). Predicting proximal health responses to reminders of death: The influence of coping style and health optimism. *Psychology & Health, 21,* 593–614. doi:10.1080/14768320500537662

Arndt, J., Schimel, J., & Goldenberg, J.L. (2003). Death can be good for your health: Fitness intentions as a proximal and distal defense against mortality salience. *Journal of Applied Social Psychology, 33,* 1726–1746. doi:10.1111/j.1559-1816.2003.tb01972.x

Becker, E. (1971). *The birth and death of meaning.* New York, NY: Free Press.

Becker, E. (1973). *The denial of death.* New York, NY: Free Press.

Bowlby, J. (1969). *Attachment.* New York, NY: Basic Books.

Brodsky, J. (Producer), & Arkin, A. (Director). (1971). *Little murders* [Motion picture]. United States: Twentieth Century Fox Film Corporation.

Cooper, D.P., Goldenberg, J.L., & Arndt, J. (2010). Examination of the terror management health model: The interactive effect of conscious death thought and health-coping variables on decisions in potentially fatal health domains. *Personality and Social Psychology Bulletin, 36,* 937–946. doi:10.1177/0146167210370694

Cox, C.R., & Arndt, J. (in press). How sweet it is to be loved by you: The role of perceived regard in the terror management of close relationships. *Journal of Personality and Social Psychology.*

Cox, C.R., Arndt, J., Pyszczynski, T., Greenberg, J., Abdollahi, A., & Solomon, S. (2008). Terror management and adult's attachment to their parents: The safe haven remains. *Journal of Personality and Social Psychology, 94*, 696–717. doi:10.1037/0022-3514.94.4.696

Cox, C.R., Cooper, D.P., Vess, M., Arndt, J., Goldenberg, J.L., & Routledge, C. (2009). Bronze is beautiful but pale can be pretty: The effects of appearance standards and mortality salience on tanning outcomes. *Health Psychology, 28*, 746–752. doi:10.1037/a0016388

Crocker, J., & Wolfe, C. (2001). Contingencies of worth. *Psychological Review, 108*, 593–623. doi:10.1037/0033-295X.108.3.593

Dechesne, M., Greenberg, J., Arndt, J., & Schimel, J. (2000). Terror management and sports fan affiliation: The effects of mortality salience on fan identification and optimism. *European Journal of Social Psychology, 30*, 813–835. doi:10.1002/1099-0992(200011/12)30:6<813::AID-EJSP17>3.0.CO;2-M

Florian, V., Mikulincer, M., & Hirschberger, G. (2001). Validation of personal identity as a terror management mechanism: Evidence that sex-role identity moderates mortality salience effects. *Personality and Social Psychology Bulletin, 27*, 1011–1022. doi:10.1177/0146167201278008

Goldenberg, J.L., & Arndt, J. (2008). The implications of death for health: A terror management health model for behavioral health promotion. *Psychological Review, 115*, 1032–1053. doi:10.1037/a0013326

Greenberg, J., Arndt, J., Simon, L., Pyszczynski, T., & Solomon, S. (2000). Proximal and distal defenses in response to reminders of one's mortality: Evidence of a temporal sequence. *Personality and Social Psychology Bulletin, 26*, 91–99. doi:10.1177/0146167200261009

Greenberg, J., Pyszczynski, T., & Solomon, S. (1986). The causes and consequences of a need for self-esteem: A terror management theory. In R.F. Baumeister (Ed.), *Public self and private self* (pp. 189–212). New York, NY: Springer-Verlag. doi:10.1007/978-1-4613-9564-5_10

Greenberg, J., Pyszczynski, T., Solomon, S., Pinel, E., Simon, L., & Jordan, K. (1993). Effects of self-esteem on vulnerability-denying defensive distortions: Further evidence of an anxiety-buffering function of self-esteem. *Journal of Experimental Social Psychology, 29*, 229–251. doi:10.1006/jesp.1993.1010

Greenberg, J., Solomon, S., Pyszczynski, T., Rosenblatt, A., Burling, J., Lyon, D., . . . Pinel, E. (1992). Assessing the terror management analysis of self-esteem: Converging evidence of an anxiety-buffering function. *Journal of Personality and Social Psychology, 63*, 913–922. doi:10.1037/0022-3514.63.6.913

Hansen, J., Winzeler, S., & Topolinski, S. (2010). When death makes you smoke: A terror management perspective on the effectiveness of cigarette on-pack warnings. *Journal of Experimental Social Psychology, 46*, 226–228. doi:10.1016/j.jesp.2009.09.007

Harmon-Jones, E., Simon, L., Greenberg, J., Pyszczynski, T., Solomon, S., & McGregor, H. (1997). Terror management theory and self-esteem: Evidence that increased self-esteem reduces mortality salience effects. *Journal of Personality and Social Psychology, 72*, 24–36. doi:10.1037/0022-3514.72.1.24

Hart, J., Shaver, P.R., & Goldenberg, J.L. (2005). Attachment, self-esteem, worldviews, and terror management: Evidence for a tripartite security system. *Journal of Personality and Social Psychology, 88,* 999–1013. doi:10.1037/0022-3514.88.6.999

Hayes, J., Schimel, J., Arndt, J., & Faucher, E.H. (2010). A theoretical and empirical review of the death-thought accessibility concept in terror management research. *Psychological Bulletin, 136,* 699–739. doi:10.1037/a0020524

Hayes, J., Schimel, J., & Williams, T.J. (2008). Evidence for the death-thought accessibility hypothesis II: Threatening self-esteem increases the accessibility of death thoughts. *Journal of Experimental Social Psychology, 44,* 600–613. doi:10.1016/j.jesp.2008.01.004

Jackson, K.M., & Aiken, L.S. (2006). Evaluation of a multicomponent appearance-based sun-protective intervention for young women: Uncovering the mechanisms for program efficacy. *Health Psychology, 25,* 34–46. doi:10.1037/0278-6133.25.1.34

Jonas, E., Martens, A., Niesta, D., Fritsche, I., Sullivan, D., & Greenberg, J. (2008). Focus theory of normative conduct and terror management theory: The interactive impact of mortality salience and norm salience on social judgment. *Journal of Personality and Social Psychology, 95,* 1239–1251. doi:10.1037/a0013593

Kashima, E.S., Halloran, M., Yuki, M., & Kashima, Y. (2004). The effects of personal and collective mortality salience on individualism: Comparing Australians and Japanese with higher and lower self-esteem. *Journal of Experimental Social Psychology, 40,* 384–392. doi:10.1016/j.jesp.2003.07.007

Kosloff, S., Greenberg, J., Sullivan, D., & Weise, D. (2010). Of trophies and pillars: Exploring the terror management functions of short-term and long-term relationship partners. *Personality and Social Psychology Bulletin, 36,* 1037–1051. doi:10.1177/0146167210374602

Landau, M.J., Greenberg, J., & Sullivan, D. (2009). Managing terror when worldviews and self-worth collide: Evidence that mortality salience increases reluctance to self-enhance beyond authorities. *Journal of Experimental Social Psychology, 45,* 68–79. doi:10.1016/j.jesp.2008.08.007

Leary, M.R., Tchividjian, L.R., & Kraxberger, B.E. (1994). Self-presentation can be hazardous to your health: Impression management and health risk. *Health Psychology, 13,* 461–470. doi:10.1037/0278-6133.13.6.461

McCabe, S., Vail, K.E., Arndt, J., & Goldenberg, J.L. (2011). *Terror management and celebrities.* Manuscript in preparation, University of Missouri, Columbia.

Mikulincer, M., & Florian, V. (2002). The effect of mortality salience on self-serving attributions: Evidence for the function of self-esteem as a terror management mechanism. *Basic and Applied Social Psychology, 24,* 261–271. doi:10.1207/S15324834BASP2404_2

Mikulincer, M., Florian, V., & Hirschberger, G. (2003). The existential function of close relationships: Introducing death into the science of love. *Personality and Social Psychology Review, 7,* 20–40. doi:10.1207/S15327957PSPR0701_2

Murray, S. L., Holmes, J. G., & Griffin, D. W. (2000). Self-esteem and the quest for felt security: How perceived regard regulates attachment processes. *Journal of Personality and Social Psychology, 78,* 478–498. doi:10.1037/0022-3514.78.3.478

Ogilvie, D. M., Cohen, F., & Solomon, S. (2008). The undesired self: Deadly connotations. *Journal of Research in Personality, 42,* 564–576. doi:10.1016/j.jrp.2007.07.012

Ouellette, J. A., Hessling, R., Gibbons, F. X., Reis-Bergan, M., & Gerrard, M. (2005). Using images to increase exercise behavior: Prototypes versus possible selves. *Personality and Social Psychology Bulletin, 31,* 610–620. doi:10.1177/0146167204271589

Pyszczynski, T., Greenberg, J., & Solomon, S. (1999). A dual-process model of defense against conscious and unconscious death-related thoughts: An extension of terror management theory. *Psychological Review, 106,* 835–845. doi:10.1037/0033-295X.106.4.835

Pyszczynski, T., Greenberg, J., Solomon, S., Arndt, J., & Schimel, J. (2004). Why do people need self-esteem? A theoretical and empirical review. *Psychological Bulletin, 130,* 435–468. doi:10.1037/0033-2909.130.3.435

Rank, O. (1978). *Truth and reality.* New York, NY: Knopf. (Original work published 1929)

Routledge, C., Arndt, J., & Goldenberg, J. L. (2004). A time to tan: Proximal and distal effects of mortality salience on sun exposure intentions. *Personality and Social Psychology Bulletin, 30,* 1347–1358. doi:10.1177/0146167204264056

Routledge, C., Ostafin, B., Juhl, J., Sedikides, C., Cathey, C., & Liao, J. (2010). Adjusting to death: The effects of self-esteem and mortality salience on well-being, growth motivation, and maladaptive behavior. *Journal of Personality and Social Psychology, 99,* 897–916. doi:10.1037/a0021431

Schimel, J., Arndt, J., Pyszczynski, T., & Greenberg, J. (2001). Being accepted for who we are: Evidence that social validation of the intrinsic self reduces general defensiveness. *Journal of Personality and Social Psychology, 80,* 35–52. doi:10.1037/0022-3514.80.1.35

Schmeichel, B. J., Gailliot, M. T., Filardo, E., McGregor, I., Gitter, S., & Baumeister, R. F. (2009). Terror management theory and self-esteem revisited: The roles of implicit and explicit self-esteem in mortality salience effects. *Journal of Personality and Social Psychology, 96,* 1077–1087. doi:10.1037/a0015091

Sedikides, C., Gaertner, L., & Toguchi, Y. (2003). Pancultural self-enhancement. *Journal of Personality and Social Psychology, 84,* 60–79. doi:10.1037/0022-3514.84.1.60

Taubman – Ben-Ari, O., Florian, V., & Mikulincer, M. (1999). The impact of mortality salience on reckless driving: A test of terror management mechanisms. *Journal of Personality and Social Psychology, 76,* 35–45. doi:10.1037/0022-3514.76.1.35

Vail, K. E., Juhl, J., Arndt, J., Routledge, C., Vess, M., & Rutjens, B. (2011). *When death is good for life: Considering the positive trajectories of terror management*. Manuscript submitted for publication.

Vess, M., & Arndt, J. (2008). The nature of death and the death of nature: The impact of mortality salience on environmental concern. *Journal of Research in Personality, 42*, 1376–1380. doi:10.1016/j.jrp.2008.04.007

Wakefield, M., Flay, B., Nichter, M., & Giovino, G. (2003). Effects of anti-smoking advertising on youth smoking: A review. *Journal of Health Communication, 8*, 229–247. doi:10.1080/10810730305686

Wisman, A., & Koole, S. (2003). Hiding in the crowd: Can mortality salience promote affiliation with others who oppose one's worldviews? *Journal of Personality and Social Psychology, 84*, 511–526. doi:10.1037/0022-3514.84.3.511

4

CULTURE, IDEOLOGY, MORALITY, AND RELIGION: DEATH CHANGES EVERYTHING

TOM PYSZCZYNSKI AND PELIN KESEBIR

The human quest for immortality is as old as the human awareness of death. Throughout the ages, human beings have striven to transcend the inevitable end of life that awaits them and achieve immortality, be it through myth and religion, science and medicine, or family and work. In this chapter, we consider how the reality of death changes the way human psychological motives operate. Relying on terror management theory (TMT; Greenberg, Pyszczynski, & Solomon, 1986; see also Chapter 1, this volume), we argue that humanly constructed meaning systems, such as culture, ideology, morality, and religion, serve important death-denying functions. Of course, these systems also function to solve practical problems. Understanding how the world works provides clues as to what to do to get what one needs and wants. However, TMT posits that the human awareness of death adds urgency to the way humans hold on to these sources of meaning and changes the sorts of meanings that people seek. We start with a brief overview of TMT and a discussion of how culture, ideology, morality, and religion are affected by

The writing of this chapter was supported in part by a grant from the Air Force Office of Sponsored Research, FA9550-04-1-0239.

awareness of mortality. We then address recent conceptualizations that cast the problem of death as a specific instance of a more general threat, and argue that awareness of death is a unique force for humankind—one that changes the pursuit of meaning, value, and security in ways that profoundly affect the functioning of culture, ideology, and religion.

THE MEANING-MAKING ANIMAL FACES ITS MORTALITY

Although ants, bees, and chimpanzees are all social animals, only human beings are cultural animals. Only human beings are meaning-making animals that live their lives embedded in a universe of symbols, ideas, and values created by other humans. TMT was developed, in part, to explain the psychological functions served by these cultural conceptions of reality and the values they specify for appropriate human conduct. From the perspective of TMT, people use the meaning systems they learn from their cultures, referred to as *cultural worldviews*, to shield themselves from the anxiety that results from awareness of the inevitability of death. To get this protection, people must believe they are living up to the standards of value espoused by their culture, thus acquiring self-esteem in the short term, and literal or symbolic immortality in the long term. For one's worldview and self-esteem to effectively fend off anxiety, people must maintain faith in these conceptions. Because worldviews and self-concepts are humanly created ideas that often bear little relation to observable aspects of nature, they can be maintained only if others share them. Those who share one's worldview increase confidence in it, and those who do not undermine confidence (for a review of TMT research, see Chapter 1, this volume).

Cultural worldviews are shared meaning systems that provide a theory of existence, which gives meaning to life, and standards of value, which are guides for appropriate behavior and yardsticks against which people's value can be assessed. Maintaining faith in one's worldview and living up to its standards help one to manage anxiety by imbuing life with meaning and oneself with value, thus opening the door to the literal immortality promised by the religious aspects of the worldview and/or the symbolic immortality that results from being a valuable part of an eternal entity greater than oneself. The term *ideology* is often used interchangeably with the term *worldview*. For present purposes, we used the term *ideology* to refer to the aspects of cultural worldviews that provide a moral and rational basis for social, political, or economic systems and prescribe how members of that system should behave (Jost, Fitzsimons, & Kay, 2004). Ideologies are the most central and highly valued aspects of most people's worldviews. That is, they contain the most important core religious and/or secular elements of the belief system, which are revered and often viewed as "sacred truths" that are beyond debate. This is especially true when the ideology is believed to have come directly from an omniscient and omnipotent deity. Conversely, especially revered secular elements of worldviews are often given sacred status (e.g., the U.S. Constitution), and the leaders responsible for these elements are often treated with god-like reverence (e.g., the American Founding Fathers). This link between ideology and the supernatural dimension is one of the central themes of this chapter.

Most popular contemporary theories of ideology, morality, and religion are primarily social in nature. They emphasize the role these institutions play in promoting the smooth functioning of groups. Both system justification theory (Jost & Banaji, 1994) and social dominance theory (Sidanius & Pratto, 1999), for example, conceive of ideology as a motivated, system-serving belief system that legitimizes and maintains the current social order. Haidt (2007) posited that moral intuitions evolved to facilitate intragroup harmony, inhibit intragroup conflict, and bind groups together against rivals. Many recent theories similarly view religious belief as functioning to bring people together and encourage intragroup cooperation (e.g., Bloom, 2005; see also Chapter 8, this volume). Although we acknowledge the role of ideology, morality, and religion in promoting social cohesion, TMT suggests an additional function of these cultural institutions that dramatically changes the way people relate to them.

The Birth of Ideology, Morality, and Religion

Cultural worldviews probably began as attempts to answer practical questions about how the world works, answers that early humans could use to meet their needs and navigate through life—explaining how to find food, stay warm, and relate to others. Meaning systems are, by definition, social in that they are ways of sharing information among people. Relationships among people were no doubt an important topic of the earliest meaning systems. Even before this, primitive moral intuitions were evolving that, as Haidt (2007) suggested, helped maintain social cohesion and minimize conflict. With the emergence of more sophisticated intellectual capacities and language, these moral intuitions were verbalized and codified into cultural norms and values and then into comprehensive meaning systems into which these norms and values were embedded.

The emergence of the awareness of death was presumably a seismic event. Our ancestors needed to manage the potential for terror that resulted from their dawning awareness of the harsh reality of nature—that all living things eventually die. From this point on, meaning systems had to do more than simply guide action and maintain group cohesion—they became part of the emerging terror management system. The explanations of the workings of the world were thus expanded to imbue reality with supernatural powers. Deities were invented who could control nature and grant immortality to otherwise mortal humans. As others have suggested, the earliest precursors to deities and religion may have initially emerged as by-products of psychological tendencies that had been selected for other purposes in our evolutionary history, such as the "hair-triggered" attribution of agency to ambiguous stimuli and the ability to "read" the content of other minds (Atran & Norenzayan, 2004). From the perspective of TMT, however, the emerging awareness of death had a profound impact on the nature and function of the gods and religions that humankind created, which ultimately changed the dynamics of the moral intuitions and social norms used to control behavior.

Probably because of the human tendency to anthropomorphize and imagine that the gods thought much like they did, people created deities that granted immortality only to those who believed in them, followed their commands, and stayed in their good graces. This also led people to impute their own moral intuitions to the gods, who were assumed to use them as standards for judging who was worthy of immortality. Thus, the regulation of moral behavior was turned over to all-powerful deities who granted immortality only to those who behaved in a moral manner. Moral thought and action thus took on the added function of managing the newly emerged potential for existential terror. The fear of negative social consequences our prehistoric ancestors experienced when they violated their moral intuitions was given further power by the newfound fear of losing the immortality that could be granted only by the gods.

Because moral behavior became the major criterion for admittance to the afterlife by the deity, moral virtue took on added value and became the preeminent value for most cultures. This explains why moral values are so highly emphasized by most parents and other important socializing agents of the culture. Consequently, they are most people's primary basis of both self-esteem and evaluations of others (for a discussion of how the anxiety-buffering functions of worldview and self-esteem emerge out of early attachments and later socialization, see Chapter 3, this volume). In line with this view, Skitka, Bauman, and Sargis (2005) provided a broad range of evidence supporting the special status of moral beliefs in social judgments.

Consistent with the death-denying function of morality, research has shown that terror management processes affect reactions to violations of all five of Haidt and Graham's (2007) moral foundations (for a review, see Kesebir & Pyszczynski, 2011). Many studies have shown that mortality salience (MS) leads people to rate moral transgressions based on the harm/care foundation (e.g., a doctor who amputates the leg of the wrong patient) as more severe and to recommend harsher punishment for the transgressors (Florian

& Mikulincer, 1997). Other studies have shown that MS intensifies reactions to violations of the fairness dimension, for example, by increasing derogation of the victim of a random tragedy (Landau et al., 2004); conversely, learning about severely injured innocent victims elicits more death-related cognitions than learning about victims responsible for their condition (Hirschberger, 2006). In addition, when justice concerns are salient, MS increases support for violence even when the expected utility of violence is low, increases the appeal of justice-based arguments for military action, and increases the desire for justice, which mediates the link between death thoughts and increased support for military action (Hirschberger, Pyszczynski, Ein-Dor, & Kesebir, 2012). A multitude of TMT studies show that MS increases ingroup loyalty in the form of both ingroup favoritism and outgroup hostility. MS also increases support for leaders who proclaim the unique value of the ingroup (Cohen, Solomon, Maxfield, Pyszczynski, & Greenberg, 2004).

Death concerns are also at play in various aspects of the purity/sanctity dimension of morality. MS increases the intensity of reactions to disgusting stimuli, and viewing pictures of bodily waste increases the accessibility of death-related thoughts (see Chapter 5, this volume). The first demonstration of the MS effect, showing that reminders of death lead to higher bond recommendations for a woman arrested for prostitution (Rosenblatt, Greenberg, Solomon, Pyszczynski, & Lyon, 1989), can be viewed as an instance of increased punitiveness toward a violator of the purity/sanctity dimension. Research demonstrating that MS increases belief in an afterlife, increases death-thought accessibility when one's religious beliefs are challenged, and increases distress when using a crucifix in a disrespectful way provides additional converging evidence of the role of death concerns in the purity/sanctity dimension (Vail et al., 2010).

Keeping Faith in an Invisible World

Because terror management through religious beliefs resides in an imagined invisible world that cannot be experienced through normal sensory channels, the anxiety-buffering power of worldviews and the deities and moral principles they contain are especially dependent on their acceptance by other people. The emergence of immortality-granting gods increased the need for group solidarity and consensual beliefs to maintain faith in them. It "takes a village" to maintain faith in things that cannot be seen. Although there are certainly other reasons people are motivated to maintain cohesive groups, the human invention of death-denying immortality systems greatly increased the urgency of these motives. Consistent with this view, research has shown that when interviewed in front of a funeral home, people exaggerate the extent of social consensus for their attitudes, especially when they hold unpopular opinions on the issues (Pyszczynski et al., 1996). Indeed, archeologists have found evidence of large-scale human settlements replete with religious temples and images at Göbekli Tepe in Turkey, dating back 11,500 years, well before any evidence of agriculture or domestication of animals (Symmes, 2010). This suggests that the widely shared view that civilization resulted from the invention of agriculture might have it backward. The motivation to please the gods who provided access to immortality may have brought people together into larger settlements to build temples, and the need to feed these larger groups may have accelerated the emergence of other aspects of culture, such as agriculture and the domestication of animals (Solomon, Greenberg, Schimel, Arndt, & Pyszczynski, 2004).

The invention of deities probably also increased the power of those who were believed best able to communicate with this invisible world and persuade the spirits to look kindly on their followers. Priests and shamans were able to wield great power within their groups because of their alleged connections to the guardians of immortality and because of their "practical knowledge" of how to please the gods. These religious leaders either assumed great power or were closely aligned with secular leaders who were believed to be chosen by the gods for their leadership roles. In many cases, the leaders were believed to be gods themselves, as in the case of the Egyptian pharaohs and Japanese emperors. This merger of church and state provided a ready explanation and justification for the power wielded by the elite. Thus, the death-inspired invention of gods and consolidation of supernatural and political power provided a potent incentive for system-justifying behavior: Doubting the righteousness of the system put one's literal immortality in jeopardy. A similar though perhaps less potent dynamic probably occurs when one questions the secular aspects of one's culture, which puts one's symbolic immortality in jeopardy.

Death Does Not Necessarily Bring Out the Worst in People

TMT does not imply that existential threats inevitably lead people to justify the status quo, as some have argued (e.g., Jost et al., 2004). From our perspective, system-justifying behavior is motivated by the terror management function that some but not all political systems serve—for some but not all people. This suggests that an important determinant of whether people are motivated to justify the systems under which they live may be the extent to which these systems meet their terror management needs. People would be expected to justify systems only to the extent that the systems are effectively providing the meaning, value, and hope of immortality needed to manage their existential fears. When a system is believed to deny these resources, the motivation to overthrow it grows. Of course, other factors, such as hope that such rebellions will be successful, are also needed for the motivation for change to lead to concrete action. This confluence of forces may be responsible for the "Arab Spring" of 2011 in the many Middle Eastern countries undergoing rebellions against corrupt leaders.

The fear of death leads people to seek protection wherever they can most readily obtain it. TMT posits that people construct their own worldview by combining elements of the diverse ideas, values, and experiences to which they have been exposed and that the extent to which this involves wholesale introjection of the ideas and values of powerful others or a thoughtful process of self-creation varies from person to person (Pyszczynski, Greenberg, & Goldenberg, 2003). The raw materials from which individualized worldviews are constructed reflect thousands of years of human thought, experience, hopes, and dreams, distilled through the socializing forces of each individual's life. Worldviews are likely to be especially complex, multifaceted, and conflicted in multicultural societies with heavy exposure to human diversity.

Diverse research traditions have suggested that an important determinant of which worldview element a person will use when in need of existential protection is the accessibility of the various elements (Higgins, 1996). Highly valued or central aspects of one's worldview are likely to be chronically accessible and thus especially likely to guide responses to MS. A host of studies show that individual differences in political orientation predict the direction of responses to death reminders. For example, Pyszczynski et al. (2006) found that MS increased politically conservative but not liberal Americans' support for the use of extreme military tactics to fight terrorism, and Hirschberger and Ein-Dor (2006) found similar patterns among Israelis. Recent priming experiences temporarily increase the accessibility of worldview elements, thus affecting the specific response to existential threat. Research has shown that priming the values of tolerance, compassion, and secure attachments all influence responses to MS, sometimes reversing the direction of effects found in the absence of such priming (Kesebir & Pyszczynski, in press).

It also seems likely that some worldview elements are more useful for safety and security than others. Elements of worldview and self most associated with security are probably held with greater conviction. Worldview elements closely tied to literal immortality, such as those involving gods, morality, and afterlife, may be especially likely to be used to manage existential anxiety. Thus, people may be most motivated to justify systems they view as sacred. Right-wing authoritarians and religious fundamentalists, who construe their ontological beliefs as sacred and inviolate, are especially likely to respond to MS with hostility toward different worldviews (Motyl & Pyszczynski, in press). Rothschild, Abdollahi, and Pyszczynski (2009) found that priming the value of compassion led fundamentalist Christians and Muslims to decrease support for hostilities against each other only when these values were presented as part of their sacred religious texts. Research has also shown that construing natural things (e.g., water) as sacred reduces the increase in worldview defense that MS otherwise produced (Kesebir, Chiu, & Pyszczynski, 2012).

In sum, research to date strongly refutes claims that existential threat inevitably leads to a conservative or system-justifying shift. Worldviews are too complex and people acquire security in too many ways for a simple unidirectional response to threat to be useful. The emerging picture is that of a highly flexible system in which both chronic and momentary salience of worldview elements, along with the security value of each, determine how people protect themselves from existential threat.

The Utility of Illusion

The dawning awareness of death, and the invention of a supernatural dimension to make death less frightening (see Norenzayan & Hansen, 2006), also changed other aspects of the way people understood their world. An accurate understanding of reality is usually the best guide for efficacious action to meet one's needs. In a world without fear, people might indeed approximate Heider's (1958) ideal of the naïve scientist, dispassionately gathering information to be objectively processed to obtain the most accurate understanding of reality possible. However, in a world where one of the few certainties is that one will die, with uncertainty regarding when, how, and what that will be like, beliefs that fit closely with observable facts about death may be too painful to be accepted. This may have been a major impetus for the emergence of self-deception in human thought.

Of course, there are many reasons for people to shield themselves from the truth. Self-deception to maintain self-esteem, cognitive consistency, belief in a just world, feelings of relational security, and faith in one's worldview are all well known in the social psychological literature. It is notable that these are all motives that research has shown to be affected by terror management concerns (Greenberg, Solomon, & Arndt, 2008). If effective attainment of what is needed for survival and reproduction were all that mattered, there would be little impetus for distorting one's perceptions of oneself or one's environment, because this would more often than not undermine one's chances of meeting one's needs. Perhaps self-deception is functional because it increases confidence and encourages risk taking that is not justified by an accurate assessment of one's skills and the situation one is facing. However, such distortions would more often produce negative outcomes, and if negative outcomes are more potent than positive ones (Baumeister, Bratslavsky, Finkenauer, & Vohs, 2001), such deviations from accuracy would be discouraged. However, if there are powerful advantages to high self-esteem, cognitive consistency, and these other psychological motives beyond the pragmatics of achieving concrete goals, then deceiving oneself to achieve these states would be adaptive. TMT suggests that the role these motives play in managing existential terror provides that incentive. Although an accurate understanding of reality is useful when something can be done to produce a favorable outcome, when there is nothing that can be done to alter one's fate, the benefits of fanciful illusions may be much greater than the rewards for accuracy.

Alternative Conceptions of Existential Motivation

Over the past decade, alternatives to TMT have been proposed that seem to take death out of the existential equation. These alternative theories argue that the reason thoughts of death produce the effects they do has little or nothing to do with the problem of mortality per se. Rather, it is argued that people are primarily motivated to seek meaning (Heine, Proulx, & Vohs, 2006), certainty (McGregor, Zanna, Holmes, & Spencer, 2001; van den Bos & Miedema, 2000), or social coalitions (Kirkpatrick & Navarrete, 2007) and that thoughts of death are upsetting because they threaten these motives. These alternative conceptualizations pose a "chicken or egg" sort of question: Do people seek meaning to protect themselves from fear of death, or is death frightening because it threatens meaning? Do people seek certainty because certainty regarding one's protective beliefs is needed for their effective functioning, or is death threatening because it threatens certainty? Do people seek belonging and social coalitions because they reduce the fear of death, or is death threatening because it undermines social connections?

Although these alternative accounts emphasize different aspects of human experience as primary, they converge on the view that the problem of death is simply a specific instance of a threat to a more basic human need. This fits well with the long-standing tradition in psychology, and science in general, of explaining diverse phenomena with abstract constructs that encompass many specific instances of those phenomena. All theories, including TMT, do this. The TMT approach is different in that rather than trying to reduce the pursuit of meaning, certainty, or social connections to a specific instance of death denial, it posits that the fear of death affects the way other psychological needs function and the outcomes that will satisfy them. We now consider some of the most influential of these alternatives and explain why they are problematic.

Death Undermines Meaning

According to the meaning-maintenance model (MMM), "meaning is the expected relationships or associations that human beings construct and impose on their worlds . . . meaning is what connects things to other things in expected ways—anything and any way that things can be connected" (Heine et al., 2006, p. 90). The MMM posits that "humans find it problematic to be . . . confronted with meaninglessness, and therefore seek to reconstruct a sense of meaning whenever their meaning frameworks are disrupted" (p. 90). This recapitulates ideas shared by virtually all psychological theories of human thought and reasoning (e.g., Heider, 1958; Kruglanski, 1989). To this widely held assumption, the authors add a fluid compensation model whereby threats to meaning frameworks lead people to bolster and reaffirm other meaning frameworks that remain intact.

From the perspective of the MMM, the reason thoughts of death motivate people to cling to their cultural worldviews, self-esteem, and close attachments is that death undermines meaning. Heine et al. (2006) argued that "people primarily have anxieties about death because death renders life meaningless by severing individuals from their external environment, and in a sense, from themselves" (p. 98). Accordingly, although the problem of death may be especially disturbing, it is not fundamentally different from any other threat to meaning. This is perhaps best illustrated in a study by Proulx and Heine (2008), in which they compared the effect of death reminders with that of subtly replacing an experimenter with another person in a way that their participants did not notice. Intriguingly, these two inductions produced similar effects on moral-belief affirmation, measured by asking participants to set a bond for a prostitute as if they were a judge reviewing the case. This and other findings of meaning-related threats producing effects similar to MS are interpreted as supporting the claim that the problem of death is simply a specific type of threat to meaning.

The most basic problem with this analysis is that knowing one will die is itself a meaning. Consistent with Heine et al.'s (2006) definition of meaning, it is an "expected relationship . . . [that] connects things to other things in expected ways" (p. 90). If meanings entail "anything and any way that things can be connected" (p. 90), is the fact that life will end someday not a meaning? Indeed, the idea that death entails complete and total annihilation of the self, which is the meaning of death that TMT posits as most troublesome, is also a meaningful relation between things in the world. Clearly, it is not a pleasant meaning, but it fits the MMM definition of meaning, and therefore it should not be troublesome from that perspective.

Heine et al. (2006) also argued, following Baumeister (1991), that death threatens meaning because:

> (a) death undermines the predictability and controllability of one's existence, (b) death eliminates all potential that one has for earning meaning in the future, (c) death reminds people that their existence and the meaning framework that they have constructed will likely be forgotten, and (d) death nullifies the value of one's life's achievements. (p. 98)

However, if what is important for meaning is how an event fits in with the relationship between ideas and events that one uses to understand the world, physical death would not pose any of these problems for people who believe in an afterlife, especially the more popular kinds in which life after death far outshines anything one could experience or even imagine during one's physical existence. The ideas about literal immortality that are part of virtually all religions provide clear ways of predicting and controlling one's existence after death, imbue one's future with great cosmic significance and meaning, enshrine people's meaning systems and selves in perpetuity, and provide a crowning achievement of one's life: attaining one's eternal reward. To the extent that death is threatening because it challenges people's existing meaning systems, it should not be troubling to the approximately 75% of today's Americans who believe in life after death (Pew Research Center, 2010). If one believes in an afterlife, the meaning of death is simply a move to a new, presumably vastly improved, environment, with no disconnect from one's self.

We agree with the MMM view that meaning is strongly desired and that the absence of it sets in motion a host of behaviors aimed at restoring it. Yet, the TMT perspective diverges from MMM in viewing death as a unique threat that changes the quality and intensity of the pursuit of meaning. Meaning has both epistemic and existential functions. In a deathless world, people would still seek meaning and comprehensibility for purely pragmatic reasons, as a basis for controlling and manipulating their environment. However, illusory meanings that deviated from observable reality and that were frequently challenged by disconfirming evidence would soon lose their appeal. The practical utility of meaning (the need for accuracy) would be much more potent, and the soothing balm of unverifiable meanings would lose much of its power without the ultimate threat of death.

Death Undermines Certainty

In a related vein, uncertainty management theory (UMT; van den Bos, Poortvliet, Maas, Miedema, & van den Ham, 2005; see also McGregor et al., 2001) argues that death is motivating, at least some of the time, because of the uncertainties it entails: when and how it will happen and what happens afterwards. More recently, van den Bos (2009) distinguished between *informational uncertainty*, which is the type of uncertainty studied by decision theorists that "involves having less information available than one ideally would like to have in order to be able to confidently form a given social judgment," and *personal uncertainty*, which he defines as "a subjective sense of doubt or instability in self-views, worldviews, or the interrelation between the two" that "involves the implicit and explicit feelings and other subjective reactions people experience as a result of being uncertain about themselves" (p. 198). UMT views the personal form of uncertainty as most relevant to worldview defense and existential meaning.

This shift from a relatively undifferentiated concept of uncertainty in early presentations of these ideas (van den Bos & Miedema, 2000) to the focus on uncertainty about self and worldview in more recent presentations (van den Bos, 2009), suggests that UMT views threats to the psychological structures that TMT posits protect people from death-related fear as most threatening. Like the MMM, UMT posits that such threats lead to fluid compensation whereby people cope with threats to one aspect of worldview or self by bolstering unrelated aspects. This seems to imply that these various meanings or certainties regarding self and world serve a shared function of some sort, a view shared with TMT. However, UMT and the MMM, unlike TMT, argue that meaning and certainty about self and world are sought only for their own sake and that death is problematic because it undermines these meanings and certainties.

McGregor, Nash, Mann, and Phills (2010) recently advanced a similar concept, *anxious uncertainty*, which like van den Bos's (2009) concept of personal uncertainty, is distinguished from "merely informational uncertainty that does not threaten personal goals or cause anxious or ideological reactions in the threat and defense literature" (McGregor et al., 2010, p. 134). Anxious uncertainty arises from simultaneously active approach and avoidance impulses and activates *reactive approach motivation* (RAM). From this perspective, tenacious absorption in an alternative approach goal distracts from the anxiety produced by the initial approach–avoidance conflict and thereby reduces the distress of anxious uncertainty. Presumably, virtually any goal or ideal can relieve anxious uncertainty as long as it is sufficiently compelling; thus, people pursue these alternative approach goals with intense zeal. Unlike the MMM and UMT, this approach does not posit a common psychological resource that is both undermined by the threat and restored by the defense; in particular, they laud the potential of this framework to dispense with the need for "convoluted links to the concept of symbolic immortality" (p. 142).

One major problem with McGregor and colleagues' (2010) RAM approach is that the definition of anxious uncertainty is circular: It is not useful to distinguish anxious uncertainty from informational uncertainty by saying that the former is the type that threatens personal goals and causes anxious or ideological reactions. It is also unclear how the fear of death involves a simultaneously active approach and avoidance tendency; as far as we can tell, the fear of death is all about avoidance. The RAM model also leaves out the fact that death reminders increase avoidance motivation, leading to behaviors such as physical distancing from foreigners (Ochsmann & Mathy,

1994), distancing from one's ethnic group when it is associated with negative qualities (Arndt, Greenberg, Schimel, Pyszczynski, & Solomon, 2002), and increased anxiety when handling cultural icons in a disrespectful manner (Greenberg, Simon, Porteus, Pyszczynski, & Solomon, 1995). Indeed, one of the most widely replicated effects of MS is more negative evaluations of outgroup members and those who criticize one's worldview, which certainly seems to entail avoidance reactions. Under certain theoretically specified conditions, MS has been shown to lead to avoidance even of things that are normally extremely appealing, such as the physical aspects of sex and other pleasurable physical sensations (see Chapter 5, this volume). The fact that most behaviors, including any that involve a choice, can be construed as either approaching one choice or avoiding the other might be used to explain away this problem, but doing so makes it impossible to make precise predictions from this theory: Is derogating an outgroup member approaching one's own group or avoiding another? Does exercise approach health or avoid illness? It is also unclear why zealous engagement in an avoidance goal would not provide relief from the anxious uncertainty created by an approach–avoidance conflict.

We agree with UMT that people often crave a sense of certainty. Although we also recognize that certainty serves other functions, such as increasing the likelihood that one will take action to pursue one's goals, we argue that certainty fulfills an important terror management function. One's worldview, self-esteem, and attachments are only effective in providing protection from existential fears when people hold them with confidence and certainty.

In our view, one of the major problems with all existing alternatives to TMT is that their proponents seem to focus on only the mortality salience hypothesis, rather than the TMT literature in its totality or the real world behavioral phenomena that TMT aims to explain. TMT was not developed to explain why MS produces diverse effects in laboratory studies; rather it was designed to explain why people need self-esteem, faith (or certainty) in their worldviews, and other people to support these two psychological entities. It was also designed with the hope of shedding light on the role that human awareness of the inevitability of death plays in diverse forms of human behavior, an issue that with few exceptions was ignored in previous psychological theorizing. The MS hypothesis is simply one of several distinct hypotheses deduced from the theory to guide empirical research on it. A viable alternative to TMT would need to address the questions that TMT tries to answer as well as explain the findings across the diverse hypotheses and applications that have been used to test it. We have never argued that understanding the death-denying aspects of self-esteem, culture, interpersonal relations, morality, or religion is all that needs to be known about these topics. Rather, we argue that it is impossible to understand these issues without a consideration of the role they play in shielding people from the existential terror that results from death awareness.

CONCLUDING REMARKS

The point of this chapter is that human awareness of the inevitability of death changes everything. Specifically, we argued that the dawning awareness of mortality had a unique impact on human psychology that changed why and how humans relate to meaning systems such as ideology, morality, and religion. We argued that the zeal and dedication with which people cling to these aspects of their culture, especially the resistance of such beliefs to compelling evidence that challenges the basis for these meanings, cannot be explained by rational or pragmatic forces alone. We emphasized the urgency and unique direction that death anxiety adds to human motivation. Despite abiding perceptions about death anxiety bringing out the worst in people, recent TMT research has made it increasingly clear that this is not true. We believe that further research on how people can use their awareness of death as a source of meaning and growth instead of a source of paralyzing dread and ultimately harmful defenses is needed, and we hope to see future TMT research move in that direction.

REFERENCES

Arndt, J., Greenberg, J., Schimel, J., Pyszczynski, T. & Solomon, S. (2002). To belong or not to belong, that is the question: Terror management and identification with gender and ethnicity. *Journal of Personality and Social Psychology, 83*, 26–43. doi:10.1037/0022-3514.83.1.26

Atran, S., & Norenzayan, A. (2004). Religion's evolutionary landscape: Counterintuition, commitment, compassion, communion. *Behavioral and Brain Sciences, 27*, 713–730. doi:10.1017/S0140525X04000172

Baumeister, R. F. (1991). *Meanings of life*. New York, NY: Guilford Press.

Baumeister, R. F., Bratslavsky, E., Finkenauer, C., & Vohs, K. D. (2001). Bad is stronger than good. *Review of General Psychology, 5*, 323–370. doi:10.1037/1089-2680.5.4.323

Bloom, P. (2005, December). Is God an accident? *Atlantic Monthly, 296*, 105–112.

Cohen, F., Solomon, S., Maxfield, M., Pyszczynski, T., & Greenberg, J. (2004). Fatal attraction: The effects of mortality salience on evaluations of charismatic, task-oriented, and relationship-oriented leaders. *Psychological Science, 15*, 846–851. doi:10.1111/j.0956-7976.2004.00765.x

Florian, V., & Mikulincer, M. (1997). Fear of death and the judgment of social transgressions: A multidimensional test of terror management theory. *Journal of Personality and Social Psychology, 73*, 369–380. doi:10.1037/0022-3514.73.2.369

Greenberg, J., Pyszczynski, T., & Solomon, S. (1986). The causes and consequences of a need for self-esteem: A terror management theory. In R. F. Baumeister (Ed.), *Public self and private self* (pp. 189–212). New York, NY: Springer-Verlag. doi:10.1007/978-1-4613-9564-5_10

Greenberg, J., Simon, L., Porteus, J., Pyszczynski, T., & Solomon, S. (1995). Evidence of a terror management function of cultural icons: The effects of mortality salience on the inappropriate use of cherished cultural symbols. *Personality and Social Psychology Bulletin, 21*, 1221–1228. doi:10.1177/01461672952111010

Greenberg, J., Solomon, S., & Arndt, J. (2008). A basic but uniquely human motivation: Terror management. In J. Y. Shah & W. L. Gardner (Eds.), *Handbook of motivation science* (pp. 114–134). New York, NY: Guilford Press.

Haidt, J. (2007, May 18). The new synthesis in moral psychology. *Science, 316*, 998–1002. doi:10.1126/science.1137651

Haidt, J., & Graham, J. (2007). When morality opposes justice: Conservatives have moral intuitions that liberals may not recognize. *Social Justice Research, 20*, 98–116. doi:10.1007/s11211-007-0034-z

Heider, F. (1958). *The psychology of interpersonal relations*. New York, NY: Wiley. doi:10.1037/10628-000

Heine, S. J., Proulx, T., & Vohs, K. (2006). The meaning maintenance model: On the coherence of social motivations. *Personality and Social Psychology Review, 10*, 88–110. doi:10.1207/s15327957pspr1002_1

Higgins, E. T. (1996). Knowledge activation: Accessibility, applicability, and salience. In E. T. Higgins & A. W. Kruglanski (Eds.), *Social psychology: Handbook of basic principles* (pp. 133–168). New York, NY: Guilford Press.

Hirschberger, G. (2006). Terror management and attributions of blame to innocent victims: Reconciling compassionate and defensive responses. *Journal of Personality and Social Psychology, 91*, 832–844. doi:10.1037/0022-3514.91.5.832

Hirschberger, G., & Ein-Dor, T. (2006). Defenders of a lost cause: Terror management and violent resistance to the disengagement plan. *Personality and Social Psychology Bulletin, 32*, 761–769. doi:10.1177/0146167206286628

Hirschberger, G., Pyszczynski, T., Ein-Dor, T., & Kesebir, P. (2012). *A psychological casus belli: Fear of death fuels the desire for justice and encourages political violence*. Unpublished manuscript.

Jost, J. T., & Banaji, M. R. (1994). The role of stereotyping in system-justification and the production of false consciousness. *British Journal of Social Psychology, 33*, 1–27. doi:10.1111/j.2044-8309.1994.tb01008.x

Jost, J. T., Fitzsimons, G., & Kay, A. C. (2004). The ideological animal: A system justi?cation view. In J. Greenberg, S. L. Koole, & T. Pyszczynski (Eds.), *Handbook of experimental existential psychology* (pp. 263–283). New York, NY: Guilford Press.

Kesebir, P., Chiu, C.-Y., & Pyszczynski, T. (2012). *The sacred: An existential anxiety buffer*. Unpublished manuscript.

Kesebir, P., & Pyszczynski, T. (2011). A moral–existential account of the psychological factors fostering intergroup conflict. *Social and Personality Psychology Compass, 5,* 878–890. doi:10.1111/j.1751-9004.2011.00397.x

Kesebir, P., & Pyszczynski, T. (in press). The role of death in life: Existential aspects of human motivation. In R. Ryan (Ed.), *The Oxford handbook of motivation*. New York, NY: Oxford University Press.

Kirkpatrick, L., & Navarrete, C. D. (2007). Reports of my death have been greatly exaggerated: A critique of terror management theory from an evolutionary perspective. *Psychological Inquiry, 17,* 288–298. doi:10.1080/10478400701366969

Kruglanski, A.W. (1989). *Lay epistemics and human knowledge: Cognitive and motivational bases*. New York, NY: Plenum Press.

Landau, M.J., Johns, M., Greenberg, J., Pyszczynski, T., Martens, A., Goldenberg, J.L., & Solomon, S. (2004). A function of form: Terror management and structuring the social world. *Journal of Personality and Social Psychology, 87,* 190–210. doi:10.1037/0022-3514.87.2.190

McGregor, I. Nash, K., Mann, N., & Phills, C.E. (2010). Anxious uncertainty and reactive approach motivation. *Journal of Personality and Social Psychology, 99,* 133–147. doi:10.1037/a0019701

McGregor, I., Zanna, M.P., Holmes, J.G., & Spencer, S.J. (2001). Compensatory conviction in the face of personal uncertainty: Going to extremes and being oneself. *Journal of Personality and Social Psychology, 80,* 472–488. doi:10.1037/0022-3514.80.3.472

Motyl, M., & Pyszczynski, T. (2010). The existential underpinnings of the cycle of terrorist and counterterrorist violence and pathways to peaceful resolutions. *International Review of Social Psychology, 22,* 267–291.

Norenzayan, A., & Hansen, I.vG. (2006). Belief in supernatural agents in the face of death. *Personality and Social Psychology Bulletin, 32,* 174–187. doi:10.1177/0146167205280251

Ochsmann, R., & Mathy, M. (1994). *Depreciating of and distancing from foreigners: Effects of mortality salience*. Unpublished manuscript, Universität Mainz, Mainz, Germany.

Pew Research Center. (2010, February 17). *Religion among the millennials*. Retrieved from http://pewforum.org/Age/Religion-Among-the-Millennials.aspx

Proulx, T., & Heine, S. J. (2008). The case of the transmogrifying experimenter: Af?rmation of a moral schema following implicit change detection. *Psychological Science, 19,* 1294–1300. doi:10.1111/j.1467-9280.2008.02238.x

Pyszczynski, T., Abdollahi, A., Solomon, S., Greenberg, J., Cohen, F., & Weise, D. (2006). Mortality salience, martyrdom, and military might: The Great Satan versus the Axis of Evil. *Personality and Social Psychology Bulletin, 32,* 525–537. doi:10.1177/0146167205282157

Pyszczynski, T., Greenberg, J., & Goldenberg, J. (2003). Freedom vs. fear: On the defense, growth, and expansion of the self. In M. R. Leary & J. P. Tangney (Eds.), *Handbook of self and identity* (pp. 314–343). New York, NY: Guilford Press.

Pyszczynski, T., Wicklund, R. A., Floresku, S., Koch, H., Gauch, G., Solomon, S., & Greenberg, J. (1996). Whistling in the dark: Exaggerated consensus estimates in response to incidental reminders of mortality. *Psychological Science, 7*, 332–336. doi:10.1111/j.1467-9280.1996.tb00384.x

Rosenblatt, A., Greenberg, J., Solomon, S., Pyszczynski, T., & Lyon, D. (1989). Evidence for terror management theory I: The effects of mortality salience on reactions to those who violate or uphold cultural values. *Journal of Personality and Social Psychology, 57*, 681–690. doi:10.1037/0022-3514.57.4.681

Rothschild, Z., Abdollahi, A., & Pyszczynski, T. (2009). Does peace have a prayer? The effect of mortality salience, compassionate values, and religious fundamentalism on hostility toward out-groups. *Journal of Experimental Social Psychology, 45*, 816–827. doi:10.1016/j.jesp.2009.05.016

Sidanius, J., & Pratto, F. (1999). *Social dominance: An intergroup theory of social hierarchy and oppression.* New York, NY: Cambridge University Press.

Skitka, L. J., Bauman, C. W., & Sargis, E. G. (2005). Moral conviction: Another contributor to attitude strength or something more? *Journal of Personality and Social Psychology, 88*, 895–917. doi:10.1037/0022-3514.88.6.895

Solomon, S., Greenberg, J., Schimel, J., Arndt, J., & Pyszczynski, T. (2004). Human awareness of mortality and the evolution of culture. In M. Schaller & C. Crandall (Eds.), *The psychological foundations of culture* (pp. 15–40). New York, NY: Erlbaum.

Symmes, P. (2010, February 19). History in the remaking: A temple complex in Turkey that predates even the pyramids is rewriting the story of human evolution. *Newsweek.* Retrieved from http://www.newsweek.com/2010/02/18/history-in-the-remaking.html

Vail, K. E., Rothschild, Z. K., Weise, D. R., Solomon, S., Pyszczynski, T., & Greenberg, J. (2010). A terror management analysis of the psychological functions of religion. *Personality and Social Psychology Review, 14*, 84–94. doi:10.1177/1088868309351165

van den Bos, K. (2009). Making sense of life: The existential self trying to deal with personal uncertainty. *Psychological Inquiry, 20*, 197–217. doi:10.1080/10478400903333411

van den Bos, K., & Miedema, J. (2000). Toward understanding why fairness matters: The influence of mortality salience on reactions to procedural fairness. *Journal of Personality and Social Psychology, 79*, 355–366. doi:10.1037/0022-3514.79.3.355

van den Bos, K., Poortvliet, M., Maas, M., Miedema, J., & van den Ham, E. (2005). An enquiry concerning the principles of cultural norms and values: The impact of uncertainty and mortality salience on reactions to violations and bolstering of cultural worldviews. *Journal of Experimental Social Psychology, 41*, 91–113. doi:10.1016/j.jesp.2004.06.001

5

A BODY OF TERROR: DENIAL OF DEATH AND THE CREATURELY BODY

JAMIE L. GOLDENBERG

The fear of death weighs heavily on the human psyche. But as Ernest Becker (1973) posited, and as research on terror management theory (TMT; see, e.g., Solomon, Greenberg, & Pyszczynski, 2004; see also Chapter 1, this volume) has empirically validated, people manage the potential for terror associated with death by immersing themselves in a symbolic, cultural world imbued with meaning, where they matter. In the arts, sports, one's career, parenthood, friendship, love, fame, charity, and of course, religion, people find meaning and prescriptions for personal value (see Chapter 4, this volume). In this way, people live their lives in a symbolic, cultural realm that extends beyond them as individuals and their inevitably doomed existence. In religion or spirituality, too, people find an even more literal solution; death is less of a problem to the extent that it does not represent the end of existence (i.e., there is life after death). By these means, people symbolically, even quite literally, manage the threat associated with death.

I would like to thank Phil Shaver, Nathan Heflick, and Kasey Lynn Morris for their useful feedback during the preparation of this manuscript.

Alas, there is a flaw in this system of defense against the problem of human mortality. It is not just the physical reality of death that people must guard against. That is easy, in a sense, because death is a reality only once in each person's life. One can deny, deny, deny; and only at the very end, or during a close encounter (or perhaps during a terror management experiment), be forced to reckon with the truth of one's mortal existence. But the body—the bleeding, stinking body—offers a constant reminder of humankind's physical, and—by virtue of this—mortal, nature. Herein resides the problem, the contradiction of being "Gods with anuses," as Becker (1973, p. 51) so aptly put it. Human beings are caught in a perpetual struggle between, on the one hand, the need to deny mortality with symbolic, cultural, or spiritual solutions, and on the other, reminders that they are flesh-and-blood creatures with animalistic needs and desires, and therefore as definitively mortal as any other animal.

It follows that people will distance themselves from the physicality of the body by concealing its more creaturely aspects or by imbuing the physical body with symbolic significance. Moreover, these reactions should be exacerbated when existential concerns are pressing, and the salience of the physical body should interfere with defenses against fear of death. In this chapter, I discuss research testing these hypotheses, shedding light on discomfort with, and inhibitions surrounding, the body; the condemnation and objectification of women's bodies, in particular; and, finally, on the belief in life after death. I conclude with a discussion of questions that remain, highlighting directions for future inquiry.

A BODY OF TERROR

"We are born between urine and faeces," Sigmund Freud (1930/1969) wrote, and indeed, from his perspective, development of the person, or personality, is rooted in this recognition (i.e., anal stage of development), and from then on, the ongoing struggle between humankind's animal nature (i.e., the id), and efforts to repress it (i.e., the superego, or civilization). Although many of Freud's conclusions have been discounted, people's fundamental inability to accept their animal nature has been recognized again and again. Subsequent psychological thinkers, such as Becker (1973) and Norman O. Brown (1959), however, reinterpreted Freud's observations and insights, concluding that the cause for the conflict was not the superego, or even civilization, but rather, the uniquely human awareness of mortality. From the perspective of Becker and TMT, the body and its animal nature is a problem because it reminds people of their physical, and consequently mortal, nature. By virtue of this, the body should be more of a threat when thoughts of mortality and/or human creatureliness are salient. A decade ago, in collaboration with my fellow TMT researchers, I began a programmatic investigation of the existential underpinnings of ambivalence toward the body.

Sex

Sex seemed like the obvious place to begin. One does not need to look too deeply into the psychological, or popular, literature—even without ever having read Freud or having seen a Woody Allen film—to realize there is a great deal of ambivalence surrounding sex. In collaboration with my colleagues, I reasoned that despite its clear intrinsic appeal, sex may be a problem because of its physical, creaturely aspects. Specifically, we hypothesized that the physical aspects of sex make human physicality salient and, therefore, should make thoughts of death accessible. In addition, people should distance themselves from physical sex when mortality is made salient.

In the first experiments on this topic, Goldenberg, Pyszczynski, McCoy, Greenberg, and Solomon (1999) supported these hypotheses but uniquely among individuals high in neuroticism. In the first study, a reminder of mortality (called *mortality salience* [MS]) caused participants high in neuroticism to report that the physical aspects of sex (e.g., "feeling my genitals respond sexually") were less appealing than when mortality had not been made salient. A second study revealed that, for individuals high in neuroticism, thinking about physical sex increased the accessibility of death-related thoughts on an implicit word fragment completion measure (e.g., completing "C O F F _ _" with "coffin" instead of "coffee"). Finally, we replicated this finding and showed that providing meaning by associating sex with love reduced death-thought accessibility in response to thinking about physical sex. As expected, there were no similar effects in response to the romantic (symbolic, not physical) aspects of the sexual experience (e.g., "expressing love for my partner").

We reasoned that these previous findings were unique among individuals high in neuroticism because these individuals are less able to imbue physical activities, such as sex, with meaning (without an explicit cue, e.g., priming love). Our position, however, suggests that sex, stripped of meaning, is problematic because of its creaturely connotations regardless of level of neuroticism. If this is correct, then reminding individuals of their similarity to other animals, thereby undermining their sense of symbolic meaning, should lead to effects in the general population similar to those found among neurotics.

We (Goldenberg, Cox, Pyszczynski, Greenberg, & Solomon, 2002) found evidence to support this in another two studies. First, thinking about the physical (but not romantic) aspects of sex led to an increase in the accessibility of death-related thoughts when participants had first been exposed to an essay highlighting the biological similarities between humans and animals (e.g., "Whether you're talking about lizards, cows, horses, insects, or humans, we're all made up of the same basic biological products . . . skin, blood, organs, and bones . . . "). Then, in a second study, when participants were primed with this same (human creatureliness) essay, priming MS resulted in decreased attraction to the physical but, again, not to the romantic aspects of sex. In each study, exposing participants to an essay distinguishing humans from animals (e.g., "Humans have language and culture . . . art, music, and literature . . . live in an abstract world of the imagination . . . ") eliminated the association between sex and death.

Thus, there is evidence to support the position that when sex is viewed in creaturely terms (because of creatureliness being primed before people think about sex, or without any priming among individuals high in neuroticism), thoughts of death become more accessible; also, the salience of mortality promotes a negative reaction to this otherwise pleasurable aspect of existence. When the threatening connotations of sex were removed by either priming human uniqueness or studying participants who scored relatively low in neuroticism, death thoughts did not become accessible, and reminders of mortality did not have this same aversive effect. Indeed, MS increased (nonsignificantly) the appeal of physical sex under these conditions. It is clear, then, that reactions to sex are complex (a point long understood). Beyond that, our studies indicate that it is death—or rather the awareness of it—that underlies the complexities.

Excrement

Sex is one of the most basic human behaviors—without it our species would cease to exist—and although sex occurs more often than death (for most people), it too is usually restricted to certain situations, times of day, and so on. Sex is usually imbued with meaning—if not by virtue of love, then because of sexual prowess or desirability. However, the body has other needs that are (for most people) more frequent and certainly less likely to convey meaning and value. Along the same lines as our research on sex, we predicted that people would respond more negatively to the physical body and its by-products when mortality was salient.

Supporting this hypothesis, Goldenberg et al. (2001, Study 1) found that MS increased people's disgust reactions to the bodily products subscale (e.g., an unflushed bowel movement) of Haidt, McCauley, and Rozin's (1994) disgust-sensitivity measure. More recently, Cox, Goldenberg, Pyszczynski, and Weise (2007) conducted two additional related studies. In the first, implicit death-thought accessibility was heightened in response to (rather extreme) images depicting human bodily products, and this was the case regardless of whether participants had or had not previously been primed with human creatureliness. In another study using milder verbal body-product stimuli, death-thought accessibility was heightened, as in the sex studies, only when human creatureliness was first primed.

Thus, consistent with reactions to sexual behavior, negative reactions to the body's even-more-unmentionable behaviors, too, appear to be driven by a threat associated with concerns about human creatureliness and death. In contrast to sex, at least with respect to the more extreme examples, the threat was found in the absence of any explicit association being drawn to human creatureliness.

Aggression

On the basis of this theoretical framework, we considered that perhaps the threat associated with creatureliness could be used to ameliorate an often harmful human behavior: aggression. Human aggression, like sex, is often robed in meaning, and it can be used as a means to feel as though one is a person of value; but at the same time, it represents an animalistic aspect of human nature. We reasoned that if we could highlight the creatureliness of aggression, we could reduce the tendency to behave aggressively.

In collaboration with Motyl and colleagues (Motyl et al., 2011), I conducted a series of experiments testing this hypothesis. In the first, participants exposed to the human creatureliness essay (compared with human uniqueness) showed elevated death-thought accessibility after hitting a punching bag for 90 seconds. Priming creatureliness had no effect in a condition in which participants listened to music instead of punching. As hypothesized, priming creatureliness also caused participants to punch the punching bag with less frequency and force and to appear (to raters blind to the creatureliness condition), and report being, uncomfortable while punching in two additional experiments. Finally, participants primed to view violence as animalistic reported reduced support for going to war against Iran. These studies suggest that portraying violence as instinctual and creaturely may serve the potentially beneficial purpose of reducing the intensity of aggressive behavior and the support of violent solutions to international conflicts.

Embodiment

The findings presented thus far show that existential concerns cause people to distance themselves psychologically from sex, aggression, and other more "disgusting" aspects of the body. But what about physical experiences that are, perhaps, less sensational but rather merely sensory in nature? In three experiments, Goldenberg, Hart, et al. (2006) demonstrated that priming thoughts about one's death caused people to avoid physical sensory experiences, including pleasurable ones. Again, this response was found to be moderated by neuroticism. In response to MS, highly neurotic individuals spent less time submerging their arm in ice-cold water and using an electric foot massager but did not avoid stimulation in nonphysical domains (e.g., listening to music). As in the studies examining reactions to sex, there was a trend for low neurotic individuals to embrace the behaviors by actually performing them longer when mortality was salient. In another study, Goldenberg, Heflick, and Cooper (2008) found that not only did individuals high in neuroticism do less of a physical exercise designed to promote body awareness when mortality was primed, they also experienced increased guilt after doing so. Thus, even physical experiences that on the surface do not appear to pose any threat can be problematic when, under the surface, existential concerns become active.

THE BODY OF WOMEN

The preceding section spoke of threats associated with the human body and its behaviors; in another line of research, Tomi-Ann Roberts and I have addressed reactions specific to the female body (Goldenberg & Roberts, 2004, 2010). In short, we argued that women's bodies pose a special problem for creatures oriented toward denying their creatureliness. Women's bodies, compared with men's, are connected to nature and reproduction in ways that are more obvious. As evolutionary theorists (e.g., Buss & Schmitt, 1993) have explained, mammalian females bear the brunt of the reproductive burden. In the human species, women shed their uterine lining monthly; when pregnant, they carry a fetus in their womb for 9 months, after which, their breasts lactate to sustain the infant. The extent of men's obligatory investment, often delivered as the punch line of a joke, is 5, or maybe 15, minutes. Consequently, women are not only likely to be the more "invested" parent (Trivers, 1972) but there may also be an additional psychological investment required in the reactions to certain aspects of women's bodies.

These aspects—menstruation, pregnancy, and breastfeeding—are likely to be threatening, especially when existential concerns are salient; but also, women's bodies, because of the threat, are likely to be imbued with symbolic meaning and value to soften their threatening quality. As with the construct "ambivalent sexism" (Glick & Fiske, 1996), our theoretical position accounts for explicitly negative attitudes toward women and their bodies and also for seemingly (but not really) positive reactions to women, including their objectification. In contrast to ambivalent sexism, however, our analysis does not view benevolence toward women as rooted primarily in a need to pacify women but rather in men's need to pacify themselves. That is, men not only need women but they also want them, and desiring a creature is in itself a threat (Landau et al., 2006). In addition, from our perspective, mortality-influenced reactions to women's bodies are not unique to men, because women, too, experience a threat associated with their own bodies.

Menstruation

There is a long history of derisive reactions to female menstruation, with women being cast out from society (e.g., being confined to menstrual huts) or generally considered dirty and contaminating during menstruation (e.g., requiring mikvah baths, being kept from touching hunting tools). Contemporary Western attitudes are also negative and center mostly on concerns about sanitation and secrecy. In line with the current theoretical perspective, it seems likely that the disdain with which menstruation is viewed may be because of its creatureliness. Moreover, in contrast to pregnancy, and even breastfeeding, one would be hard pressed to find evidence of menstruation being imbued with meaning or value.

Converging with the anthropological evidence, contemporary empirical research reveals negative views of menstruation and menstruating women (e.g., Rozin, Haidt, McCauley, Dunlop, & Ashmore, 1999). For example, in a study conducted by Roberts, Goldenberg, Power, and Pyszczynski (2002), a female confederate seemed to inadvertently drop a wrapped tampon out of her backpack. Not only was the woman viewed as less competent and less likable than when the same woman, in another condition, dropped another feminine item—a hair barrette—from her bag, but the mere presence of the tampon led participants, both male and female, to distance themselves physically from the woman by sitting farther away. Although I am not aware of any studies examining reactions to menstruation as a function of existential concerns, the hypothesis is straightforward: Priming mortality should increase negative attitudes toward menstruation.

Pregnancy

Pregnancy, too, should be a blatant reminder of women's creatureliness, and existential concerns should therefore be expected to exacerbate negative attitudes toward pregnancy. Supporting this hypothesis, in the first of two experiments, Goldenberg, Cox, Arndt, and Goplen (2007) primed human creatureliness with the essay highlighting the similarities between humans and animals and then examined reactions to one of two *Vanity Fair* magazine covers: Demi Moore posing nude and pregnant or nude (wearing nothing but body paint) but not pregnant. In line with our position, priming creatureliness led to more negative reactions to the pregnant image but did not affect reactions to the one in which Moore was not pregnant. In a second experiment, participants evaluated actor Gwyneth Paltrow's competence in response to viewing a photo of her fully clad, pregnant or not, again as a function of a creatureliness manipulation. This study showed that not only do concerns about creatureliness inspire negative reactions to a pregnant depiction but also that a woman's competence is devalued under such conditions.

Breastfeeding

In a series of experiments, Cox, Goldenberg, Arndt, and Pyszczynski (2007) also examined reactions to breastfeeding as a function of existential concerns. In two experiments, the salience of mortality enhanced negative reactions to breastfeeding. In the first, after being reminded of death, breastfeeding in public was rated as a more severe transgression; in the second, MS led participants to dislike and sit farther away from a woman they believed had just breastfed (rather than bottle-fed) her baby in private. A separate study demonstrated a causal effect of creaturely concerns on breastfeeding reactions by showing that people expressed increased negativity toward a picture of a breastfeeding female after exposure to the human creatureliness essay. This study used two nearly identical *Redbook* magazine covers: one showing actor Pierce Brosnan with his wife and child, and the other showing the same pose except that his wife was breastfeeding. Finally, Cox et al. (2007) provided evidence that not only do creatureliness and MS exacerbate negative reactions to breastfeeding, but also when mortality is primed, concerns about human creatureliness become more accessible in response to a woman breastfeeding, but not bottle-feeding, her baby (in the next room).

Women as Objects

There is evidence to support the claim that the reproductive aspects of women's bodies can provoke a threat that is exacerbated by experimental primes highlighting the awareness of human mortality and/or creatureliness. It follows from TMT that a solution to this problem lies in humankind's capacity to imbue that which is threatening with symbolic meaning. Tomi-Ann Roberts and I (e.g., Goldenberg & Roberts, 2004) proposed that the objectification of women accomplishes this goal. In Roberts et al. (2002), the study in which a woman dropped a tampon, there was evidence for this. Both male and female participants responded to the tampon not only with negative evaluations of the woman who dropped it but also with a tendency to objectify women in general. That is, it was deemed more important for women to be beautiful (than competent) when one woman had inadvertently revealed her menstrual status. These findings provide direct support for a causal influence of women's creatureliness on their subsequent objectification. In an ongoing series of studies, we also found that women objectify themselves in response to a depiction of a pregnant woman (Morris, Goldenberg, & Heflick, 2011).

Characteristics of Objects

What does it mean to be "objectified"? And why is it that objectification ameliorates the threat associated with the creatureliness of women's bodies? The answer, we suspect, has to do with the fact that objects, devoid of life, are antithetical not only to human but also to animal existence. Haslam (e.g., 2006) discussed objectification as a special kind of dehumanization, which he dubbed *mechanistic dehumanization* (i.e., likening people to machines). This can be contrasted with a more traditional treatment of dehumanization wherein people are viewed as similar to animals. Thus, objectification can be considered a type of dehumanization (see also Nussbaum, 1999), though objectified women are dehumanized, from the current perspective, not by being compared to animals but to nonliving, nonbreathing, noncreaturely, and most important, nonmortal, things.

In a series of studies, we (Heflick & Goldenberg, 2009; Heflick, Goldenberg, Cooper, & Puvia, 2011) examined perceptions of women when their appearance was the focus of other people's attention. We reasoned that if the tendency is to objectify women more than men, focusing on a woman's appearance should induce perceptions of her as more object-like, whereas focusing on a man's appearance would not. We focused on the traits of competence, warmth, and morality, which from a number of perspectives are associated with humanness (e.g., Haslam, Bain, Douge, Lee, & Bastian, 2005; see also Heflick, Goldenberg, Cooper, et al., 2011) and therefore should be deemphasized to the extent that a person is perceived as more like an object and less human.

Female perceptual targets included the following: at-the-time U.S. vice-presidential candidate Sarah Palin, actor Angelina Jolie, First Lady of the United States Michelle Obama, CNN's morning show host Robin Meade, and two unknown female weather forecasters who differed in attractiveness. Participants were instructed to evaluate each woman on the basis of either her appearance or who she was as a person. Across the board, the women were perceived as less competent and/or warm and/or moral (depending on which was assessed) as a consequence of focusing on their appearance. In contrast, Barack Obama, ABC news lead anchor Brian Williams, and two unknown male weather forecasters who differed in attractiveness did not suffer comparable effects of appearance focus.

In addition, the study using Sarah Palin included having participants rate her (and Angelina Jolie) on a handful of traits that they then judged in terms of how much each one characterizes human nature (i.e., what it means to be human). The correlation between the perceived typicality of each trait for the target and the extent that each trait was perceived as human was used as an indicator of humanity assigned to the target. As hypothesized, appearance focus led participants to perceive both women as lower in the characteristics they associated with human nature. Moreover, when Sarah Palin was the target, appearance focus reduced participants' likelihood of voting for the McCain–Palin ticket in the 2008 U.S. presidential election, an effect that was mediated by perceptions of competence and human nature.

Although these studies do not directly test the proposed connection between women's creatureliness and their subsequent objectification, they do fit with the idea that women are objectified when their appearance is the focus and that objectification involves a stripping away of important human qualities.

THE BODY ETERNAL

So far, I have shown that people tend to deny or disapprove of the body's physicality and to hide it or surround it with cultural symbols. In line with TMT, I view these tendencies as defenses against awareness of death. But clearly, a belief in literal immortality is particularly well suited to assuage mortality concerns (Greenberg, Landau, Solomon, & Pyszczynski, in press). With this consideration in mind, we asked: How can people believe in life after death in the face of indisputable evidence that the physical body dies? The answer: Separate some aspect of the self (e.g., soul, spirit) from the undeniably mortal body.

We (Heflick, Goldenberg, Hart, & Kamp, 2011) have begun a program of research to examine how viewing the self and the body dualistically interacts with mortality concerns to create the cognitive and motivational conditions necessary for belief in an afterlife. We argue that the threat of physical mortality fuels a need for an afterlife but that belief in an afterlife is accomplished only to the extent that individuals can and do conceptualize the body and the self dualistically.

We designed three studies to test this line of reasoning. In each study, we either enhanced dualism (by priming participants to distance themselves psychologically from their bodies) or hindered it (by grounding them in their bodies). For example, in one study we instructed participants to place their feet on a vibrating foot massager, which made them more aware of, and presumably less separable from, their bodies (i.e., perceive themselves nondualistically). This was contrasted with a neutral condition in which participants simply placed their feet on a massager positioned *off*. Participants were primed with MS or a control topic and completed a measure of afterlife belief. As hypothesized, belief was lowered in response to MS when the focus was on physical sensations; there was no effect when the massager was turned off.

To test whether a sense of dualism enhances belief in an afterlife in response to MS, we used brain–computer interface (BCI) technology (Farwell & Donchin, 1988). With BCI, the brain's electrical signals are read and used to communicate with an external device, in this case a computer screen. We fitted each participant with an electrode cap and then had them focus on letters as they flashed on a computer. The letters were then displayed with varying accuracy on a second monitor. To the extent that the BCI results were accurate—and therefore the participant believed that he or she was typing mentally rather than physically—we assumed that he or she was encouraged to believe in mind–body dualism. Participants for whom the BCI performed with lower levels of accuracy were assumed to experience less evidence for dualism. MS was manipulated in this study by varying the words participants encountered in the BCI task: *dealt* or *death*. The results were as expected: Participants primed with *death* reported belief in an afterlife to the extent that they perceived the BCI as accurate. That is, as in the first study, dualism and MS interacted to affect afterlife belief, although this time we showed that enhancing dualism under MS increased this belief.

In addition, a separate study included a manipulation aimed at both enhancing and hindering dualism. Participants were simply asked to write about the nonphysical, or physical, aspects of the self. As expected, enhancing dualism resulted in more afterlife belief relative to nondualism when mortality was salient. Thus, in sum, how people relate to their physical selves has implications not just for their ideas and experiences in this life but also for beliefs about one's existence, or lack thereof, in a world beyond.

THE BODY IN QUESTION

In sum, a large body of research is consistent with the position that the threat of human creatureliness and mortality underlie negative reactions to the human body. Evidence was presented with respect to the body generally and specifically in response to the aspects of women's bodies relevant to reproduction. The findings are also consistent with the idea that imbuing the body with meaning reduces the threat and that objectification, therefore, may be rooted in a need to strip women's bodies of their creatureliness. Finally, evidence was presented depicting how being grounded in a physical body can interfere with conceptualizations of life after death. Questions remain, however, and these may serve as a guide for future inquiry.

Inconsistencies?

Within these studies, there are inconsistencies concerning whether it is necessary to prime creatureliness in the context of MS and whether MS effects are found solely among highly neurotic individuals. In addition, in some studies, priming creatureliness had effects in the absence of any mortality reminder. The reason for these differences is not entirely clear. One possibility concerns the nature of the bodily behaviors examined in this work. There is variability in the degree to which behaviors are imbued with symbolic meaning and other potentially buffering qualities. For example, sex, even in its most physical aspects, is cloaked in uniquely human meanings, such as the appreciation of pleasure and intensity of human-to-human connection. It makes sense, then, that the connotation of human creatureliness may not be the same for all people (i.e., nonneurotics) or without directing the focus to the creaturely implication of the behavior. In contrast, in response to the body's activities that are not typically imbued with meaning—an unflushed bowel movement, perhaps—MS evoked a negative reaction in the absence of any moderators. Thus, although the research findings are generally consistent—people (especially neurotic people) distance themselves psychologically from the physical aspects of the body when existential factors (creatureliness, MS, or both) are rendered salient—further research is needed to clarify when particular combinations of variables are necessary to produce these effects.

Cultural Restrictions?

When made aware of their mortality, people respond with increasingly negative reactions to the body and its behaviors, including behaviors that are ordinarily quite desirable, such as sex. However, these same bodily behaviors are often surrounded by taboos. Given that mortality reminders promote greater efforts to conform to cultural standards (e.g., Greenberg, Simon, Porteus, Pyszczynski, & Solomon, 1995), could negative reactions to the body's physicality simply be a result of cultural restrictions? There is evidence to suggest that this is not the case. Most notably, mortality concerns lead people to distance themselves from sensory experiences that are not in the slightest bit taboo (e.g., submersing one's arm in ice-cold water). Moreover, effects are found not only in response to MS but also in response to reminders of the similarities between humans and animals, suggesting that concerns about human creatureliness play a critical role in the distancing-from-the-body reactions.

One cannot help but notice, however, that a disproportionate number of societal norms and taboos focus on the body and its behaviors. Why might this be? The current perspective suggests that cultural restrictions so often target the body because of its inherent existential threat. Thus, it is not that the restrictions cause discomfort (or at least this is not the whole story) but that the discomfort causes the restrictions. Therefore, concerns about mortality and human creatureliness may underlie not just individuals' inhibitions but also possibly the norms themselves (Goldenberg, Hart, et al., 2006).

This question of whether the threat emanates from external (cultural) versus internal (existential) pressures is also relevant in the context of negative reactions to the unique aspects of women's bodies that are involved in reproduction. Although it makes sense that women's bodily investment in the continuation of the species would render their bodies threatening, it is hard to test this as distinct from the influence of gender inequality. Men are, and have traditionally been, in a position of greater economic, political, and social power. Thus, they have the power to name that which should be concealed and that which is the-bigger-the-better. Could it be there is no specific inherent threat in women's bodies but rather that societal norms have made it so? It will be a challenge for future research to delineate more clearly the existential and cultural influences on the reactions to women's bodies.

Beautification Versus Sexualization?

The treatment of objectification as I have described it differs somewhat from portrayals of objectification in which women are explicitly sexualized. Clearly, when women are sexualized, they are sometimes likened to animals with, for example, derogatory and also seemingly complimentary slang names (e.g., bitch, fox). There are also empirical findings revealing that sexualized women are implicitly likened to animals (Vaes, Paladino, & Puvia, 2011). Yet, my colleagues and I have argued that the objectification of women strips them not only of their humanness but also their creatureliness, or animalness, thereby reducing the threat caused by women's association with nature. How do we reconcile these positions?

One possibility (see Heflick, Goldenberg, Cooper, et al., 2011) is that objectification comes in two forms: the explicitly sexual and a more seemingly benevolent kind (Glick & Fiske, 1996). From this perspective, the appearance-focus manipulation in the Heflick, Goldenberg, Cooper, et al. (2011) studies was likely objectifying (for women) without necessarily being sexualizing. Objectifying without sexualizing women may result in mechanistic dehumanization (Haslam, 2006), which in a sense purifies women by turning them into noncreaturely objects. In contrast, it is possible that more explicit sexualization of women would result in animalistic dehumanization, consistent with the findings of Vaes et al. (2011). We are currently collecting data to test these ideas.

Soulless Objectified Women?

Another question arises when considering the merger between the objectification of women and the findings revealing that afterlife beliefs are hindered by a focus on the body. As described by objectification theory (Fredrickson & Roberts, 1997), women more than men learn that their value is contingent on their physical appearance. As a consequence, they are prone to adopt an external perspective on themselves, focusing on their body's appearance. Our perspective suggests that in such a state of self-objectification, mortality reminders may reduce belief in an afterlife for women. That is, to the extent that the mind-set "you are your body" is salient, the idea that one can exist beyond the body's death becomes an untenable defense in response to MS. Similarly, objectifying (other) women may have an additional consequence beyond being perceived as less competent, warm, and moral. It may be that when others focus on a woman's appearance, she is, as a consequence of being a physical thing, assumed by others to have no afterlife and no soul. Heflick, Goldenberg, Hart, et al. (2011) recently speculated about this possibility and are in the process of designing studies to test this. The consequences are chilling in light of arguments excusing animal cruelty on the basis of the belief that animals have no souls.

Approaching the Body?

I would like to conclude with two related questions: Why do people approach the body in addition to avoiding it, and why do they not do it more? Research has revealed a general tendency for people to distance themselves psychologically from the body, but in many studies, people low in neuroticism or exposed to a prime highlighting human uniqueness respond to MS with the opposite tendency—for example, expressing increased interest in the physical aspects of sex (Goldenberg et al., 1999, 2002). In other writings (e.g., Goldenberg, Kosloff, & Greenberg, 2006), my colleagues and I have considered the possibility that physical experiences offer a means to affirm life, and thus under the right (protected) conditions, it makes sense that the body could be embraced as a solution to the threat associated with the awareness of death.

Embracing physical experience in response to MS, however, has been less reliable as a response than distancing from the body; the trend (e.g., to express more interest in sex) has been nonsignificant, when found at all. We suspect that although the body can offer a means to combat fear of death—because it is through the body that one can feel most fully alive—a more basic tendency is to escape it. That is, the more defensive strategy is to flee from the body. We have previously argued (Pyszczynski, Greenberg, & Goldenberg, 2003) that although integrative or growth-oriented outcomes are possible in response to MS, defensive needs take precedence.

Women's bodies, too, offer a potentially life-affirming solution to the problem of death, because they create, carry, and sustain life. Yet, reactions to the female body, exacerbated by MS, can be negative, as we have seen. Indeed, when reactions to women's bodies are less blatantly negative (i.e., when they are objectified), such responses quite literally suck the life out of women, as our recent work on perceptions of objectified women shows.

Future research should be directed at ways to promote less defensiveness in response to MS generally and specifically with respect to the physical body. If individuals who score low on neuroticism are less defensive, what is it about them that makes them so? One idea might be that neurotic individuals tend to be oriented toward avoidance (i.e., predisposed toward avoiding potentially punishing stimuli in contrast to approaching rewarding stimuli; Elliot & Thrash, 2002). Thus, we might find that people who are more approach oriented (e.g., extraverts; Elliot & Thrash, 2002), rather than merely less avoidance oriented (i.e., low neurotics), would respond to MS by embracing rather than avoiding, or objectifying, the body. It might also be possible that people can learn to be more sensitive to the rewards of the body—for example, by engaging in physical activities that subtly increase body awareness, such as yoga (see Daubenmier, 2005), in the context of salient death thought. Findings that yoga decreases self-objectification (Daubenmier, 2005) are consistent with, and encouraging with respect to, this general position.

We have previously demonstrated health risks associated with avoidance of the body in response to MS (e.g., women avoiding cancer-screening breast exams; Goldenberg & Arndt, 2008; Goldenberg, Arndt, Hart, & Routledge, 2008). It may also be that a less defensive orientation—helping people learn to approach the body in response to the awareness of death—can set the stage for not just more positive, accepting attitudes toward the body but also better bodily health as well.

REFERENCES

Becker, E. (1973). *The denial of death*. New York, NY: Free Press.

Brown, N. O. (1959). *Life against death: The psychoanalytical meaning of history*. Middletown, CT: Wesleyan University Press.

Buss, D. M., & Schmitt, D. P. (1993). Sexual strategies theory: An evolutionary perspective on human mating. *Psychological Review, 100*, 204–232. doi:10.1037/0033-295X.100.2.204

Cox, C. R., Goldenberg, J. L., Arndt, J., & Pyszczynski, T. (2007). Mother's milk: An existential perspective on negative reactions to breastfeeding. *Personality and Social Psychology Bulletin, 33*, 110–122. doi:10.1177/0146167206294202

Cox, C. R., Goldenberg, J. L., Pyszczynski, T., & Weise, D. (2007). Disgust, creatureliness, and the accessibility of death related thoughts. *European Journal of Social Psychology, 37*, 494–507. doi:10.1002/ejsp.370

Daubenmier, J. J. (2005). The relationship of yoga, body awareness, and body responsiveness to self-objectification and disordered eating. *Psychology of Women Quarterly, 29*, 207–219. doi:10.1111/j.1471-6402.2005.00183.x

Elliot, A. J., & Thrash, T. M. (2002). Approach–avoidance motivation in personality: Approach and avoidance temperaments and goals. *Journal of Personality and Social Psychology, 82*, 804–818. doi:10.1037/0022-3514.82.5.804

Farwell, L. A., & Donchin, E. (1988). Talking off the top of your head: Toward a mental prosthesis utilizing event-related brain potentials. *Electroencephalography and Clinical Neurophysiology, 70*, 510–523. doi:10.1016/0013-4694(88)90149-6

Fredrickson, B. L., & Roberts, T. (1997). Objectification theory: Toward understanding women's lived experiences and mental health risks. *Psychology of Women Quarterly, 21*, 173–206. doi:10.1111/j.1471-6402.1997.tb00108.x

Freud, S. (1961). *Civilization and its discontents*. New York, NY: Norton. (Original work published 1930)

Glick, P., & Fiske, S. T. (1996). The ambivalent sexism inventory: Differentiating hostile and benevolent sexism. *Journal of Personality and Social Psychology, 70*, 491–512. doi:10.1037/0022-3514.70.3.491

Goldenberg, J. L., & Arndt, J. (2008). The implications of death for health: A terror management model of behavioral health promotion. *Psychological Review, 115*, 1032–1053. doi:10.1037/a0013326

Goldenberg, J. L., Arndt, J., Hart, J., & Routledge, C. (2008). Uncovering an existential barrier to breast self-exam behavior. *Journal of Experimental Social Psychology, 44*, 260–274. doi:10.1016/j.jesp.2007.05.002

Goldenberg, J. L., Cox, C. R., Arndt, J., & Goplen, J. (2007). "Viewing" pregnancy as existential threat: The effects of creatureliness on reactions to media depictions of the pregnant body. *Media Psychology, 10*, 211–230. doi:10.1080/15213260701375629

Goldenberg, J. L., Cox, C., Pyszczynski, T., Greenberg, J., & Solomon, S. (2002). Understanding human ambivalence about sex: The effects of stripping sex of its meaning. *Journal of Sex Research, 39*, 310–320. doi:10.1080/00224490209552155

Goldenberg, J. L., Hart, J., Pyszczynski, T., Warnica, G. M., Landau, M., & Thomas, L. (2006). Terror of the body: Death, neuroticism, and the flight from physical sensation. *Personality and Social Psychology Bulletin, 32*, 1264–1277. doi:10.1177/0146167206289505

Goldenberg, J. L., Heflick, N. A., & Cooper, D. P. (2008). The thrust of the problem: Bodily inhibitions and guilt as a function of mortality salience and neuroticism. *Journal of Personality, 76*, 1055–1080. doi:10.1111/j.1467-6494.2008.00513.x

Goldenberg, J. L., Kosloff, S., & Greenberg, J. (2006). Existential underpinnings of approach and avoidance of the physical body. *Motivation and Emotion, 30,* 127–134. doi:10.1007/s11031-006-9023-z

Goldenberg, J. L., Pyszczynski, T., Greenberg, J., Solomon, S., Kluck, B., & Cornwell, R. (2001). I am not an animal: Mortality salience, disgust, and the denial of human creatureliness. *Journal of Experimental Psychology: General, 130,* 427–435. doi:10.1037/0096-3445.130.3.427

Goldenberg, J. L., Pyszczynski, T., McCoy, S. K., Greenberg, J., & Solomon, S. (1999). Death, sex, and neuroticism: Why is sex such a problem? *Journal of Personality and Social Psychology, 77,* 1173–1187. doi:10.1037/0022-3514.77.6.1173

Goldenberg, J. L., & Roberts, T. A. (2004). The beast within the beauty: An existential perspective on the objectification and condemnation of women. In J. Greenberg, S. L., Koole, & T. Pyszczynski (Eds.), *Handbook of experimental existential psychology* (pp. 71–85). New York, NY: Guilford Press.

Goldenberg, J. L., & Roberts, T. A. (2010). The birthmark: An existential account of why women are objectified. In R. Calogero, S. Tantleff-Dunn, & J. K. Thompson (Eds.), *The objectification of women: Innovative directions in research and practice* (pp. 77–100). Washington, DC: American Psychological Association.

Greenberg, J., Landau, M., Solomon, S., & Pyszczynski, T. (in press). The case for terror management as the primary psychological function of religion. In D. Wulff (Ed.), *Handbook of the psychology of religion.* London, England: Oxford University Press.

Greenberg, J., Simon, L., Porteus, J., Pyszczynski, T., & Solomon, S. (1995). Evidence of a terror management function of cultural icons: The effects of mortality salience on the inappropriate use of cherished cultural symbols. *Personality and Social Psychology Bulletin, 21,* 1221–1228. doi:10.1177/01461672952111010

Haidt, J., McCauley, C. R., & Rozin, P. (1994). Individual differences in sensitivity to disgust: A scale sampling seven domains of disgust elicitors. *Personality and Individual Differences, 16,* 701–713. doi:10.1016/0191-8869(94)90212-7

Haslam, N. (2006). Dehumanization: An integrative review. *Personality and Social Psychology Review, 10,* 252–264. doi:10.1207/s15327957pspr1003_4

Haslam, N., Bain, P., Douge, L., Lee, M., & Bastian, B. (2005). More human than you: Attributing humanness to self and others. *Journal of Personality and Social Psychology, 89,* 937–950. doi:10.1037/0022-3514.89.6.937

Heflick, N. A., & Goldenberg, J. L. (2009). Objectifying Sarah Palin: Evidence that objectification causes women to be perceived as less competent and less fully human. *Journal of Experimental Social Psychology, 45,* 598–601. doi:10.1016/j.jesp.2009.02.008

Heflick, N. A., Goldenberg, J. L., Cooper, D. P., & Puvia, E. (2011). From women to objects: Appearance focus, target gender, and perceptions of warmth, morality and competence. *Journal of Experimental Social Psychology, 47,* 572–581. doi:10.1016/j.jesp.2010.12.020

Heflick, N. A., Goldenberg, J. L., Hart, J. J., & Kamp, S. M. (2011). *Death awareness and body–self dualism: The why and how of afterlife belief.* Manuscript submitted for publication.

Landau, M. J., Goldenberg, J. L., Greenberg, J., Gillath, O., Solomon, S., Cox, C., . . . Pyszczynski, T. (2006). The siren's call: Terror management and the threat of sexual attraction. *Journal of Personality and Social Psychology, 90,* 129–146. doi:10.1037/0022-3514.90.1.129

Morris, K. L., Goldenberg, J. L., & Heflick, N. A. (2011). *The effects of priming women's reproduction on self-objectification.* Manuscript in preparation, University of South Florida, Tampa.

Motyl, M., Hart, J., Cooper, D. P., Heflick, N. A., Goldenberg, J. L., & Pyszczynski, T. (2011). *Creatureliness priming reduces aggression and support for war.* Manuscript in preparation.

Nussbaum, M. C. (1999). *Sex and social justice.* New York, NY: Oxford University Press.

Pyszczynski, T., Greenberg, J., & Goldenberg, J. L. (2003). Freedom vs. fear: On the defense, growth, and expansion of the self. In M. R. Leary & J. P. Tangney (Eds.), *Handbook of self and identity* (pp. 314–343). New York, NY: Guilford Press.

Roberts, T. A., Goldenberg, J. L., Power, C., & Pyszczynski, T. (2002). "Feminine protection": The effects of menstruation on attitudes toward women. *Psychology of Women Quarterly, 26,* 131–139. doi:10.1111/1471-6402.00051

Rozin, P., Haidt, J., McCauley, C., Dunlop, L., & Ashmore, M. (1999). Individual differences in disgust sensitivity: Comparisons and evaluations of paper-and-pencil versus behavioral measures. *Journal of Research in Personality, 33,* 330–351. doi:10.1006/jrpe.1999.2251

Solomon, S., Greenberg, J., & Pyszczynski, T. (2004). The cultural animal: Twenty years of terror management theory and research. In J. Greenberg, S. L., Koole, & T. Pyszczynski (Eds.), *Handbook of experimental existential psychology* (pp.13–34). New York, NY: Guilford Press.

Trivers, R. L. (1972). Parental investment and sexual selection. In B. Campbell (Ed.), *Sexual selection and the descent of man, 1871–1971* (pp. 136–179). Chicago, IL: Aldine.

Vaes, J., Paladino, M. P., & Puvia, E. (2011). Are sexualized females complete human beings? Why males and females dehumanize sexually objectified women. *European Journal of Social Psychology, 41,* 774–785.

6

THE IMPERMANENCE OF ALL THINGS: AN EXISTENTIALIST STANCE ON PERSONAL AND SOCIAL CHANGE

GILAD HIRSCHBERGER AND DAN SHAHAM

Change is a given. Be it due to external forces or internal psychological processes, people are in a constant state of flux, confronted with various challenges and threats on an ongoing basis. Change is also inextricably linked to the human existential plight: Our existence is part of a cycle, a process. Every day thousands of people die and thousands more are born. Within a mere century, the entire population of the planet will have been replaced. Yet, people seem relatively oblivious to these dramatic facts as they strive to achieve a sense of permanence and stability in their lives (Levine & Levine, 1982). It would be incorrect, however, to conclude that people are generally resistant to change. In fact, change is a celebrated value in contemporary societies and is equated with progress and improvement. Lack of change signifies stagnation and decay. Thus, the sands of time may be a threatening reminder of the emptying hourglass of life, and change may signify the loss of youth and vitality. Permanence, however, may be equally threatening because it is through progress and rejuvenation that people achieve meaning, which may enable them to transcend the ephemeral nature of their physical existence.

This work was partially funded by an Israel Science Foundation grant awarded to the first author.

This chapter is an attempt to understand, through terror management theory (TMT; see Chapter 1, this volume), how change may pose both an existential threat and a remedy for such threats. We review the terror management and existentialist literature, focusing on the issue of change, and present a series of new studies examining the relation between the prospect of change and existential concerns. These studies examine change in three different domains— vocational, interpersonal, and political—with the goal of demonstrating that the relation between change and existential threat can be attributed to change per se and is not confined to a specific change domain. We also discuss existential concerns associated with facing the most prominent personal manifestation of change, aging, and examine how the antiaging industry capitalizes on people's desperate need to hold onto the fleeting moment of youth. We conclude with a discussion of how an existentialist perspective on change can help address the various social and political challenges confronting contemporary societies.

REACTIONS TO CHANGE

Change is a transformation from one state to another and involves the interruption of a given state of affairs (Fox, 1998). The momentary disequilibrium resulting from change may be experienced as aversive because it destabilizes psychological equanimity. Humans, like other living organisms, strive at a basic biological level to maintain a stable and constant inner state, *homeostasis* (Cannon, 1935). This biological imperative is mirrored at the individual and social levels, where stability is considered an answer to the basic need for security and safety (Maslow, 1970). Personal daily routines and habits, as well as cultural rituals and traditions, are examples of the ways in which people maintain stability in the face of constant change in almost every aspect of life.

Among the central reasons for negative reactions to change are the discomfort of uncertainty and a decreased sense of control (Fox, 1998). *Resistance to change* (RTC) is defined as a negative attitude toward change that includes affective, behavioral, and cognitive components (Oreg, 2006). Change is a central ingredient in modern life, and for an organization to be successful, it must react quickly and efficiently to a rapidly changing and dynamic environment. A survey, however, found that only 41% of the changes implemented in over 1,500 companies could be described as successful and that psychological, not technological, reasons best explained the failures in implementing change (IBM, 2008). The growing understanding that human RTC is an obstacle to personal, social, and organizational change has prompted the publication of popular books, such as *Who Moved My Cheese? An Amazing Way to Deal with Change in Your Work and in Your Life* (Johnson, 1998), that attempt to explain why RTC is a hopeless strategy, whereas accepting change and accommodating to it provide rewards such as wealth and prosperity. RTC, however, may not be just an attitudinal problem that can be argued away; it may also reflect more enduring dispositions that are resistant to rational persuasion.

Prospect theory (Kahneman & Tversky, 1979) provides an example of the cognitive determinants of RTC. It focuses on the discovery that people's attitudes toward risks involving gains may be quite different from their attitudes toward risks involving losses. For example, when people are given a choice between receiving $1,000 with certainty or having a 50% chance of receiving $2,500, they may well choose the certain $1,000 rather than the uncertain $2,500, even though the mathematical expectation of gain from the uncertain option is $1,250, 25% more than the certain $1,000. This *risk aversion* may reflect a universal human predisposition to resist change, especially change associated with risk and with potential losses.

A Resource Model of Reactions to Change

The cognitive model of risk aversion offered by prospect theory seems also to be reflected in physiological reactions to change. Novel situations loaded with uncertainty and unpredictability may elicit a stress response manifested in autonomic, hormonal, and immunological functioning (e.g., Lovallo & Thomas, 2000). This physiological response, however, depends on a cognitive appraisal of the situation, such that the stress response will be triggered only when an individual appraises a situation as one that he or she does not have adequate resources to deal with (Lazarus & Folkman, 1984). According to the resource and perception model (Harber, Einev-Cohen, & Lang, 2008), reactions to stress are moderated by psychosocial resources. When people feel that they have resources such as self-efficacy (Bandura, 1997), perceived control (Seligman, 1975), and attachment security (see Chapter 16, this volume) at their disposal, they are likely to appraise a situation as an opportunity and a challenge. When they feel that their resources are depleted, however, change will most likely be perceived as a threat and the stress response will be exacerbated (Blascovich & Mendes, 2000).

The Existential Meaning of Change

If you don't get what you want, you suffer; if you get what you don't want, you suffer; even when you get exactly what you want, you still suffer because you can't hold on to it forever. Your mind is your predicament. It wants to be free of change. Free of pain, free of the obligations of life and death. But change is law and no amount of pretending will alter that reality.
—Socrates, in D. Millman's *The Way of the Peaceful Warrior: A Book That Changes Lives*

The cognitive, physiological, and psychosocial models of change explain how people react to change, which types of change are more aversive, and how psychological resources influence reactions to change. It is not entirely clear from these perspectives, however, why change poses such a fundamental human problem. In this chapter, we argue that change is perceived as a threat because it is inextricably linked to the passage of time, to a transition from a younger state to an older state, and to a realization that one is inching closer to death. The idea that change signifies death or that death is a form of change is a major pillar of Socratic philosophy (Vlastos, 1971).

The Buddhist tradition (Rinpoche, 1992) seems to complement the Socratic view in claiming that one of the reasons people experience so much anguish about death is that they generally ignore the reality of impermanence. People desperately want everything to stay the same, and change is experienced as loss and suffering. Change acts as a daily reminder of the unavoidability of death and of the temporary state of existence. Each change is a continuous "small death," an unsettling reminder that time flows and that attempts to cling to the here and now are futile: "Changes . . . are the pulse of death, the heartbeat of death" (Rinpoche, 1992, p. 46). The Buddhist tradition contends that only if we liberate ourselves from our flawed and destructive illusion of permanence and accept that, ironically, impermanence is the only real thing we can hold on to, will we be able to confront death without fear.

TERROR MANAGEMENT AND RESISTANCE TO CHANGE

Philosophical analyses of existence and impermanence, which are only briefly and incompletely discussed in this chapter, are supplemented by psychological theory and research that attempt to explain how the transient nature of being affects human behavior. In his essay "On Transience," Freud (1916/1942) recalled a walk he took with the poet Rainer Maria Rilke. It was a beautiful summer day, and Freud was happy to be outdoors. Rilke, however, was somber and seemed incapable of enjoying the leisurely stroll. According to Freud, Rilke felt that "all this beauty was fated to extinction, that it would vanish when winter came, like all human beauty and all the beauty that men have created or may create" (p. 38). Freud, however, was unsympathetic to Rilke's response and contended that the hallmark of psychological health is the ability to appreciate life and beauty regardless of how fragile and transient it may be.

On the basis of Freud's psychoanalytic theory, Ernest Becker (1973, 1975) wrote, many years after the theory's creation, that the human inability to contend with the problem of death and impermanence is not just dysfunctional for individual mental health but also has detrimental social consequences. Becker's writings laid the foundations for TMT (see Chapter 1, this volume) and related experimental investigations into the psychology of death and impermanence.

Terror management research has dealt, directly and indirectly, with the problems of change and impermanence. In the most direct examination to date of permanence as a terror management defense, Landau et al. (2004) demonstrated that priming thoughts of personal death (mortality salience [MS]) increased preference for a more benign, representative, consistent, and orderly cognitive structuring of the social world. This seemed to hold true primarily for participants who scored high on a measure of the need for personal structure, suggesting that they typically perceive uncertain and unstable situations as threatening. These results suggest that significant change is linked to death by the mere disruption of an orderly state of affairs but that change is not uniformly threatening. Whereas some individuals responded to MS with greater clinging to familiar social constructions, others did not.

Individual differences in the effects of MS on change have also been detected in other research. In a prospective study of political change, for example, Hirschberger and Ein-Dor (2006) examined reactions to the 2005 disengagement of Israel from Gaza among Gaza strip settlers and their supporters 3 months before the withdrawal took place. They found that MS increased support for violent means to sabotage the disengagement plan (i.e., violent RTC), but this effect was obtained only among settlers who were unable to come to terms with the unfolding reality and relied on denial as a defense mechanism. Others who opposed the plan but did not deny that it would take place did not show this effect.

Links between existential concerns and RTC were also evident in research on the terror management function of close relationships (Mikulincer, Florian, & Hirschberger, 2003). In one study, participants expressed high levels of intimacy strivings toward a relationship partner who harshly criticized them (Hirschberger, Florian, & Mikulincer, 2003). The study suggested that when death is salient, the need for security and stability increases to the extent that people are willing to endure insult and pain to maintain emotional closeness. Similarly, thoughts of change and instability in close relationships led to an increase in the cognitive accessibility of death-related thoughts (Florian, Mikulincer, & Hirschberger, 2002). These findings indicate that stable close relationships satisfy, among other things, a need for permanence, and when this need for permanence is disrupted, people experience a surge of death concerns.

The terror management literature has thus far supported the contention that change is existentially threatening and that MS typically leads to RTC. It seems, however, that this effect is not uniform and that some individuals find change more existentially threatening than others. In the next section, we describe new research that sheds further light on the relation between change and death. The first group of studies examines whether change elicits greater concerns about death than a condition with no change and whether this effect is moderated by individual difference variables. The second group examines the impact of MS on RTC. The third group of studies focuses on a common and inevitable human change—aging—and examines the effects of MS on the appeal of antiaging products and treatments.

DOES CHANGE ELICIT DEATH-RELATED COGNITIONS?

Most terror management research has focused on the MS paradigm and has examined how death primes influence social cognitions, emotions, and behaviors. However, a significant body of terror management research has examined the terror management process from the opposite direction to determine whether destabilizing or threatening terror management defenses causes an upsurge of death-related cognitions (see Hayes, Schimel, Arndt, & Faucher, 2010, for a recent review). This research paradigm, designed to test a death-thought accessibility (DTA) hypothesis, is based on the reasoning that if a construct serves to protect individuals from thoughts of death, threatening its validity should compromise its defensive function and lead to an increase in the accessibility of death-related cognitions.

In our research, we used the DTA paradigm to examine whether the prospect of change compromises the need for stability and certainty and thus induces an increase in thoughts of death. We examined this hypothesis in three different domains—interpersonal, vocational, and political—to increase our confidence that the results address change in general and are not confined to a particular domain.

Because the extant research on terror management and processes of change suggests that change is existentially threatening only to some individuals, we predicted that reactions to change would be moderated by individual difference variables. Specifically, on the basis of resource models of reactions to change (e.g., Harber et al., 2008; Lazarus & Folkman, 1984), we suggested that the effects of change would depend on the perceived psychological resources at the disposal of the individual confronting change. The perception of resources would be associated with acceptance of change, whereas the lack thereof would be associated with RTC. Applying this reasoning to our current research, we hypothesized that change would elicit death-related cognitions only among those low in psychological resources and not those high in resources. We further speculated that those high in psychological resources might perceive change as an opportunity for progress and that for them stability would connote stagnation and decay. If this reasoning is correct, we would expect that among such individuals, DTA would be higher in the stability condition than in the change condition.

In the first study in this series, we focused on a domain of change that might elicit the stress of uncertainty but is usually perceived as positive: the prospect of spending an academic year abroad. In this study, we had first-year undergraduate participants either read a scenario formatted as a newspaper article reporting that the minister of education decided to keep everything in the forthcoming year as planned (no change condition) or an article describing a new 1-year mandatory study abroad program in which students would be required to spend 1 year abroad at the same cost as their studies in Israel (change condition). The accessibility of death-related thoughts was assessed by a Hebrew version of the word-completion task, which had been constructed originally in English (e.g., Greenberg, Pyszczynski, Solomon, Simon, & Breus, 1994) and then used successfully in Hebrew (e.g., Florian et al., 2002) in Israeli research. In our study, the task consisted of 19 Hebrew word fragments (missing one letter) that participants were asked to complete with the first word that came to mind. Eight of the 19 Hebrew fragments could be completed with either neutral or death-related Hebrew words. For example, participants saw the Hebrew fragment –VEL and could complete it with the Hebrew word HVEL (cord) or with the death-related EVEL (mourning). The possible death-related words were the Hebrew words for death, mourning, cadaver, grave, killing, dying, grief, and skeleton. The dependent measure was the number of death-related Hebrew words a participant used to complete the fragments. This score could range from 0 to 8. We also measured participants' need for cognitive closure (NFC; Webster & Kruglanski, 1994) as a moderator, because NFC indicates the extent to which participants need a stable and structured world and the ways in which they deal with uncertainty. We hypothesized that change would lead to higher DTA only among those high in NFC.

The results partially supported the hypotheses and indicated that participants high in NFC tended to show an increase in DTA in the change condition compared with the no-change condition. However, people low in NFC exhibited the opposite trend and had lower DTA in the change condition compared with the control condition. Although uncertainty management theory (UMT) does not make specific predictions about DTA, the finding that change (with the uncertainty it entails) was existentially soothing for participants low in NFC and that lack of change or stagnation was existentially threatening for them seems to violate the assumption that avoiding uncertainty is a central human motivation.

In the second study, we attempted to replicate these results in the context of political change: the possibility of a peace agreement between Israel and its neighbors. Although Israel has much to gain from peace, it also has much to lose (e.g., land, settlements). According to prospect theory (Kahneman & Tversky, 1979), people are more reluctant to lose what they already have than to gain something that they still do not have. Therefore, we predicted that political change would elicit higher levels of DTA after controlling for political orientation. Participants were randomly assigned to one of two scenarios: The first was a political change scenario suggesting that Israel was about to sign a comprehensive peace agreement with Syria and the Palestinians, which would include a withdrawal from territories. The no-change scenario described a continuation of the status quo between Israel and these two parties with no significant change expected in the near future. The results replicated those from the academic relocation study and indicated that participants high in NFC reacted to political change with significantly elevated DTA, whereas people low in NFC reacted to the change scenario with lower DTA (at a marginal significance level) compared with the no-change condition, after controlling for political orientation. These results enable us to generalize the results of the first study to other domains of change and support our contention that the results reflect a reaction to change and not a reaction to a specific change domain. The results also suggest that reactions to political change are not just a function of political ideology but also of psychological reactions to change and uncertainty.

Following the first two studies on academic and political change, we examined whether we could extend the findings to the interpersonal realm. Marriage constitutes a significant life change that is often perceived as positive, although it entails certain costs, such as the loss of freedom and the sacrifice of potential opportunities. In this study, we examined whether thoughts of relational change (marriage) compared with a control condition (continued singlehood) would influence DTA. In addition to manipulating the occurrence of change, we also manipulated judgments of change, such that half of the participants read a passage suggesting that change is good, and the other half read a passage suggesting that stability is good. We also examined whether attachment orientations (see Chapter 16, this volume) would moderate the effects of relationship change on DTA, because attachment orientations have been found to be important predictors of processes in close relationships (Mikulincer & Shaver, 2007).

The results indicated that whereas participants low on attachment-related avoidance exhibited low levels of DTA when presented with relational change and primed with prochange values, participants high on avoidance responded to these conditions with elevated DTA. Thus, nonavoidant people seem to find existential comfort in close relationships, as Mikulincer et al. (2003) showed. People who are more avoidant, however, respond to the prospect of marriage with an upsurge of death-related cognitions. For them, not only does the prospect of marriage fail to provide a sense of security in the face of existential threat but it also seems to be the source of stress that amplifies existential concerns.

These first three studies on change and the accessibility of death-related thoughts support our prediction that change is existentially threatening. However, the results indicate that this holds true only for individuals low in psychological resources. People high on NFC responded to academic and political change with elevated death-related cognitions. People scoring high on attachment-related avoidance responded to changes in close relationships with elevated death concerns. Those with substantial psychological resources (being low on NFC and attachment-related avoidance), however, exhibited the opposite pattern and responded to change with lower DTA. These individuals displayed higher levels of death cognitions in the no-change condition. It seems that for them, lack of change is existentially threatening, whereas the prospect of change quells their existential concerns. The results of these studies raise doubts about the claim of UMT that uncertainty poses the greatest human threat and that uncertainty can explain MS effects. The three studies suggest that change and uncertainty are existentially threatening, but only for some individuals. For others, the prospect of change, with all of the uncertainty it entails, was experienced as existentially comforting.

DOES MORTALITY SALIENCE ALWAYS INCREASE RESISTANCE TO CHANGE?

In the next step of our investigation, we examined whether priming thoughts of personal death would influence RTC in the same three domains already studied. We reasoned that if change is perceived by some as an existential threat and by others as an existential remedy, as suggested in the first three studies, MS would not be expected to have a uniform effect on RTC and would increase RTC in some cases and decrease it in others. In the first study examining this hypothesis, we randomly assigned participants to either an MS or a pain salience condition, asked them to read the academic relocation vignette, and then had them complete an RTC scale (Oreg, 2006) modified to relate to academic relocation. To better understand the role of uncertainty in these effects, we constructed a measure of perceived uncertainty and examined whether it moderated the MS effect. Results revealed a significant interaction between MS and perceived uncertainty, indicating that in the control condition persons high on perceived uncertainty were more resistant to change than those low on perceived uncertainty. However, MS reduced RTC among the highly uncertain individuals to the level of individuals low on uncertainty.

These results indicate that highly uncertain individuals are typically resistant to academic relocation. MS, however, reduces their RTC in this domain.

In the next study, we replicated the design of the first MS study and replaced the academic relocation scenario with the political change scenario. Here the results were slightly different. As in the first study, individuals who were highly uncertain were more resistant to change than individuals low on uncertainty. In this study, however, MS did not reduce RTC among highly uncertain individuals, as in the academic change study. Rather, MS increased resistance to political change among those who were low on uncertainty, raising this resistance to the level of people who scored high on uncertainty. These effects were obtained even after controlling for political orientation.

Following the first two studies, we examined reactions to relational change. In this study (Seagel, 2011), however, we examined single men (age > 30) who were not involved at the time in a long-term relationship. To examine reactions to change, we asked them to indicate when they would like to marry, on a scale ranging from 1 (*never*) to 7 (*sometime in the next year*). We measured attachment orientation as a moderator. Results indicated that MS increased the desire to get married in the near future among men who were low on attachment-related avoidance. Men who were high on avoidance, however, responded to MS with a significant decrease in the desire to get married.

The three studies conducted on MS and RTC complement the three studies on change and DTA and indicate that MS may either increase or decrease RTC. The studies suggest that individual differences moderate the relation between existential concerns and reactions to change. Although the findings generally replicate from one change domain to another, our studies also suggest that the nature of the targeted domain is an important factor in determining RTC. Specifically, participants high in uncertainty were more resistant to change compared with participants low in uncertainty in both the academic and the political domains. The effects of MS, however, were opposite in these two domains. In the academic domain, MS reduced the RTC of highly uncertain individuals to the level of those low in uncertainty. In the political domain, MS increased the RTC of those low in uncertainty to the extent that they became as resistant as highly uncertain individuals. Although we cannot be sure about the reasons for these differences, they can be explained from the perspective of prospect theory. The political change we examined seems to be associated with greater losses than gains (Gayer, Landman, Halperin, & Bar-Tal, 2009), and this can explain why the political change scenario primarily increased DTA and why MS increased RTC. The academic relocation scenario, however, may have elicited some anxiety, but the benefits of studying abroad were probably more salient than the costs. This may explain why the academic change scenario significantly decreased DTA among some individuals and why MS in this case decreased RTC.

FOREVER YOUNG: DEATH AND ANTIAGING

The idea is to die young as late as possible.
—Ashley Montagu, *Growing Young*

Our research on academic, political, and interpersonal change illustrates the effects of existential concerns on reactions to change. Spending an academic year abroad, experiencing historical political transformations, or committing to a close relationship are events we may or may not experience in our lifetime. If we live long enough, however, we are bound to experience an inescapable universal transformation, the process of aging. Although aging is a natural and inevitable part of the life cycle, it is perceived negatively in many societies, and older people often suffer from discrimination (Cuddy & Fiske, 2002). Terror management research on aging has indicated that older people elicit high levels of DTA compared with young people and that MS leads to the derogation of older people and to distancing from them (Martens, Greenberg, Schimel, & Landau, 2004). Because aging is so strongly associated with impermanence and death, we postulated that when death was salient, people would be motivated to fight the aging process. The antiaging industry successfully capitalizes on the desire to stay young forever and markets products that enjoy great popularity despite questions about their effectiveness. In a series of two studies, Lazovsky-Feine (2010) examined whether MS increases the appeal of antiaging products.

In the first study, female participants were randomly assigned to MS or pain salience conditions and then completed a questionnaire tapping the appeal of various cosmetic treatments, some of which pertained directly to antiaging (e.g., Botox, facial lift) and some that were not related to aging (e.g., hair removal, manicure or pedicure). MS significantly increased the appeal of antiaging treatments, but it had no significant effects on the other cosmetic treatments.

The second study was an attempt to replicate the results of the first study using a behavioral paradigm. In this study, research assistants randomly distributed fliers to women walking through a university campus. The fliers that served as the MS prime mentioned either death or back pain. This MS procedure has been successfully used in previous research (Hirschberger, Ein-Dor, & Almakias, 2008). These women were then solicited by another research assistant standing at a booth to try a new antiaging cream, *Toujour Lisse*, which they were told had been scientifically proven to slow the aging process of the face and skin. Participants were presented with a jar of cream that had been weighed prior to the experiment and were asked to apply the cream on the face of a mannequin as if it were their own face. Then they rated their interest in antiaging products. Results indicated that in the MS condition, the jar was significantly lighter than in the control condition, meaning that when death was salient participants applied more cream. This effect occurred primarily among participants who were not college educated. MS also increased participants' self-reported interest in antiaging products.

The results of these two studies on the appeal of antiaging products as an existential defense indicate that primes of death increase the motivation to fight the natural aging process and to stay young for as long as possible. These findings are in line with the other studies we presented on change, and they add further evidence for the role of existential concerns in reactions to change. Although the results of the research presented here provide a general picture of the effects of MS on reactions to change, a picture that emphasizes individual differences in resources, there are also some notable differences between the change domains. It seems that the change domains of academic relocation and marriage elicited not only existential fear and RTC but also acceptance of change among some individuals. The political and aging domains, however, seemed to elicit greater existential fear and RTC. We suggest, on the basis of prospect theory (Kahneman & Tversky, 1979), that marriage and relocation may be associated with gains for many individuals. A political settlement between Israel and its neighbors seems to be primarily associated with loss, and aging is associated in the eyes of many people with degeneration and decay, which also connotes loss. In accordance with prospect theory, the results indicate that for domains associated with gains, MS decreases RTC, but for domains associated with loss, MS increases RTC.

CONCLUSION

The dogmas of the quiet past are inadequate to the stormy present. The occasion is piled high with difficulty, and we must rise—with the occasion. As our case is new, so we must think anew, and act anew. We must disenthrall ourselves, and then we shall save our country.
—Abraham Lincoln in Roy P. Basler's *Collected Works of Abraham Lincoln*

The writing of this chapter takes place during turbulent times in the Middle East. Mass protests are spreading like fire throughout the region. Some of the dictatorial regimes are collapsing, others are using brute force against their people to hold on to power; all are unstable. At present, uncertainty abounds, and no one can be sure about the outcome of this geopolitical earthquake. What seems to be certain, however, is that the people of the Middle East are desperate for change. Many evidently prefer the uncertainty of political upheaval to the certainty of living in a dictatorship, and they are willing to make great sacrifices to advance the change they desire. These events constitute a real-life demonstration of one of the central points of the research on terror management and change: When change accords with personal meaning, when it is consistent with personal values and beliefs, and when it holds the promise of a better future, it will offer greater existential benefits than would stability and permanence.

The results of the research presented here suggest that both contextual and individual-difference factors determine whether change is experienced as existentially threatening or comforting. Change that reflects cultural or religious values and beliefs will likely quell existential anxiety because cultural worldviews serve as terror management mechanisms (see Chapter 1, this volume). When change does not bolster cultural worldviews, however, and when losses loom larger than gains, the change is likely to be experienced as existentially threatening and to elicit greater RTC.

Some people shrink in the face of change. For them, the passage of time feels like being washed down a river with little control over what lies ahead. RTC may temporarily assuage their existential concerns and provide a comforting illusion of safety and stability. But as long as the wheels of time keep turning, so will the prospect of permanence and stagnation fail to provide existential solace. The unrealistic desire for permanence leads to desperate attempts to slow and reverse the effects of time (e.g., the signs of aging), but these efforts are doomed to fail. Others, who realize they cannot resist the powerful flow of the river, attempt to take control, keep balance, and seize the opportunity for making meaningful personal decisions in the inevitable process of continuous transformation.

REFERENCES

Bandura, A. (1997). *Self efficacy: The exercise of control*. New York, NY: Freeman.

Basler, R. P. (Ed.). (2008). *The collected works of Abraham Lincoln*. Rockville, MD: Wildside Press.

Becker, E. (1973). *The denial of death*. New York, NY: Free Press.

Becker, E. (1975). *Escape from evil*. New York, NY: Free Press.

Blascovich, J., & Mendes, W. B. (2000). Challenge and threat appraisals: The role of affective cues. In J. Forgas (Ed.), *Feeling and thinking: The role of affect in social cognition* (pp. 59–82). Cambridge, England: Cambridge University Press.

Cannon, W. (1935). Stress and strains of homeostasis. *The American Journal of the Medical Sciences, 189,* 13–14. doi:10.1097/00000441-193501000-00001

Cuddy, A. J., & Fiske, S. T. (2002). Doddering but dear: Process, content, and function in stereotyping of older persons. In T. D. Nelson (Ed.), *Ageism: Stereotyping and prejudice against older people* (pp. 3–26). Cambridge, MA: MIT Press.

Florian, V., Mikulincer, M., & Hirschberger, G. (2002). The anxiety-buffering function of close relationships: Evidence that relationship commitment acts as a terror management mechanism. *Journal of Personality and Social Psychology, 82*, 527–542. doi:10.1037/0022-3514.82.4.527

Fox, S. (1998). *The psychology of resistance to change*. Ramat Gan, Israel: Bar-Ilan University Press.

Freud, S. (1942). On transience (J. Strachey, Trans.). *The International Journal of Psychoanalysis, 23*, 84–85. (Original work published 1916)

Gayer, C. C., Landman, S., Halperin, E., & Bar-Tal, D. (2009). Overcoming psychological barriers to peaceful conflict resolution: The role of arguments about losses. *The Journal of Conflict Resolution, 53*, 951–975. doi:10.1177/0022002709346257

Greenberg, J., Pyszczynski, T., Solomon, S., Simon, L., & Breus, M. (1994). The role of consciousness and accessibility of death-related thoughts in mortality salience effects. *Journal of Personality and Social Psychology, 67*, 627–637. doi:10.1037/0022-3514.67.4.627

Harber, K. D., Einav-Cohen, M., & Lang, F. (2008). They heard a cry: Psychosocial resources moderate perception of others' distress. *European Journal of Social Psychology, 38*, 296–314. doi:10.1002/ejsp.448

Hayes, J., Schimel, J., Arndt, J., & Faucher, E. H. (2010). A theoretical and empirical review of the death-thought accessibility concept in terror management research. *Psychological Bulletin, 136*, 699–739. doi:10.1037/a0020524

Hirschberger, G., & Ein-Dor, T. (2006). Defenders of a lost cause: Terror management and violent resistance to the disengagement plan. *Personality and Social Psychology Bulletin, 32*, 761–769. doi:10.1177/0146167206286628

Hirschberger, G., Ein-Dor, T., & Almakias, S. (2008). The self-protective altruist: Terror management and the ambivalent nature of prosocial behavior. *Personality and Social Psychology Bulletin, 34*, 666–678. doi:10.1177/0146167207313933

Hirschberger, G., Florian, V., & Mikulincer, M. (2003). Striving for romantic intimacy following partner complaint or partner criticism: A terror management perspective. *Journal of Social and Personal Relationships, 20*, 675–687. doi:10.1177/02654075030205006

IBM. (2008). *Making change work—global cluster*. Sommers, NY: IBM Global Services.

Johnson, S. (1998). *Who moved my cheese? An amazing way to deal with change in your work and in your life*. London, England: Putnam.

Kahneman, D., & Tversky, A. (1979). Prospect theory: An analysis of decision under risk. *Econometrica, 47*, 263–291. doi:10.2307/1914185

Landau, M. J., Johns, M., Greenberg, J., Pyszczynski, T., Martens, A., Goldberg, J., & Solomon, S. (2004). A function of form: Terror management and structuring the social world. *Journal of Personality and Social Psychology, 87*, 190–210. doi:10.1037/0022-3514.87.2.190

Lazarus, R. S., & Folkman, S. (1984). *Stress, appraisal, and coping*. New York, NY: Springer.

Lazovsky-Feine, M. (2010). *The cosmetic war against aging: A terror management perspective* (Unpublished master's thesis). Bar-Ilan University, Israel.

Levine, S., & Levine, O. (1982). *Who dies: An investigation of conscious living and conscious dying.* New York, NY: Anchor Books.

Lovallo, W.R., & Thomas, T.L. (2000). Stress hormones in psychophysiological research. In J.T. Cacioppo, L.G. Tassinary, & G.G. Berntson (Eds.), *Handbook of psychophysiology* (2nd ed.; pp. 342–367). Cambridge, England: Cambridge University Press.

Martens, A., Greenberg, J., Schimel, J., & Landau, M.J. (2004). Ageism and death: Effects of mortality salience and similarity to elders on distancing from and derogation of elderly people. *Personality and Social Psychology Bulletin, 30,* 1524–1536. doi:10.1177/0146167204271185

Maslow, A.H. (1970). *Motivation and personality* (2nd ed.) New York, NY: Harper & Row.

Mikulincer, M., Florian, V., & Hirschberger, G. (2003). The existential function of close relationships: Introducing death into the science of love. *Personality and Social Psychology Review, 7,* 20–40. doi:10.1207/S15327957PSPR0701_2

Mikulincer, M., & Shaver, P. (2007). *Attachment in adulthood: Structure, dynamics, and change.* New York, NY: Guilford Press.

Millman, D. (1980). *The way of the peaceful warrior: A book that changes lives.* Novato, CA: HJ Kramer.

Montagu, A. (1981). *Growing young.* New York, NY: McGraw-Hill.

Oreg, S. (2006). Personality, context, and resistance to organizational change. *European Journal of Work and Organizational Psychology, 15,* 73–101. doi:10.1080/13594320500451247

Rinpoche, S. (1992). *The Tibetan book of living and dying.* San Francisco, CA: HarperCollins.

Seagel, H. (2011). *An existential perspective on late bachelorhood: Relational strivings and relationship avoidance as terror management strategies* (Unpublished doctoral dissertation). Bar-Ilan University, Israel.

Seligman, M.E.P. (1975). *Helplessness.* San Francisco, CA: Freeman.

Vlastos, G. (1971). *The philosophy of Socrates: A collection of critical essays.* New York, NY: Anchor Books.

Webster, D.M., & Kruglanski, A.W. (1994). Individual differences in need for cognitive closure. *Journal of Personality and Social Psychology, 67,* 1049–1062. doi:10.1037/0022-3514.67.6.1049

II
THE THREAT OF
MEANINGLESSNESS

7

MEANING: UBIQUITOUS AND EFFORTLESS

LAURA A. KING

It may be one of the great achievements of the Cognitive Revolution that psychology approaches meaning much like Hamlet in concluding that "there is nothing either good or bad but thinking makes it so." As Lazarus (1984) argued, thinking determines the meaning of experience, and meaning is, therefore, a remarkably malleable commodity. The meaning of any event or experience is whatever one cognitively construes it to be. That is, thinking is where meaning comes from. From this perspective, meaning is, by its nature, a question to be answered, a problem to be solved, or a construct to be created (for similar views, see Chapters 4, 10, and 11, this volume).

In this chapter, I present a different approach to meaning, namely, that meaning is rarely proximally or effortfully constructed. Rather than being shattered, violated, or absent, meaning is often present. Meaning is everywhere, widely available, and routinely accessed in an effortless fashion as an inherent aspect of experience. Essentially, I argue that thinking is one way in which meaning is created but that thinking is rarely needed (or particularly useful) in the experience of meaning. Although we often talk of "making sense" of experience, I argue that more often than otherwise, sense is not made but, indeed, sensed.

Understanding this often-present experience of sense is important for at least two reasons. First, focusing on meaning when it is missing, violated, challenged, or threatened risks leaving us with little information about the 98% of the time when life makes sense. In thinking about meaning as an experience that emerges from thinking, we have forgotten what meaning feels like most of the time. Second, this focus has also left us with a dearth of knowledge about the criteria against which constructed meanings ought to be evaluated. How can we know when meaning-making efforts will satisfy the longing for meaning? What might distinguish good constructed meanings from those that do not fulfill that longing?

I begin this chapter by briefly reviewing William James's idea of the subjective rationality of experience and drawing links from this perspective to intuitive information processing. I then provide a brief taste of the origins of a sense of meaning and argue that engagement in thought is rarely required for the experience of meaning. I identify the intuitive information processing system (Epstein, 1994) as responsible for the experience of this unintentional meaning and describe the role of positive affect (PA) in the functioning of this meaning-detection system. I then present evidence concerning the detection of the presence of meaning. I conclude this analysis by noting its implications for constructed meanings and the experience of meaning in life.

SENSING SENSE

William James (1893) described the *fringe of consciousness* as nonsensory experiences that emerge around conscious thoughts. The fringe of consciousness contains metacognitive experiences that provide consciousness with continuity and a sense of the relations among the elements of experience. James suggested that at the heart of the nonsensory fringe of the stream of consciousness is the feeling of the "subjective rationality of experience" or the "rightness of direction" of one's thoughts. This feeling of rightness is responsible for our perception that experiences make sense (Mangan, 2000, 2001). Mangan (2001) described the feeling of "right direction" as "the feeling of meaning" (p. 13). The feeling of meaning pertains to a feeling about an event or experience that one has found to "feel right." Like other aspects of the fringe of consciousness (e.g., feelings of familiarity, knowing, or causation), feelings of rightness are evident instantly, although they may be amorphous and fuzzy (Mangan, 2001). The feeling of meaning is present when experience fits with its context and one's expectations (King & Hicks, 2009a) and absent when experience violates these (Heine, Proulx, & Vohs, 2006; see also Chapter 4, this volume). When experiences feel right, they also feel better. Subtle facial musculature activity suggestive of PA occurs when stimuli make sense (Topolinski, Likowski, Weyers, & Strack, 2009) or when expectancies are not violated (Harmon-Jones & Allen, 2001; Winkielman & Cacioppo, 2001).

The clear overlap between James's description of the fringe of consciousness and our contemporary understanding of intuitive information processing has been recognized (e.g., Nickerson, 1990; Reber & Schwarz, 2002; Reber, Wurtz, & Zimmerman, 2004; Topolinski & Strack, 2009b). *Intuitive processing* is generally characterized as rapid, internally generated, top-down, requiring little in terms of awareness, and based, phenomenologically, on vague gut feelings, hunches, or vibes (Epstein, 1994). I return to this system more specifically later, but in the next few sections, I argue that given the adaptive importance of the experience of sense, it is just such a system that functions in the detection of the presence of meaning.

THE SIMPLEST MEANINGS OF LIFE

To undertake a consideration of the presence of meaning or the subjective rationality of experience, we can begin with what I hope is not a controversial assumption: Like all other animals, human beings live in a lawful physical world. That world is characterized by invariants. For instance, the existence and physical characteristics of objects have a constancy that our perceptual systems are wired to accommodate. Further, objects fall down (not up), causes precede their effects, morning follows night, and spring follows winter. For all creatures, adaptation requires the capacity to detect the relevant invariants of existence. At the simplest level, the experience of "sense" is centered in the durability of this natural lawfulness. To the physical invariants noted earlier, we might add that the day after Monday is Tuesday, and no matter what else is going on, we can all "hang on, baby" because, inevitably, "Friday is coming." In this sense, meaning is a local, proximal concern that is generally present in our workaday, predictable lives. Often psychologists describe meaning in terms of expectancies. The existence of these invariants suggests that we have expectancies because we live in a world that invites them and more often than not conforms to them. Perceptions of these invariants may represent our first expectancies.

In today's increasingly post-Piagetian psychology of infant cognitive development, we see that, for humans, the detection of the invariants in our world does not require "thinking," in the usual sense. For example, in a series of meticulous studies, Luo and Baillargeon (2005) presented infants ranging from 2 to 3.5 months of age with physically possible and impossible situations. The infants watched a puppet show in which the "set" was a panel (a castle) with a square cut out of its middle (the open castle door)—leaving an open space through which the back of the stage could be seen. A puppet entered the stage from one side, traversed the stage, going behind the leftmost side of the castle. In the possible situations, she traveled behind the left side of the castle, was seen appearing in the cutout, and then continued behind the right side, emerging again, and finally exiting the stage. In the impossible situations, the infants saw the puppet make the same journey, but in this case, after going behind the first side of the castle, she did not appear in the cutout. Instead, she emerged directly out of the opposite side, exiting the stage. That is, in this impossible situation, the puppet "magically" appeared, without ever revealing herself in the open door of the castle. Infants looked reliably longer at the impossible than at the possible situations, indicating that they noticed this violation of natural physical laws (Luo & Baillargeon, 2005). We might say that prior to these violations, the world was making sense, even for infants as young as 2 months old. In its simplest form, sense exists without the intervention of higher level cognitive efforts.

Adaptation requires not only noticing invariants in the environment but also the capacity to detect and learn from regularities and predictable associations. Sophisticated cognitive architecture, the likes of which characterize conscious thought, is unnecessary for such learning. Certainly, since Pavlov and Skinner, we have known that learned associations do not require a system that includes intentionality but simply one that detects lawfulness and predictability in the environment.

SYMBOLIC MEANINGS

Of course, when human beings talk of meaning, we are not concerned, generally, with infant perception of the laws of physics or with the nonconscious detection of regularity in the environment. We refer to the underlying meaning of a stimulus, to the idea that stimuli serve as representations of other deeper meanings. We recognize that pictures and words are symbols that reflect a referent. Such representational thought is at the basis of language itself. Talking, comprehending, and reading words imply that one has the capacity to recognize that symbols (words) have referents (meanings). Right now, the reader of this chapter is, one hopes, immersed in meaning. The automaticity of this encounter is demonstrated in the classic Stroop effect (Stroop, 1935).

The *Stroop effect* refers to the reliable delay that ensues when a person is asked to name the color in which a word is printed, when the word itself names a different color (e.g., the word *blue* printed in red ink). At its base, the Stroop effect demonstrates that overlearned symbolic meanings are not only automatically perceived but also difficult to avoid. Only with effortful regulation of this automatic meaning-relevant response can a person avoid the delay in responding. In other words, conscious effort is not required to recognize semantic meaning, but it is required to avoid meaning. The "underlying" meaning of a word is not sought out. It springs forth instantaneously as our first habitual response, superseding even the physical properties of the object perceived. Though clearly the product of distal effortful processes (e.g., a person who cannot read would not show the Stroop effect at all), semantic meaning, once acquired, operates automatically.

Symbolic meaning can also be seen to function automatically in the operation of metaphors. A host of fascinating studies have emerged around the notion of embodied cognition, pointing to the fact that our bodies traffic in metaphorical meanings in ways that are, again, not mediated by awareness. Bodily movements conveying metaphors can have an array of effects on thoughts and behaviors. For example, Schwarz and Lee (2011) found that participants who were asked to hold both palms facing upward and alternately move them up and down (a movement that conveyed the metaphor of weighing both sides) were more likely, relative to those performing a control movement, to attend to both sides of an argument and endorse greater balance in their lives (Schwarz & Lee, 2011). It is notable that such effects arise in the absence of awareness of the metaphorical significance of the movements and, indeed, the presence of awareness wipes out these effects, suggesting that conscious thought, rather than facilitating the emergence of meaning, may well interfere with its nonconscious (and potentially visceral) flow.

Research on judgments of semantic coherence likewise suggests that intentionality is not involved in and may even impede the discrimination of semantic sense from nonsense. In this research, participants are often given loosely related linguistic triads and asked to guess as quickly as possible whether the triad has a fourth word that unites the other three (participants are not asked to produce the common associate but only whether they feel like one exists). For example, the triad *snow*, *base*, and *dance* is coherent (common associate, "ball"), whereas the triad *mouth*, *lines*, and *sixteen* is incoherent (there is no common associate). It is interesting that when relying on intuitive hunches, people are generally better than chance at accurately discriminating between coherent and incoherent triads, whereas thinking carefully about these judgments leads to poorer performance (Topolinski & Strack, 2008).

Topolinski and Strack (e.g., 2009a) proposed a fluency-affect model of these judgments that focuses on metacognitive processing ease and subtle indicators of PA. They noted that coherent triads are more fluently processed than incoherent triads (Topolinski & Strack, 2009b). This fluid processing is reflected in subtle changes in facial musculature indicating PA. According to Topolinski and Strack (2009a), this fluency-triggered affect leads to the experiential "gut feeling" that drives accurate intuitive judgments.

Clearly, the question posed by semantic coherence judgments is, centrally, "Is this triad sense or nonsense?" The Topolinski-Strack model (and the host of empirical studies supporting it; see, e.g., Topolinski & Strack, 2009a; also, Reber et al., 2004; Wurtz, Reber, & Zimmerman, 2008) suggests that such discrimination occurs automatically and is based not on thoughtful consideration but rather on nonconscious and subtle experiences of metacognitive ease and free-floating affect.

Thus far, I have argued that meaning happens to us automatically through the detection of regularities in a lawful world, through reading, in the bodily operation of metaphors, and in vague hunches driven by processing ease. Importantly, research suggests that, in adults, nonconscious violation of expectancies can lead to systematic differences in later responses, supporting the notion that the presence of meaning is monitored on a nonconscious level (e.g., Proulx & Heine, 2008).

A CIRCUMSCRIBED LESSON FROM THE MEANING MAINTENANCE MODEL

The meaning maintenance model (Heine et al., 2006) focuses on the ways that expectancy violations lead to meaning reinstatement (i.e., attempts to defend or uphold meaning). Of most relevance here, this research demonstrates that violations of expectancy can influence subsequent behavior even in the absence of awareness of the violation. For instance, in a pair of clever experiments (Proulx & Heine, 2008) participants came to a lab and were greeted by a female experimenter, who escorted them to a computer to complete a variety of measures. During the lab assessment, the experimenter walked behind a file cabinet. For those in the control condition, she returned and administered the dependent measures, which in this case involved assigning bail to a prostitute (i.e., a person who had violated cultural norms, thought to be a source of meaning). For those in the violation condition everything was the same, with the exception that the experimenter who emerged from behind the cabinet was a different woman. This new experimenter was dressed identically to the previous one and administered the dependent measure. Only 10% of the participants noticed that the experimenter was a different woman. Analyses excluding these individuals showed that those who had experienced the "transmogrifying experimenter" set higher bails for the prostitute (Proulx & Heine, 2008).

For the purposes of the present discussion, the key conclusion one might draw from this work is perhaps more limited than that favored by the meaning maintenance model. Whether setting a higher bail in fact "reinstated" previously "violated" meaning was motivated by a chronic need for meaning or reflected, instead, misattribution, cognitive conflict, or dissonance, the bottom line is that nonconscious violations were registered, suggesting that the presence of meaning itself may be monitored by an ongoing process in the background of mental life.

In all of the examples I have used so far, the detection of meaning has, itself, made sense. Infants looked longer at impossible situations. Accurate discrimination between objective sense and nonsense is demonstrated in linguistic triad studies. College students responded to an objectively real (if undetectable) violation of sense in a systematic way. Before exploring the underlying processes that may support automatic experiences of meaning, we might consider one additional issue with particular relevance to intuitive processing: the potential irrational qualities of meaning.

THE INNATELY MEANINGFUL

Taken to its extreme, the notion that thinking creates meaning suggests that nothing is inherently meaningful. Nevertheless, some experiences can feel innately meaningful. Sometimes the meaning of a life event feels all but inescapable based solely on the experience of temporal proximity. These meaningful moments emerge around events that approximate physical laws but are not, in fact, products of them (e.g., Kozak, Marsh, & Wegner, 2006). Imagine a person experiencing a particularly strong sneeze while walking past a skyscraper. If, by chance, the building collapses immediately after the sneeze, the implications are clear (if decidedly unrealistic). In more common circumstances, random coincidence has the capacity to invite the feeling that things were "meant to be."

The psychological power of random events in the human experience of meaning has long been recognized. Both Freud and Jung noted the ways in which coincidence can be a strangely compelling fish in the stream of consciousness. As Freud (1919/1953) noted, the experience of the *uncanny* "forces upon us the idea of something fateful and inescapable when otherwise we would have spoken only of 'chance'" (p. 230). Likewise, Jung (1950/1997) described *synchronicity* as taking "the coincidence of events as meaning something more than mere chance" (p. xxv). Similarly, a long history of modern research on counterfactual thinking suggests that when an unlikely twist of fate or a random occurrence is brought into a story, the events feel fated or meant to be (e.g., Markman & McMullen, 2003).

In research on narrative constructions of meaning, my collaborators and I collected narratives from parents of children with Down syndrome (DS; King, Scollon, Ramsey, & Williams, 2000). Participants wrote the story of finding out that they would be parenting a child with DS. For 17% of these parents, the story began, not with a prenatal test or a few moments after the child was born but instead months before, when the fact that the child had DS was foreshadowed by an objectively random event. For example, one woman began her story with an experience at a baby shower. She and her husband were given the book *What to Expect When You're Expecting* (an enormously popular book for new parents). The husband opened the book "at random" and started reading. They both "recoiled in horror" as they realized he was reading about DS. Other parents mentioned dreams or vague hunches that occurred and persisted despite no medical evidence of any problems. Interestingly, those who included such foreshadowing were more likely to have found positive meaning in the experience (i.e., reporting greater personal growth as a result of parenting a child with DS; King et al., 2000).

Rationality tells us that these experiences are random. These foreshadowing moments could happen to any number of expectant parents, some portion of whom might have a child with DS. Logic tells us that the odds of such events occurring by chance are far higher than these parents might imagine. Nevertheless, these and other more common encounters with apparent magic (i.e., the thought that a traffic light turned red specifically because we were in a hurry) persist in the imagination and tug powerfully on the strings of meaning, suggesting that meaning itself may be a far less rational process than might be assumed in a world where all meanings are constructed.

At last, then, we consider, directly, the system that is responsible for the detection of meaning. It is one that is automatic and runs in the background, at the fringe, of mental life. It applies as a default mode of information processing (because the presence of sense itself is the default). It has the capacity to detect regularities and subtle variations in ease of processing. It can also be, at times, apparently not terribly rational and neither good at nor convinced by mathematical probabilities.

INTUITION, RATIONALITY, AND MEANING

Dual process models of information processing often describe one system that is rapid, heuristic, and intuitive (System 1) and another that is slower, effortful, and analytical (System 2; e.g., Bargh, 2004; Evans, 2010; Stanovich & West, 2000). Both systems of processing are important to adaptive behavior, and these two systems are generally thought to work together, dynamically, to allow humans to function.

Exhibit 7.1 provides a brief summary of the characteristics of these two systems. I note just a few of their differences that are particularly relevant to meaning. First, the intuitive system is generally more subjective than the rational system. The intuitive meaning of a life event, for instance, is inher-

EXHIBIT 7.1
Two Sides of Human Information Processing and Meaning

System 1 (intuitive)	System 2 (rational)
Rapid, nonconscious	Analytical, effortful, intentional, slow
Gut feelings, hunches, heuristics	Logical operations and rules
Just knowing	Knowing and knowing why
Subjective	Objective
Facilitated by positive affect	Facilitated by negative affect
Default	Used when needed and to override
Sensing sense	System 1 impulses
	Making sense

ently subjective whereas rational conclusions have objective weight. Regardless of who does the math, $2 + 2 = 4$. Also, as noted in the exhibit, the two sides of information processing relate differently to affect. Negative affect signals that analytical problem solving (i.e., System 2 processing) is required. In contrast, PA signals that all is well and one can indeed follow one's hunches (i.e., System 1 processing; e.g., Clore & Palmer, 2009). Finally, as I have proposed, these two systems may be viewed as serving different functions in the experience of meaning, with System 1 generally functioning as the meaning-detection system and System 2 being more relied on in the process of meaning construction.

My colleagues and I have used cognitive experiential self theory (CEST; Epstein, 1994) to explore the role of intuition in the experience of meaning. CEST presents these two styles of information processing as individual differences in habitual processing style, with the intuitive style being reflected in the characteristics noted in Exhibit 7.1. The processing style that characterizes the intuitive system has been measured using the Faith in Intuition (FI) Scale (Pacini & Epstein, 1999), and scores on this measure do predict intuitive processing (e.g., reliance on heuristics; e.g., Epstein, Pacini, Denes-Raj, & Heier, 1996; Shiloh, Salton, & Sharabi, 2002).

A note about the role of PA is warranted here. As noted previously, the two sides of human information processing generally work together to produce adaptive behavior. Exhibit 7.1 includes the notion that System 1 is the default system and System 2 (which is generally a more costly processing style, in terms of effort and energy) is used more judiciously when needed. One of its functions is to override System 1 impulses when these are likely to be inaccurate (as in the case of biases associated with, say, heuristic processing) or ineffective (as in the case of doing math problems). In our research, we have found that reporting oneself as intuitive is not sufficient to demonstrate the effects of this individual difference on beliefs and behavior. Rather, PA appears to be required to strongly shift the balance of processing over to the intuitive system, allowing these individual differences to manifest in behavior without interference from rational impulses. In this sense, we might think of PA as giving the "go ahead" to the intuitive system for whatever task is at hand (King, Burton, Hicks, & Drigotas, 2007).

In a number of studies, we have examined the ways that PA and individual differences in reliance on intuitive processing predict the experience of meaning. We began by examining these variables as predictors of paranormal or magical meanings. For example, when presented with videotapes of purported UFOs and ghosts, intuition predicted ratings of the believability and meaningfulness among participants in a positive (vs. neutral) mood condition (King et al., 2007, Study 1). Similarly, in studies of susceptibility to sympathetic magic, intuition and naturally occurring PA interacted to predict poorer performance in hitting a picture of a baby with darts, and induced PA (vs. neutral mood) predicted sitting farther from a person who had purportedly stepped in excrement, for those who were high on intuition (King et al., 2007, Studies 2 and 3). More recently, the relationship of naturally occurring PA to referential thinking (ascribing personal meaning to patently meaningless events, such as thinking that traffic lights turned red because one was in a hurry) was similarly moderated by individual differences in intuition (King & Hicks, 2009b).

These studies indicate that when one is in a good mood, the intuitive system is more likely to ascribe (in these cases, nonrational) meaning to experience. Might the convergence of PA and intuitive processing represent a more general meaning-detection system?

POSITIVE AFFECT, INTUITION, AND COMMONPLACE FEELINGS OF MEANING

In a series of studies, we examined whether PA and intuitive processing style predict feelings of meaning for a variety of stimuli (each evaluated by independent samples), including ambiguous quotations, Zen koans, and Japanese Kanji characters (Hicks, Cicero, et al., 2010, Study 1). For all the stimuli, participants were asked to rate their feelings of meaning (e.g., "It makes sense to me"). For all the stimuli, a consistent pattern emerged, such that self-rated feelings of meaning were predicted by the interaction of PA and individual differences in reliance on intuitive processing, with PA being especially associated with feelings of meaning for those high on intuition. In a subsequent study, we found similar patterns for real-life negative events. As an example (Hicks, Cicero, et al., 2010, Study 2), within days of the storm's landfall, a sample of students rated the extent to which the events surrounding Hurricane Katrina fit with their preexisting expectations. In this case, once again, PA informed feelings of meaning for those who were high on intuition.

Of course, these studies are limited by the fact that subjective rationality is innately subjective. Indeed, feelings of meaning may differ from other aspects of the fringe of consciousness in one important way: The subjective feeling of meaning may lack an objective referent against which to judge its accuracy. Feelings of knowing or feelings of familiarity can be tested against objective reality. For the subjective feeling of the sense of some experience, however, an objective measure of accuracy may be difficult to specify, suggesting that the subjective rationality of experience may be definitively subjective (as William James himself asserted). To address this specific concern, we conducted a final study that used the semantic coherence judgment paradigm described previously.

In this study (Hicks, Cicero, et al., 2010, Study 3), participants were randomly assigned to a positive or neutral/freestanding mood condition. Those in the positive mood condition received an unexpected payment of $20 for their participation before completing the dependent measures. Participants then completed the same task used in the Topolinski and Strack (2009a) studies described earlier. They were told to guess as quickly as possible whether presented triads were coherent or incoherent. Figure 7.1 shows the results for the key dependent measure of interest, A', a measure of signal detection. As can be seen in the figure, in the positive mood condition, reliance on intuitive processing was associated with superior discrimination of sense from nonsense.

Of course, these semantic coherence judgments are limited. They are thought to represent widely shared overlearned patterns of meaning (Kahneman

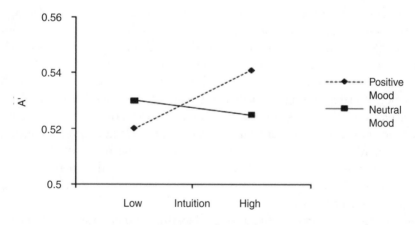

Figure 7.1. Discrimination of sense from nonsense as a function of intuitive processing style and mood induction condition. Adapted from "Positive Affect, Intuition, and the Feeling of Meaning," by J. A. Hicks, D. C. Cicero, J. Trent, C. M. Burton, and L. A. King, 2010, *Journal of Personality and Social Psychology, 98,* pp. 967–979. Copyright 2010 by the American Psychological Association.

& Klein, 2009). Thus, it is ambiguous whether individuals who were successful at these judgments would be equally able to discern meaning based not on a lifetime of learning but during the process of learning itself. I have argued that the intuitive system ought to play a role in the discernment of regularities in the environment. Thus, more recently, these findings have been generalized to implicit learning (Cicero, Hicks, & King, 2011).

In one study, participants were asked to copy letter strings that (unbeknownst to them) followed specific artificial grammar rules. Induced PA interacted with individual differences in intuition to predict accuracy in recognizing letter strings that conformed to those rules on a subsequent task. In a second study, induced PA interacted with individual differences in intuition to predict accuracy in estimates of the reward contingencies associated with various discriminative stimuli in an operant conditioning paradigm. These findings lend support to the notion that, unfettered by the influence of rationality, the intuitive system not only recognizes overlearned meanings but also plays a role in acquiring the meaning of stimuli, even through subtle processes that do not implicate awareness.

IMPLICATIONS FOR MADE MEANINGS AND MEANING IN LIFE

I close this chapter by addressing two topics that are perhaps more central to the psychology of meaning than anything I have covered so far: meaning making and meaning in life. The literature on meaning making is mixed, to say the least (see Park, 2010, for a thorough review; see also Chapter 8, this volume). Among individuals who have experienced similar traumatic events, some search for meaning (others never do), and some searchers find meaning (whereas other searchers never do). Further, even among those who have "made meaning," consistent evidence for the salubrious effects of this sense making has not emerged (Park, 2010). A better understanding of the presence of meaning might clarify these issues. It is presumed that both the intuitive and rational systems take part in the construction of meaning when it occurs. However, whether that construction feels meaningful is judged by the standards of the intuitive system. The system that naturally detects the presence of meaning in our world is the one that answers the question, "Does this feel right?" Thus, we might consider the extent to which constructed meanings reflect the kinds of processes that have been shown to appeal to this system as indications of meaning. Constructed meanings should be satisfying to the extent that they approximate the presence of meaning when it occurs naturally. Thus, a constructed meaning ought to be viable to the extent that it feels right, just as an object falling down (not up) feels exactly and intuitively right.

The experience of meaning in life is certainly an important aspect of psychological well-being. Our research suggests that although individual differences in intuition may not determine all aspects of the assessment of meaning in life, judgments of meaning in life are strongly influenced by intuitive factors, such as PA (King, Hicks, Krull, & Del Gaiso, 2006), heuristics (King, Hicks, & Abdelkhalik, 2009), and accessible information (e.g., Hicks & King, 2009). Perhaps most important, our research demonstrates a robust, durable (Hicks, Trent, Davis, & King, in press; Trent & King, 2010), and causal role for PA in the experience of meaning in life (see Hicks & King, 2009, for a review). Indeed, this research shows that when a host of other sources of meaning in life are absent, a good mood can cause life to feel meaningful (e.g., Hicks, Schlegel, & King, 2010).

Our research on the detection of meaning and the experience of meaning in life has led us to the conclusion that in thinking about meaning, meaning in life, and happiness, psychologists have often confused causes and effects. Faced with traumatic life events, a meaning maker might note, "If I could just make sense of this, I would feel better." Our research suggests that the situation may be more accurately expressed as, "If I could just feel better, this would make sense." In thinking about meaning in life and happiness, the self-help literature seems to convey the message, "If life had meaning, I could be happy." Our work suggests a different conclusion: "If I were happy, life would have meaning." Although we often bring our powerful cognitive capacities to bear on meaning when it is violated or feels absent, these vivid moments of searching for and constructing meaning should not crowd out the quieter and less remarked on reality of meaning when it is present. Meaning is often not a problem to be solved but an aspect of experience that is simply and intuitively present.

REFERENCES

Bargh, J. A. (2004). Being here now: Is consciousness necessary for human freedom? In J. Greenberg, S. L. Koole, & T. Pyszczynski, (Eds.), *Handbook of experimental existential psychology* (pp. 385–397). New York, NY: Guilford Press.

Cicero, D. C., Hicks, J. A., & King, L. A. (2011). *Extracting the meaning of experience: Positive affect and individual differences in intuition.* Manuscript submitted for publication.

Clore, G. L., & Palmer, J. (2009). Affective guidance of intelligent agents: How emotion controls cognition. *Cognitive Systems Research, 10,* 21–30. doi:10.1016/j.cogsys.2008.03.002

Epstein, S. (1994). Integrating the cognitive and psychodynamic unconscious. *American Psychologist, 49,* 709–724. doi:10.1037/0003-066X.49.8.709

Epstein, S., Pacini, R., Denes-Raj, V., & Heier, H. (1996). Individual differences in intuitive–experiential and analytical–rational thinking styles. *Journal of Personality and Social Psychology, 71*, 390–405. doi:10.1037/0022-3514.71.2.390

Evans, J.S.B.T. (2010). *Thinking twice: Two minds in one brain.* New York, NY: Oxford University Press.

Freud, S. (1953). The uncanny. In J. Strachey (Ed. & Trans.), *The standard edition of the complete psychological works of Sigmund Freud* (Vol. 17, pp. 219–252). London, England: Hogarth Press. (Original work published 1919)

Harmon-Jones, E., & Allen, J.J.B. (2001). The role of affect in the mere exposure effect: Evidence from psychophysiological and individual differences approaches. *Personality and Social Psychology Bulletin, 27*, 889–898. doi:10.1177/0146167201277011

Heine, S.J., Proulx, T., & Vohs, K.D. (2006). The meaning maintenance model: On the coherence of human motivations. *Personality and Social Psychology Review, 10*, 88–110. doi:10.1207/s15327957pspr1002_1

Hicks, J.A., Cicero, D.C., Trent, J., Burton, C.M., & King, L.A. (2010). Positive affect, intuition, and the feeling of meaning. *Journal of Personality and Social Psychology, 98*, 967–979. doi:10.1037/a0019377

Hicks, J.A., & King, L.A. (2009). Meaning in life as a judgment and lived experience. *Social and Personality Psychology Compass, 3*, 638–653. doi:10.1111/j.1751-9004.2009.00193.x

Hicks, J.A., Schlegel, R.J., & King, L.A. (2010). Social threats, happiness, and the dynamics of meaning in life judgments. *Personality and Social Psychology Bulletin, 36*, 1305–1317. doi:10.1177/0146167210381650

Hicks, J.A., Trent, J., Davis, W., & King, L.A. (in press). Positive affect, meaning in life, and future time perspective: An application of socioemotional selectivity theory. *Psychology and Aging.*

James, W. (1893). *The principles of psychology* (Vol. 1). New York, NY: Holt.

Jung, C.G. (1997). Foreword. In R. Wilhelm & C.F. Baynes (Trans.), *I ching or The book of changes* (pp. XXI–XL). Princeton, NJ: Princeton University Press. (Original work published 1950)

Kahneman, D., & Klein, G. (2009). Conditions for intuitive experience: A failure to disagree. *American Psychologist, 64*, 515–526. doi:10.1037/a0016755

King, L.A., Burton, C.M., Hicks, J.A., & Drigotas, S.M. (2007). Ghosts, UFOs, and magic: Positive affect and the experiential system. *Journal of Personality and Social Psychology, 92*, 905–919. doi:10.1037/0022-3514.92.5.905

King, L.A., & Hicks, J.A. (2009a). The detection and construction of meaning in life events. *The Journal of Positive Psychology, 4*, 317–330. doi:10.1080/17439760902992316

King, L.A., & Hicks, J.A. (2009b). Positive affect, intuition, and referential thinking. *Personality and Individual Differences, 46*, 719–724. doi:10.1016/j.paid.2009.01.031

King, L. A., Hicks, J. A., & Abdelkhalik, J. (2009). Death, life, scarcity, and value: An alternative approach to the meaning of death. *Psychological Science, 20*, 1459–1462. doi:10.1111/j.1467-9280.2009.02466.x

King, L. A., Hicks, J. A., Krull, J., & Del Gaiso, A. K. (2006). Positive affect and the experience of meaning in life. *Journal of Personality and Social Psychology, 90*, 179–196. doi:10.1037/0022-3514.90.1.179

King, L. A., Scollon, C. K., Ramsey, C. M., & Williams, T. (2000). Stories of life transition: Happy endings, subjective well-being, and ego development in parents of children with Down Syndrome. *Journal of Research in Personality, 34*, 509–536. doi:10.1006/jrpe.2000.2285

Kozak, M. N., Marsh, A. A., & Wegner, D. M. (2006). What do you think you're doing? Action identification and mind attribution. *Journal of Personality and Social Psychology, 90*, 543–555. doi:10.1037/0022-3514.90.4.543

Lazarus, R. (1984). On the primacy of cognition. *American Psychologist, 39*, 124–129. doi:10.1037/0003-066X.39.2.124

Luo, Y., & Baillargeon, R. (2005). When the ordinary seems unexpected: Evidence for incremental physical knowledge in young infants. *Cognition, 95*, 297–328. doi:10.1016/j.cognition.2004.01.010

Mangan, B. (2000). What feeling is the "feeling of knowing?" *Consciousness and Cognition, 9*, 538–544. doi:10.1006/ccog.2000.0488

Mangan, B. (2001). Sensation's ghost: The non-sensory "fringe" of consciousness. *Psyche, 7*, 1–35.

Markman, K. D., & McMullen, M. N. (2003). A reflection and evaluation model of comparative thinking. *Personality and Social Psychology Review, 7*, 244–267. doi:10.1207/S15327957PSPR0703_04

Nickerson, R. S. (1990). William James on reasoning. *Psychological Science, 1*, 167–171. doi:10.1111/j.1467-9280.1990.tb00190.x

Pacini, R., & Epstein, S. (1999). The relation of rational and experiential information processing styles to personality, basic beliefs, and the ratio-bias phenomenon. *Journal of Personality and Social Psychology, 76*, 972–987. doi:10.1037/0022-3514.76.6.972

Park, C. L. (2010). Making sense of the meaning literature: An integrative review of meaning making and its effects on adjustment to stressful life events. *Psychological Bulletin, 136*, 257–301. doi:10.1037/a0018301

Proulx, T., & Heine, S. J. (2008). The case of the transmogrifying experimenter: Reaffirmation of moral schemas following implicit change detection. *Psychological Science, 19*, 1294–1300. doi:10.1111/j.1467-9280.2008.02238.x

Reber, R., & Schwarz, N. (2002). The hot fringes of consciousness: Perceptual fluency and affect. *Consciousness & Emotion, 2*, 223–231. doi:10.1075/ce.2.2.03reb

Reber, R., Wurtz, P., & Zimmerman, T. D. (2004). Exploring "fringe" consciousness: The subjective experience of perceptual fluency and its objective basis. *Consciousness and Cognition, 13*, 47–60. doi:10.1016/S1053-8100(03)00049-7

Schwarz, N. B., & Lee, S. W. S. (2011, January). On the one hand, on the other hand: How hand movements tune the mind. In R. Mayo (Chair), *Cognitive tuning: How contextual and embodied cues shift reasoning and decision-making*. Symposium conducted at the meeting of the Society for Personality and Social Psychology, San Antonio, TX.

Shiloh, S., Salton, E., & Sharabi, D. (2002). Individual differences in rational and intuitive thinking styles as predictors of heuristic responses and framing effects. *Personality and Individual Differences, 32*, 415–429. doi:10.1016/S0191-8869(01)00034-4

Stanovich, K. E., & West, R. F. (2000). Individual differences in reasoning: Implications for the rationality debate. *Behavioral and Brain Sciences, 23*, 645–665. doi:10.1017/S0140525X00003435

Stroop, J. R. (1935). Studies of interference in serial verbal reactions. *Journal of Experimental Psychology, 18*, 643–662. doi:10.1037/h0054651

Topolinski, S., Likowski, K. U., Weyers, P., & Strack, F. (2009). The face of fluency: Semantic coherence automatically elicits a specific pattern of facial muscle reactions. *Cognition and Emotion, 23*, 260–271. doi:10.1080/02699930801994112

Topolinski, S., & Strack, F. (2008). Where there's a will—there's no intuition: The unintentional basis of semantic coherence judgments. *Journal of Memory and Language, 58*, 1032–1048. doi:10.1016/j.jml.2008.01.002

Topolinski, S., & Strack, F. (2009a). The architecture of intuition: Fluency and affect determine intuitive judgments of semantic and visual coherence and judgments of grammaticality in artificial grammar learning. *Journal of Experimental Psychology: General, 138*, 39–63. doi:10.1037/a0014678

Topolinski, S., & Strack, F. (2009b). Scanning the "Fringe" of consciousness: What is felt and what is not felt in intuitions about semantic coherence. *Consciousness and Cognition, 18*, 608–618. doi:10.1016/j.concog.2008.06.002

Trent, J., & King, L. A. (2010). Predictors of rapid vs. thoughtful judgments of meaning in life. *The Journal of Positive Psychology, 5*, 439–451. doi:10.1080/17439760.2010.534106

Winkielman, P., & Cacioppo, J. T. (2001). Mind at ease puts a smile on the face: Psychophysiological evidence that processing facilitation elicits positive affect. *Journal of Personality and Social Psychology, 81*, 989–1000. doi:10.1037//0022-3514.81.6.989

Wurtz, P., Reber, R., & Zimmermann, T. D. (2008). The feeling of fluent perception: A single experience from multiple asynchronous sources. *Consciousness and Cognition, 17*, 171–184. doi:10.1016/j.concog.2007.07.001

8

RELIGION AS A SOURCE OF MEANING

CRYSTAL L. PARK AND DONALD EDMONDSON

Chapter 7 of this volume described an exciting perspective on the role of intuitive information processing on the detection of the meaning of experiences and of life itself. It is certainly true that most meaning making is automatic and intuitive, and arises because the experience "feels right." In this chapter, we attempt to describe the global meaning systems against which the metacognitive arbiter of "right feeling" makes its determinations—religious meaning systems and the cognitive efforts that occur when experiences fail the meaning test; that is, when life experiences fail to conform to the fundamental expectations that constitute religious meaning systems. We also briefly discuss the interesting possibilities for expanding our understanding of the workings of religious meaning systems implied by the incorporation of affective states and intuitive processing into research in this area.

The universal human need for meaning is a widely accepted notion. The need is generally described as a drive to understand one's experience and to feel that one's life has significance and purpose. In a slight reformulation, Park, Edmondson, and Hale-Smith (in press) recently asserted that this need is better understood as a need for a functional meaning system that can meet meaning-related needs for significance, comprehension, and transcendence. That is, rather than positing that people "need" meaning, it seems more useful to think about how people have a need for many functions related to meaning. Indeed, a host of more specific meaning-related needs have been identified, including agency (Gray & Wegner, 2010), control (Kay, Gaucher, McGregor, & Nash, 2010), certainty (Hogg, Adelman, & Blagg, 2010), identity (Ysseldyk, Matheson, & Anisman, 2010), social validation (Park et al., in press), values (Baumeister, 1991), and coping with trauma and awareness of our own mortality (see Chapters 1, 3, and 4, this volume).

Although people have many options for meeting their needs for understanding, significance, and transcendence, religion is one of the most common and powerful sources of meaning, present throughout history and thriving in the 21st century (see Chapter 4, this volume). This chapter conceptualizes religion as a pervasive influence on the beliefs, goals, values, and subjective sense of fulfillment that collectively form a global sense of meaning, and describes the many ways that religion is drawn on to meet the pressing need for a functional meaning system. The chapter begins with an explication of a theoretical model of meaning in both daily life and in times of crisis and then presents conceptual and empirical support for the roles that religion can play in providing meaning in these contexts. The chapter concludes with remaining questions regarding religion as a source of meaning.

THE MEANING-MAKING MODEL

Developed to integrate the various predominant strands of theory and research on meaning, the *meaning-making model* posits that there are two important aspects of meaning: global and situational meaning (Park, 2010; see Figure 8.1). *Global meaning* is a framework through which people structure their experiences and assign meanings to specific experiences (*situational meaning*). Global meaning comprises three aspects: beliefs, goals, and feelings (Park & Folkman, 1997). *Global beliefs* are broad assumptions that people make regarding their own nature as well as their understanding of other people and the universe (Janoff-Bulman, 1989; Koltko-Rivera, 2004). *Global goals* refer to people's motivation or purpose for living, choice of goals, standards for judging behavior, and basis for self-esteem. Global goals are high-level ideals, states, or objects that people seek to maintain and toward which they work (Klinger, 1998). The affective aspect of global meaning is the subjective experience of a sense of meaning or purpose in life (Steger, 2009), which may be derived, in part, from seeing one's actions as oriented toward a desired future goal and making progress toward achieving it (McGregor & Little, 1998; Steger, 2009; but see Chapter 7, this volume, for a different perspective on the affective component of meaning).

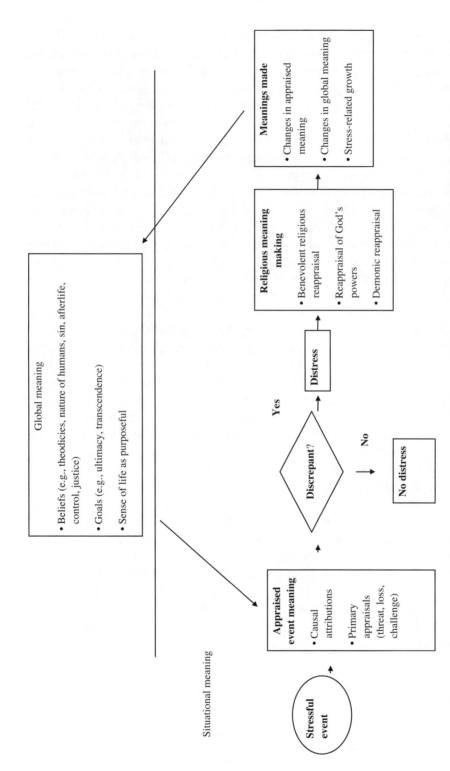

Figure 8.1. Religion, meaning, and meaning making. The roles of religion in global meaning and situational meaning-making processes.

Global meaning influences individuals' interpretations of both ordinary encounters and highly stressful events. In the course of everyday life, global meaning informs individuals' understanding of themselves and their lives and directs their personal projects and, through them, their general sense of well-being and life satisfaction (e.g., Emmons, 1999). Further, when individuals encounter potentially stressful events, they assign meanings to them that are compared with global meaning. Stress is experienced when appraised meanings violate aspects of one's global meaning system (Janoff-Bulman, 1992).

Determining that an appraised event violates one's global meaning can lead to a loss of a sense of control or a loss of the sense that the world is comprehensible, creating distress. The meaning-making model posits that the level of distress experienced is predicated on the extent of discrepancy between one's global beliefs and goals, on the one hand, and one's appraised situational meaning of the event, on the other (Park & Folkman, 1997). Distress, in turn, initiates a search for restoration of coherence among aspects of global meaning and the meaning assigned to the event (Park, Edmondson, & Mills, 2010).

These attempts to restore global meaning following its disruption or violation are termed *meaning making*. Meaning making is the process by which one comes to see or understand a situation in a different way and/or reconsiders one's beliefs and goals so as to restore consistency among them (Davis, Wortman, Lehman, & Silver, 2000). When the appraised meaning of an event is discrepant with its global meaning, people typically attempt to change or distort their views of events to assimilate them into their global meaning. However, people may also change their global sense of meaning to accommodate events. Meaning making reduces the sense of discrepancy between appraised and global meanings and restores a sense that the world is comprehensible and that life is worthwhile.

Meaning making is generally considered adaptive to the extent that satisfactory meanings are produced (Michael & Snyder, 2005), but continued unsuccessful efforts to reduce discrepancy can segue into rumination, intrusive thoughts, and long-term distress (Park, 2010). Many outcomes, or *meanings made*, can result from meaning making, including changes in one's appraisal of a stressful event (e.g., viewing it as less damaging or perhaps even fortuitous), changes made in one's global meaning system (e.g., viewing the world as less controllable), and stress-related growth (e.g., experiencing increased appreciation for life, stronger connections with family and friends, or greater self-awareness of one's strengths).

Religion and Global Meaning in Ordinary Circumstances

Zinnbauer and Pargament (2005) proposed a general working definition of *religiousness* as a search for significance in ways related to the sacred (p. 36).

This definition suggests the close link between religiousness and meaning. Worldwide, about 85% of people report having some form of religious belief, with only 15% describing themselves as atheist, agnostic, or nonreligious (Zuckerman, 2005). In the United States, the majority of Americans attend religious services at least once a month, pray at least once a day, state that religion is an important part of their lives, and believe in heaven, hell, angels, demons, and miracles (e.g., Pew Forum on Religion and Public Life, 2010; see also Slattery & Park, 2011). Yet, although research in the psychology of religion has proceeded apace over the past decades (Paloutzian & Park, in press), many researchers tend to overlook, minimize, or altogether ignore this influence on human behavior, whether out of bias or ignorance (Pargament, in press). This inattention to the high levels of religious interest and behavior in the lives of most people by many mainstream researchers is unfortunate, because it results in an incomplete understanding of human nature.

The need to acknowledge and understand religious influences is important in many areas of human life but is perhaps nowhere more relevant than in attempting to understand meaning (Batson & Stocks, 2004). Religious meaning systems are well suited to provide global meaning. For example, Hood, Hill, and Williamson (2005) identified four criteria by which religion is uniquely capable of providing global meaning: comprehensiveness, accessibility, transcendence, and direct claims. *Comprehensiveness* refers to the vast scope of issues that religion can subsume, including beliefs about the world (e.g., human nature, the social and natural environments, an afterlife), contingencies and expectations (e.g., rewards for proper behavior), goals (e.g., benevolence, virtue), actions (e.g., charity, violence), and emotions (e.g., love, joy, peace; Hood, Hill, & Spilka, 2009).

Religion is accessible in that it is widely promoted and comes in many forms, so that people can usually find a way of being religious or spiritual that suits them (Hood et al., 2005). Religions provide opportunities for transcending people's own concerns or experiences and connecting them with something greater. Finally, religions make bold and authoritative claims regarding their ability to provide a sense of significance. All these characteristics lead to the unmatched ability of religion to serve as a source of global meaning (Hood et al., 2009). Religion can provide individuals with comprehensive and integrated frameworks of meaning that explain many worldly events, experiences, and situations in satisfactory ways (Spilka, Hood, Hunsberger, & Gorsuch, 2003). Religious meaning systems provide ways to understand mundane, day-to-day occurrences as well as extraordinary ones (Park, 2005).

Religion and Global Beliefs

When religion is incorporated into people's global meaning systems, their understanding of God or the divine (e.g., as loving and benevolent, wrathful, or distant) will inform their beliefs about the nature of people (e.g., inherent goodness, made in God's image, sinful), this world (e.g., the coming apocalypse, the illusory nature of reality), and, perhaps, the next (e.g., heaven, reincarnation; McIntosh, 1995; see also Chapter 4, this volume).

Religion is the core of many individuals' identities, affecting how they understand themselves as religious or spiritual beings (e.g., as unworthy of God, as chosen; Pargament, 1997; Slattery & Park, 2011) as well as determining their social identification with a particular religious group (Ysseldyk et al., 2010). Religious identity can also provide a source of self-esteem and a sense of moral superiority (Sedikides & Gebauer, 2010).

Religion can strongly influence beliefs about control (Rothbaum, Weisz, & Snyder, 1982; Young & Morris, 2004). Some forms of religiousness exhort believers to take explicit action when conditions call for it and to work closely with God as partners (Pargament, 1997), whereas other religious traditions explicitly encourage a surrender of control and a handing over of control to powerful others, which can be seen as a form of secondary control (Exline, 2002). In research that manipulated participants' sense of personal control, greater belief in a God who has control over events was reported by those whose sense of personal control was undermined (Kay et al., 2010), suggesting that religion serves a compensatory control function.

Individuals' understanding of human suffering, termed *theodicy*, is strongly informed by their religious beliefs (Hall & Johnson, 2001). Hall and Johnson (2001) discussed how individuals can hold only two of the following three propositions simultaneously: God is all-powerful, God is all good, and evil exists. They noted that people struggle to find some way to believe that these three statements are not logically incompatible or defend the plausibility of God's existence in light of these seemingly contradictory propositions. Such a struggle to make meaning or hold onto one's beliefs in a powerful and loving God when one has personally experienced evil or severe trauma can be very challenging (Pargament, 1997).

A variety of solutions to this dilemma have spawned a variety of theodicies. Hall and Johnson (2001) noted that one influential Christian viewpoint holds that goodness can occur only in a world where evil also exists, particularly those virtues that an individual comes to practice only through suffering because of evil, such as patience, mercy, forgiveness, endurance, faith, courage, and compassion. In this meaning system, one can come to see one's traumatic or stressful experience as an opportunity to grow through suffering (e.g., to build one's soul, to become more Christ-like, to grow in agape love; Hall & Johnson, 2001). Another solution may be to view suffering as necessary for reaching future goals, such as the ultimate goal of salvation (Baumeister, 1991).

Although religiousness and spirituality have generally been found to influence global beliefs in positive ways, religious beliefs can be negative in their content or influence on the believer as well. For example, aversive religious cognitions, such as religious extremism, have been implicated in terrorism (see Chapter 11, this volume), and beliefs about an angry, uncaring, or punitive God can have powerfully destructive implications for personal and social functioning (Exline & Rose, in press). In terms of influences on a believer, some research suggests that although a sense of secondary control can be helpful, it also poses the risk of religious fatalism, by which people may abdicate responsibility for acting to alleviate problems (e.g., Franklin, Schlundt, & Wallston, 2008; Norenzayan, & Lee, 2010).

Religion and Global Goals

Religion is central to many people's life purposes. Such purposes can include connecting to the sacred, achieving enlightenment, finding salvation, knowing God, and experiencing the transcendent (Emmons, 1999). Other goals may follow from these overtly religious ones, such as living an upstanding life, working for peace and justice in the world, and devoting oneself to raising a family. It must be noted, of course, that people often embrace troubling goals, such as supremacy and destruction, in the name of religion as well (see Chapter 11, this volume).

Global goals are pursued through a variety of lower level, more concrete goals. *Personal strivings* refer to the recurrent or ongoing goals that a person characteristically tries to attain or maintain. According to Emmons (2005), *spiritual strivings* refer to goals that involve self-transcendence and that concern ultimate questions of meaning and existence. Prototypic of these types of strivings are those that reflect knowing and serving God. However, in addition to these explicitly religious motives, people can imbue virtually any personal striving with spiritual significance and character (Mahoney et al., 2005).

Religion and the Subjective Sense of Meaning in Life

Although religion and meaning in life may seem obviously related, surprisingly few studies have specifically documented this link, and most of the research has examined bivariate relations using fairly simple measures of both religion and sense of purpose. Results of these studies indicate that religiousness is related to a sense of meaning in life (e.g., Tomer & Eliason, 2000). For example, a series of studies of college students, examining dimensions of religiousness and meaning in life, yielded consistent correlations of moderate strength (Steger & Frazier, 2005).

Relations between religiousness and meaning may be moderated by demographic factors. Religiousness appears to be more strongly related to a sense of life's meaning in elderly people, especially for older Black adults as compared with older White adults (Krause, 2008). Further, different aspects of religiousness and spirituality may be differentially related to a sense of meaning in life. Intrinsic religiousness has been found to be more strongly related to meaning in life than extrinsic religiousness (e.g., Francis & Hills, 2008).

Recent research suggests that the connections between religiousness or spirituality and a sense of meaning in life may be even more complex in that religiousness may change the basis of meaning in life by shifting people's focus away from hedonic concerns and toward eudemonic concerns about living according to one's core values or authentic self (Koole, McCullough, Kuhl, & Roelofsma, 2010; see also Ryan & Deci, 2000; Chapter 12, this volume). Consistent with this notion, studies of undergraduates indicate that positive affect predicts meaning in life more strongly among students with lower religious involvement or students who were not primed with positive religious words relative to those who were primed (Hicks & King, 2008).

RELIGION AND MEANING IN STRESSFUL CIRCUMSTANCES

According to the meaning-making model, crises trigger processes of meaning making, through which individuals reduce discrepancies between their appraised meaning of a particular stressful event and their global beliefs and goals (Baumeister & Vohs, 2002; Park, 2010). Religion is often an integral part of this meaning-making process and appears to exert its most pronounced influence in times of greatest stress (McIntosh, Silver, & Wortman, 1993; Pargament, 1997). This influence is due to at least two factors: (a) for most people, religion is part of their global beliefs and goals, which may be threatened or violated by traumatic events; and (b) most religions provide ways of understanding, reinterpreting, and adding value to difficulties and suffering as well as ways to see in these travails the work of a loving God (Pargament, 1997; Park, 2005). For people experiencing injustice, suffering, or trauma, a religious belief system and its associated goals may be the most unfailing way to make meaning from their experiences.

Religion as a framework of meaning can strongly influence individuals' initial appraisals. Following a stressful event, individuals have a number of ways of making meaning, which generally involve changing the appraised meaning of events by understanding them in a different and less stressful way (e.g., by understanding the suffering as having redeeming value or by searching for positive aspects of the event) or by changing the global beliefs and goals that were violated, to bring them more in line with their current understanding of what happened (Pargament, 1997; Park, 2010). Finally, religion can be highly involved in the products of these processes, including the positive changes that individuals report following stressful experiences (Park, 2009).

Initial Appraisals

Depending on individuals' specific views, events can be experienced and understood in different ways; religious beliefs provide many alternatives for interpreting an event. For example, notions that there is a larger plan, that events are not random, or that personal growth can arise from struggle can inform the meaning of an event. Some individuals believe that God would not harm them or call on them more than they can handle, whereas others believe that God is trying to communicate something important through the event or that the event is a punishment from God (Furnham & Brown, 1992).

Religiousness can influence how people understand and respond to specific traumatic events. For example, one study found that, among students who were strongly adversely affected by the 2005 hurricanes along the Gulf Coast, higher religiousness was related to greater appraisal of the hurricanes as threatening and as more of a loss and less of a challenge. Further, those who were more religious were more likely to perceive God as responsible for the hurricanes (Newton & McIntosh, 2009).

Event appraisals also include causal attributions—people's understandings of why a given event occurred. Attributions for negative events can be naturalistic or religious (Spilka et al., 2003). For example, naturalistic explanations for illnesses can include stress, injury, pathogens, and weakened immune systems, whereas religious attributions can include God's efforts to teach, challenge, or punish the afflicted or to teach a lesson to others (Spilka et al., 2003). However, it is quite common for individuals to make naturalistic attributions for the immediate cause of the event but also invoke religious or metaphysical explanations for the more distal causes (see Park & Folkman, 1997). For example, a cancer diagnosis may be understood as caused by dietary or environmental factors but may also be seen in a broader context as due to God's will or as a punishment for previous sinful behavior (Weeks & Lupfer, 2000).

Religious attributions appear to be particularly likely for aversive or harmful events (Gray & Wegner, 2010) and those of high ambiguity and threat (Spilka et al., 2003). The likelihood that an individual will make religious or nonreligious attributions for particular experiences or encounters also depends, in large part, on the relative availability of global religious and naturalistic beliefs (Gray & Wegner, 2010; Spilka et al., 2003) as well as the extent to which the explanatory power of each type of attribution is satisfactory (Spilka et al., 2003).

Determination of Discrepancy or Distress

After appraising the initial meaning of an event, individuals must determine the extent to which that meaning is congruent with their general views of the world and their desires and goals. Little research has explicitly focused on how people evaluate the discrepancies between their global meaning system and their appraisals of potentially traumatic events (Park, Mills, & Edmondson, 2012). Several studies have suggested that more religious people perceive traumatic events as more discrepant with their global meaning systems; these sudden and inexplicable aversive events can shatter the devout individual's positive global meaning system (Park, 2005, 2008; Park & Cohen, 1993).

Religion and Meaning-Making Coping

Discrepancies between global and situational meanings produce distress and drive efforts to restore congruence through meaning making, which can involve changing the appraised meaning of the stressor to make it less aversive or changing global beliefs and goals to accommodate the experience (see Park, 2010, for a review). Meaning-making efforts often have a religious aspect. For example, religious reappraisals of stressful events are common (Harrison, Koenig, Hays, Eme-Akwari, & Pargament, 2001).

Religion and Meanings Made

The products of meaning making can be changes in the appraised meaning of the stressful event and, sometimes, changes in global meaning. Because religious beliefs, like other basic beliefs, tend to be relatively stable, people confronting crises are thought to be more likely to reappraise their perceptions of situations to fit their preexisting beliefs than to change their religious beliefs (Pargament, 1997). Religion can be involved in both meanings made that involve changes in appraised meaning and those that involve changes in global meaning.

Changes in Appraised Meaning

Religion can be involved in changing the meaning of a stressful situation by offering additional possibilities for causal attributions and by illuminating other aspects of the situation. The motivation to reduce distress generally leads to reappraising stressful situations in a more positive light by giving them a more acceptable meaning that is more consistent with global meaning, although negative reappraisals are sometimes made. Reattribution, in which the original causal attribution for an event is revised, is one of the most commonly studied changes in situational meaning made (Davis, Nolen-Hoeksema, & Larson, 1998). For example, people may initially feel that God neglected to care for them or even deliberately and unjustly caused their stressful event, but over time they may come to see it as the will of a loving or purposeful God, even if it is a God who is inscrutable and beyond human understanding (Spilka et al., 2003).

Religion offers many avenues for positive reattribution and is frequently invoked in the search for a more acceptable reason for an event's occurrence than what one may have originally entertained. For example, people can come to see the stressful event as a spiritual opportunity, as the result of a punishing God, or as the result of human sinfulness (Pargament, 1997).

Although religion commonly facilitates the making of more positive meanings, reinterpretations are not always positive. For example, people sometimes come to believe that God harmed them, either through deliberate action or through passivity and neglect. These negative results of the making-meaning process can lead to mistrust, anger, hurt, and disappointment toward God, or even doubt regarding God's existence (Exline & Rose, in press).

Changes in Global Meaning

Traumatic events are sometimes so discrepant with global meaning that situational reappraisal cannot restore congruence with an individual's pre-existing global meaning. In these instances, people may reduce the discrepancy between their understanding of an event and their global meaning by changing their fundamental global beliefs or goals. For example, those with faith may come to view God as less powerful (Kushner, 1982) or cease to believe in God altogether. Others may come to believe that they are unable to comprehend everything that happens in the world or that their own nature is sinful (Exline & Rose, in press). Individuals may change or reprioritize their global goals by, for example, rededicating themselves to their religious commitments or pledging to be more devout. Negative events may be easier to bear when understood within a benevolent religious framework, and attributing death, illness, and other major losses to the will of God or to a loving God are generally linked with better outcomes (Pargament, 1997).

Stress-Related Growth

One outcome of meaning making that often straddles the global/situational meaning distinction is stress-related growth. *Stress-related growth* refers to positive life changes that people perceive they have experienced as a result of a negative event. Some of these changes are profound, such as reorienting their lives and rededicating themselves to their reconsidered priorities. Other types of stress-related growth involve smaller changes, such as being more intimate with loved ones, handling stress more effectively, taking better care of themselves, seeing their own identities more clearly, feeling closer to

God, appreciating more the everyday aspects of life, and having the courage to try new things (Park, 2009; see also Chapter 9, this volume). Growth appears to come from looking for positive aspects of negative events and identifying some redeeming features of the experience, which may involve changes in both situational and global meaning (Park & Fenster, 2004).

Many religious traditions contend that spiritual growth occurs primarily during times of suffering. Through suffering, people develop character, coping skills, and a repertoire of life experiences that may enable them to manage future struggles more successfully. Many religions also attempt to cultivate virtues such as compassion, which cause people to be more attuned to the suffering of others (Exline, 2002). In fact, one of the most consistent findings regarding predictors of positive life change following life stressors is that religiousness, measured by various dimensions, such as intrinsic religious motivation and religious coping, strongly predicts reports of growth (Shaw, Joseph, & Linley, 2005). Further, this stress-related growth is often religious in nature. Growth following stressful encounters generally involves perceptions of increased coping skills, increased social support, and deepened or renewed perspectives and philosophies of life (Park, 2009), and religion is often an element of each of these changes. For example, research has demonstrated that, following a stressful encounter, many people report feeling closer to God, more certain of their faith, and more religious; they often report using more religious coping and increasing their commitment to their religion and their involvement in their religious community (e.g., Cole, Hopkins, Tisak, Steel, & Carr, 2008).

It should be noted that reports of stress-related growth (also known as posttraumatic growth, adversarial growth, benefit finding, and similar monikers) represent perceptions of positive change rather than positive change per se (Park, 2009). The extent to which these perceptions are accurate is a point of controversy in the literature. Some research has demonstrated little correspondence between reports of change (on a growth inventory) and actual change (measured pre–post on a variety of indices such as religiousness and interpersonal relationships; Frazier et al., 2009). Some researchers contend that the veridicality of such reports is beside the point and that the perception of growth is the important construct, whereas others argue that the focus should be on actual change (see Park, 2009, for a more detailed review of this issue).

FUTURE RESEARCH DIRECTIONS

Although the need for meaning and the pervasive role of religion in maintaining life meaning have long been the focus of social scientists, empirical progress in this area has suffered from a lack of clarity regarding meaning. Framing the "need for meaning" as the "need for a functional meaning system" helps to anchor the issues of meaning and religiousness or spirituality in ways that allow delineation of many specific types of meaning, contexts, and processes, allowing for more sophisticated empirical research. Advances will come from future research in this area. Such research should be longitudinal and, ideally, prospective in design. Meaning making and meanings made must be assessed at different times, and processes of meaning making should be assessed carefully (see Park, 2010, for an overview of methodological issues).

Several research directions seem particularly promising. First, the complex relations between religious and secular aspects of global meaning and meaning-making processes are virtually unexamined. Most extant studies focus on circumscribed sets of variables, but in human lives, religious and nonreligious aspects of global meaning are intermingled, and the extent to which religiousness underlies secular meaning systems may be a key individual-difference factor. Further, little research has linked these global meaning systems with processes of meaning making. More sophisticated research that follows individuals over time as they deal with major life stressors, comparing religious and secular meaning-making processes and meanings made, will be important for understanding the unique role of religious meaning.

Another important direction for future research is delving deeper into the issue of discrepancy, which is the construct on which the meaning making is explicitly based. Yet the conditions under which people experience violations of their global religious meaning systems remain unknown. Sometimes individuals' religious meaning systems are strong enough to protect them from experiencing violations (e.g., by believing that God has a plan, albeit one that may be beyond human understanding), yet stronger religiousness predicts more violations and cognitive processing, at least following bereavement (e.g., McIntosh et al., 1993). Chapter 7 of this volume offers some interesting insights into this question. Though the processes involved in detecting meaning violation because of traumatic experiences, and reconstructing meaning in its wake, may be quite different from those involved in judging the type of meaning implied by semantic similarities or the plausibility of supernatural events, positive affect and individual differences in reliance on intuition may play an important role in determining whose meaning systems will "feel" violated, and who will search for meaning in the wake of trauma.

Some researchers have recently framed religiousness as culture (e.g., Cohen, 2009). This perspective opens many doors to research examining meaning systems as cultural elements. Further, most of the research on religion and meaning has been conducted in the United States with primarily Christian participants. The need to examine global and situational meaning and the roles of religion in diverse populations across the world is obvious.

Finally, future research should focus more explicitly on the content of religious beliefs and goals. Most research in the area of religion and meaning has, to date, used fairly generic measures of religiousness that provide little information on the specifics of what a person believes or holds as important, let alone how the how different beliefs and goals predict violations and meaning-making processes. The recent focus on specific theodicies (Hale-Smith, Park, & Edmondson, in press) is a welcome advance; similar developments in conceptualizing other types of beliefs and goals will help to illuminate religious meaning systems.

REFERENCES

Batson, C.D., & Stocks, E.L. (2004). Religion: Its core psychological function. In J. Greenberg, S.L. Koole, & T. Pyszczynski (Eds.), *Handbook of experimental existential psychology* (pp. 141–155). New York, NY: Guilford Press.

Baumeister, R.F. (1991). *Meanings of life*. New York, NY: Guilford Press.

Baumeister, R.F., & Vohs, K.D. (2002). The pursuit of meaningfulness in life. In C.R. Snyder & S.J. Lopez (Eds.), *The handbook of positive psychology* (pp. 608–618). New York, NY: Oxford University Press.

Cohen, A.B. (2009). Many forms of culture. *American Psychologist, 64*, 194–204. doi:10.1037/a0015308

Cole, B.S., Hopkins, C.M., Tisak, J., Steel, J.L., & Carr, B.I. (2008). Assessing spiritual growth and spiritual decline following a diagnosis of cancer: Reliability and validity of the spiritual transformation scale. *Psycho-Oncology, 17*, 112–121. doi:10.1002/pon.1207

Davis, C.G., Nolen-Hoeksema, S., & Larson, J. (1998). Making sense of loss and benefiting from the experience: Two construals of meaning. *Journal of Personality and Social Psychology, 75*, 561–574. doi:10.1037/0022-3514.75.2.561

Davis, C.G., Wortman, C.B., Lehman, D.R., & Silver, R. (2000). Searching for meaning in loss: Are clinical assumptions correct? *Death Studies, 24*, 497–540. doi:10.1080/07481180050121471

Emmons, R.A. (1999). *The psychology of ultimate concerns*. New York, NY: Guilford Press.

Emmons, R.A. (2005). Striving for the sacred: Personal goals, life meaning, and religion. *Journal of Social Issues, 61*, 731–745. doi:10.1111/j.1540-4560.2005.00429.x

Exline, J.J. (2002). Stumbling blocks on the religious road: Fractured relationships, nagging vices, and the inner struggle to believe. *Psychological Inquiry, 13*, 182–189. doi:10.1207/S15327965PLI1303_03

Exline, J.J., & Rose, E. (in press). Spiritual struggle. In R.F. Paloutzian & C.L. Park (Eds.), *Handbook of the psychology of religion and spirituality* (2nd ed.). New York, NY: Guilford Press.

Francis, L.J., & Hills, P.R. (2008). The development of the Meaning in Life Index (MILI) and its relationship with personality and religious behaviours and beliefs among UK undergraduate students. *Mental Health, Religion & Culture, 11*, 211–220. doi:10.1080/13674670701243758

Franklin, M. D., Schlundt, D. G., & Wallston, K. A. (2008). Development and validation of a religious health fatalism measure for the African-American faith community. *Journal of Health Psychology, 13*, 323–335. doi:10.1177/1359105307088137

Frazier, P., Tennen, H., Gavian, M., Park, C. L., Tomich, P., & Tashiro, T. (2009). Does self-reported posttraumatic growth reflect genuine positive change? *Psychological Science, 20*, 912–919. doi:10.1111/j.1467-9280.2009.02381.x

Furnham, A., & Brown, L. B. (1992). Theodicy: A neglected aspect of the psychology of religion. *International Journal for the Psychology of Religion, 2*, 37–45. doi:10.1207/s15327582ijpr0201_4

Gray, K., & Wegner, D. (2010). Blaming God for our pain: Human suffering and the divine mind. *Personality and Social Psychology Review, 14*, 7–16. doi:10.1177/1088868309350299

Hale-Smith, A., Park, C. L., & Edmondson, D. (in press). Measuring religious beliefs about suffering: Development of the Views of Suffering Scale. *Psychological Assessment*.

Hall, M. E. L., & Johnson, E. L. (2001). Theodicy and therapy: Philosophical/ethological contributions to the problem of suffering. *Journal of Psychology and Christianity, 20*, 5–17.

Harrison, M. O., Koenig, H. G., Hays, J. C., Eme-Akwari, A. G., & Pargament, K. I. (2001). The epidemiology of religious coping: A review of recent literature. *International Review of Psychiatry, 13*, 86–93. doi:10.1080/09540260120037317

Hicks, J. A., & King, L. A. (2008). Religious commitment and positive mood as information about meaning in life. *Journal of Research in Personality, 42*, 43–57. doi:10.1016/j.jrp.2007.04.003

Hogg, M. A., Adelman, J., & Blagg, R. (2010). Religion in the face of uncertainty: An uncertainty-identity theory account of religiousness. *Personality and Social Psychology Review, 14*, 72–83. doi:10.1177/1088868309349692

Hood, R. W., Jr., Hill, P. C., & Spilka, B. (2009). *The psychology of religion: An empirical approach* (4th ed.). New York, NY: Guilford Press.

Hood, R. W., Jr., Hill, P. C., & Williamson, W. P. (2005). *The psychology of religious fundamentalism*. New York, NY: Guilford Press.

Janoff-Bulman, R. (1989). Assumptive worlds and the stress of traumatic events: Applications of the schema construct. *Social Cognition, 7*, 113–136. doi:10.1521/soco.1989.7.2.113

Janoff-Bulman, R. (1992). *Shattered assumptions: Towards a new psychology of trauma*. New York, NY: Free Press.

Kay, A. C., Gaucher, D., McGregor, I., & Nash, K. (2010). Religious belief as compensatory control. *Personality and Social Psychology Review, 14*, 37–48. doi:10.1177/1088868309353750

Klinger, E. (1998). The search for meaning in evolutionary perspective and its clinical implications. In P. T. P. Wong & P. S. Fry (Eds.), *The human quest for meaning* (pp. 27–50). Mahwah, NJ: Erlbaum.

Koltko-Rivera, M. E. (2004). The psychology of worldviews. *Review of General Psychology, 8,* 3–58. doi:10.1037/1089-2680.8.1.3

Koole, S. L., McCullough, M., Kuhl, J., & Roelofsma, P. (2010). Why religion's burdens are light: From religiosity to implicit self-regulation. *Personality and Social Psychology Review, 14,* 95–107. doi:10.1177/1088868309351109

Krause, N. (2008). The social foundation of religious meaning in life. *Research on Aging, 30,* 395–427. doi:10.1177/0164027508316619

Kushner, H. S. (1982). *When bad things happen to good people.* New York, NY: HarperCollins.

Mahoney, A., Pargament, K. I., Cole, B., Jewell, T., Magyar, G. M., Tarkeshwar, N., . . . Phillips, R. (2005). A higher purpose: The sanctification of strivings in a community sample. *International Journal for Psychology of Religion, 15,* 239–262. doi:10.1207/s15327582ijpr1503_4

McGregor, I., & Little, B. R. (1998). Personal projects, happiness, and meaning: On doing well and being yourself. *Journal of Personality and Social Psychology, 74,* 494–512. doi:10.1037/0022-3514.74.2.494

McIntosh, D. N. (1995). Religion-as-schema, with implications for the relation between religion and coping. *International Journal for the Psychology of Religion, 5,* 1–16. doi:10.1207/s15327582ijpr0501_1

McIntosh, D. N., Silver, R. C., & Wortman, C. B. (1993). Religion's role in adjustment to a negative life event: Coping with the loss of a child. *Journal of Personality and Social Psychology, 65,* 812–821. doi:10.1037/0022-3514.65.4.812

Michael, S. T., & Snyder, C. R. (2005). Getting unstuck: The roles of hope, finding meaning, and rumination in the adjustment to bereavement among college students. *Death Studies, 29,* 435–458. doi:10.1080/07481180590932544

Newton, A. T., & McIntosh, D. N. (2009). Associations of general religiousness and specific religious beliefs with coping appraisals in response to Hurricanes Katrina and Rita. *Mental Health, Religion & Culture, 12,* 129–146. doi:10.1080/13674670802380400

Norenzayan, A., & Lee, A. (2010). It was meant to happen: Explaining cultural variations in fate attributions. *Journal of Personality and Social Psychology, 98,* 702–720. doi:10.1037/a0019141

Paloutzian, R. F., & Park, C. L. (Eds.). (in press). *Handbook of the psychology of religion and spirituality* (2nd ed.). New York, NY: Guilford Press.

Pargament, K. I. (1997). *The psychology of religion and coping.* New York, NY: Guilford Press.

Pargament, K. I. (in press). Envisioning an integrative paradigm for the psychology of religion and spirituality: An introduction to the *APA Handbook of Psychology, Religion, and Spirituality.* In K. I. Pargament, J. J. Exline, J. Jones, & A. Mahoney

(Eds.), *Handbook of the psychology of religion and spirituality*. Washington, DC: American Psychological Association.

Park, C. L. (2005). Religion and meaning. In R. F. Paloutzian & C. L. Park (Eds.), *Handbook of the psychology of religion and spirituality* (pp.295–314). New York, NY: Guilford Press.

Park, C. L. (2008). Testing the meaning making model of coping with loss. *Journal of Social and Clinical Psychology, 27*, 970–994. doi:10.1521/jscp.2008.27.9.970

Park, C. L. (2009). Overview of theoretical perspectives. In C. L. Park, S. Lechner, M. H. Antoni, & A. Stanton (Eds.), *Positive life change in the context of medical illness: Can the experience of serious illness lead to transformation?* (pp. 11–30). Washington, DC: American Psychological Association. doi:10.1037/11854-001

Park, C. L. (2010). Making sense of the meaning literature: An integrative review of meaning making and its effects on adjustment to stressful life events. *Psychological Bulletin, 136*, 257–301. doi:10.1037/a0018301

Park, C. L., & Cohen, L. H. (1993). Religious and nonreligious coping with the death of a friend. *Cognitive Therapy and Research, 17*, 561–577. doi:10.1007/BF01176079

Park, C. L., Edmondson, D., & Hale-Smith, A. (in press). Why religion? Meaning as the motivation. In K. I. Pargament, J. J. Exline, J. Jones, & A. Mahoney (Eds.), *Handbook of the psychology of religion and spirituality*. Washington, DC: American Psychological Association.

Park, C. L., Edmondson, D., & Mills, M. A. (2010). Religious worldviews and stressful encounters: Reciprocal influence from a meaning-making perspective. In T. W. Miller (Ed.), *Handbook of stressful transitions across the lifespan* (pp. 485–501). New York, NY: Springer. doi:10.1007/978-1-4419-0748-6_25

Park, C. L., & Fenster, J. R. (2004). Stress-related growth: Predictors and processes. *Journal of Social and Clinical Psychology, 23*, 195–215.

Park, C. L., & Folkman, S. (1997). The role of meaning in the context of stress and coping. *Review of General Psychology, 1*, 115–144.

Park, C. L., Mills, M., & Edmondson, D. (2012). PTSD as meaning violation: Testing a cognitive worldview perspective. *Psychological Trauma: Theory, Research, Practice, and Policy, 4*(1), 66–73. doi:10.1037/a0018792

Pew Forum on Religion and Public Life. (2010). *U. S. Religious Landscape Survey*. Retrieved from http://religions.pewforum.org/

Rothbaum, F., Weisz, J. R., & Snyder, S. S. (1982). Changing the world and changing the self: A two-process model of perceived control. *Journal of Personality and Social Psychology, 42*, 5–37. doi:10.1037/0022-3514.42.1.5

Ryan, R. M., & Deci, E. L. (2000). Self-determination theory and the facilitation of intrinsic motivation, social development, and well-being. *American Psychologist, 55*, 68–78. doi:10.1037/0003-066X.55.1.68

Sedikides, C., & Gebauer, J. E. (2010). Religiosity as self-enhancement: A meta-analysis of the relation between socially desirable responding and religiosity. *Personality and Social Psychology Review, 14*, 17–36. doi:10.1177/1088868309351002

Shaw, A., Joseph, S., & Linley, P. A. (2005). Religion, spirituality, and post-traumatic growth: A systematic review. *Mental Health, Religion & Culture, 8,* 1–11. doi:10.1080/1367467032000157981

Slattery, J. M., & Park, C. L. (2011). Meaning making and spiritually oriented interventions. In J. Aten, M. R. McMinn, & E. V. Worthington (Eds.), *Spiritually oriented interventions for counseling and psychotherapy* (pp. 15–40). Washington, DC: American Psychological Association.

Spilka, B., Hood, R. W., Jr., Hunsberger, B., & Gorsuch, R. (2003). *The psychology of religion: An empirical approach* (3rd ed.). New York, NY: Guilford Press.

Steger, M. F. (2009). Meaning in life. In S. J. Lopez (Ed.), *Oxford handbook of positive psychology* (2nd ed.; pp. 679–687). Oxford, England: Oxford University Press.

Steger, M. F., & Frazier, P. (2005). Meaning in life: One link in the chain from religion to well-being. *Journal of Counseling Psychology, 52,* 574–582. doi:10.1037/0022-0167.52.4.574

Tomer, A., & Eliason, G. (2000). Beliefs about self, life, and death: Testing aspects of a comprehensive model of death anxiety and death attitudes. In A. Tomer (Ed.), *Death attitudes and the older adult* (pp. 137–153). Philadelphia, PA: Brunner-Routledge.

Weeks, M., & Lupfer, M. B. (2000). Religious attributions and proximity of influence: An investigation of direct interventions and distal explanations. *Journal for the Scientific Study of Religion, 39,* 348–362. doi:10.1111/0021-8294.00029

Young, M. J., & Morris, M. W. (2004). Existential meanings and cultural models: The interplay of personal and supernatural agency in American and Hindu ways of responding to uncertainty. In J. Greenberg, S. L. Koole, & T. Pyszczynski (Eds.), *Handbook of experimental existential psychology* (pp. 215–230). New York, NY: Guilford Press.

Ysseldyk, R., Matheson, K., & Anisman, H. (2010). Religiosity as identity: Toward an understanding of religion from a social identity perspective. *Personality and Social Psychology Review, 14,* 60–71.

Zinnbauer, B. J., & Pargament, K. I. (2005). Religiousness and spirituality. In R. F. Paloutzian & C. L. Park (Eds.), *Handbook of the psychology of religion and spirituality* (pp. 21–42). New York, NY: Guilford Press.

Zuckerman, P. (2005). Atheism: Contemporary rates and patterns. In M. Martin (Ed.), *The Cambridge companion to atheism* (pp. 47–67). Cambridge, England: Cambridge University Press.

9

BECOMING AND DEVELOPING: PERSONAL GROWTH IN THE WAKE OF PARENTHOOD AND GRANDPARENTHOOD

ORIT TAUBMAN – BEN-ARI

The previous two chapters in this section of the volume discussed two alternative ways of finding meaning in personal experiences: intuitively sensing what "feels right" at a given moment (Chapter 7) and using religion as a meaning-making mechanism mainly when confronting traumatic life events (Chapter 8). In this chapter, I also focus on life events that can challenge existing meaning systems but that, unlike other traumatic situations, provide a natural opportunity to intuitively sense and detect the meaning that emerges from the situation itself and to experience personal growth. More specifically, I focus on transitions to parenthood and grandparenthood and the factors that might allow people to sense the meaning that emerges from these transitions.

The transition to parenthood is one of the most significant role changes in an individual's life (e.g., Feeney, Hohaus, Noller, & Alexander, 2001). However, although the birth of a child is generally viewed as a joyful event, it may also generate stress and thus shares certain features with negative life experiences (e.g., Cowan & Cowan, 1999; Feeney et al., 2001). The transition to grandparenthood is second only to parenthood in terms of its significance in the family life cycle. Similarly, it is typically associated with positive outcomes (e.g., Rowe & Kahn, 1998) but may well be a source of stress (e.g., Mann & Leeson, 2010).

Nevertheless, with any stress-related event, the upheaval resulting from the loss of cherished roles, along with new and challenging demands, may provide an opportunity to create a better life structure and enable individuals to find new strengths and appreciate the value of supportive others. In other words, the need to adapt to demanding circumstances in the transition to parenthood or grandparenthood may also engender personal growth (Calhoun & Tedeschi, 2006; see also Chapter 8, this volume). Thus, although many of the chapters in this book deal with existential concerns and treat them as threats that often lead to defensiveness and demoralization, the current chapter focuses on the opportunity embedded in difficult or challenging experiences to initiate beneficial and appreciated periods of personal growth.

Three broad areas of growth are generally reported following stressful events: enhanced interpersonal relationships and greater appreciation of others; changes in self-perception, in the direction of increased resilience and maturity; and reexamination of life philosophy and the setting of new priorities. Analysis of the items on the Posttraumatic Growth Inventory (PTGI), a scale developed by Tedeschi and Calhoun (1996) to assess positive changes in the wake of adversity, has led to the conceptualization of these three areas in terms of five dimensions: new possibilities, relating to others, personal strength, spiritual change, and appreciation of life. The PTGI has been used and validated in a wide variety of studies and with diverse populations (e.g., Calhoun & Tedeschi, 2006).

It is important to note that the term *growth* refers to a perceptible sense of improvement and not to a return to baseline. Growth is not an enhancement in well-being or a decrease in level of distress (Calhoun & Tedeschi, 2006), nor is it the learning of new behavioral or cognitive skills that might improve the individual's quality of life in a specific area. It is, rather, an indication that a person has developed beyond his or her previous level of adaptation, psychological functioning, or understanding of life (Zoellner & Maercker, 2006). Moreover, studies examining the relationship between growth and both negative and positive characteristics of mental health, including depressive symptoms, anxiety, and anger, on the one hand, and self-esteem and adaptation on the other, have found no systematic associations between them (Zoellner & Maercker, 2006). Thus, growth does not appear to reflect changes in well-being in the sense of emotional state and hedonic tone but as a genuine personal development that enables individuals to better understand their place in the world, including the meaning of life and their commitment to the challenges with which it presents them (Joseph & Linley, 2008).

Although most of the literature on growth deals with traumatic life events, such as the death of a loved one or a serious illness, as noted earlier, growth is not exclusively related to negative experiences; it may also follow a challenge to, and consequent reexamination of, one's core beliefs (Tedeschi, Calhoun, & Cann, 2007). Because growth refers to positive psychological changes experienced as a result of struggling with demanding circumstances—circumstances that require adaptive resources and challenge the way people understand the world and their place in it—I argue that positive experiences can also be life altering and entail stress. That is, they may challenge an individual's schemas and life meaning and therefore lead to growth.

Indeed, the literature on the adaptation to motherhood provides indications of this possibility, showing that during the transition to motherhood, women may gain self-esteem, new meaning in life, a sense of competence, and awareness of the positive features of themselves and their social environment (Wells, Hobfoll, & Lavin, 1999). In one early study, almost 60% of mothers whose newborns had been in a neonatal intensive care unit reported some benefits, including improved relationships with family and friends, emotional growth, and an appreciation of just how precious their child was. Others felt that their vulnerability made them more emotionally expressive and appreciative of their inner resources, thereby improving their use of a social support system they had previously ignored (Affleck, Tennen, Allen, & Gershman, 1986). Although the term *growth* was not yet used in these studies, they indicated that the kinds of growth identified in trauma victims might also be found in new mothers.

The following sections rely on a series of recent studies conducted by my colleagues and me. They take the research on stress and growth one step further, allowing for a multidimensional perspective on the complex experience of growth following the transition to parenthood or grandparenthood. I first attempt to show that parents and grandparents indeed experience growth. Next, I discuss internal and external factors that may play a role in the experience of growth of parents and grandparents. Finally, I offer some personal insights regarding growth and the implications of our findings for future research and practice.

DO PARENTS AND GRANDPARENTS
REALLY EXPERIENCE GROWTH?

As explained previously, personal growth consists of perceived positive changes in interpersonal relationships, self-perceptions, and priorities. These outcomes were mentioned spontaneously by parents and grandparents when describing their thoughts and feelings about their current status, either in response to open-ended questions on self-report questionnaires (Taubman – Ben-Ari, Findler, & Sharon, 2011) or in face-to-face interviews (Findler, 2009). Typical indications of such growth are presented here in the participants' own words.

Enhanced Interpersonal Relationships and Greater Appreciation of Others

- "Following the birth, our partnership became stronger. The shared process of concern for the child and taking care of him sometimes causes stress and crises, but mostly it brings the parents closer together as a couple."—Father of a 6-month-old son
- "I think that being a grandmother brought my husband and me together in a new and very special way, something very strong. Today we share experiences that we are very happy with, and this is a strong bond."—Grandmother of 2-year-old and 4.5-month-old boys
- "I have learned that I have the strength to cope with difficult situations thanks to the great support I got and am still getting from my family [siblings and parents]. My husband and I cooperate in every situation and deal with everything together."—Mother of a 4-year-old girl

These examples reveal how new parents and grandparents perceive their relationships with others. Parents tend to focus on their newfound understanding of the importance of the people around them, their appreciation for the help and support they have received, and the positive effects on their marital and intergenerational relationships. They also refer to an increased ability to ask for help and to allow themselves to rely on others, an experience many of them were not open to before they became parents. Grandparents tend to speak about the strengthening of their relations with their son or daughter and the new generation and about how fulfilling and satisfying the experience is. They also experience becoming part of a new community, the "fellowship" of grandparents. Both groups mention a stronger or deeper connection with others.

Changes in Self-Perception in the Direction of Increased Resilience and Maturity

- "I feel I'm better able to express abilities and capabilities that I didn't call on before. I can make better, more rational decisions. I feel I'm more responsible and empowered in many ways."—First-time father
- "The transition to grandparenthood enabled me to come to terms with my parenting and maybe give myself another chance to give, influence, and be an important figure in my grandchildren's lives."—First-time grandmother

- "The experience of motherhood is empowering and life-changing. I put my sense of guilt behind me (as far as possible) and live most of the time with a feeling of satisfaction and love for my children. I've become more efficient, competent, and sensitive to communications with the people around me. My time management is more effective."—Mother of a 4-year-old boy
- "I feel that my relationship with my granddaughter comes from a calmer and more mature place than the relationship I had with my own children."—First-time grandfather

Clearly, both parents and grandparents learn something new about their abilities and find capacities in themselves they were unaware of even a short time before the transition. They learn that they are stronger than they thought and discover traits they are proud of, including greater responsibility, efficiency, and sensitivity to others' needs. These new insights give them a sense of empowerment. Grandparents also mention the opportunity they have been given to "fix" the mistakes they made as parents, to be better as grandparents than they were as parents.

Reexamination of Life Philosophy and Setting New Priorities

- "I see things from a different perspective. My priorities have changed. Things I focused on in the past have given way to a stronger focus on the family."—Father of a 2-year-old girl
- "My priorities have changed. The most important thing for me right now is to be with my daughter and give her everything she needs, physically, emotionally, mentally. . . . That comes before everything else—the rest of the family (my brothers and sisters, for instance), work, hobbies, friends."—First-time mother

Transitioning to a new familial role affects self-development, priorities, rethinking of existing schemes and structures, and setting new goals in life. Parenthood often brings with it a shift from a focus on self-fulfillment through a career to nesting and enriching the family space. Importantly, although the examples have been organized to illustrate certain dimensions of growth, their categorization into separate themes is at times artificial; many of them are associated with more than one dimension, suggesting that the whole is greater than the sum of its parts.

In view of the indications of growth revealed with qualitative methods, I undertook a series of systematic quantitative studies. As will become evident, most studies assessing growth in the transition to parenthood and grandparenthood use the PTGI (Tedeschi & Calhoun, 1996) as a measurement tool, adapting the general instructions to fit the specific life transition examined.

One of my studies therefore sought to determine whether the PTGI is indeed a suitable instrument to measure personal changes following childbirth. I content-analyzed mothers' responses to open-ended questions regarding positive changes that occurred following the birth of their child (or children, in the case of twins) and compared the themes that emerged with the PTGI items. I studied two samples of mothers. The first consisted of 150 relatively new first-time mothers. The second sample was more diverse, comprising 157 mothers in various subgroups (first-time and non-first-time mothers, mothers of twins and singletons, mothers of pre- and full-term babies). In both samples, compatibility was found between the spontaneous responses and the PTGI items (Taubman – Ben-Ari, Findler, & Sharon, 2011). In other words, the positive changes that mothers report after giving birth do appear to indicate growth as originally conceptualized by Tedeschi and Calhoun (1996).

This conclusion was also borne out by a study of psychological growth in British women following childbirth: Sawyer and Ayers (2009) found that half of the women in their sample reported at least a moderate degree of growth. They compared their findings with those of studies of other life events and found that the growth level of the mothers was similar to those reported following accidents and assaults (Snape, 1997) and mixed traumatic events (Wild & Paivio, 2004), although lower than the levels reported by individuals suffering chronic illness or bereavement (Cordova, Cunningham, Carlson, & Andrykowski, 2001; Polatinsky & Esprey, 2000).

So far, all the reviewed studies have relied on self-reports, which may be affected by self-serving biases or socially desirable responding. I therefore decided to see whether signs of growth would also be detected by external evaluators. I examined the association between self-reported and other-reported personal growth in three samples. In the first sample, both first-time mothers and their own mothers completed the PTGI, with the grandmothers reporting on changes in their daughters following the transition to motherhood. Significant positive correlations were found between the two groups on the five factors as well as on the total growth scores (Taubman – Ben-Ari, Findler, & Sharon, 2011). The next two samples were grandparents. In the first, spouses' responses to the PTGI were compared, and in the second, grandparents' self-reports were compared with reports of their child who had recently become a parent. The self-reports of new grandparents and their growth as perceived by their spouses were positively correlated, and these results were replicated by positive correlations between grandparents' own reports and their offspring's reports about their parents' growth (Taubman – Ben-Ari, Findler, & Ben Shlomo, in press b). Thus, reported growth is not just an artifact of self-reports; it can also be seen by external observers. In light of these findings, I turned to the next question: Which individuals are more likely to experience growth in the wake of parental and grandparental life transitions?

WHAT FACTORS MAY ENABLE THE EXPERIENCE
OF GROWTH AMONG PARENTS?

- "I discovered that I have strengths and characteristics I didn't know about before, such as patience, an extraordinary ability to educate and set limits, and a capacity to cope with the different situations the children confront me with."—Mother of 4-year-old twins, a boy and a girl

Perceived Stress and Cognitive Appraisals

One of the basic premises of growth theories is that some degree of stress is required to initiate and maintain growth, whether or not the individual is fully aware of the stress. However, few of the studies of growth on the part of parents have directly considered the issue of stress.

Certain special circumstances of childbirth have been shown to elicit stress. For example, parenthood resulting from fertility treatments is considered stressful, and people suffering from infertility often report distress (e.g., Chen, Chang, Tsai, & Juang, 2004). Likewise, giving birth to a premature baby is recognized to be stressful (e.g., Goldberg & DeVitto, 2002). When a baby is born prematurely, before the parents are psychologically ready for parenthood, they may experience not only disappointment that their expectations for a normal delivery and healthy infant were not fulfilled but also the additional emotional burden of anxiety over the infant's survival, health, and development (Pederson, Bento, Chance, Evans, & Fox, 1987). This is exacerbated by the realization that they cannot care for their own baby, particularly if the infant is removed to special facilities, in which case the parents may be forced to come to terms with a hospital stay of unknown length and the possibility of life-threatening complications or compromised development (DeMier, Hynan, Harris, & Manniello, 1996).

Most relevant to the present discussion, individuals in these stressful circumstances often report greater growth than those in more normal situations. Mothers of preterm twins reported greater growth than mothers of either full-term twins or singletons 1 year after giving birth (Taubman – Ben-Ari, Findler, & Kuint, 2010), and first-time parents of preemies reported greater growth than parents of full-term babies, both at 1 month (Spielman & Taubman – Ben-Ari, 2009) and 2 years (Taubman – Ben-Ari & Spielman, 2012) after delivery. Similarly, first-time parents who underwent fertility treatments reported greater growth 6 to 12 months after the birth than those who had conceived spontaneously (Bar-Shua, 2011). Thus, in all of these studies, the group likely to have experienced higher levels of stress also reported greater growth. This suggests that stressful circumstances make it possible to perceive childbirth as a crisis, with its inherent potential for stress-related growth.

Two of the studies also examined the relationship between stress and growth directly, revealing a more complex picture. In one (Taubman – Ben-Ari & Spielman, 2012), first-time fathers and mothers of pre- or full-term babies were asked to report on their parental stress 2 years after the birth. A significant positive association was found between growth and certain dimensions of parental stress among mothers, although not among fathers. In the other study (Bar-Shua, 2011), first-time parents were examined 6 to 12 months after delivery, with those who had undergone fertility treatments compared with those who had conceived spontaneously. Whereas women's level of parental stress was not significantly associated with their reported growth, the higher their spouse's level of stress, the greater their own perceived growth. In addition, the greater parental stress the man reported, the higher his experienced growth. Higher parental stress reported by the woman was related to lower perceived growth among the men in the spontaneous conception group, but to higher levels of experienced growth among the men in the fertility treatments group. Although these findings are not entirely consistent, they indicate that a parent's growth may be related not only to his or her own stress level but also to that experienced by the spouse and may be exacerbated by objective circumstances as well. This suggests that an important issue for understanding of growth is the way a situation is appraised by the individual.

Cognitive appraisal is the process by which a person decides whether a particular event or experience is relevant to his or her well-being, and if so, how. *Primary appraisal* concerns whether something has occurred that may affect the individual's social image or self-esteem. This includes *threat appraisal*—the belief that a transaction with the environment may endanger the person's well-being—and *challenge appraisal*, where there is a possibility for mastery or benefit. *Secondary appraisal* relates to perception of coping options and evaluation of the personal resources available for contending with the situation. In effect, this is an appraisal of self-efficacy (Folkman & Lazarus, 1985).

A series of studies indicates the importance of cognitive appraisal to the growth of new mothers. One study found that appraising motherhood as a challenge was associated with more reported personal growth during pregnancy among expectant first-time mothers. Furthermore, although growth 2 months after delivery was related most strongly to the general level of growth during pregnancy, appraisal of motherhood as a challenge during pregnancy was the only factor measured before the birth that was significantly associated with growth after delivery (Taubman – Ben-Ari, Ben Shlomo, Sivan, & Dolizki, 2009).

The importance of cognitive appraisal was confirmed in another study of first-time mothers conducted 3 to 24 months after birth, which showed that lower appraised threat was related to higher perceived growth, especially for those who reported more social support (Taubman – Ben-Ari, Ben Shlomo, & Findler, in press). Thus, it appears that cognitive appraisals of motherhood begin to play a role during pregnancy and are able to predict growth not only during that period but also following the birth of the child. The studies indicate that growth is enhanced by perceiving the situation as more of a challenge and less of a threat, especially when these appraisals are backed up by support from significant others. Nevertheless, perceived stress and the evaluation of the situation as a threat or a challenge do not explain fully why some people grow more than others in the wake of parenthood. Certain background variables and internal resources are also important.

Sociodemographic Variables and Internal Resources

The few studies that have examined both mothers and fathers have consistently found that mothers report greater growth than fathers. This was found both among first-time parents of full- and pre-term children about 1 month of age (Spielman & Taubman – Ben-Ari, 2009) and 2 years of age (Taubman – Ben-Ari & Spielman, 2012) and in parents of infants ages 6 to 12 months, regardless of conceiving either spontaneously or following fertility treatments (Bar-Shua, 2011). In the last of these studies, mothers scored higher than fathers not only on the total growth measure but also on each of three areas of growth (change in self-perception, change in perceived relations with others, and change in life philosophy). These results are in line with the majority of studies of gender differences in growth following adverse events, indicating that women reported higher levels of benefit (e.g., Park, Cohen, & Murch, 1996; Tedeschi & Calhoun, 1996). One explanation for the perception of more growth among women is their ability to embrace and admit their feelings more than men do, allowing women to recognize positive changes when they occur (McMillen & Fisher, 1998).

The transition to parenthood inevitably has a stronger impact on mothers than fathers, including the physiological changes of pregnancy, birth, and (in many cases) nursing, and often the need to give up some independence and a former way of life (Nicolson, 1999). These larger life changes may be associated with a more powerful sense of personal growth. Other sociodemographic variables have yielded less conclusive results. Some studies have found age to be an important variable for mothers, with younger mothers reporting greater growth (Sawyer & Ayers, 2009; Taubman – Ben-Ari et al., 2010; in press). If younger mothers are less mature and self-confident than older mothers, the transition to motherhood may initiate a self-learning process that reveals personal strengths. Other studies suggest that less education among women (Taubman – Ben-Ari et al., 2010) and lower economic status among men, especially those using fertility treatments (Bar-Shua, 2011), may be associated with growth following childbirth.

Psychological variables are also relevant to growth. Numerous studies of well-being, adaptation to demanding circumstances, and mental health have shown that certain personality traits, or ego resources, enable positive responses to stress. Among new mothers, one of those variables is self-esteem (Rosenberg, 1979), which is positively associated with psychological adjustment, including the view that motherhood is not threatening to one's health (Terry, McHugh, & Noller, 1991). A study of first-time parents questioned about a month after their child's birth found that self-esteem was associated with greater reported growth among mothers but not among fathers (Spielman & Taubman – Ben-Ari, 2009). However, a study examining expectant mothers found that although self-esteem was related to women's mental health, it was not associated with perceived growth (Taubman – Ben-Ari et al., 2009).

Other studies have revealed that among first-time mothers who had given birth 3 to 24 months earlier, self-esteem was related to reported meaning in life but not to growth (Taubman – Ben-Ari et al., in press). In another study (Taubman – Ben-Ari & Spielman, 2012), although self-esteem was not associated with growth among first-time mothers of 2-year-old children, it was inversely related to personal growth among fathers who perceived their child to have an easy temperament. These results follow studies that have also found no systematic associations of growth with self-esteem and other characteristics of mental health (Zoellner & Maercker, 2006).

Another internal resource used to manage stressful situations is attachment orientation, consisting of two dimensions: avoidance and anxiety (Brennan, Clark, & Shaver, 1998; see also Chapter 16, this volume). Those high on avoidance are characterized by a distrust of others' goodwill and a preference for emotional distance, relying mostly on themselves and failing to rely on others to relieve distress. Those scoring high on attachment anxiety have a strong need for closeness combined with an overwhelming fear of rejection and tend to dwell on their emotional state and rely on emotion-focused coping strategies.

Although some studies have found no association between attachment orientations and growth among mothers up to 1 year after giving birth (Taubman – Ben-Ari et al., 2009, 2010), others have found attachment anxiety to be related to growth among first-time mothers and fathers 6 to 12 months (Bar-Shua, 2011) and 2 years (Taubman – Ben-Ari & Spielman, 2012) after the birth. In another study, this association was found only among first-time fathers about a month after their child's birth (Spielman & Taubman – Ben-Ari, 2009). Avoidant attachment was associated with greater growth only among fathers of 2-year-olds (Taubman – Ben-Ari & Spielman, 2012).

The suggestion that attachment anxiety may be a factor in parents' growth is in line with research showing that in times of turmoil, attachment-anxious individuals feel more threatened and consequently make strong efforts to obtain comfort and support from their attachment figures (see Chapter 16, this volume). During the stressful transition to parenthood, these tendencies, along with the presence of a baby who is totally dependent on them, may cause such people to feel overwhelmed. Their ability to "survive" the experience may result in enhanced self-confidence, a heightened sense of trust, and a fuller understanding of the meaning of life and the value of a family (Cadell, Regehr, & Hemsworth, 2003), which may be interpreted as growth.

External Resources

Besides internal resources, there are also important resources in the external environment (e.g., Calhoun & Tedeschi, 2006; Park et al., 1996; Prati & Pietrantoni, 2009). One of these is social support, which may include love, caring, solidarity, and the satisfaction of personal needs, including material or instrumental needs (Wandersman, Wandersman, & Kahn, 1980). Regarding new parents, a prospective study found that marital relationship quality during a first pregnancy was associated with women's reports of growth during that period, and greater support from their mothers was associated with greater self-reported growth a few months after the birth (Taubman – Ben-Ari et al., 2009). Another study, which compared mothers of preterm twins, full-term twins, and full-term singletons a year after the birth, revealed a connection between support from the maternal grandmother and a mother's reported growth, especially among mothers of full-term twins. In addition, more contact between mothers and grandmothers was associated with reports of greater growth (Taubman – Ben-Ari et al., in press). Associations have also been found between women's perceived marital quality and growth, mainly among mothers with less education and those who harbor negative feelings toward their children (Taubman – Ben-Ari et al., 2010), and between men's marital satisfaction and their growth following childbirth (Bar-Shua, 2011). It seems that a supportive mother or spouse can facilitate growth by creating a positive atmosphere for coping with stresses, by lessening the mother's practical and mental burdens, and by allowing her to share her difficulties with significant others.

WHAT FACTORS MAY ENABLE THE EXPERIENCE OF GROWTH AMONG GRANDPARENTS?

- "A new layer has been added to my life. I have something else in common with some of my friends, and I have another person to care for and think about. I feel a new unconditional love for my granddaughter."—First-time grandfather of a 6-month-old girl

Recent increases in the life span of people in developed countries mean more years of shared life between generations and more grandparents living to see their grandchildren grow up (Silverstein & Long, 1998). The few studies of personal growth among grandparents have yielded interesting insights regarding factors relevant to such growth.

Perceived Stress and Cognitive Appraisals

One study of grandfathers focused on stresses that might be evoked by the grandparent–grandchild relationship and its connection to the five growth dimensions. It included three stress factors: grandfather's distress, dysfunctional grandfather–grandchild relations, and perception of the grandchild as difficult (based on Abidin's, 1990, research on parental stress). The study indicated that lower grandfather–grandchild relationship dysfunction was associated with two areas of growth: relating to others and appreciation of life. Perceiving the grandchild as difficult, especially among older grandfathers, was related to self-reported personal growth, supporting the theoretical notion that coping with stress is associated with perceiving oneself as strong (Taubman – Ben-Ari, Findler, & Ben Shlomo, in press a).

As with parents, cognitive appraisals are also important in affecting the experience of growth among grandparents. Challenge appraisals are associated with greater self-reported growth among both grandmothers (Taubman – Ben-Ari et al., in press) and grandfathers (Taubman – Ben-Ari et al., in press a), suggesting that when an event is perceived positively, despite the difficulties involved, it is more likely to generate a sense of growth. However, threat appraisals were also associated with greater growth among grandmothers (Taubman – Ben-Ari et al., in press), leaving us, so far, with a complex, unclear picture.

Sociodemographic Variables and Internal Resources

Gender differences were investigated in one study of grandparents' personal growth, revealing that grandmothers reported more growth than grandfathers (Taubman – Ben-Ari et al., in press b). Age was positively associated with growth among grandmothers (Taubman – Ben-Ari et al., in press, in press b) but not grandfathers (Taubman – Ben-Ari et al., in press a; Taubman – Ben-Ari, Findler, & Ben Shlomo, 2011). Results regarding education indicate that it was inversely related to growth among new grandmothers and grandfathers (Taubman – Ben-Ari et al., in press b) and to four of the five growth dimensions (the exception being spiritual change) among grandfathers in another sample (Taubman – Ben-Ari et al., in press a).

In regard to internal resources, lower self-esteem has been found to be associated with higher growth among first-time grandmothers (Taubman –

Ben-Ari et al., in press) and with higher spiritual change among first-time grandfathers (Taubman – Ben-Ari et al., in press a). In line with the same reasoning, higher attachment anxiety was associated with greater growth among expectant maternal grandmothers (Ben Shlomo, Taubman – Ben-Ari, Findler, Sivan, & Dolizki, 2010).

Being older, less educated, and having lower self-esteem or higher attachment anxiety are all expressions of lower personal resources, which may point to the fact that when people with fewer personal resources encounter situations in which they do not necessarily anticipate effective coping and good adjustment, they have a greater chance of discovering new aspects of their abilities and strengths.

External Resources

External resources also appear to play a part in grandparents' growth. More meetings between first-time maternal grandmothers and their daughters are associated with greater reported growth among them (Taubman – Ben-Ari et al., in press). In addition, on the basis of independent reports of both partners, spouses' growth was found to contribute to the explained variance in growth among both grandmothers and grandfathers, beyond the contribution of background variables and internal resources (Taubman – Ben-Ari et al., in press b). Thus, spouses' growth might represent an opportunity to share the experience of grandparenthood with a significant other, which is in line with a series of findings indicating that sharing life events with other people is associated with positive adaptation and growth (e.g., Tedeschi & Calhoun, 1996).

FURTHER INSIGHTS ABOUT GROWTH AND THOUGHTS FOR THE FUTURE

- "I've learned that my physical abilities are much greater than I thought; that I can handle work and family. I have more patience for other people. Everything is measured by different standards. I am less easily upset by the stresses of work and daily life. Everything seems less significant. The family and the children are more important than anything else."—Mother of 4-year-old twins, a boy and a girl

To sum up, fewer personal resources, appraising parenthood or grandparenthood as a challenge rather than a threat, and having a more supportive environment all appear to encourage growth in new parents and grandparents, though parents do seem to report higher growth than grandparents. It goes without saying that the transition to parenthood is a decisive turning point in a person's life. Such a major change is likely to involve a reevaluation of priorities and reexamination of core beliefs and life philosophy. Although the transition to grandparenthood is also a special event in an individual's life, which may also instigate a rethinking of priorities, new insights about self and others, and a reexamination of beliefs, it is not as dramatic as the transition to parenthood. Whereas recent studies substantially expand our knowledge regarding the growth of parents and grandparents, many questions remain unanswered.

Is Growth Solely a Subjective, Individualistic Experience, or Can It Be Shared?

The available evidence indicates that one person's growth can be observed by significant others (Taubman – Ben-Ari, Findler, & Ben Shlomo, 2011; Taubman – Ben-Ari et al., in press a) and is enhanced by being experienced together with someone else. A spouse's growth is positively associated with one's own personal growth among grandparents (Taubman – Ben-Ari et al., in press b), and a similar association was found in mother–daughter pairs (Taubman – Ben-Ari et al., in press). However, we still know little about the conditions that promote or interfere with shared personal growth.

Is There a Developmental Pattern in Personal Growth?

When can personal growth be detected for the first time? Does it change with time or does it develop? Taubman – Ben-Ari et al.'s (2009) prospective study of mothers' personal growth during the third trimester of pregnancy and shortly after delivery and Ben Shlomo et al.'s (2010) related study of maternal grandmothers revealed that patterns established during pregnancy tend to foreshadow later stages of motherhood and grandmotherhood. Moreover, growth measured during pregnancy was a better predictor of growth after the birth than any of the other personal or environmental resources measured following delivery. This suggests that the critical period for personal growth and its continuation is pregnancy. Moreover, mothers, although not grandmothers, reported more growth after the birth of the child than during pregnancy. Similarly, Taubman – Ben-Ari and Spielman's (2012) longitudinal study revealed correlations between the levels of growth at the three waves of data collection, with greater growth 2 years after the birth of a first child than 1 month after the child's delivery. These findings suggest that, as observed in other contexts and with other kinds of samples (e.g., Anderson & Lopez-Baez, 2008), the first signs of growth among parents and grandparents occur early in the process of a life transition. Moreover, once initiated, growth seems to increase with time.

How Is Growth Related to Other Positive Outcomes?

Is growth distinct from well-being, meaning in life, positive perceptions of parenthood, and so on? Are the trajectories of growth similar to those for other positive or adaptive outcomes? Results so far suggest that growth is a distinct construct (Ben Shlomo et al., 2010; Taubman – Ben-Ari et al., 2009). For example, during pregnancy and shortly after the birth of a first child, internal resources were associated with mental health and the perceived costs of becoming a mother, whereas cognitive appraisal of challenge and support systems were associated with a mother's personal growth (Taubman – Ben-Ari et al., 2009). These results also indicate that distress in the form of perceived costs (and perhaps other negative consequences as well) can coexist with growth as separate outcomes of the same event.

Similarly, among first-time mothers and fathers, growth and parental self-efficacy were associated with different variables (Spielman & Taubman – Ben-Ari, 2009), as were growth and meaning in life among both first-time mothers and grandmothers (Ben Shlomo, & Findler, 2011; Taubman – Ben-Ari et al., 2009). Stable variables (self-esteem, social support) were found to be related mainly to meaning, whereas more event-specific variables (e.g., the perception of motherhood or grandmotherhood as a challenge or threat) were related to growth. Hence, although meaning is often thought to be part of growth, the findings suggest that growth is generated by change and is sensitive to circumstances, whereas meaning is more stable and may be experienced continuously throughout life.

The finding that growth in the transitions to parenthood and grandparenthood is not identical to other concepts such as well-being, mental health, meaning in life, and positive emotions is consistent with results from studies of traumatic events (Zoellner & Maercker, 2006). Although people who undergo a life crisis may suffer a reduction in well-being as a result, they can nevertheless grow from the experience (Taubman – Ben-Ari et al., 2010).

CONCLUDING REMARKS

Our understanding of self-perceptions of personal growth is still limited. Some of the research findings are counterintuitive, such as the fact that individuals who seem to have fewer internal resources feel they have grown the most following a stressful life event. This contrasts with what is usually found in studies of other positive outcomes, wherein individuals characterized by more resources tend to react more adaptively. Until research provides further insight, the interpretation of such findings must remain speculative.

Should growth during positive life transitions be encouraged? Interventions have traditionally been aimed at preventing negative emotional reactions, distress, and psychopathology. Should growth become an additional target for practitioners? Bearing in mind that not everyone needs to grow from a stress-related experience, it would seem that facilitating the personal growth of new parents and grandparents may be beneficial not only for them but also for the next generation whose care they are undertaking.

REFERENCES

Abidin, R.R. (1990). *The Parenting Stress Index short form*. Charlottesville, VA: Pediatric Psychology Press.

Affleck, G., Tennen, H., Allen, D.A., & Gershman, K. (1986). Perceived social support and maternal adaptation during the transition from hospital to home care of high-risk infants. *Infant Mental Health Journal, 7*, 6–18. doi:10.1002/1097-0355(198621)7:1<6::AID-IMHJ2280070103>3.0.CO;2-V

Anderson, W.P., Jr., & Lopez-Baez, S.I. (2008). Measuring growth with the posttraumatic growth inventory. *Measurement and Evaluation in Counseling & Development, 40*, 215–227.

Bar-Shua, E. (2011). *Personal growth in the transition to parenthood following fertility treatments*. Unpublished manuscript.

Ben Shlomo, S., Taubman – Ben-Ari, O., Findler, L., Sivan, E., & Dolizki, M. (2010). Becoming a grandmother: Maternal grandmothers' mental health, loss, and growth. *Social Work Research, 34*, 45–57.

Brennan, K.A., Clark, C.L., & Shaver, P.R. (1998). Self-report measurement of adult attachment: An integrative overview. In J.A. Simpson & W.S. Rholes (Eds.), *Attachment theory and close relationships* (pp. 46–76). New York, NY: Guilford Press.

Cadell, S., Regehr, C., & Hemsworth, D. (2003). Factors contributing to posttraumatic growth: A proposed structural equation model. *American Journal of Orthopsychiatry, 73*, 279–287. doi:10.1037/0002-9432.73.3.279

Calhoun, L.G., & Tedeschi, R.G. (2006). The foundations of posttraumatic growth: An expanded framework. In L.G. Calhoun & R.G. Tedeschi (Eds.), *Handbook of posttraumatic growth: Research and practice* (pp. 3–23). Mahwah, NJ: Erlbaum.

Chen, T.H., Chang, S.P., Tsai, C.F., & Juang, K.D. (2004). Prevalence of depressive and anxiety disorders in assisted reproductive technique clinic. *Human Reproduction, 19*, 2313–2318. doi:10.1093/humrep/deh414

Cordova, M.J., Cunningham, L.L.C., Carlson, C.R., & Andrykowski, M.A. (2001). Posttraumatic growth following breast cancer: A controlled comparison study. *Health Psychology, 20*, 176–185. doi:10.1037/0278-6133.20.3.176

Cowan, C.P., & Cowan, P.A. (1999). *When partners become parents: The big life change for couples*. Hillsdale, NJ: Erlbaum.

DeMier, R.L., Hynan, M.T., Harris, H.B., & Manniello, R.L. (1996). Perinatal stressors as predictors of symptoms of posttraumatic stress in mothers of infants at high risk. *Journal of Perinatology, 16,* 276–280.

Feeney, J.A., Hohaus, L., Noller, P., & Alexander, R.P. (2001). *Becoming parents: Exploring the bonds between mothers, fathers, and their infants.* New York, NY: Cambridge University Press.

Findler, L. (2009). *The experience of grandparenthood among grandparents of children with/without an intellectual disability.* Manuscript submitted for publication.

Folkman, S., & Lazarus, R. (1985). If it changes it must be a process: Study of emotion and coping during three stages of a college examination. *Journal of Personality and Social Psychology, 48,* 150–170. doi:10.1037/0022-3514.48.1.150

Goldberg, S., & DeVitto, B. (2002). Parenting children born preterm. In M. E. Bornstein (Ed.), *Handbook of parenting* (Vol. 1, pp. 329–354). Mahwah, NJ: Erlbaum.

Joseph, S., & Linley, P.A. (2008). Positive psychological perspective on posttraumatic stress: An integrative psychosocial framework. In S. Joseph & P. A. Linley (Eds.), *Trauma, recovery, and growth: Positive psychological perspective on posttraumatic stress* (pp. 3–20). Hoboken, NJ: Wiley.

Mann, R., & Leeson, G. (2010). Grandfathers in contemporary families in Britain: Evidence from qualitative research. *Journal of Intergenerational Relationships, 8,* 234–248. doi:10.1080/15350770.2010.498774

McMillen, J.C., & Fisher, R.H. (1998). The perceived benefit scales: Measuring perceived positive life changes after negative events. *Social Work Research, 22,* 173–187.

Nicolson, P. (1999). Loss happiness and postpartum depression: The ultimate paradox. *Canadian Psychology/Psychologie canadienne, 40,* 162–178. doi:10.1037/h0086834

Park, C.L., Cohen, L.H., & Murch, R.L. (1996). Assessment and prediction of stress related growth. *Journal of Personality, 64,* 71–105. doi:10.1111/j.1467-6494.1996.tb00815.x

Pederson, D.R., Bento, S., Chance, G.W., Evans, B., & Fox, A.M. (1987). Maternal emotional responses to preterm birth. *American Journal of Orthopsychiatry, 57,* 15–21. doi:10.1111/j.1939-0025.1987.tb03504.x

Polatinsky, S., & Esprey, Y. (2000). An assessment of gender differences in the perception of benefit resulting from the loss of a child. *Journal of Traumatic Stress, 13,* 709–718. doi:10.1023/A:1007870419116

Prati, G., & Pietrantoni, L. (2009). Optimism, social support, and coping strategies as factors contributing to posttraumatic growth: A meta-analysis. *Journal of Loss and Trauma, 14,* 364–388. doi:10.1080/15325020902724271

Rosenberg, M. (1979). *Conceiving the self.* New York, NY: Basic Books.

Rowe, J.W., & Kahn, R.L. (1998). *Successful aging.* New York, NY: Pantheon Books.

Sawyer, A., & Ayers, S. (2009). Post-traumatic growth in women after childbirth. *Psychology & Health, 24,* 457–471. doi:10.1080/08870440701864520

Silverstein, M., & Long, J. D. (1998). Trajectories of grandparents' perceived solidarity with adult grandchildren: A growth curve analysis over 23 years. *Journal of Marriage and the Family, 60*, 912–923. doi:10.2307/353634

Snape, M. C. (1997). Reactions to a traumatic event: The good, the bad and the ugly? *Psychology Health & Medicine, 2*, 237–242. doi:10.1080/13548509708400581

Spielman, V., & Taubman – Ben-Ari, O. (2009). Parental self-efficacy and personal growth in the transition to parenthood: A comparison between parents of premature and of full-term babies. *Health & Social Work, 34*, 201–212.

Taubman – Ben-Ari, O., Ben Shlomo, S., & Findler, L. (in press). Personal growth and meaning in life among first-time mothers and grandmothers. *Journal of Happiness Studies.*

Taubman – Ben-Ari, O., Ben Shlomo, S., Sivan, E., & Dolizki, M. (2009). The transition to motherhood: A time for growth. *Journal of Social and Clinical Psychology, 28*, 943–970. doi:10.1521/jscp.2009.28.8.943

Taubman – Ben-Ari. O., Findler, L., & Ben Shlomo, S. (2011). *Personal growth in grandparents—An examination of scales.* Unpublished manuscript.

Taubman – Ben-Ari, O., Findler, L., & Ben Shlomo, S. (in press a). Growth and the transition to grandfatherhood. *The International Journal of Aging and Human Development.*

Taubman – Ben-Ari, O., Findler, L., & Ben Shlomo, S. (in press b). When couples become grandparents: Factors influencing the growth of each spouse. *Social Work Research.*

Taubman – Ben-Ari, O., Findler, L., & Kuint, J. (2010). Personal growth in the wake of stress: The case of mothers of pre-term twins. *The Journal of Psychology: Interdisciplinary and Applied, 144*, 185–204. doi:10.1080/00223980903472268

Taubman – Ben-Ari, O., Findler, L., & Sharon, N. (2011). Personal growth in mothers: Examination of the suitability of the Posttraumatic Growth Inventory as a measurement tool. *Women and Health, 51*, 604–622.

Taubman – Ben-Ari, O., & Spielman, V. (2012). *Personal growth of parents two years after the birth of their first child: A comparison of parents of pre- and full-term babies.* Manuscript submitted for publication.

Tedeschi, R. G., & Calhoun, L. G. (1996). The posttraumatic growth inventory: Measuring the positive legacy of trauma. *Journal of Traumatic Stress, 9*, 455–471. doi:10.1002/jts.2490090305

Tedeschi, R. G., Calhoun, L. G., & Cann, A. (2007). Evaluating resource gain: Understanding and misunderstanding posttraumatic growth. *Applied Psychology, 56*, 396–406. doi:10.1111/j.1464-0597.2007.00299.x

Terry, D. J., McHugh, T. A., & Noller, P. (1991). Role dissatisfaction and the decline in marital quality across the transition to parenthood. *Australian Journal of Psychology, 43*, 129–132. doi:10.1080/00049539108260136

Wandersman, L. P., Wandersman, A., & Kahn, S. (1980). Social support in the transition to parenthood. *Journal of Community Psychology, 8*, 332–342. doi:10.1002/1520-6629(198010)8:4<332::AID-JCOP2290080407>3.0.CO;2-H

Wells, D. J., Hobfoll, E. S., & Lavin, J. (1999). When it rains, it pours: The greater impact of resource loss compared to gain on psychological distress. *Personality and Social Psychology Bulletin, 25*, 1172–1182. doi:10.1177/01461672992512010

Wild, N. D., & Paivio, S. C. (2004). Psychological adjustment, coping, and emotion regulation as predictors of posttraumatic growth. *Journal of Aggression, Maltreatment & Trauma, 8*, 97–122. doi:10.1300/J146v08n04_05

Zoellner, T., & Maercker, A. (2006). Posttraumatic growth in clinical psychology— A critical review and introduction of two component model. *Clinical Psychology Review, 26*, 626–653. doi:10.1016/j.cpr.2006.01.008

10

DERIVING SOLACE FROM A NEMESIS: HAVING SCAPEGOATS AND ENEMIES BUFFERS THE THREAT OF MEANINGLESSNESS

MARK J. LANDAU, DANIEL SULLIVAN, ZACHARY K. ROTHSCHILD, AND LUCAS A. KEEFER

People often believe that individuals and groups are systematically plotting their downfall, and furthermore, they tend to perceive these enemy figures as exceptionally intelligent, powerful, and resourceful. For example, although most Americans believe that the failed Times Square bomb attempt in 2010 was planned by Faisal Shahzad, many Pakistanis believe that the culprit was a secret American "think tank" that controls virtually every aspect of the American government and is responsible for pretty much everything that goes wrong in Pakistan (Tavernise, 2010). Similarly, millions of Americans tune in to watch television personalities such as Glenn Beck "connect the dots" in an attempt to expose President Barack Obama as an evil mastermind orchestrating a diabolical plot against the American way of life. At a more personal level, 70% of Americans report having had, at some point in their lives, a powerful enemy who sought to sabotage their goals and inflict harm (Holt, 1989). Although enemies can certainly exist and pose a legitimate threat to one's well-being, people nevertheless seem almost irrationally motivated to single out powerful enemies in their environment.

On the surface this tendency is puzzling. Why would people want to believe that powerful others aim to cause them harm? In this chapter, we propose that having enemies, although superficially undesirable, fulfills a protective function for the individual by providing a buffer against the threat of meaninglessness. Briefly, our analysis states that people are always potentially aware that they live in a meaningless world, one in which they can be negatively affected by myriad hazards stemming from impersonal forces beyond their capacity to understand or control. To keep this threatening awareness at bay, people "narrow down" the multifarious sources of potential misfortune to a focal individual or group that can be understood and perhaps controlled.

In this chapter, we present this analysis in more detail and show how it has been empirically supported. Specifically, we summarize research showing that experimentally increasing the salience of uncontrollable hazards leads people to attribute exaggerated influence to their enemies and that exposure to powerful scapegoats and enemies has the somewhat counterintuitive effect of decreasing perceptions of risk in one's environment and bolstering feelings of personal control. We conclude by discussing future research directions and practical implications.

MEANING, MEANINGLESSNESS, AND FETISHISM

Our analysis of enemy perceptions is based on Ernest Becker's (1969) broad theoretical account of the motivations behind *fetishism*, a construct that appears in the psychoanalytic literature (e.g., Freud, 1927/1963) and can be linked to a host of so-called perverse behaviors, including sadomasochism, obsessive–compulsive tendencies, and paranoia. Becker reformulated traditional psychoanalytic explanations of fetishism using insights from existential psychiatry into people's experience of meaning and meaninglessness. He began with the notion that people are fundamentally motivated to view themselves and their actions as valuable. People maintain subjective certainty of their personal value by perceiving themselves as capable of effectively negotiating their environment. *Meaning* is the perception that one's environment affords clearly defined and reliable standards for such effective action (see also Chapter 7, this volume). That is, the individual sees meaning in the world to the extent that he or she can decipher dependable "rules" or contingencies that can be followed to establish a sense of personal efficacy and, thus, confidently held feelings of personal value. As Becker (1969) put it, "To negotiate dependable action is to imbibe in meaning; to build up a world of known and expected consequences is to create meaning" (p. 8).

Driven by the psychological imperative to attain personal value, people create and adhere to systems of meaning that afford reliable routes to valued action (Park & Edmonson, Chapter 8, this volume). For example, they subscribe to a cultural worldview, which is a set of socially constructed beliefs that provides an account of the nature of reality, principles to live by, and prescriptions for sanctioned conduct (see Chapter 4, this volume). The individual internalizes the worldview through an immersive socialization process that reinforces prevailing norms, values, and ideals through life-long participation in collective ceremonies, rituals, and rites of passage and through constant engagement with cultural products that embody those ideologies. In this way, the worldview provides the individual with the broad outlines of what it means to live a valuable life (see Chapter 8, this volume, for similar ideas on the function of religion).

In addition to the cultural worldview, people derive meaning from well-structured (i.e., clearly defined, consistent, stable) conceptions of the people, objects, and events that they encounter in their environment. Although these conceptions refer to relatively mundane aspects of one's environment and experience, they are the foundation that allows people to maintain adequate faith in the validity of their worldview and to live up to the worldview's standards of value. For example, as Goffman (1959) articulated so well, to dependably negotiate social interactions and influence how the self is viewed by others, a person has to perceive other people's characteristics and behaviors as fairly consistent from one moment to the next. Similarly, to anticipate the consequences of one's actions and feel secure that long-term projects will unfold reliably over time, the person must believe that favorable and unfavorable outcomes have clear causes and do not occur on an arbitrary and random basis. Conversely, if people lacked these structured conceptions—if, for example, other people's behavior seemed contradictory or arbitrary, if the flow of time appeared disordered, or if events were experienced as haphazard—they would perceive their environment as meaningless and consequently have difficulty establishing and maintaining a confident sense of personal value.

The more people can feel confident that their cultural worldview prescribes legitimate routes to attain value and that their environment has a predictable structure, the more they can view their life as meaningful. Of course, the sense that life is meaningful need not be a radical epiphany. Most of the time, people take their cultural worldview and structured social conceptions for granted—they accept the identities, long-term projects, and routines that are offered to them by virtue of their membership in certain social groups, and in this way, they maintain a secure sense that they are doing something significant.

However, because these systems of meaning are essentially symbolic constructs that resist conclusive verification, they can be threatened by social experiences and environmental conditions (see Chapter 4, this volume). Such threats put people at risk for feelings of meaninglessness or the sense that one lacks the infrastructure necessary for effective action and the attainment of lasting personal value. For example, when people encounter someone who subscribes to an alternative worldview, they may question the validity of their own worldview ("If they have it right, what happens to me?"). People might also witness other people meet with favorable and unfavorable outcomes regardless of their adherence to the worldview's prescriptions for valued action, and this can undermine their confidence that by following those prescriptions, they will be rewarded with lasting value. A similar threat to meaning may occur when people witness or fall victim to randomly occurring catastrophes, accidents, and chance occurrences that undermine the stable order on which all long-term strivings for value are predicated.

To minimize the threat of meaninglessness, Becker (1969) claimed, people often rely on fetishism, a broad psychological strategy that involves reducing one's conception of the world and oneself to exceedingly narrow dimensions that afford well-defined, concrete opportunities to effectively act in a valued manner. Because people view their fetishes as affording a stable basis for establishing their personal value, they invest them with undue psychological importance and rely on them to understand and relate to the world. Becker illustrated the process of fetishism in his account of people's occasional desire for fetishes in the sexual realm. On this account, if, say, a man feels insecure in his ability to relate to his sexual partner's ambiguous emotions or spontaneous displays of intimacy, he may compensate by "boiling down" the sexual encounter to a narrow dimension, such as an isolated aspect of his partner (e.g., a high-heeled shoe) that affords clearly defined (albeit limited) routes to effectively act in a valued manner.

SCAPEGOATING AND ENEMYSHIP AS BUFFERS AGAINST THE THREAT OF MEANINGLESSNESS

Becker (1969) extended his analysis of fetishism beyond the sexual realm to explain the motivations that shape people's perceptions of enemies, both real and imagined. He argued that people may feel threatened by the limits to their ability to anticipate and control the hazards lurking in their environment, because this implies that their well-being (and their being at all) is subject to the influence of impersonal and indeterminate forces beyond their control. To avoid being overwhelmed by feelings of meaninglessness in the face of uncontrollable hazards, people may view negative outcomes as stemming from the intentional actions of a focal individual or group that can be effectively controlled, managed, or (at minimum) understood. Becker summarized the process thus:

> The paranoid fantasy builds on one's insecure power base, his helplessness in the world, his inability to take command of his experience, to get on top of the evil in the world. . . . One feels overwhelmed and has to make sense out of his precarious position. And the way to do this is to attribute

definite motives to *definite* people. This seems to straighten the situation out, to put one back into things. There is now a focus, a center, with lines running from others to oneself and to one's objects and loved ones. There is something one can *do* from his position of utter helplessness . . . and even if he can't do anything, or especially if he can't do anything, at least he can order the world in his thought, see and make connections between things that are so unconnected. . . . Above all, he masks his feelings of impotence in the face of events; his helplessness is now no longer his own tragic shortcoming, but a realistic reaction to the real actions of others. (p. 126; emphasis in original)

To put the matter more plainly, we need fetishized, human sources of evil and misfortune because they help avert the more profoundly distressing realization that we are incapable of controlling the myriad chaotic forces in the natural and social world that threaten to block our goals, harm us, or annihilate us altogether.

This analysis helps to explain *scapegoating*, or the tendency to attribute blame to a person or group for a particular negative outcome that is due, at least in part, to other causes (T. Douglas, 1995). If people are confronted with a hazardous event or circumstance that lacks an easily comprehensible and controllable cause, they may avoid the potential threat of meaninglessness by projecting responsibility for that negative outcome onto a focal individual or group that can be understood and controlled. That is, focusing attention on the scapegoat as the primary causal agent behind hazard or misfortune affords the reassuring (yet often erroneous) sense that negative outcomes do not "just happen"—rather, they are due to the actions or mere existence of an individual or group that can be pointed at, monitored, and even destroyed.

In addition to explaining the motivation behind scapegoating in response to a particular hazard, Becker's (1969) analysis suggests that people seek out powerful enemies to cope with the more general awareness that multiple sources of potential hazard are spread diffusely throughout their environment. To the extent that an enemy is perceived to be an influential source of misfortune, having an enemy allows people to avert the threat of meaninglessness by perceiving their environment as containing less randomly distributed risk. Hence, people may imbue real or imagined enemies with undue power as a way of transferring ambient danger onto a more concrete and comprehensible adversary. Becker's analysis thus explains enemyship in general as the attempt to maintain clear meaning in the world by fetishizing an isolated individual or group as the source of all hazard and misfortune (including those hazards with which the enemy cannot be logically connected).

This analysis yields additional insights into how people tend to perceive their scapegoats and enemies. In the case of scapegoats, the central issue is whether the scapegoat is *viable*, meaning whether the target person or group in question is perceived as sufficiently powerful and malevolent to perpetrate the threatening outcome that needs to be explained (Glick, 2005). Because scapegoats are relied on to explain how a particular threatening event (that either has occurred or is likely to occur) is traceable to a human source, those seeking to blame the scapegoat need to understand exactly how the scapegoat was capable of perpetrating that event. If a person or group appears patently incapable of having caused the event—for instance, if they appear too weak to have exerted the amount of influence necessary—then they are *nonviable* as a scapegoat and will not restore feelings of control and a sense of clear meaning in the face of the threatening event.

Moving beyond the case of using a scapegoat to defuse a single threatening occurrence, the fetishization of enemy figures as a response to myriad sources of chaotic hazard involves seeing the enemy not only as possessing power in an absolute sense but also as possessing a certain kind of power. According to M. Douglas (1966), people often see their enemies as having ambiguous natures and possessing ambiguous powers. By describing an enemy as *ambiguously* powerful, we imply the following: that the enemy's characteristics and actions do not lend themselves to clear interpretation but rather can be interpreted in a number of possible ways (e.g., the enemy may not be what he appears to be or the enemy may be driven by different possible motivations), that the full extent and variety of the enemy's powers are only poorly understood, and that the enemy seems to exist and operate outside of conventional patterns, meaning his character and actions are covert, atypical, and even potentially "magical." This is to be contrasted with those agents whom we imbue with *explicit* power, most typically ourselves, our heroes, and the government. Individuals and entities perceived to be explicitly powerful are seen as having a character and performing actions that are clearly interpretable, possessing capabilities that are well understood in respect to both their nature and their extent, and conforming to conventional categories and patterns for character and behavior (e.g., they operate within the bounds of physics as we understand them).

From our perspective, enemies are typically perceived as ambiguously (as opposed to explicitly) powerful for two reasons. First, because ambiguity is associated with the absence of clear meaning, people can rely on ambiguous enemies to help define the borders of their meaningful worldview. The ambiguous enemy represents the boundary line where that which is good and meaningful passes into that which is evil and meaningless. Thus, ambiguous enemies help define us and our sense of meaning by showing us what we are not. Second, the present perspective further suggests that people fetishize their enemies and imbue them with ambiguous power because this makes their enemies seem capable of perpetrating the widest possible range of misdeeds. Although superficially it may seem preferable to see one's enemy as having explicitly defined, well-understood powers, our analysis counterintuitively suggests that ambiguously powerful enemies serve as better fetish objects—and thus provide individuals more help in maintaining a sense of meaning in a chaotic world—because they can be seen as responsible for a wider possible array of seemingly random threats.

The notion that enemies are often construed as ambiguously powerful points to an important distinction between the closely related defensive processes of scapegoating and fetishistic enemyship. Scapegoating involves blaming a person or group for a particular threatening event. Accordingly, for a scapegoat to maintain meaning in the face of potential meaninglessness, the scapegoat must be perceived as capable of having perpetrated the event in question. This often involves imbuing the scapegoat with explicitly defined capabilities to demonstrate the scapegoat's responsibility for a specific outcome. By contrast, fetishistic enemyship involves using enemy figures (either persons or groups) to maintain a sense of meaning when one becomes aware that multiple diffuse and uncertain threats exist in one's environment. To serve this function, enemies are preferably seen as ambiguously powerful: They are capable of perpetrating a wide range of misdeeds. Of course, there have been some historical instances in which scapegoats have been blamed for a particular event and simultaneously imbued with ambiguous powers. The psychological processes of scapegoating and enemyship sometimes overlap. By and large, however, our analysis suggests that when people are confronted with a particular inexplicable threatening event, they will look for a viable scapegoat to blame, whereas when people are confronted with the reality that their environment is full of multifarious hazards, they will imbue focal enemies with ambiguous powers in an attempt to restore meaning.

RESEARCH FINDINGS

Summarizing our theoretical analysis, the threat of meaninglessness stems from the awareness that one's environment contains multiple, randomly occurring hazards that are difficult or impossible to fully understand, anticipate, and control. People can shield themselves from this threat by tracing the causes of hazards—both particular hazards and hazards in general—to the willful actions of a scapegoat or enemy. This analysis yields three testable hypotheses:

1. Framing a particular threatening event as caused by chaotic forces beyond one's control should prompt people to attribute greater responsibility for that event to a scapegoat (and, consequently, express a stronger desire to punish the scapegoat).

2. Increasing the salience of uncontrollable hazards in general should lead people to attribute increased power and influence to an enemy, even if the enemy's perceived influence is superficially unrelated to the salient hazards.

3. When people are exposed to a particular chaotic hazard, subsequent exposure to a scapegoat who can be viably blamed for the particular hazard should bolster people's feelings of personal control. Similarly, when people are exposed to the idea that multiple diverse potential hazards exist in their environment, subsequent exposure to an ambiguously powerful enemy should have the somewhat counterintuitive effect of bolstering their feelings of personal control.

We (Rothschild, Landau, Sullivan, & Keefer, in press) recently tested the first of these hypotheses in a series of studies looking at people's tendency to attribute responsibility to scapegoats for particular hazards, in this case harmful climate change. In one study, participants told that climate change was due to unknown chaotic forces (chaos threat condition) attributed more responsibility for climate change to oil companies and reported a greater desire to punish those companies, compared with participants who were not primed with chaotic causes of climate change (no threat condition). Consistent with our analysis, this effect was mediated by decreased feelings of personal control but not by feelings of guilt or other negative self-relevant perceptions.

But what role does the specifically chaotic nature of harmful events play in increasing scapegoating? A second study addressed this question by adding to the chaos threat and no-threat conditions a third condition in which participants were provided with an outgroup (other than the scapegoat target) that could be causally linked to climate change. In this new nonchaotic threat condition, the threat of climate change was made salient, but the cause of this threat was clearly identified. To further isolate control restoration as the underlying motivational process, we tested whether the effect of priming a chaotic hazard on increased scapegoating would be attenuated if participants had the opportunity to affirm perceptions of personal control in a domain superficially unrelated to climate change.

Supporting hypotheses, results showed that participants primed with chaotic causes behind harmful climate change were more likely to blame and penalize international corporations for their role in climate change than were participants in the no-threat and nonchaotic threat conditions. Also supporting hypotheses, this effect was significantly attenuated if participants affirmed their personal control but not if they affirmed their moral character, despite these affirmations being equivalent in overall valence. These findings suggest that people compensate for the salience of a particular hazard that seems out of their control by projecting power onto a scapegoat who can serve as a comprehensible source of that hazard, and they do so specifically to restore perceived personal control after it has been threatened.

We then tested the first part of the third hypothesis described earlier: If people encounter a chaotic hazard and are then presented with a viable scapegoat, they should report a stronger sense of personal control than those presented with a target that is not a viable scapegoat for the same chaotic hazard. Consistent with this hypothesis, we found that when participants were led to believe that global warming is due to unknown causes and were subsequently given the chance to blame oil companies for global warming (a viable scapegoat), they reported feeling significantly more control over their lives compared with participants given the chance to blame the Amish for global warming (a nonviable scapegoat).

In a related line of research, we (Sullivan, Landau, & Rothschild, 2010) investigated people's perceptions of enemies in the personal and political realms. To assess the second broad hypothesis described earlier, in one study, we tested whether reminding participants of a wide variety of unpredictable hazards in their environment would prompt them to attribute undue influence to a focal enemy figure. We found that when participants dispositionally low in perceived control contemplated negative events that could befall them at any time (e.g., airborne infections), they attributed increased influence to an enemy figure in their personal life; however, these participants did not attribute increased influence to a person who was annoying but not maliciously inclined, suggesting that priming potential hazards specifically influenced perceptions of others with malicious intent and not simply disliked others.

We replicated this effect on the eve of the 2008 U.S. presidential election, finding that participants primed with uncontrollable hazards expressed greater belief that the candidate opposing their preferred candidate was orchestrating a conspiracy to steal the election. However, participants primed with uncontrollable hazards were no more likely to view their political enemy in more generally negative terms (i.e., as less kind), suggesting that attributing power to an enemy is a uniquely effective means of managing the threat of meaninglessness. Note that perceiving Barack Obama or John McCain as perpetrating a conspiracy does not bear any obvious relation to the potential hazards participants were primed with, such as natural disasters and the suffering of family members. Thus, these findings suggest that attributing surreptitious power to a focal enemy figure can function in a flexible manner to assuage the threatening awareness of one's vulnerability to chaotic hazards.

It is important to note that threat inductions similar to those used by Sullivan et al. (2010) have been shown in other lines of research to increase affirmation of benevolent sources of power and influence. For example, prior research shows that threatening people's sense that they have control over outcomes in their life increases their investment in a controlling God and political and institutional sources of order (Kay, Gaucher, Napier, Callan, & Laurin, 2008). These findings have been interpreted as providing support for the compensatory control model, which posits that perceiving the self as in control, and perceiving external systems as in control, are intersubstitutable means of maintaining a consistent level of perceived order in one's environment and avoiding threatening cognitions about randomness.

Taking these findings into account, Sullivan et al. (2010) examined the conditions under which people respond to the salience of uncontrollable hazards by ascribing power to an enemy versus affirming benevolent systems of institutional control. On the basis of relevant anthropological work (M. Douglas, 1966), we hypothesized that one important moderator is the perception that the benevolent system in question in fact possesses the necessary resources to act in one's best interests. If the external system appears ineffectual, then people will not invest in it as a means of minimizing the threat of meaninglessness; instead, they will find alternate, personal means of maintaining the perception that the world is ordered and meaningful, such as ascribing increased power and influence to an enemy.

We tested this hypothesis by manipulating whether American participants saw the United States as a relatively ordered system in which economic and law enforcement institutions can be relied on for security or a relatively disordered system in which the economy is fragile and the government unreliable. When participants were primed to view governmental institutions as intact and capable, those primed with uncontrollable hazards ascribed increased power and influence to the U.S. government (e.g., replicating Kay et al., 2008), but their enemy perceptions were unaffected. In contrast, when the same governmental institutions were portrayed as ineffectual and unable to provide protection from external threats, participants primed with uncontrollable hazards did not affirm that system; rather, they were more likely to view a personal enemy as responsible for seemingly random misfortunes in their life (e.g., lost computer files, contracting food poisoning).

In another study that assessed the second part of the third broad hypothesis described earlier, we reasoned that if people contemplate uncontrollable hazards but, in addition, are exposed to an ambiguously powerful enemy capable of perpetrating a wide range of seemingly chaotic hazards, they should perceive less harmful risk in their environment and, consequently, perceive themselves as having more control. That is, whereas common sense would suggest that exposure to a powerful and malicious enemy would increase perceptions of risk, our analysis suggests that narrowing down chaotic threats to an enemy figure will eliminate the increased perception of risk engendered by the salience of uncontrollable hazards and thus bolster perceived personal control.

Consistent with this reasoning, participants led to focus on uncontrollable hazards in their environment, but then presented with a portrayal of an enemy (Al-Qaeda) as possessing ambiguous, ill-defined powers, perceived less risk in their environment than did participants who were not primed with chaotic hazards. This effect did not occur, however, among participants exposed to a portrayal of Al-Qaeda as possessing explicitly defined powers, supporting the significance of the attribution of ambiguous powers to enemies. Participants who saw Al-Qaeda as ambiguously powerful also reported higher personal control than participants in the comparison conditions. Also supporting predictions, a mediation analysis showed that this increase in perceived control was mediated by decreased risk perceptions. Thus, contemplating a powerful enemy when one is motivated to minimize threats to meaning can increase one's perceived mastery of the world, but only when the capabilities of that enemy are not completely known.

Summing up the primary research findings reviewed in this section: When people are confronted with a particular hazardous event portrayed as due to chaotic causes, or when they are reminded of the multiple potential hazards lurking in their environment, they compensate by ascribing increased power and influence to a malicious individual or group. Support for the unique role of control motivation in scapegoating comes from evidence that the effect of priming hazards on scapegoating is mediated by perceived personal control and is attenuated if people affirm their perceived control in another domain. Furthermore, after being confronted with a particular hazard or multiple potential hazards, being provided with a malicious scapegoat or enemy figure bolsters global perceptions of personal control. Finally, the reviewed studies provide evidence concerning both the circumstances under which people are likely to engage in enemyship as a control-restorative strategy (namely, when the broader social system appears disordered) and the type of enemy that best serves this function (an ambiguously, as opposed to an explicitly, powerful enemy).

FUTURE RESEARCH DIRECTIONS

Although scapegoating and enemyship have been the topics of a considerable body of theoretical work, they have been largely neglected in contemporary empirical research. The research just reviewed represents an attempt to understand whether and how these tendencies are motivated by a more distal psychological motive to maintain a buffer against the threat of meaninglessness. We operationalized this threat by reminding individuals that there are uncontrollable hazards in their environment that could seriously jeopardize all their efforts to negotiate their surroundings and establish their personal value. However, prior research has effectively threatened meaning using other procedures, such as exposure to relatively trivial expectancy violations (e.g., mismatched colors on a deck of cards; Proulx & Heine, 2009), exposure to information that is critical of one's cultural ideology (e.g., Schimel, Hayes, Williams, & Jahrig, 2007), and even the mere contemplation of death (Vess, Routledge, Landau, & Arndt, 2009). Confronting people with any of these threats to meaning might increase the tendencies to ascribe power to, and perhaps even create, scapegoats and enemy figures in order to restore perceived order and control. These possibilities remain to be tested.

Beyond this fairly straightforward direction for future work, there remain a number of unanswered questions concerning the motivations underlying enemy perceptions. In particular, future research should focus on the likely possibility that perceptions of scapegoats and enemies are shaped by motives other than the need to maintain meaning per se. For example, Becker (1969) noted that sometimes people generate paranoid fantasies to compensate for their own feelings of guilt and inadequacy. In such instances people may very well feel that the world is meaningful—that is, that their culture and immediate social environment afford reliable standards for valued action—yet they nevertheless perceive that they have personally fallen short of those standards. One means of compensating for this perceived failure is to invest in the belief that an enemy figure was responsible for that failure. For instance, a woman might convince herself that she could have become successful in her career if it had not been for the malicious intentions of a jealous coworker or the surreptitious sabotaging efforts of a bitter ex-lover.

In the same vein, classic theoretical perspectives on scapegoating suggest that people may scapegoat to compensate for feelings of personal inadequacy. Allport (1950/1983) in particular emphasized that scapegoating functions in part to alleviate the burden of responsibility for illegitimate harm committed by oneself or one's ingroup. This motive is conceptually distinct from the meaning-related motive we have emphasized so far. The question then arises: Which motive underlies scapegoating? Do people scapegoat to reduce the overwhelming indeterminacy of the world, or do they scapegoat to project negative feelings of moral culpability onto an external source?

Recently we took initial steps to address this question. Rather than argue that one motive is reducible to the other, we investigated the possibility that both motives contribute independently to scapegoating. That is, people may scapegoat to minimize concerns with either chaos or personal inadequacy, but these processes may nevertheless have distinct predictors, mediators, moderators, and downstream consequences. In fact, we tested this analysis in the three scapegoating studies reviewed previously (Rothschild et al., in press). What we did not mention earlier was that all the studies included a moral threat condition (for comparison with the chaotic threat condition) in which participants were exposed to an induction that framed ecological destruction as the direct result of participants' own behavior or that of their ingroup. Consistent with our dual-motive analysis, we found increased scapegoating in response to the salience of both a chaotic hazard and a moral threat; however, the effect of moral threat on increasing scapegoating was mediated by feelings of personal guilt, not personal control, and furthermore this effect was eliminated if participants affirmed their moral value, but not their personal control, in an unrelated domain.

Also, when climate change was framed as chaotic, perceiving a viable scapegoat increased feelings of personal control; when climate change was initially framed as being the ingroup's fault, perceiving a viable scapegoat decreased feelings of personal guilt as well as personal control. In other words, although scapegoating in some situations represents an attempt to create meaningful order out of apparent meaninglessness specifically to bolster feelings of personal control, in other situations scapegoating represents a defensive process meant to avoid feelings of guilt over one's actions, even at the apparent expense of personal control (i.e., by relinquishing control over a negative outcome to a scapegoat).

Differentiating these motivational paths becomes important when considering the downstream consequences of scapegoating. For example, it is possible that scapegoating to reduce guilt will be more likely to breed apathy and inaction than scapegoating to bolster control. Once people have projected their guilt over their own harmful actions onto a scapegoat, they may feel freed from responsibility for preventing or reversing those harmful actions. One study provided initial support for this possibility. We found that participants presented with a viable scapegoat after initially being told that their ingroup was responsible for climate change reported significantly less willingness to help stop climate change compared with participants presented with a nonviable scapegoat, as well as those initially told that the cause of climate change was unknown (control threat). This raises the possibility that people may be more strongly motivated to take personal or collective action in response to threats to meaning than they are in response to the threat of personal culpability—at least when they are provided with a scapegoat for these threats.

Another question that should be addressed in future research is whether focalizing the source of an unexplained event onto a scapegoat represents a unique buffer against meaninglessness or whether it is ultimately interchangeable with other means of maintaining perceived meaning. For instance, if climate change is framed as a natural process resulting from scientifically well-understood but impersonal causal forces, would such an explanation serve to buffer the threat of meaninglessness in the same way as blaming a viable scapegoat, or would it fail because it does not afford the individual with clear routes for exercising control? If focalizing blame on a definite intentional agent does provide a superior resolution to the threat of a salient chaotic hazard, when given the choice, individuals faced with a such an event should prefer to blame a scapegoat as compared with adopting an alternative explanatory framework (e.g., scientific explanation) that does not provide a causal agent as the focal source of the misfortune.

PRACTICAL IMPLICATIONS

In this section, we discuss practical implications of the theory and research reviewed thus far. First, we consider how the focalization of evil or guilt onto a convenient source shapes the ways in which societal problems are communicated in the public discourse and addressed by political policy. Next, we consider how individuals might maintain the perception that life is meaningful without resorting to the harmful tendency to create enemies and scapegoats.

Implications for Policy and Public Discourse

The research reviewed earlier helps to explain why people often prefer solutions to complex societal problems that focus on a single person or group viewed as the sole cause of those problems. This preference is reflected in Americans' attitudes toward solutions to terrorism. According to a 2006 national Gallup poll (Carroll, 2006), Americans believed that capturing or killing Osama Bin Laden should have been a higher priority in combating terrorism than attempting to improve communication between Middle Eastern countries and the United States, establishing a stable democratic government in Iraq, or resolving the conflict between Israel and Arab nations. Under the administration of President Barack Obama, the U.S. government seems to have responded to the public's priorities by making the apprehension of Bin Laden a top priority (Obama, 2011). Although killing Bin Laden may have been one part of a solution to the problem of terrorism, an overly narrow preoccupation with Bin Laden as the wellspring of evil may have resulted in inadequate attention paid to other, more complex dimensions of the problem. Indeed, at the time of writing, Bin Laden has been killed, yet the operations of Al Qaeda and the war in Afghanistan continue. Governmental policies and mass communications that support such simplified focalizations of threat may appease the public's concerns in the short term but may ultimately leave the underlying causes of a problem unaddressed.

These implications are also relevant to how the media, politicians, and the public have communicated and attempted to solve the problem of global climate change. In recent years, there has been growing awareness and concern about the hazardous effect of climate change, which is widely recognized as at least partly the result of human behavior (Krosnick & MacInnis, 2011). Opinion polls indicate that the American public is all too eager to blame climate change on large corporations and industries and to support policies that penalize those institutions (Kempton, Boster, & Hartley, 1995; Lorenzoni & Langford, 2002). For example, in the recent court case of *Comer v. Murphy Oil USA* (2009), New Orleans residents claimed that oil and gas companies had caused the emission of greenhouse gases that contributed to global warming and, as a consequence, added to the ferocity of Hurricane Katrina, which destroyed those residents' private property.

At the same time that people are willing to blame large corporations for the effects of environmental hazards, most of them are unwilling to accept personal responsibility for the problem or to change their lifestyle in ways that might help curb the harmful effects of climate change (Kempton et al., 1995; Lorenzoni & Langford, 2002). Insofar as climate change is partly the result of consumers' lifestyle choices, it is unlikely to be ameliorated so long as the public remains unwilling to make significant changes to their everyday behaviors.

Common sense and many psychological theories seem to suggest that these tendencies to displace blame for climate change to large corporations, and to avoid personal responsibility for the problem, stem from people's motivation to view themselves in a positive light. We do not doubt the validity of this explanation, and in fact, our research on scapegoating (Rothschild et al., in press) provides evidence that the motivation to maintain one's perceived moral value is indeed a driving force behind blame displacement. Nevertheless, our research suggests that these tendencies are also driven by a motivation to assuage deep-seated concerns with chaos and control. Even if one accepts that climate change is due in large part to human behavior, it remains a global hazard of enormous scope and extreme complexity, and its potential consequences for humanity are, for most people, ambiguous and remote (Langford, 2002). The myriad causal factors influencing climate change make it difficult to pinpoint an exact source of the problem or easily relate its hazardous effects to individuals' everyday actions (Lorenzoni & Pidgeon, 2006). In addition, the politicization of climate change and the systematic dissemination of misinformation have only served to infuse more uncertainty into an already complex and seemingly chaotic threat. Indeed, opinion polls on the topic of climate change show that people report feeling that the environment is an issue beyond their personal control (Pew Research Center, 2006). Our research shows that a negative outcome perceived as chaotic and ambiguous threatens people's conception of the world as meaningful and controllable, and they can compensate for this threat by focalizing blame onto a target that provides a simple causal explanation for that outcome.

The leading prospective governmental policies on climate change, which target corporations and industry, offer further evidence of a motivated urge to focalize the source of a complex and multidetermined hazard onto a single agent. Standing international agreements such as the Kyoto Protocol attempt to establish international guidelines for emissions. In practice, these guidelines often take the form of government regulations of industry, or of emissions trading systems (e.g., cap-and-trade policies), which are focused specifically on industry (Hood, 2010). Our work suggests that such policies may overly focalize blame onto an outgroup target and in this way reduce people's willingness to change their own lifestyles.

Our research also points to avenues for developing strategies that are more effective in encouraging people to change their lifestyles for the better. One study reported in Rothschild et al. (in press) showed that making people aware of their personal contribution to climate change can indeed increase their willingness to engage in reparative actions (e.g., driving less) so long as they are also made aware of clear actionable behaviors and are not provided with an opportunity to displace blame onto a scapegoat. This suggests that effective strategies for encouraging proenvironmental behaviors outside of the laboratory should (a) inform people of their personal contribution to climate change, (b) provide actionable steps for behavioral change that allow for the perception of effective control over the problem, and (c) discourage people from displacing responsibility onto popular scapegoats such as corporations.

One way to inform individuals about their personal contribution to climate change might be to provide personalized environmental footprint reports, similar to those used by governments and international organizations to monitor national climate change contributions. Manufacturers could also be mandated to add environmental footprint information on all products, similar to current food labeling laws enacted to place responsibility and control in the hands of the consumer. This policy would empower individuals to make informed decisions and thus bolster their perception of personal control over the problem. It would have the added advantage of making it salient to consumers just how much the environmental impact of corporations is interwoven with their own lifestyle choices. In this way, this strategy might prevent people from displacing responsibility. Politicians and the media could facilitate this shift in perspective by refraining from providing the public with convenient scapegoats for climate change, even though singling out such scapegoats may provide the comforting illusion of meaning in the world.

Implications for Personal Well-Being

Of course, in addition to further investigating the causes and consequences of people's perceptions of scapegoats and enemies, we should also investigate factors that remove the causes or mitigate the consequences. In other words, we should better determine how to encourage people to embrace more complex and diverse conceptions of the world and themselves to circumvent unnecessarily rigid focalization of evil or guilt onto a convenient source. In this regard, it is critical for future research to continue to explore strategies that facilitate less defensive reactions to the unpredictability of existence and that more flexibly maintain the perception that life is meaningful (see Chapters 7, 8, and 9, this volume, for these alternative strategies). The question becomes how to sustain strong convictions about life's meaning while imposing the least harm on those outside of one's own cultural circle and on future generations.

Fortunately, some important research along these lines is already emerging. One possibility for reducing scapegoating and enemyship is to encourage people to zealously pursue more socially constructive fetishes. The same urges to concretize the abstract and find clear paths to self-value that have fueled destructive forms of enemyship and violence have, arguably, also catalyzed many of the great innovations and discoveries in art, science, and technology (Van Zuylen, 2005). All these endeavors essentially amount to creating and discovering new knowledge structures that will serve as firm bases for viewing the world as meaningful and one's life as significant.

Related to this possibility, it is likely that the need to rely on scapegoats and enemies to defend one's sense of self-worth could be lessened to the extent that people are encouraged to develop more intrinsic standards of value and to move beyond an inflexible reliance on extrinsic standards for value and meaning. The conditions that allow people to develop and express such intrinsic standards are articulated in self-determination theory (e.g., Chapter 12, this volume). People pursuing intrinsic goals or possessing more intrinsic beliefs may adopt an open-minded approach to extracting meaning from life and may therefore display less defensive reactions to events that threaten to undermine the symbolic edifice of meaning that people share within a culture (Jonas & Fischer, 2006, report evidence supporting this possibility). Thus, people with more internalized sources of meaning and value may be able to manage their anxiety in ways that do not require rigid fetishism.

Becker's analysis shows that the psychological investment in enemy figures reflects an impoverished behavioral repertoire—the sense that one's powers to act in the world are crippled or blocked. Ultimately, people should be encouraged to cultivate increasingly complex and flexible conceptions of reality and themselves, even if this means accepting that feelings of meaninglessness will always be a part of this reality. In fact, contemplating those aspects of life that might make it seem meaningless need not always lead to rigidly defensive responses. Some recent work suggests that deeper conscious recognition of existentially threatening outcomes can actually foster greater attention to intrinsic values, potentially leading to some of the positive outcomes associated with such a focus. Drawing on the posttraumatic growth literature, Cozzolino, Staples, Meyers, and Samboceti (2004) conducted a series of studies indicating that a more open and in-depth confrontation with the idea of life's finality can inspire greater attention to self-transcendent values and goals. Future research might similarly find that encouraging a focused consideration of chaos and meaninglessness may eliminate the need to defend against those existential realities by creating enemies and scapegoats.

Of course, sustained concentration on thoughts of chaos and potentially lethal catastrophes would likely interfere with the thousands of routine acts that are required simply to navigate the social and physical world every day. Still, the possible benefits of a more honest acknowledgement of life's potential inherent meaninglessness are worth exploring. As M. Douglas (1966) and others have noted, whole cultural realms of endeavor—such as art—have developed largely as "safe" zones in which individuals can temporarily contemplate and engage with the potential absurdities and hardships of existence as well as life's inherent complexity and resistance to clear interpretation. By fostering widespread participation in such educational and reflective pursuits, we may help change people's psychological relationship to their own relative powerlessness and lead them to sources of strength without the crutch of their enemies.

REFERENCES

Allport, G. W. (1983). *The ABCs of scapegoating* (9th ed.). London, England: Antidefamation League of Britain. (Original work published 1950)

Becker, E. (1969). *Angel in armor*. New York, NY: Free Press.

Carroll, J. (2006, October). The American people's priorities for fighting terrorism. *Gallup*. Retrieved from http://www.gallup.com/poll/24865/American-Peoples-Priorities-Fighting-Terrorism.aspx

Comer v. Murphy Oil USA, 585 F. 3rd 855 (5th Cir. 2009).

Cozzolino, P. J., Staples, A. D., Meyers, L. S., & Samboceti, J. (2004). Greed, death, and values: From terror management to transcendence management theory. *Personality and Social Psychology Bulletin, 30*, 278–292. doi:10.1177/0146167203260716

Douglas, M. (1966). *Purity and danger*. Baltimore, MD: Penguin Books. doi:10.4324/9780203361832

Douglas, T. (1995). *Scapegoats: Transferring blame*. New York, NY: Routledge. doi:10.4324/9780203410684

Freud, S. (1963). Fetishism. In J. Strachey (Trans.), *The standard edition of the complete psychological works of Sigmund Freud* (Vol. 21, pp. 152–157). London, England: Hogarth. (Original work published 1927)

Glick, P. (2005). Choice of scapegoats. In J. F. Dovidio, P. Glick, & L. A. Rudman (Eds.), *On the nature of prejudice* (pp. 244–261). Malden, MA: Blackwell. doi:10.1002/9780470773963.ch15

Goffman, E. (1959). *The presentation of self in everyday life*. Garden City, NY: Doubleday.

Holt, T. R. (1989). College students' definitions and images of enemies. *Journal of Social Issues, 45*, 33–50. doi:10.1111/j.1540-4560.1989.tb01541.x

Hood, C. (2010). *Reviewing existing and proposed emissions trading systems*. Paris, France: International Energy Agency.

Jonas, E., & Fischer, P. (2006). Terror management and religion: Evidence that intrinsic religiousness mitigates worldview defense following mortality salience. *Journal of Personality and Social Psychology, 91*, 553–567. doi:10.1037/0022-3514.91.3.553

Kay, A. C., Gaucher, D., Napier, J. L., Callan, M. J., & Laurin, K. (2008). God and the government: Testing a compensatory control mechanism for the support of external systems. *Journal of Personality and Social Psychology, 95*, 18–35. doi:10.1037/0022-3514.95.1.18

Kempton, W., Boster, J., & Hartley, J. (1995). *Environmental values in American culture*. Cambridge, MA: MIT Press.

Krosnick, J. A., & MacInnis, B. (2011). *National survey of American public opinion on global warming*. Palo Alto, CA: Stanford University with Ipsos and Reuters.

Langford, I. H. (2002). An existential approach to risk perception. *Risk Analysis, 22*, 101–120. doi:10.1111/0272-4332.t01-1-00009

Lorenzoni, I., & Langford, I. (2002). Dealing with climate change: Role of institutions in the eyes of the public. In F. Bierman et al. (Eds.), *Proceedings of the 2001 Berlin Conference on the Human Dimensions of Global Environmental Change* (pp. 342–351). Potsdam, Germany: Potsdam Institute for Climate Impact Research.

Lorenzoni, I., & Pidgeon, N. F. (2006). Public views on climate change: European and USA perspectives. *Climatic Change, 77*, 73–95. doi:10.1007/s10584-006-9072-z

Obama, B. (May 2, 2011). Osama bin Laden killed. *The Telegraph*. Retrieved from http://www.telegraph.co.uk/news/worldnews/barackobama/8487354/Osama-bin-Laden-killed-Barack-Obamas-speech-in-full.html

Pew Research Center. (2006). *Little consensus on global warming*. Retrieved from http://www.people-press.org/2006/07/12/little-consensus-on-global-warming/2/

Proulx, T., & Heine, S. J. (2009). Connections from Kafka: Exposure to meaning threats improves implicit learning of an artificial grammar. *Psychological Science, 20*, 1125–1131. doi:10.1111/j.1467-9280.2009.02414.x

Rothschild, Z., Landau, M. J., Sullivan, D., & Keefer, L. A. (in press). A dual-motive model of scapegoating: Displacing blame to reduce guilt or increase control. *Journal of Personality and Social Psychology*.

Schimel, J., Hayes, J., Williams, T., & Jahrig, J. (2007). Is death really the worm at the core? Converging evidence that worldview threat increases death-thought accessibility. *Journal of Personality and Social Psychology, 92*, 789–803. doi:10.1037/0022-3514.92.5.789

Sullivan, D., Landau, M. J., & Rothschild, Z. (2010). An existential function of enemyship: Evidence that people attribute influence to personal and political enemies to compensate for threats to control. *Journal of Personality and Social Psychology, 98*, 434–449. doi:10.1037/a0017457

Tavernise, S. (May 25, 2010). U.S. is a top villain in Pakistan's conspiracy talk. *The New York Times*. Retrieved from http://www.nytimes.com/2010/05/26/world/asia/26pstan.html?scp=1&sq=U.S.%20is%20a%20top%20villain%20in%20Pakistan%E2%80%99s%20conspiracy%20talk&st=cse

Van Zuylen, M. (2005). *Monomania: The flight from everyday life in art and literature*. Ithaca, NY: Cornell University Press.

Vess, M., Routledge, C., Landau, M. J., & Arndt, J. (2009). The dynamics of death and meaning: The effects of death-relevant cognitions and personal need for structure on perceptions of meaning in life. *Journal of Personality and Social Psychology, 97*, 728–744. doi:10.1037/a0016417

11

TERRORISM AS MEANS TO AN END: HOW POLITICAL VIOLENCE BESTOWS SIGNIFICANCE

ARIE W. KRUGLANSKI, MICHELE GELFAND,
AND ROHAN GUNARATNA

Nowhere is meaning making more important than in the realm of *self-meaning*. Coming to terms with one's place in the universe, feeling that one's existence has significance, sensing the appreciation and respect of others whom one reveres and trusts all constitute a universal motivating force propelling people into actions all over the world (see Chapters 8, 9, and 19, this volume). The universal quest for meaning has made innumerable positive contributions to humankind, in the domains of art, science, and culture more generally. Victor Frankl in his renowned 1959 volume (*Man's Search for Meaning*) poignantly illustrated how maintenance of meaning carried him and others through the horrors of a Nazi concentration camp and was ultimately responsible for their survival. But the quest for meaning has a dark side as well. There is a potential Mr. Hyde lurking in the search for meaning, the hideous twin of the beloved Dr. Jekyll. In this chapter, we explore the destructive potential of the quest for significance as it manifests itself in the contemporary scourge of international terrorism.

The topic of modern terrorism has been of interest to social scientists at least since the late 1960s and 70s, when a wave of bombings, hijackings, and kidnappings catapulted the subject to the top of the world's concerns. This interest spiked following the tragedy of 9/11 and has grown as the world realizes that the problem is not going away anytime soon and may undermine the security of most nations. The study of terrorism is proceeding apace around the world; numerous institutes and associations have sprung up devoted to research on the topic, and the number of conferences, symposia, and publications on terrorism and political violence exhibits an accelerated growth curve. But what exactly is the state of our knowledge concerning terrorism?

In this chapter, we provide a motivational analysis of terrorists' behavior, grounded in the notion of a quest for meaning. As a preview of what is to come, we first survey an early phase in the psychological analysis of terrorism, centered on explaining the phenomenon in terms of the terrorists' personalities or the situations in which they find themselves. Subsequently, we move to consider a later explanatory paradigm wherein researchers offered analyses of terrorism focused exclusively on either personal trauma and suffering or the terrorism-justifying ideology, or the social process, that led individuals to become terrorists. Next, we offer our own integrative analysis wherein the quest for meaning, the ideology, and the mechanism of social influence jointly instill the motivation for terrorism. Finally, we review initial empirical evidence relevant to our theoretical integration.

THE DISTAL FOCUS: PERSON- VERSUS ENVIRONMENT-BASED EXPLANATIONS OF TERRORISM

Early psychological research on terrorism focused on categories of variables assumed relevant to behavior, namely, the person or the environment. Researchers' initial instinct was to commit the "fundamental attribution error" and ascribe terrorist behavior to specific personality traits or specific psychopathologies (e.g., Atran, 2003; Kennedy, 2009). Given the terrorists' bizarre cruelty, seeming callousness, and readiness to engage in violence against civilians, the first hypothesis that came to mind was that because their behavior was so unusual, their deviant personalities must be to blame. However, the research results quickly disabused terrorism researchers of this notion. The consensus in the field today is that there is no unique terrorist personality profile, nor is there a unique terrorist psychopathology.

If not a unique form of psychopathology or personality disorder, perhaps the environment explains why someone would become a terrorist. This may seem plausible as well as charitable, as it depersonalizes terrorism and hence removes the burden of responsibility from individual terrorists. Yet, here too researchers struck out: The hypotheses that poverty, poor education, and political oppression are the root causes of terrorism have proven unsustainable on empirical grounds.

Of course, personality and environment are not irrelevant to terrorism. In fact, we have mounting evidence that they are relevant. For instance, Merari, Diamant, Bibi, Broshi, and Zakin (2009), who conducted clinical interviews with failed suicide bombers in Israeli jails, found that they were characterized by dependent and rigid personalities. Of course, this does not mean that all people who have dependent and rigid personalities will become terrorists. Thus, the relation between personality and terrorism seems to be moderated by circumstances. Another example: Our research team has carried out research with terrorism suspects in Filipino detention centers (members of the Abu Sayyaf organization affiliated with Jemmah Islamiyah and Al Qaeda, and members of the Raja Sulaiman organization of Christian converts to Islam). We found, for example, that stable individual differences in the need for cognitive closure are highly correlated with Islamic extremism (Kruglanski, Gelfand, & Gunaratna, 2011). Again, we know many people who are high in the need for closure who do not support Islamic extremism. In fact, in research we carried out in the Netherlands (Orehek et al., in press), we found that need for closure is significantly correlated with anti-Muslim attitudes. Thus, the relation between need for cognitive closure and Islamist extremism also appears to be moderated by circumstances.

In yet another study carried out with detained members of the Liberation Tigers of Tamil Eelam (LTTE) in Sri Lanka (arguably one of the most violent terrorist organizations in the history of the phenomenon), we found that stable individual differences in collectivism and collective narcissism were correlated with support for armed struggle against the Sinhalese majority (Kruglanski, Gelfand, Malshanti, et al., 2011). Again, it seems clear that these relations must be moderated rather than general, for there are surely numerous collectivists and collective narcissists (those who believe their group to be the best) who do not support terrorism and are even strongly opposed to it.

Similarly, it would be a mistake to conclude that situational factors such as poverty, political oppression, or poor education are irrelevant to terrorism. Rather, their relation to terrorism also seems to be moderated by circumstances. Thus, for example, Krueger and Laitin (2008) found that many recently active terrorists come from countries in which regimes are politically oppressive, or "tight." However, we also know of circumstances (e.g., in the former Soviet Union or Nazi Germany) where political oppression was considerable, yet there was no terrorism. Similarly, there have been numerous instances of terrorism in major Western democracies (e.g., in the United States, Canada, Spain, Italy, Germany, and France), where there was terrorism without political oppression. So the question again is, What are the moderating circumstances, and under what conditions does political oppression produce terrorism and under what conditions does it not?

GETTING PROXIMAL: ON STATES, IDEOLOGIES, AND NETWORKS AS EXPLANATIONS OF TERRORISM

Whereas the personality and environment factors studied originally were rather general, researchers have recently tended to cleave terrorism along more proximal joints by drawing distinctions between emotional states, ideologies, and social networks as explanations of terrorism. For instance, Speckhard and Akhmedova (2005) found in their sample of Chechen women terrorists that personal trauma and frustration caused by the loss of a significant other (e.g., a husband or fiancé) constituted the tipping point that pushed these "black widows" toward terrorism. Pedahzur (2005) noted that several Palestinian terrorists suffered serious personal problems before volunteering to blow themselves up in suicidal missions.

Of interest, investigators who stress the role of emotional states and personal problems as causes of terrorism typically view them as the exclusive causes, downplaying the role of ideology as epiphenomenal. Other investigators disagree and believe that ideology is essential. For instance, Ginges, Atran, Medin, and Shikaki (2007) in their work on "sacred values" highlighted the ideological bases of terrorists' attitudes and viewed these as the unique explanation of their behavior. Certainly, the various de-radicalization programs that have sprung up in several Muslim nations (Saudi Arabia, Yemen, Egypt, Singapore, Iraq) are premised on the belief that ideology matters and that religious and moral counterarguments are essential to reversing extremism.

Finally, some investigators, such as Marc Sageman, who published a well-known book in 2004, have highlighted the role of social processes and argued that an individual's social networks are the most important ingredient of terrorism (at least the recent Jihadist terrorism). How do we reconcile these seemingly incompatible views (emphasizing personal traumas, ideologies, or social networks)? Like the wise rabbi in the joke, who told two combative disputants that each of them was right, we too believe that everyone is right, though not exclusively right. Personality can matter under some circumstances, and so can the environment. Emotional states can matter, and so can ideologies, though not in all cases, and the social networking of individuals can matter as well. The big question is when they matter and under what conditions.

One way of addressing this issue is by harking back to the basics and outlining a general analysis of terrorists' behavior. We assume that, like other behaviors, terrorists' behavior is goal driven and constitutes the means through which individuals choose to pursue their goal. We assume that this self-regulatory process of goal pursuit is carried out against a backdrop of cultural meanings that determine what goals are worthy of pursuit and what means are effective and legitimate for that purpose. We also assume that this process is unfolding dynamically within a persuasive social context that convinces the individual to adopt certain goals, relinquish others, and choose certain means with which to pursue the goals.

The foregoing characterization is, admittedly, rather general. It applies to all behavior, not just terrorist behavior. Is there a unique goal that terrorists in general are pursuing? Or do different terrorists pursue different goals altogether, meaning that a person can engage in terrorism for any number of reasons.

The literature on this topic has proposed a variety of possible motives, including honor, redressing humiliation, heavenly rewards, devotion to a leader, vengeance, group pressure, even feminism (Bloom, 2005; Gambetta, 2005; Stern, 2003). But in a recent paper, we argued that there is a way to integrate all of the specific motives under a more general motivational rubric that we called the *quest for significance* (Kruglanski, Chen, Dechesne, Fishman, & Orehek, 2009). The quest for significance refers to a general motivational force beyond mere survival, and it has been recognized by psychological theorists under various labels, such as *competence* or *effectance* (e.g., Elliot & Dweck, 2005; White, 1959), *self-esteem*, and *mastery*. We also delineated three general cases in which the quest for significance can be aroused: (a) when one has suffered a considerable loss of significance (e.g., because one or one's group has been severely humiliated; this applies to the Chechen widows who were rendered powerless and hence demeaned by having their husband or fiancé forcefully taken from them, or the Palestinian women humiliated by their infertility or infidelity, or the Muslim immigrants to Europe who feel they are victims of Islamophobia); (b) when one faces a threat of significance, should one fail to comply with the pressure to engage in terrorism (e.g., Japanese kamikaze pilots, many of whom did not want to die but who could not live with the dishonor of refusing the mission, as well as individuals who commit themselves publically to an act of martyrdom and see no way of undoing this commitment without tremendous loss of face); and (c) when one sees an opportunity for a considerable significance gain, becoming "famous overnight" and acquiring the status of a martyr or hero (see Chapter 1, this volume, for a similar analysis of these cases). This explains why individuals who seemingly have not been personally humiliated, poor, uneducated, or particularly discriminated against (e.g., Muhammad Atta, Bin Laden, and many others) choose to engage in terrorism.

It should be clear that the goal of attaining or restoring personal significance can vary as a function of personality (some people are more sensitive than others to the issue of significance); hence, personality matters, but also as a function of the situation (e.g., being humiliated oneself or belonging to a humiliated group, being threatened with humiliation). Hence, situation matters as well. Also, arousal of the quest for significance is typically accompanied by an emotional state of some sort (shame, anger, frustration, elation). Thus, personality, situation, and emotional states are all relevant to the tendency to engage in terrorism insofar as they relate to the goal of maintaining significance, our main explanatory construct.

Of course, arousal of a goal alone is not enough to explain a given behavior. In addition, one needs a means to that goal. Typically, such means are suggested by a *terrorism-justifying ideology*. In other words, the ideology dictates what an individual needs to do in order to attain significance (see Chapter 4, this volume). Such an ideology is grounded in the shared reality of one's group. It is a collective belief system to which an individual subscribes. In the case of threats to the group from its (real or imagined) enemies, the gain or restoration of significance often has to do with defending the group and making personal sacrifices on the group's behalf. In exchange for this benefit, the group accords one the status of martyr or hero whose exploits are to be forever engraved in the group's collective memory. In other words, ideology can be important.

There has been considerable debate among terrorism scholars as to whether ideology in general and religion in particular are necessarily involved in terrorism (see Chapter 8, this volume). So let us quickly disavow what we are *not* saying. We are not suggesting that anyone who engages in terrorism is privy to an intricate "ideology." A jihadist terrorist need not be a theological expert on the Quran, and in fact, many Quranic scholars strongly oppose terrorism. Hence, no systematic relation should be expected between religiosity and terrorism. Those who subscribe to moderate Islam believe that the road to personal significance is moderation and charity rather than violence. However, an extremist interpretation of the religion offers terrorism as a means to significance. In short, ideology is relevant to terrorism only in identifying a means to personal significance, no more and no less. And it does not have to be any particular ideology; for instance, it can be an ethnonationalist ideology such as the ideology of the LTTE organization that we have recently studied.

Perhaps the most elementary form of a suggested means to significance is a pronouncement by a worshipped and beloved leader. For instance, those who have studied the suicide bombers of the LTTE have reported that in many cases it was the say-so of the leader, Velupillai Prabhakaran, and the feeling that he deeply respected the Black Tiger volunteers who decided to sacrifice their lives that motivated them to embark on a suicidal mission. To those volunteers, the leader was the utmost "epistemic authority" (Kruglanski et al., 2005) concerning the proper means to attain significance and glory.

This brings us to a final theoretical point concerning the role of distal culture and of the proximal social process in defining what constitutes significance. One's culture outlines what is societally valued (for instance, in our research in the Middle East, we find that "honor" is valued considerably more than it is in the United States and that having honor is what constitutes significance). And one's local social process brings one into contact with, and renders accessible and salient, the notion that terrorism is a means to personal significance. So social networking is typically important, just as Sageman (2004) suggested. Similarly, charismatic, firebrand leadership can be important, and propaganda can be important, although in some cases (atypical ones to be sure) an individual may arrive on her or his own at the idea that terrorism is a means to significance (as may have been the case with Ted Kaczynski, the ill-fated Unabomber, or Igal Amir, the assassin of Yitzhak Rabin). In those cases, what is crucial is the compelling means suggestion accomplished through networking, charisma, propaganda, or one's own deliberation.

EMPIRICAL EVIDENCE

Recently, we collected evidence concerning aspects of our theory related to the loss of significance and its association with support for violence and self-sacrifice on behalf of one's group. Specifically, we hypothesized that a loss of significance would generally lead one to become attuned to one's group's norms and likely to abide by them, something we refer to as a *collectivistic shift*. In particular, we hypothesized that self-identification as a group member (i.e., thinking of oneself as "we" rather than an "I") would (a) restore one's sense of significance and immunize one to significance loss and (b) dispose one to defend one's group and engage in violence against the group's perceived enemies. Therefore, ultimately, a loss of personal significance would prompt support for martyrdom and self-sacrifice for a common cause.

Let us examine these elements one by one. That personal failure (loss of significance) leads one to a collectivistic shift—that is, greater attunement to one's group—is suggested by several studies. For instance, in an Internet survey of 12 Arab countries, Pakistan, and Indonesia, we found that participants reporting lower life success tended more strongly to self-identify as members of collectivities (nation or religion). In experimental studies, individuals who were given failure versus success feedback scored higher on a measure of interdependence and lower on a measure of independence. On a different task, those given failure (vs. success) feedback chose more often to work in a group rather than alone.

In addition, we found that collective self-identity immunizes one to an extent against feelings of insignificance. This is manifested specifically through people's reduced defense against notions of mortality and death, which (according to terror management theorists, such as Greenberg, Chapter 1, this volume) convey the possibility of utter insignificance (the prospect of becoming a "speck of dust in an uncaring universe," as Arndt puts it in Chapter 3, this volume). Thus, in one study, participants were asked to circle either singular first-person pronouns (I, me, my) or collective pronouns (we, us, our). The latter scored lower on a scale of death anxiety, and they pulled death-related words faster toward them (indicating stronger approach) and pushed death-related words away from them more slowly than persons in the individualistic condition.

In Internet surveys conducted in 12 Arab countries, Indonesia, and Pakistan and in representative face-to-face research in Egypt, Morocco, Indonesia, and Pakistan, we found that individuals who identified collectivistically (as members of their religion or nation) tended more strongly to support the killing of American civilians.

We have some evidence that in circumstances in which the group norms support violence against an outgroup, feelings of personal insignificance, anger, and shame are associated with support for armed struggle in a sample of LTTE members. In circumstances in which one is made to feel bad about oneself, one's support for martyrdom seems to increase. In a study relevant to this proposition, we had religious participants exposed to stimuli assumed to arouse forbidden sexual thoughts and hence sexual guilt. The participants looked at sexual stimuli or neutral stimuli, and we measured their sexual guilt. Those exposed to sexual stimuli evidenced greater sexual guilt. What is more intriguing, they also evinced greater support for martyrdom as measured by our scale.

CONCLUSION

The understanding that at some level terrorist behavior is governed by the same principles as any other behavior, and more specifically that it is goal driven, serves an important function. It directs our analytic gaze beyond the observable surface specifics and allows us to peer deeper into the underlying dynamics of the process that can result in terrorist behavior. It suggests certain questions that need to be answered if we are to understand the psychology of terrorism. What is the fundamental personal goal that individuals are trying to achieve when they engage in terrorist behavior? (We have concluded that the main goal is personal significance.) What are the conditions under which such a goal is likely to be adopted? (We answered this question by suggesting that it is likely when significance has been lost or threatened and there is an opportunity for considerable gains in significance.) These insights integrate a variety of disparate personality and cultural and environmental factors. To mention just one cultural factor, research that one of us and our multi-university research initiative team has carried out in the Middle East

(Gelfand, 2011) suggests that dishonor and loss of face are particularly important causes of significance loss in the Middle East, more so than in the United States, and that these experiences might, therefore, constitute particularly important incitements to violence and terrorism in that part of the world.

Our framework also directs investigators to ask what the perceived means to the goal of significance are, and what the circumstances are under which they are suggested. What is the role of ideology in this regard; how deep an ideological conviction does it necessitate? What is the role of charismatic leadership in means suggestion, and what is the function of the social process in this regard? One important implication of our analysis is that strong ideology alone does not necessarily produce violence, not even a fundamentalist ideology; it is the explicit ideological justification of violence that matters, not ideology per se. It is not the social networks alone that matter either, or the leader's charisma, but rather the content of the message carried by the networks and advocated by the leader. In short, recognizing that terrorist behavior is an instance of human behavior allows us to apply to it general psychological knowledge concerning goal-directed behavior. In this case, then, the "banality of evil," or the "normalcy of terrorism," is good news in that it affords a well-grounded understanding of radicalization and terrorism with potentially important practical implications for counteracting these dangerous phenomena.

REFERENCES

Atran, S. (2003, March 7). Genesis of suicide terrorism. *Science, 299,* 1534–1539. doi:10.1126/science.1078854

Bloom, M. (2005). *Dying to kill: The allure of suicide terrorism.* New York, NY: Columbia University Press.

Elliot, A. J., & Dweck, C. S. (Eds.). (2005). *Handbook of competence and motivation.* New York, NY: Guilford Press.

Frankl, V. E. (1959). *Man's search for meaning.* Boston, MA: Beacon Press.

Gambetta, D. (2005). *Making sense of suicide missions.* Oxford, England: Oxford University Press. doi:10.1093/acprof:oso/9780199276998.001.0001

Gelfand, M. J. (2011). Unpublished raw data. University of Maryland.

Ginges, J., Atran, S., Medin, D., & Shikaki, K. (2007). Sacred bounds on rational resolution of violent political conflict. *Proceedings of the National Academy of Sciences of the United States of America, 104,* 7357–7360. doi:10.1073/pnas.0701768104

Kennedy, D. B. (2009). Terrorists behind bars. *American Jails, 23,* 31–39.

Krueger, A. B., & Laitin, D. D. (2008). Kto Kogo?: A cross-country study of the origins and targets of terrorism. In P. Keefer & N. Loayza (Eds.), *Terrorism and economic development* (pp. 148–173). New York, NY: Cambridge University Press.

Kruglanski, A. W., Chen, X., Dechesne, M., Fishman, S., & Orehek, E. (2009). Fully committed: Suicide bombers' motivation and the quest for personal significance. *Political Psychology, 30,* 331–357. doi:10.1111/j.1467-9221.2009.00698.x

Kruglanski, A. W., Gelfand, M. J., & Gunaratna, R. (2011). Unpublished raw data. University of Maryland.

Kruglanski, A. W., Gelfand, M. J., Malshanti, M., Gunaratna, R., Belanger, J., & Sharvit, K. (2011). Unpublished raw data. University of Maryland.

Kruglanski, A. W., Raviv, A., Bar-Tal, D., Raviv, A., Sharvit, K., Ellis, S., & Mannetti, L. (2005). Says who? Epistemic authority effects in social judgment. In M. P. Zanna (Ed.), *Advances in experimental social psychology* (Vol. 37, pp. 346–392). New York, NY: Academic Press.

Merari, A., Diamant, I., Bibi, A., Broshi, Y., & Zakin, G. (2009). Personality characteristics of "self martyrs"/"suicide bombers" and organizers of suicide attacks. *Terrorism and Political Violence, 22,* 87–101. doi:10.1080/09546550903409312

Orehek, E., Doosje, B., Kruglanski, A. W., Cole, A., Saddler, T., & Jackson, J. (2010). Need for closure and the social response to terrorism. *Basic and Applied Social Psychology, 32,* 279–290. doi:10.1080/01973533.2010.519196

Pedahzur, A. (2005). *Suicide terrorism.* London, England: Polity Press.

Sageman, M. (2004). *Understanding terror networks.* Philadephia, PA: University of Pennsylvania Press.

Speckhard, A., & Akhmedova, K. (2005). Talking to terrorists. *The Journal of Psychohistory, 33,* 125–156.

Stern, J. (2003). *Terror in the name of God: Why religious militants kill.* New York, NY: HarperCollins.

White, R. W. (1959). Motivation reconsidered: The concept of competence. *Psychological Review, 66,* 297–333. doi:10.1037/h0040934

III
THE CHALLENGE
OF FREEDOM

12

BEYOND ILLUSIONS AND DEFENSE: EXPLORING THE POSSIBILITIES AND LIMITS OF HUMAN AUTONOMY AND RESPONSIBILITY THROUGH SELF-DETERMINATION THEORY

RICHARD M. RYAN, NICOLE LEGATE, CHRISTOPHER P. NIEMIEC, AND EDWARD L. DECI

Social psychologists are skilled at showing that nonconscious processes determine our behavior, that implicit threats automatically drive us toward inhumanity and defense, and that attempts to exercise choice and volition are not only mentally depleting but also often illusory. But is that the full story? In this chapter, we review evidence concerning people's illusions of will and vulnerabilities to defense and contrast it with findings from self-determination theory (SDT). The latter findings highlight individuals' power to act in accord with integrated values and, through mindfulness and autonomy, to resist habitual and defensive responding. These inherent human potentials are, of course, balanced by manifold vulnerabilities to threats and controls made salient in research within the SDT tradition, as well by findings from other social psychological perspectives. In short, findings that people can be defensive or unconsciously controlled do not mean that they are always defensive and controlled. Psychology can shed valuable light on existential philosophy's "other side"—namely, the human potential to act autonomously.

THE CONTEMPORARY IMAGE OF HUMANITY
IN SOCIAL PSYCHOLOGY

If we were to peer into the mirror held up to us by contemporary experimental social psychology, the reflection would be sad indeed. We would see fearful, weak, defensive, and nonconsciously driven animals who suffer illusions of free will. We would see creatures dominated by implicit processes operating outside of their awareness and who are mentally depleted by even simple efforts at self-regulation. In fact, with regard to any sense of human freedom, volition, or will, the message from today's social psychology seems to be that these cherished ideas are at best fragile and more likely merely illusory.

Authors such as Wegner (2008) and Bargh (2008) have specifically portrayed free will and self-causation as inherently antideterministic and, hence, unscientific concepts, thus rendering them indefensible and implying that the idea of committed choices is without empirical support. Indeed, a cover of *American Psychologist* (November 1999) went so far as to proclaim, "Behavior—It's Involuntary," as if this were an empirical conclusion. Even Freud, so often said to have held a pessimistic view of humanity, might reel at the fragile automaton envisioned within social psychology today, for his (1923/1961) metaphor of a powerful unconscious at least allowed for a rider, the partially conscious ego, that could sometimes guide the steed.

Even in the chapters of this volume on meaning, mortality, and choice, the message from terror management theory (TMT; Greenberg, Solomon, & Pyszczynski, 1997) suggests that our personal beliefs, life goals, and cultural values are largely products not of growth and conscious purpose but of blind defense. That is, nonconscious defenses against the awareness of mortality drive people to adopt identities, develop affiliations and attachments, aggress against outgroup members, and convince themselves that their lives have purpose and meaning (see Chapters 1, 2, 3, 4, and 6, this volume). Thus, the consciousness that some philosophies consider to be liberating is viewed in TMT as awakening realities that are, apparently, too hard to handle. Protecting the psyche from anxiety thus becomes in TMT the primary, rather than a secondary, source of human motivation and culture.

REALLY? ARE HUMANS SO WEAK, DEFENSIVE,
AND CONTROLLED?

Before social psychology indulges in its final celebratory dance on the graves of free will, human meaning, and self, let us consider the specific constructs being so eagerly toppled. Perhaps the free will that theorists are speaking of is not the kind of autonomy or self-regulatory capacity that humans need to thrive. If, for example, *free will* were defined as the capacity to make choices through processes that defy scientific principles of causation, we too would be happy to applaud its demise. However, we maintain that the "feeling of free will," when properly considered, is not merely illusory; it is rather an experiential state with important consequences that accompanies some forms of motivated behavior. In fact, substantial evidence suggests that people's feelings of "authorship" (e.g., Wegner, 2008) or autonomy (e.g., Ryan & Deci, 2000) reliably predict many positive functional outcomes such as effective performance and wellness (Deci & Ryan, 2012). Such feelings and attributions are typically not epiphenomenal or deluded (although they can be tricked by clever experimenters) but rather constitute reliable and functionally important experiences and adaptive sensibilities.

Our concern is not only about free will; it also extends to the portrait of a defensive humanity highlighted in this volume's chapters on TMT. To be sure, we believe that TMT points to an important aspect of life highlighted by existential philosophers in which anxiety about mortality can drive defensive behavior. Yet, even though many of the dynamic defensive processes revealed by TMT are robust, there is another side of existentialism, a side that Warnock (1970) reminded us is existentialism's central message. As she stated, existentialists

> aim, above all, to show people *that they are free*, to open their eyes to something which has always been true, but which for one reason or another may not always have been recognized, namely not only that men are free to choose, not only what to do on a specific occasion, but what to value and how to live. (pp. 1–2, emphasis in original)

Is there any empirical evidence to support this positive message of existentialism? Or must one conclude that people are indeed the passive, weak, and defensive creatures some experimental social psychologists have portrayed? Are we capable of being in the center of our lives, responsible for what we do? Or is that merely illusion and defense?

In what follows, we consider the philosophical and empirical support for existentialism's most central message and review evidence derived from self-determination theory (SDT; Ryan & Deci, 2000) suggesting that people can and do exercise autonomy and act with integrity, whereas at other times they succumb to vulnerabilities to being controlled, defensive, or inauthentic (see also Chapter 14, this volume, on this point). First, we reexamine recent arguments against free will to contrast them with more useful and functionally relevant conceptions of volition and autonomy. Second, we briefly review a large body of evidence showing that the human experience of behaving autonomously is related to effective, positive functioning, findings that are consistent across cultures, gender, domains, and economic status. Third, we review recent experimental evidence that people who are more integrated and autonomous are more resilient to threat, depletion, terror, and non-conscious influences. That is, when more self-determined, people show less vulnerability to eroding influences. Fourth, we show that this is true even with respect to reminders of personal mortality. Without denying that mortality salience (MS) can, under some conditions, evoke defenses and self-esteem-protective behavior, we show that defense is not inevitable and that not everyone is equally susceptible.

Finally, we revisit the popular trend in psychology to deflate the human image, asking why such a tendency has emerged particularly within experimental social psychology. We remind readers of the "can versus do" bias (McCall, 1977) of experimental psychology—namely, that although in controlled experiments one can produce certain behaviors, this does not ensure that those same factors typically do initiate or control those behaviors outside the lab. Thus, we understand that people can be fooled into a false sense of volition, but that does not mean they are always fooled. We can evoke defenses that push people to cling to beliefs, but it does not follow that this is why beliefs are typically developed or held. In short, there is a tendency within experimental social psychology to make logical leaps from findings that people can be controlled to assertions that they are pervasively controlled. Sadly, this fosters bodies of knowledge that are disconnected from a fuller, more coherent model of human functioning that places vulnerabilities in juxtaposition to inherent growth tendencies and capacities for autonomy. We conclude by pointing to the evolved integrative propensities that are at the forefront of human motivation as a core existential strength. We note that findings from social psychology concerning human fallibilities and defenses highlight our limitations and the dynamic forces that can derail positive human potentials. Yet, as salient as these vulnerabilities may be, they need to be put into a theoretical context that recognizes the possibilities of "free-range" human beings.

ON THE ILLUSIONS BEHIND THE "ILLUSION OF FREE WILL": LET THE STRAW MEN BURN

Some kinds of free will may not be worth having. The most popular attacks on free will and self-regulation from social psychologists should not disturb anyone who is listening carefully, because the concepts they knock down are not consistent with practical living.

For example, we do not need a free will that is defined as an original or first cause of action. This is the definition of free will provided by Bargh (2008), who stated with all the authority of science that "subjective feelings of free will are one of the 'positive illusions' . . . we hold dear. [It] is irrelevant to the scientific status or truth-value . . . it is still an illusion" (p. 133). His argument is based on the premise that free will is only represented by thoughts and decisions that arise from neither the brain nor one's environment. For Bargh, will is "free" only when it is "uncaused"—there being no prior cues, influences, or prompts. In fact, Bargh's free will must also be immaterial. Citing evidence from Libet (2004) that brain activity can be detected before a conscious thought, Bargh construed this to mean that the "brain," rather than the self or will, "causes" consciousness—a logical trick only a dualist can master.

Should we be surprised that intentions are in fact inspired from within our minds or by cues from without? For an action to be done freely, must the motive first arise in immaterial thought and not in my brain or body, my unconscious musings, or even my environment? If I freely decide to go out with a friend, does that necessitate that the friend did not invite me, that it must be *my*, and only *my*, idea? Indeed, does any action arise without preceding conditions? This Procrustean bed appears to be required for Barghian free will. In fact, however, prior inputs are always involved in will or autonomy, simply because as living organisms we are inherently intertwined with the world (Mackenzie, 2000). Making choices and regulating behaviors inevitably occur with respect to multiple and concurrent inputs and influences. To act with autonomy and integrity is an act of synthesis, not one of creating intentions ex nihilo.

Another form of free will we have no desire to defend is a free will that is infallible. Wegner (2008) argued that self and volition are akin to "magic"— masking the "real" automatic mechanisms of mind. Wegner's bases for this claim overlap considerably with those of Bargh (2008), but he brings an additional form of evidence to condemn free will: demonstrations that our sense of will can be tricked. Specifically, Wegner noted that actions perceived to be self-caused typically share common features, including consistency (intentions and outcomes must be consistent), priority (intention must precede the action), and exclusivity (no other plausible causes are apparent). He and his colleagues then showed that when people are in ambiguous experimental situations (e.g., involving Ouija boards, voodoo curses) and are given cues of consistency, priority, and exclusivity, they often misattribute actions or outcomes to their own intentions.

But, speaking of magic, these demonstrations do not show what they claim to reveal. They are, in fact, analogous to optical illusions. To create an optical illusion, one inserts cues into visual stimuli that typically inform vision but that instead mislead the perceiver. For example, occlusions typically convey depth, and an illusion fools us by making a foreground object appear occluded by something that is, in fact, farther away. It's a great trick, but how many visual researchers have concluded that because we can design such optical illusions, the human capacity for visual perception is therefore an illusion? Yet Wegner appears to apply this logic: If people can be fooled about the antecedents of their behavior, then all attributions to self or volition are erroneous.

It is also not necessary that free will be independent of a brain. Reductionists argue that causation of volitional action is of necessity based in brain activity, and they then derive from that idea that volition therefore does not exist. After all, the brain did it! Examples of this line of thinking abound in neuroscience discourse, with Pinker (2002) providing an illustrative quote:

> Each of us feels that there is a single "I" in control. But that is an illusion that the brain works hard to produce. . . . The brain does have supervisory systems in the prefrontal lobes and anterior cingulate cortex, which can push the buttons of behavior and override habits and urges. But these systems are gadgets with specific quirks and limitations; they are not implementations of the rational free agent traditionally identified with the soul or the self. (p. 43)

This is remarkable thinking. First, who doubts that autonomous, volitional action in which the I "feels in control" requires a brain (and a cardiovascular system and some other essential organs as well)? So too does engaging controlled or alienated actions. But what is this "rational free agent," "soul" construct Pinker introduces? It certainly sounds implausible! Yet, note in Pinker's account that as he eviscerates the "I/soul," the brain becomes, linguistically, a new homunculus or agent. The brain is "producing illusions" and "pushing the gadgets."

In our view, autonomy is not separate from the organism—rather, autonomy is one form of functioning, as is being controlled. Accordingly, empirical research is increasingly pinpointing the distinctive processes involved in autonomous regulation versus controlled regulation. As Walton, Devlin, and Rushworth (2004) stated, neural mechanisms "differ depending on whether we are told what to do or are able to exercise our volition" (p. 1259). Rather than contradicting theorizing about autonomy, localization efforts support and extend theorizing (Reeve & Lee, 2012), showing, for example, that volitional action involves a great degree of higher order supervisory capacities (e.g., Brass & Haggard, 2007) or the processes underlying intrinsic motivation and its undermining (e.g., Murayama, Matsumoto, Izuma, & Matsumoto, 2010).

When one conceives of an "I," not as a mysterious immaterial force but as a whole organism that is functioning in a relatively unified, integrated way—acting as a synthesis—and in doing so, experiencing self-regulation and autonomy, then one is closer to the organismic view of the self. The self is organization and is opposed not by brain or environment but by controlling forces or contingencies that are inconsistent with its functioning or needs and thus disrupt its tendency toward volitional functioning.

In short, the versions of free will that are being torched all along main street social psychology are highly combustible conceptualizations, well worth burning. Luckily, the volitional and self-regulation capacities humans actually need to thrive are not disconnected from a world, need not be infallible, and certainly require both brain and body. No one has yet made a convincing argument that this type of free will is without import or use.

AUTONOMY: THE FUNCTIONAL FORM OF WILLING IN HUMAN BEINGS

One of the most noteworthy characteristics of the concepts of free will attacked by experimental psychologists is how they are "all or none." Behavior is either free or determined, accurate or illusion, immaterial or "real." These absolutist formulations of volition and self-regulation contrast with our everyday phenomenology of autonomy and self-determination (see, e.g., Pfander, 1908/1967). When acting in real life, people may sometimes feel "totally" free, but more often individuals experience varied degrees of volition or choice. It is in fact the relative autonomy of almost all actions that defines the sense of self and its involvement in intentional behaviors. As de Charms (1968) suggested, the *perceived locus of causality* for actions is a fundamental human sensibility and concern. Behavior that has an *internal perceived locus of causality* is experienced as either self-initiated or self-supported (i.e., as willingly done). Behavior that has an *external perceived locus of causality* is experienced as controlled and sustained by forces outside the phenomenal self (see Ryan & Connell, 1989).

The concept of autonomy as reflecting this relative sense of self-endorsement and self-support of one's actions, versus the sense of one's behaviors as being imposed or alien, has a deep history within philosophical thought. It is reflected in existential phenomenology from Pfander (1908/1967) to Ricoeur (1966), in analytic philosophy from Frankfurt (1971) to Friedman (2003), and in varied Eastern philosophies, within which even Confucian analytics value autonomy as integration (e.g., Cheng, 2004). Philosophical traditions thus have been concerned with the kind of autonomy we do have: autonomy as the reflective endorsement of one's actions, grounded in the congruence between actions and one's abiding values, interests, and priorities. In addition, these traditions make clear that autonomy is not independence. One can be autonomously or heteronomously dependent, interdependent, or independent.

This idea of autonomy is instantiated within the SDT model of self-regulation. Specifically, the regulation of behavior is seen in SDT as varying along a continuum of relative autonomy. At the more heteronomous end of the continuum is behavior that is *externally regulated*: Behaviors are experienced as controlled by an external agent, as when one is doing something to get an externally administered reward or avoid a punishment. To the degree that such behaviors are not backed by the self (i.e., are not internalized), they become reward- or control-dependent. Thus, when external rewards or contingencies lapse, so does maintenance of the behavior. In contrast to external regulation, *introjected regulation* represents regulations that have been partially internalized, with behavior being motivated by avoidance of shame or guilt for failing, or by rewards of self-esteem and ego inflation for success. Introjected regulation often takes the form of *ego involvement* (Nicholls, 1984), in which self-esteem is hinged on attaining certain outcomes, resulting in an internally controlling state (Ryan, 1982). As such, introjected, like external, regulation is relatively controlled.

Moving toward the more autonomous side of this continuum of regulation, we next consider *identified regulation*, in which the individual has consciously identified with the value of a given behavior, accepts this value as his or her own, and feels responsible for its enactment. Identified regulations represent a relatively autonomous form of motivation because people feel volition when acting in accord with abiding values. Closely related to identification is the most autonomous form of extrinsic motivation, *integrated regulation*, in which one not only has identified with the value and regulation of the behavior but also has brought it into coherence with other values and identifications. Integrated extrinsic motivation shares many qualities with intrinsic motivation; people experience both as highly volitional, and these motivations are associated with positive experience. Yet these motivations do differ in that the basis of *intrinsic motivation* is interest—people engage in these behaviors because they are inherently engaging and fascinating—whereas with integrated regulation people perform the behaviors because they are instrumental and viewed as valued and important.

Indeed, intrinsic motivation, doing an activity for its inherent interest, represents a prototype of human proactivity that is experienced as highly autonomous and not a function of anxiety or defense. People are active, curious creatures; they seek out novelty and discrepancy and take pleasure in assimilating. Evolution has liberally endowed us with this growth-oriented potential, which far better characterizes our bases for learning and developing than do secondary motives such as anxiety reduction (Deci & Ryan, 1985; Ryan, Brown, & Creswell, 2007).

THE RELATIVE AUTONOMY CONTINUUM

Clearly, individuals differ in the relative autonomy they experience when enacting different behaviors or life roles. A person may feel externally regulated in one circumstance, yet identified with the importance of his or her role in another. Even the same action can vary depending on how it is incited: The slave who moves the stone for a master feels differently from an inspired sculptor moving her block. People can also have mixed motives, for example, feeling both compelled to help someone in order to avoid guilt (introjection) and also valuing being helpful (identification). Given these complexities, underlying this taxonomy of motives or regulatory processes is a *continuum of autonomy* that is useful in assessing the overall relative autonomy of behavior, when all regulations and motives are considered.

Studies by Ryan and Connell (1989), Vallerand (1997), and others (e.g., Legault, Green-Demers, Grant, & Chung, 2007) have shown that these varied types of motivation exhibit properties consistent with an underlying dimension of autonomy. They form a quasi-simplex pattern in which subscales conceptually closer to each other along the continuum are more highly correlated than those farther apart. The pattern has been supported in domains as varied as sports, religion, school, health care, and politics, among others (e.g., Ryan & Deci, 2000), and by multiple analytical methods (e.g., Roth, Kanat-Maymon, Assor, & Kaplan, 2006).

The relative autonomy of one's behavior within a domain, setting, or time period can be derived from weighting each type of one's relevant motives. In addition, insofar as each type of regulation has a distinct character, each involves different dynamic processes and predicts different outcomes. From these two ideas a large literature has been spawned, providing evidence both for the strong functional association between one's overall relative autonomy and the quality, persistence, and experiential accompaniments of behavior, and for the distinct character and consequences of the different regulatory styles we have conceptualized as lying along the autonomy continuum. Rather than attempt to capture this extensive literature, we simply refer the reader to various comprehensive reviews (e.g., Deci & Ryan, 2012; Ryan & Deci, 2000) and present only a few illustrative examples here.

First, regarding the differentiation of regulatory styles, many studies have shown contrasting outcomes associated with the different regulatory styles (Deci & Ryan, 2000). Given the simplex-like relations between styles, the most interesting comparisons are, however, those between styles relatively close in relative autonomy, such as introjected and identified regulation, which are close on the continuum but different in phenomenology and process. For example, Ryan, Rigby, and King (1993) showed that introjected motivation for religious behavior was either not related or negatively related to well-being, whereas identified regulation was associated with greater wellness. Weinstein and Ryan (2010) obtained similar contrasting results for introjected versus identified motivations for prosocial behavior and also found that recipients of help motivated by a helper's introjection benefited less than those receiving help provided more autonomously. Koestner, Losier, Vallerand, and Carducci (1996) compared people whose involvement in political concerns was based in introjected versus identified forms of internalization. They found identification to be associated with more active political information seeking, having a more complex viewpoint, and being more likely to actually vote, whereas introjection was associated with more vulnerability to persuasion, reliance on others' opinions, and conflicting emotions about election results. In education, Yamauchi and Tanaka (1998) assessed introjection and identification in Japanese elementary students, finding introjection to strongly predict performance goals and identification to strongly predict learning goals.

These are just a few examples of a rich literature relating different motives to different behavioral and wellness outcomes in varied cultures (e.g., Chirkov, Ryan, Kim, & Kaplan, 2003). There are now several hundred studies showing that the more autonomous the regulation of values, practices, and goals, the better one's performance and the greater one's well-being. In line with these findings, researchers have correspondingly shown that controlled regulation is in part associated with lower wellness because of its greater defensiveness (e.g., Hodgins et al., 2010), thus supporting the interplay of human growth and autonomy with control and defense.

SOCIAL CONDITIONS AND AUTONOMOUS MOTIVATION

Having discussed the benefits of autonomous motivation, we now argue that this high-quality form of functioning can be either facilitated or hindered by social conditions. A large literature confirms that *autonomy-supportive contexts*—those that take interest in the other person's perspective, afford choice when possible, provide a meaningful rationale when choice is constrained, and minimize pressure—support autonomous motivation, whereas *controlling contexts*—those that pressure the person to think, feel, or behave in particular ways—foster external and introjected forms of behavioral regulation. In education, for example, studies have shown that controlling contexts are associated with children's memorization of material without understanding it well and without retaining it for long, whereas autonomy-supportive contexts are associated with conceptual understanding that is well maintained over time (Grolnick & Ryan, 1987). In the domain of sport, studies have shown that autonomy-supportive contexts are associated with greater persistence and wellness (Pelletier, Fortier, Vallerand,

& Brière, 2001). Again, this suggests that autonomy is a form of human functioning that can be facilitated by contexts that nurture the process of organismic integration but can also be disrupted by conditions that forestall this process (see Chapter 13, this volume, for more findings on conditions that facilitate or inhibit autonomy). In other words, external and internal controls interfere with the natural guidance system of the organism, thereby diminishing optimal autonomous functioning, whether conscious or nonconscious.

The causal status of these relations has been variously demonstrated but is perhaps best supported through intervention studies. A number of randomized clinical trials based on SDT have demonstrated that the provision of an autonomy-supportive treatment environment increases behaviors such as healthy eating, smoking cessation, and improved dental hygiene, relative to a more controlling environment (Ryan, Patrick, Deci, & Williams, 2008). Further, these and other studies have made clear that the ever-present possibility of individual autonomy and the simultaneous integration of the individual into a larger group or society lies in the process of internalization, which occurs most readily within autonomy-, competence-, and relatedness-supportive contexts.

It is worth noting, however, that even in relatively autonomy-supportive contexts, people will sometimes choose not to internalize a cultural value if it is counter to their deeply held beliefs, a phenomenon that represents an important "pushback" from human nature, one that can keep people from being overrun by a culture with inhumane values. Indeed, it is quite laudatory that segments of the populace in some societies have resisted being controlled by laws or regulations that would compromise their autonomy. In this dialectic, then, we can begin to see the unfolding of history in a narrative of humankind's progressive series of internalizations and resistances to them in the context of historical, cultural evolution. Put differently, when we see the progressive tendencies within cultural groups to move toward liberation—away from slavery and toward rights and capabilities—we can also see a dialectical exchange between what is transmitted and what is fitting. Further, we can understand this as highlighting the importance of human autonomy as a basic human tendency to act in accord with one's interests and values and to resist forces, be they conscious or nonconscious, that coerce people into actions that represent passivity and defense. Surely, there is plenty of passivity and defense, and resisting society's values and demands may take considerable time, but the inherent tendency to internalize fitting mores and beliefs and to resist the less-fitting ones is an aspect of human nature that disconfirms the idea that psychological freedom and autonomy are illusions. In fact, they are real and important not only for individuals but also for groups and cultural evolution.

AUTONOMY AND DEFENSE: BEHAVIORAL AND DUAL PROCESS CONSIDERATIONS

An intriguing new area for research on volition has been inspired by dual process approaches (e.g., Aarts, Custers, & Holland, 2007). In general, these approaches suggest that humans have both explicit (i.e., reflective) and implicit (i.e., nonconscious) motives, attitudes, and feelings that determine behavior and that these different sets of processes may often be inconsistent with each other, a point of considerable import to volition researchers.

In considering dual process issues with respect to autonomy, a series of studies by Legault et al. (2007) is particularly relevant. They measured both implicit and explicit prejudice as well as motives for regulating prejudice using the SDT taxonomy. They found that motivations for regulating prejudice that were more autonomous were associated with lower levels of both explicit and implicit prejudice. In other words, although people have implicit prejudices that can motivate prejudiced behaviors, those who are autonomously committed to not acting in a prejudiced way can more effectively coordinate their implicit and explicit attitudes.

Similarly, Thrash and Elliot (2002) measured implicit and explicit achievement motivation, and found them to be largely uncorrelated, though there was greater implicit–explicit convergence among individuals high in self-determination. As well, Brown and Ryan (2003) found that explicit measures of people's current feelings were uncorrelated with parallel implicit measures (using the Implicit Attitudes Test), but this lack of relation was moderated by mindfulness, such that highly mindful people showed robust positive correlations between implicit and explicit measures of emotions, whereas low mindful people showed a significant negative relation.

How do implicit and explicit discrepancies come about? We believe that a frequent root cause is social control and the suppression it fosters, potentiating defensive incongruence. Weinstein and colleagues (in press) recently investigated *reaction formation* (Freud, 1915/1961), a defense in which individuals adopt beliefs that directly oppose socially unacceptable inner impulses or desires. They examined whether parents who were more controlling fostered implicit–explicit discrepancies regarding a potentially stigmatizing issue—namely, a nonheterosexual orientation—and whether such discrepancies could in turn prompt defensive negative attitudes toward one's own implicit desires that power aggression toward homosexual others. Four studies revealed that (a) when people perceived their parents as controlling, they evidenced more incongruence in self-reported and implicitly assessed sexual orientations; (b) those with greater discrepancies between implicit and explicit orientations endorsed more antigay attitudes; and

(c) perceiving parents as homophobic moderated these relations, such that participants with parents high in control and homophobia displayed the highest incongruence in their explicit and implicit sexual orientations and the highest bias against gay individuals. These data suggest that parental control fosters implicit–explicit incongruence, whereas parental autonomy support fosters congruence regarding sexual orientations. Those who are more congruent are less vulnerable to defensive responding.

Other evidence has shown that autonomy support encourages authentic self-expression (e.g., Lynch, La Guardia, & Ryan, 2009) across cultures, whereas autonomy thwarting fosters conditional self-esteem and suppression of conflicting feelings (Roth, Assor, Niemiec, Ryan, & Deci, 2009). There is also evidence that when people's autonomy is supported with opportunities for true choice, their self-regulation is not mentally depleting, as Baumeister, Bratslavsky, Muraven, and Tice (1998) suggested, whereas if they are controlled or lacking a sense of choice, regulating behavior is depleting (Moller, Deci, & Ryan, 2006).

TERROR MANAGEMENT AND DEFENSIVENESS: IS A DEFENSIVE STRATEGY INEVITABLE?

Although we earlier wrote off certain attacks on free will as irrelevant to our functional conception of autonomy, TMT's portrait of a primarily defensive human existence demands a different kind of consideration. In TMT, there is not a denial of freedom but rather an argument that our most fundamental motivations are defensive in nature. The issue becomes not whether, but how much of our cherished senses of volition, meaning, and purpose are instead nonconsciously driven attempts to run for cover from anxiety. TMT suggests that such defensive processes supply the primary explanation of important cultural pursuits, including meaning making, group affiliations, and other human endeavors.

As reviewed by Greenberg (Chapter 1, this volume), TMT assumes that humans, like other animals, have an instinct for self-preservation, and yet they alone possess the ability to know that their own death is inevitable and forthcoming. This coupling of instinct with awareness creates the circumstance for existential terror. The central human question then becomes how such terror will be managed, and TMT's normative answer is that people employ defenses, both proximal and distal (see Pyszczynski, Greenberg, & Solomon, 1999). Numerous studies have now verified the common reactions to mortality salience (MS) conditions: proximal defense, characterized by death-thought suppression (low accessibility); a subsequent increase in death-related thoughts (high accessibility); and distal defense, characterized by worldview protection (e.g., favoring ingroup members) and self-esteem striving (see Burke, Martens, & Faucher, 2010).

In contrast, SDT maintains that such defensive responding in the face of existential threat is not inevitable. Indeed, Niemiec et al. (2010) argued that *mindfulness*—a receptive, nonjudgmental state of mind associated with greater autonomy (Brown & Ryan, 2003; see also Chapter 14, this volume)—would moderate these defensive responses following MS. They conducted seven experiments showing that whereas less mindful individuals showed higher worldview defense under MS, more mindful individuals showed no greater worldview defense or self-esteem striving under MS than in control conditions. Further, more mindful individuals showed higher death-thought accessibility immediately following MS, which then decreased after a delay, suggesting that they processed the mortality cues more openly and completely in the moment and then let go of the experience without engaging in defense. In short, even robust TMT effects are not inevitable; when mindful, people are less defensive and more autonomous.

As existential thought has always maintained, people can, through being more openly aware and developing values that are more integrated, be resistant to influences that erode autonomy. At the same time, it is important to recognize that not all automatic or nonconscious actions are necessarily controlled and defensive; they can be congruent and consistent with autonomous functioning, as many SDT-based priming studies have shown.

"CAN VERSUS DO" AND THE BIAS OF EXPERIMENTAL SOCIAL PSYCHOLOGY

We began this essay by remarking that social psychology has disseminated a portrait of humanity as weak, defensive, and lacking in volitional capacities. This viewpoint derives support from experimental studies showing that people can be fooled about volition, can be deceived as to their degree of control, can be threatened and exhibit defensive reactions, and can be cued to behave without intention or self-endorsement. But one cannot logically leap from "can" to "do" (McCall, 1977). Just because people can be derailed does not mean they are always off track.

Experimental methods are designed to manipulate behavior—that is, to control it. When experiments succeed, investigators are often tempted to think that the behavior similarly and always occurs through such manipulations or controls outside of the experimental setting. It is a tempting but illogical leap. Thus, because some people were fooled into thinking their intentions were causal when they were not, it was concluded that people's intentions are never causal. Because MS can produce defensive, affiliation-seeking responses in the lab, some suggest that group affiliations are merely defensive responses to the terror of mortality. Obviously, such conclusions do not follow from the data, and experimental studies alone cannot address how much "can" translates into "do." Even when behavior can be controlled, as indicated by experiments, the same behavior may also occur through varied other processes, including intrinsic ones that were not revealed in such experiments.

In fact, we have long been studying experimental evidence of vulnerabilities (for example, the undermining of intrinsic motivation by rewards; e.g., Deci, Koestner, & Ryan, 1999) or the fostering of introjects through contingent regard (e.g., Roth et al., 2009), but we have also argued consistently that these vulnerabilities need to be integrated into a fuller view of an active, and actively coping, human being. Within SDT, our model portrays an intrinsically motivated, integrative, human nature, which in times of threat or low mindfulness is vulnerable to non-self-determined behavior. In addition, we see self-determination or autonomy not as an "all or none" phenomenon but as an ongoing experience of relative autonomy in which one more or less chooses and stands behind one's actions. The fact that humans can be both alienated and free, both controlled and autonomous, is an aspect of our existential condition that cannot be reasoned away, only acknowledged and used as a basis for authentic behavior.

REFERENCES

Aarts, H., Custers, R., & Holland, R. W. (2007). The nonconscious cessation of goal pursuit: When goals and negative affect are coactivated. *Journal of Personality and Social Psychology, 92*, 165–178. doi:10.1037/0022-3514.92.2.165

Bargh, J. A. (2008). Free will is un-natural. In J. Baer, J. Kaufman, & R. F. Baumeister (Eds.), *Are we free? Psychology and free will* (pp. 128–154). New York, NY: Oxford University Press.

Baumeister, R. F., Bratslavsky, E., Muraven, M., & Tice, D. M. (1998). Ego depletion: Is the active self a limited resource? *Journal of Personality and Social Psychology, 74*, 1252–1265. doi:10.1037/0022-3514.74.5.1252

Brass, M., & Haggard, P. (2007). To do or not to do: The neural signature of self-control. *The Journal of Neuroscience, 27*, 9141–9145. doi:10.1523/JNEUROSCI.0924-07.2007

Brown, K. W., & Ryan, R. M. (2003). The benefits of being present: Mindfulness and its role in psychological well-being. *Journal of Personality and Social Psychology, 84*, 822–848. doi:10.1037/0022-3514.84.4.822

Burke, B. L., Martens, A., & Faucher, E. H. (2010). Two decades of terror management theory: A meta-analysis of mortality salience research. *Personality and Social Psychology Review, 14*, 155–195. doi:10.1177/1088868309352321

Cheng, C.-Y. (2004). A theory of Confucian selfhood: Self-cultivation and free will in Confucian philosophy. In K.-L. Shun & D. B. Wong (Eds.), *Confucian ethics: A comparative study of self, autonomy and community* (pp. 124–147). New York, NY: Cambridge University Press. doi:10.1017/CBO9780511606960.008

Chirkov, V., Ryan, R. M., Kim, Y., & Kaplan, U. (2003). Differentiating autonomy from individualism and independence: A self-determination theory perspective on internalization of cultural orientations and well-being. *Journal of Personality and Social Psychology, 84,* 97–110. doi:10.1037/0022-3514.84.1.97

de Charms, R. (1968). *Personal causation.* New York, NY: Academic Press.

Deci, E. L., Koestner, R., & Ryan, R. M. (1999). A meta-analytic review of experiments examining the effects of extrinsic rewards on intrinsic motivation. *Psychological Bulletin, 125,* 627–668. doi:10.1037/0033-2909.125.6.627

Deci, E. L., & Ryan, R. M. (1985). *Intrinsic motivation and self-determination in human behavior.* New York, NY: Plenum Press.

Deci, E. L., & Ryan, R. M. (2000). The "what" and "why" of goal pursuits: Human needs and the self-determination of behavior. *Psychological Inquiry, 11,* 227–268. doi:10.1207/S15327965PLI1104_01

Deci, E. L., & Ryan, R. M. (2012). Motivation, personality, and development within embedded social contexts: An overview of self-determination theory. In R. M. Ryan (Ed.), *Oxford handbook of human motivation* (pp. 85–110). New York, NY: Oxford University Press.

Frankfurt, H. (1971). Freedom of the will and the concept of person. *The Journal of Philosophy, 68,* 5–20. doi:10.2307/2024717

Freud, S. (1961). The ego and the id. In J. Strachey (Ed. & Trans.), *The standard edition of the complete works of Sigmund Freud* (Vol. 19, pp. 3–66). London, England: Hogarth Press. (Original work published 1923)

Freud, S. (1961). Repression. In J. Strachey (Ed. & Trans.), *The standard edition of the complete works of Sigmund Freud* (Vol. 14, pp. 143–160). London, England: Hogarth Press. (Original work published 1915)

Friedman, M. (2003). *Autonomy, gender, politics.* New York, NY: Oxford University Press. doi:10.1093/0195138503.001.0001

Greenberg, J., Solomon, S., & Pyszczynski, T. (1997). Terror management theory of self-esteem and social behavior: Empirical assessments and conceptual refinements. In M. P. Zanna (Ed.), *Advances in experimental social psychology* (Vol. 29, pp. 61–139). San Diego, CA: Academic Press.

Grolnick, W. S., & Ryan, R. M. (1987). Autonomy in children's learning: An experimental and individual difference investigation. *Journal of Personality and Social Psychology, 52,* 890–898. doi:10.1037/0022-3514.52.5.890

Hodgins, H. S., Weisbust, K. S., Weinstein, N., Shiffman, S., Miller, A., Coombs, G., & Adair, K. C. (2010). The cost of self-protection: Threat response and performance as a function of autonomous and controlled motivations. *Personality and Social Psychology Bulletin, 36,* 1101–1114. doi:10.1177/0146167210375618

Koestner, R., Losier, G. F., Vallerand, R. J., & Carducci, D. (1996). Identified and introjected forms of political internalization: Extending self-determination theory. *Journal of Personality and Social Psychology, 70*, 1025–1036. doi:10.1037/ 0022-3514.70.5.1025

Legault, L., Green-Demers, I., Grant, P., & Chung, J. (2007). On the self-regulation of implicit and explicit prejudice: A self-determination theory perspective. *Personality and Social Psychology Bulletin, 33*, 732–749. doi:10.1177/0146167206298564

Libet, B. (2004). *Mind time: The temporal factor in consciousness.* Cambridge, MA: Harvard University Press.

Lynch, M. F., La Guardia, J. G., & Ryan, R. M. (2009). On being yourself in different cultures: Ideal and actual self-concept, autonomy support, and well-being in China, Russia, and the United States. *The Journal of Positive Psychology, 4*, 290–304. doi:10.1080/17439760902933765

Mackenzie, C. (2000). Imagining oneself otherwise. In C. Mackenzie & N. Stoljar (Eds.), *Relational autonomy* (pp. 124–150). New York, NY: Oxford University Press.

McCall, R. B. (1977). Challenges to a science of developmental psychology. *Child Development, 48*, 333–344. doi:10.2307/1128626

Moller, A. C., Deci, E. L., & Ryan, R. M. (2006). Choice and ego-depletion: The moderating role of autonomy. *Personality and Social Psychology Bulletin, 32*, 1024–1036. doi:10.1177/0146167206288008

Murayama, K., Matsumoto, M. Izuma, K. & Matsumoto, K. (2010). Neural basis of the undermining effect of monetary reward on intrinsic motivation. *Proceedings of the National Academy of Sciences, 107*, 20911–20916.

Nicholls, J. G. (1984). Achievement motivation: Conceptions of ability, subjective experience, task choice, and performance. *Psychological Review, 91*, 328–346. doi:10.1037/0033-295X.91.3.328

Niemiec, C. P., Brown, K. W., Kashdan, T. B., Cozzolino, P. J., Breen, W. E., Levesque, C. S., & Ryan, R. M. (2010). Being present in the face of existential threat: The role of trait mindfulness in reducing defensive responses to mortality salience. *Journal of Personality and Social Psychology, 99*, 344–365. doi:10.1037/a0019388

Pelletier, L. G., Fortier, M. S., Vallerand, R. J., & Brière, N. M. (2001). Associations among perceived autonomy support, forms of self-regulation, and persistence: A prospective study. *Motivation and Emotion, 25*, 279–306. doi:10.1023/ A:1014805132406

Pfander, A. (1967). *Phenomenology of willing and motivation* (H. Spiegelberg, Trans.). Evanston, IL: Northwestern University Press. (Original work published 1908)

Pinker, S. (2002). *The blank slate: The modern denial of human nature.* New York, NY: Viking.

Pyszczynski, T., Greenberg, J., & Solomon, S. (1999). A dual process model of defense against conscious and unconscious death-related thoughts: An extension of terror management theory. *Psychological Review, 106*, 835–845. doi:10.1037/0033-295X.106.4.835

Reeve, J., & Lee, W. (2012). Neuroscience and human motivation. In R. M. Ryan (Ed.), *Oxford handbook of human motivation* (pp. 365–380). New York, NY: Oxford University Press.

Ricoeur, P. (1966). *Freedom and nature: The voluntary and the involuntary* (E. Kohák, Trans.). Chicago, IL: Northwestern University Press.

Roth, G., Assor, A., Niemiec, C. P., Ryan, R. M., & Deci, E. L. (2009). The emotional and academic consequences of parental conditional regard: Comparing conditional positive regard, conditional negative regard, and autonomy support as parenting practices. *Developmental Psychology, 45*, 1119–1142. doi:10.1037/a0015272

Roth, G., Kanat-Maymon, Y., Assor, A., & Kaplan, H. (2006). Assessing the experience of autonomy in new cultures and contexts. *Motivation and Emotion, 30*, 361–372. doi:10.1007/s11031-006-9052-7

Ryan, R. M. (1982). Control and information in the intrapersonal sphere: An extension of cognitive evaluation theory. *Journal of Personality and Social Psychology, 43*, 450–461. doi:10.1037/0022-3514.43.3.450

Ryan, R. M., Brown, K. W., & Creswell, J. D. (2007). How integrative is attachment theory? Unpacking the meaning and significance of felt security. *Psychological Inquiry, 18*, 177–182. doi:10.1080/10478400701512778

Ryan, R. M., & Connell, J. P. (1989). Perceived locus of causality and internalization: Examining reasons for acting in two domains. *Journal of Personality and Social Psychology, 57*, 749–761. doi:10.1037/0022-3514.57.5.749

Ryan, R. M., & Deci, E. L. (2000). Self-determination theory and the facilitation of intrinsic motivation, social development, and well-being. *American Psychologist, 55*, 68–78. doi:10.1037/0003-066X.55.1.68

Ryan, R. M., Patrick, H., Deci, E. L., & Williams, G. C. (2008). Facilitating health behaviour change and its maintenance: Interventions based on self-determination theory. *The European Health Psychologist, 10*, 2–5.

Ryan, R. M., Rigby, S., & King, K. (1993). Two types of religious internalization and their relations to religious orientations and mental health. *Journal of Personality and Social Psychology, 65*, 586–596. doi:10.1037/0022-3514.65.3.586

Thrash, T. M., & Elliot, A. J. (2002). Implicit and self-attributed achievement motives: Concordance and predictive validity. *Journal of Personality, 70*, 729–756. doi:10.1111/1467-6494.05022

Vallerand, R. J. (1997). Toward a hierarchical model of intrinsic and extrinsic motivation. In M. P. Zanna (Ed.), *Advances in experimental social psychology* (Vol. 29, pp. 271–360). San Diego, CA: Academic Press.

Walton, M. E., Devlin, J. T., & Rushworth, M. F. S. (2004). Interactions between decision making and performance monitoring within prefrontal cortex. *Nature Neuroscience, 7*, 1259–1265. doi:10.1038/nn1339

Warnock, M. (1970). *Existentialism*. Oxford, England: Oxford University Press.

Wegner, D. M. (2008). Self is magic. In J. Baer, J. Kaufman, & R. F. Baumeister (Eds.), *Are we free? Psychology and free will* (pp. 226–247). New York, NY: Oxford University Press.

Weinstein, N., Ryan, W. S., DeHaan, C., Przybyski, A., Legate, N., & Ryan, R. M. (in press). Parental autonomy support and discrepancies between implicit and explicit sexual identities: Dynamics of self-acceptance and defense. *Journal of Personality and Social Psychology*.

Weinstein, N., & Ryan, R. M. (2010). When helping helps: Autonomous motivation for prosocial behavior and its influence on well-being for the helper and recipient. *Journal of Personality and Social Psychology, 98*, 222–244. doi:10.1037/a0016984

Yamauchi, H., & Tanaka, K. (1998). Relations of autonomy, self-referenced beliefs and self-regulated learning among Japanese children. *Psychological Reports, 82*, 803–816.

13

CONDITIONAL REGARD IN CLOSE RELATIONSHIPS

YANIV KANAT-MAYMON, GUY ROTH, AVI ASSOR, AND ABIRA REIZER

Humanistic perspectives assume that people are by nature autonomy- and freedom- seeking (e.g., Deci & Ryan, 1985; Erikson, 1950; Rogers, 1951; see also Chapter 12, this volume). Yet, these theories also assume that this basic tendency is inhibited when social contexts impose significant psychological costs on individuals' pursuit of autonomy. Examples of these costs are provided in Fromm's (1941) well-known volume *Escape from Freedom*. Fromm argued that freedom from traditional societal bonds gives people a new feeling of autonomy. At the same time, once the primary bonds that provide reassurance and security are severed, people face the world feeling alone, isolated, and anxious. This alienation from place and community, along with the insecurities and fears it entails, helps to explain why some people escape from freedom, thereby becoming an indistinguishable part of a uniform mass or submitting themselves to the rule of domineering authorities or totalitarian institutions. At the same time, Fromm acknowledged that one can take a different path and develop autonomy and authenticity through the experience of love, meaningful self-expressive work, and genuine expression of emotions.

In Chapter 12 of this volume, Ryan and coauthors use self-determination theory (SDT; Ryan & Deci, 2000) to analyze the core human tendency for autonomy seeking and the ways in which specific social contexts can inhibit this tendency and drive people away from freedom and autonomy. Assor, Kaplan, Kanat-Maymon, and Roth (2005) proposed that it is useful to distinguish between two types of contexts that can inhibit autonomy: direct controlling contexts and indirect controlling contexts. *Direct controlling contexts* inhibit autonomy by explicitly making clear that autonomy seeking is painful (e.g., imposing physical punishment, denying privileges, yelling, public humiliation). *Indirect controlling contexts* use means for inhibiting autonomy that are more subtle and somewhat less painful, such as contingent praise and guilt induction.

The present chapter focuses on one indirect controlling process—conditional regard—that until recently received little attention in empirical research despite its autonomy-inhibiting nature and its high, though often subtle, emotional costs. The concept of conditional regard was proposed by Rogers (1951) several decades ago. *Conditional regard* on the part of an agent (e.g., parent, relationship partner) is defined as providing more acceptance and affection than usual when a person displays desired behavior and withholding attention and affection when the person displays undesired behavior. Conditional regard is frequently used and widely endorsed as a socialization practice, although its effectiveness has been questioned (e.g., Assor & Roth, 2005; Assor, Roth, & Deci, 2004; Roth, Assor, Niemiec, Ryan, & Deci, 2009). In this chapter, we clarify the concept of conditional regard as a socialization practice and define two forms of conditional regard. We then review research evidence concerning the detrimental effects of these two forms of conditional regard on motivational regulation, performance quality, and well-being. Finally, we present unpublished data on the consequences of conditional regard in close relationships using hierarchical linear modeling techniques.

CONDITIONAL REGARD

In this chapter, we differentiate between two kinds of conditional regard: positive and negative. *Conditional positive regard* is the offering of acceptance, warmth, and respect only when another person fulfills a particular expectation, desire, or requirement; it conveys the message "I will approve of, like, or favor you only if you do this or act in this way." *Conditional negative regard* involves withholding affection and esteem when others do not behave according to a specific expectation or demand. Viewed from a behaviorist perspective, conditional regard is the contingent administration of reinforcements and punishments that are expected to increase the likelihood of desired behaviors (Gewirtz & Pelaez-Nogueras, 1991; McDowell, 1988).

Indeed, early research that examined the consequences of conditional regard found a link between parental conditional regard and children's subsequent enactment of targeted behaviors (Sears, Maccoby, & Levin, 1957).

However, other psychological theorists have presented less favorable views of conditional regard as a socialization technique. Rogers (1951) claimed that conditional regard undermines self-esteem and interferes with personal exploration and self-regulation. Psychoanalytic object relations theorists have argued that when children learn that they are not unconditionally loved, the desired instrumental behavior may persist but the children's satisfaction with a momentary reward is fleeting and precarious because it does not result in the unconditional love they deeply desire (Miller, 1981).

More recently, research on constructs related to conditional regard, such as love withdrawal (e.g., Elliot & Thrash, 2004) and psychological control (e.g., Barber, Stolz, & Olsen, 2005), has indicated that these socialization techniques are associated with depression, maladaptive perfectionism, delinquency, and substance abuse. However, conditional regard differs from love withdrawal and psychological control. Conditional regard includes both withdrawing attention and affection when one fails to act as expected (conditional negative regard) and increased affection and attention when one does act as expected (conditional positive regard). Moreover, conditional regard as operationalized by Assor et al. (2004) is a domain-specific practice, whereas love withdrawal is a general practice. Last, conditional negative regard is just one of three components that constitute the concept of psychological control (Barber et al., 2005).

CONDITIONAL REGARD AND SELF-DETERMINATION THEORY

In our research, we have examined correlates and consequences of conditional regard using SDT's conception of behavioral internalization (Deci & Ryan, 2000; Ryan & Deci, 2000; see also Chapter 12, this volume). Specifically, we have been interested in the possibility that conditional regard leads to a problematic type of internalization, introjection, which arouses anxiety and leads to rigid and low-quality performance in the behavioral domain on which regard was contingent.

SDT is based on the distinction between intrinsic and extrinsic motivation (see Chapter 12, this volume). *Intrinsic motivation* involves performing an activity because the activity itself is interesting and engaging. This kind of motivation supports the development of autonomy because it is self-sustaining. *Extrinsic motivation* involves performing an activity because it leads to some desired external payoff, and the actor infers that the activity itself is not sufficiently interesting to be done without extrinsic reward. Research has shown that performing activities for external rewards feels controlled, or elicited, rather than autonomous (e.g., Deci, Koestner, & Ryan, 1999).

According to SDT, the degree to which behaviors are experienced as autonomous versus controlled depends on the degree to which their motivational foundations have been internalized. SDT suggests that for an extrinsically motivated behavior to become more autonomous, that behavior's underlying regulation and value must be internalized. The theory further suggests that various types of internalization or motivation differ in the degree to which they have been internalized, and therefore differ in the degree to which the resulting behaviors are autonomous rather than controlled (Ryan & Connell, 1989). When the motivation for an activity has not been internalized, regulation is said to be external. The behavior is enacted compliantly and is experienced as controlled. Such behavior is regulated externally by threats of punishment or offers of material rewards.

SDT distinguishes among three types of internalized motivation: introjection, identification, and integration. *Introjection* involves "taking in" a value but not accepting it as one's own. Instead, one applies to oneself the contingencies of approval or worth that were previously applied by others. This causes the individual to feel an inner compulsion to behave, with his or her self-esteem being contingent on the behavior. Behaviors regulated by introjection, although more autonomous than behaviors regulated externally, are still quite controlled and represent the least autonomous form of internalization.

A more complete form of internalization is referred to as *identified* regulation. Here, the individual has identified with the importance of the activity for himself or herself and thus performs the behavior autonomously, even though he or she does not find the activity interesting. Finally, when that identification has been reciprocally assimilated with other aspects of the individual's self, the regulation is considered to be *integrated*. Integration results in the most autonomous kind of extrinsic motivation.

We posit that using conditional regard as a socializing practice leads to four kinds of negative consequences: (a) introjected regulation, (b) rigid and low-quality performance, (c) diminished well-being, and (d) negative affect in relation to the conditioning agent.

CONDITIONAL REGARD AND INTROJECTED REGULATION

When parental attention or affection is contingent on a child's conformity with expectations, he or she may feel compelled to behave in accord with parental expectations so as to maintain or even enhance parental regard and affection. This practice entwines a child's own self-regard with parental regard. STD conceptualizes actions motivated by esteem from others or one-self as internalized through introjection. Parental conditional regard tends to be converted into conditional self-esteem, which is the core of introjected regulation (Assor et al., 2004; Ryan, Deci, & Grolnick, 1995). The intro-jected parental expectations may be experienced as internal pressure, which restricts the child's sense of choice or room for deliberation. Consequently, the driving force behind behaviors rooted in parental regard is to minimize shame and guilt and/or to increase self-esteem.

Empirical studies of introjection found that American college students who experienced parental regard as contingent on academic achievement, athletic success, prosocial behavior, or suppression of negative affect reported feeling an internal pressure to behave in ways that would fulfill parental expectations with no sense of identification or choice (Assor et al., 2004). This research was then extended to the domain of religious socialization and found that in the domain of religious practice, parents' use of conditional regard to promote a child's observance of religious practices was associated with introjected internalization of the religious practices by students attending a modern orthodox Jewish school (Assor, Cohen-Melayev, Kaplan, & Friedman, 2005).

Roth et al. (2009) then differentiated between the effects of condi-tional positive regard as opposed to conditional negative regard when study-ing Jewish Israeli high school students' regulation of negative emotions and academic achievement. Conditional positive regard was associated with introjected internalization, and conditional negative regard was associated with greater anger and resistance toward parents and failed to result in any kind of internalization.

Another series of studies, by Shavit-Miller and Assor (2003), explored associations between parental conditional regard in three domains (emotional suppression, academic achievement, and prosocial behavior) and offspring's emotional states among college students in Israel and the United States. A qualitative analysis of open-ended questionnaire responses revealed that pat-terns of parental expectations that were more introjected were characteris-tic of participants whose parents were described as using more conditional regard to encourage internalization of expectations. This was especially the case for women, who often described feelings of estrangement from goals on which their parents' regard depended. These feelings were nevertheless asso-ciated with a sense of obligation to pursue the goals to procure parental love. Evidence also suggested that offspring experiencing high levels of parental conditional regard engaged in little reflection on the goals and values that parents attempted to promote and transmit.

Young women's vulnerability to parental conditional regard may be due to early gender socialization, with women's sense of self-worth and well-being

being heavily dependent on the satisfaction of relatedness needs. Women may be less able to tolerate withdrawal of parental love and may feel more responsible for parental suffering when their goals for their offspring are rejected. As a result, women may be more likely to introject parental expectations that they do not necessarily identify with, while feeling angrier and more conflicted concerning the introjected parental expectations (Assor, Kaplan, et al., 2005).

Together, the research findings suggest that using conditional regard as a socializing practice may lead to an introjected pattern of behavioral regulation that is experienced as pressured. Advocates of the use of conditional regard might argue that the process of introjection is simply a step toward a more integrated regulation. However, the research results provide no support for this position. Participants in the studies reviewed here were university students who recalled examples of conditional regard from their childhood and adolescence yet continued to display a pressured form of introjected regulation years later. Moreover, the effects of conditional regard were always accompanied by negative emotional states, suggesting that behaviors regulated by conditional regard had not been integrated in a growth-enhancing way.

CONDITIONAL REGARD AND RIGID AND LOW-QUALITY PERFORMANCE

SDT assumes that parental conditional regard leads to introjected motivation to enact the behavior on which the parental approval hinged (see Chapter 12, this volume). For example, if a child perceives that parental approval depends on success in sports, then the child may introject the goal of athletic success and devote time and energy to that goal. Ultimately, though, because investment in sports is a means of acquiring or maintaining self-esteem, the child's engagement in sports is accompanied by anxiety, feelings of pressure, and fear of failing. These negative emotions are likely to result in a constricted and uncreative mode of engagement (e.g., Roth et al., 2009).

The concern with attaining positive regard through success in a particular area of activity may cause the child to focus exclusively on winning and thereby neglect other aspects of the situation as well as other lines of activity. Moreover, the child may stick to known methods rather than taking a chance on creative or personally suitable methods. In addition, the weight placed on success may cause needless practicing (repeated training even though one knows the drill), which Covington (1992) described as *overstriving*. The relation between parental conditional regard and rigid, low-quality performance has been examined in multiple domains, as we now describe.

Academic Achievement

In two studies involving Israeli high school students, Roth et al. (2009) found that those who described their parents as encouraging academic success with conditional positive regard were perceived by teachers as exhibiting *grade-focused engagement*. This type of engagement is characterized by studying only material that may appear on a test, feeling hurt and distressed if one fails an assignment or a test, and arguing with the teacher about grades. Teacher ratings also showed that there was a negative association between positive parental conditional regard and interest-focused engagement. This type of engagement is based on an inclination to study and spend time and effort on topics and materials that are not being tested. As would be expected, feeling internally compelled to study hard (i.e., having introjected the importance of academic work) mediated the effect of positive parental conditional regard on grade-focused studying. The narrow and rigid engagement associated with positive parental conditional regard was further explored by Assor and Tal (in press). *Narrow overstriving* is characterized by a tendency to invest a lot of time in studying what is already known about the subject, which causes students to unnecessarily give up activities they really enjoy. Narrow overstriving was predicted by positive parental conditional regard, and this association was mediated by grandiose and narcissistic feelings following success and, to a lesser degree, by shame following failure.

Parental negative conditional regard in the academic domain was associated with lack of academic achievement and was unrelated to grade-focused engagement and interest-focused engagement (Roth et al., 2009). Thus, this parental practice appears to be particularly problematic in that it does not promote any kind of investment.

Emotion Regulation

Children who perceive parental regard as contingent on suppressing or hiding negative emotions are inclined to demonstrate controlling and suppressive methods of emotion regulation. In addition, avoiding one's own negative emotions tends to restrict a person's ability to identify emotions in other people. Moreover, the ability to listen and show empathy in the face of painful emotional disclosures in close relationships may be compromised. Roth et al. (2009) found that children who perceived their parent as making positive regard contingent on successful suppression of fear or anger reported that they often felt flooded and overwhelmed by negative emotions, making it difficult for them to engage in daily tasks when feeling angry or fearful. In other words, this kind of emotion regulation is actually conducive to dysregulation. Parental conditional positive regard was also associated with a suppressive regulatory style, which involves suppressing and concealing one's negative emotions. Another study by Roth and Assor (2003) yielded similar results. Although they did not distinguish between conditional positive and conditional negative regard, they still found that perceived parental conditional regard was associated with nonoptimal approaches to emotion regulation.

Eilot, Assor, and Roth (2006) obtained similar results in studies of Israeli high school students. They found a positive association between reports of parental conditional positive regard and suppressive and dysregulatory forms of anger regulation, as well as a positive association between parental conditional negative regard and emotional dysregulation.

In addition, Roth and Assor (2003) found that parental conditional regard was negatively associated with the ability to recognize feelings in facial expressions of emotions and in stories. Furthermore, parental conditional regard predicted poor ability to support a romantic partner, and this association was mediated by poor emotion recognition. In another study, Roth and Assor (2010) explored the association between parental conditional regard and empathy among kindergarten children. This study was based on parental reports on their own practice of conditional regard toward their child and an emotion regulation task completed by the children, as opposed to retrospective self-reports by the offspring as was used in previous studies. The findings revealed negative associations between both negative and positive parental conditional regard and children's ability to feel sadness, recognize sadness in others, and empathize with and help a child who looked sad.

Prosocial Behavior

The final domain to be discussed in this section is parental conditional regard as a goad to prosocial behavior. We expected that children who perceive parental love as contingent on assisting others would be disposed to help but would show relatively little empathy and sensitivity toward those they assisted. Assor et al. (2004) found that offspring's perceptions of parents' regard being contingent on helping others were associated with introjected motivation for helping others (indicated mainly by a sense of internal compulsion to help), which in turn predicted frequent (self-reported) helping. Roth (2008) studied the association between parental conditional regard and self- versus other-oriented prosocial tendencies among Israeli college students. *Self-oriented prosocial helping* was defined as helping behavior enacted for the sake of others' approval and appreciation, whereas *other-oriented prosocial helping* was defined as helping done while focusing on others' needs and preferences. Parental conditional regard was associated with self-oriented prosocial behavior but not with other-oriented helping behavior.

Overall, research suggests that conditional regard leads to restricted and impaired performance in the domains in which parental regard is contingent on a child's performance, demonstrating that although parental conditional regard encourages the fulfillment of parental expectations, the child's performance may be maladaptive, uncomfortable, and in some cases pressured and resented.

CONDITIONAL REGARD AND DIMINISHED WELL-BEING

Parental conditional regard causes children's self-esteem to depend on fulfillment of parental expectations. This approach to parenting tends to induce anxiety and perceived pressure or compulsion. The dependence of self-esteem on performing desired behaviors may result in fluctuations in self-esteem, or unstable self-esteem (Kernis & Paradise, 2002) because satisfaction is likely to be fragile and short-lived. That is, satisfaction lasts only until the pressure of the next demand (actual or imagined) is felt, and the failure to attain a particular outcome may lead to feelings of guilt and shame because failure is interpreted as implying unworthiness.

Four studies have supported the hypothesis that conditional regard is associated with negative affect and diminished well-being. Assor et al. (2004) found that successful achievement of parental expectations in the domains of academic achievement, sports, and negative emotion suppression was followed by short-lived satisfaction and then feelings of disappointment or emptiness. Furthermore, when participants did not achieve athletic success or were unable to suppress negative affect, they felt guilty and ashamed. The idea that fluctuating self-worth results from parental conditional regard was supported by Assor et al. (2004) in four different domains. In the study that focused on the academic domain, they found that parental conditional regard was related to poor self-esteem.

Assor and Tal (in press) showed that shame following academic failure was linked to both positive and negative parental conditional regard in the academic domain. Shame also mediated the effects of conditional positive and negative regard on less adaptive modes of academic coping. In an unpublished lexical decision study, Kanat-Maymon and Roth (2011) found that participants who perceived their mothers as high, compared with low, on academic conditional regard were quicker to perceive stress-related words (e.g., anxiety, shame) but not other kinds of negative words. This suggests that when facing an academic task, children who experienced conditional regard are more anxious and perturbed by the thought of shamefully failing. Another study, this one by Shavit-Miller and Assor (2003), found that confusion, guilt, low self-worth, meaninglessness, and confusion about one's purpose in life are often felt by students whose parents practiced conditional regard.

CONDITIONAL REGARD AND RELATIONSHIP QUALITY

People's use of conditional regard to pressure others to behave in a certain way can arouse negative feelings toward the agent and undermine relationship quality. Using conditional regard may cause anger and resentment toward the agent because it undermines the sense of autonomy and indicates that the agent does not trust or does not believe that one will behave in a desired way on one's own. Assor et al. (2004) found that American college students' perception of parental conditional regard in four different domains was related to perception of their parents as disapproving and to resentment toward the parents. In a subsequent study, Roth et al. (2009) studied Jewish Israeli high school students and found that perceptions of parental conditional negative regard in the domains of academic achievement and emotion regulation were associated with resentment toward the parent.

In a recent project, we extended the previous studies by testing the consequences of conditional regard in egalitarian relationships, such as relationships with peers and romantic partners, and by using a variety of measures of relationship quality (Kanat-Maymon, Roth, & Reizer, 2011). In one such study, we examined the effect of conditional negative regard on romantic relationship quality among married participants (N = 144). Perceived conditional negative regard by a romantic partner was associated with relationship dissatisfaction, as indicated by lower levels of directly assessed relationship satisfaction and less direct measures such as inclusion of other in the self, doubts regarding the relationship, and a sense of entrapment. Moreover, participants who perceived their partners as providing conditional affection reported that they were less inclined to disclose personal information and listen empathically to their partner, and more inclined to avoid conflicts with their partner.

These findings align well with previous research on the parent–child relationship. Roth et al. (2009) found that negative conditional regard was associated with resentment toward the parent, and Chapman and Zahn-Waxler (1982) found that love withdrawal was related to avoiding socializing agents. Conditional negative regard involves withdrawal of affection and attention when the other does not comply with one's expectations. This practice is experienced as highly punitive and controlling and thus as uncaring, disaffirming, and coercive. These feelings of rejection are expected to lead to relationship dissatisfaction, and our study did demonstrate the harmful effects of conditional negative regard on romantic relationship quality. The study also indicated that the harmful effects go beyond specific feelings of anger and resentment to the perception of the relationship itself as less satisfying and intimate and to the expenditure of less effort to benefit the partner and the relationship (Kanat-Maymon et al., 2011).

To systematically explore the effect of conditional positive regard on relationship quality with a range of significant others, we conducted two additional studies. The first study assessed the effects of conditional positive regard in four different relationships (with mother, father, romantic partner, and best friend; $N = 123$). The data from this study were hierarchically nested because participants rated multiple relationship partners on various measures. Thus, relationships were not independent, and shared variance across relationships on the various measures was expected. The important questions for us were, first, to what extent the within-person variance was systematic, and second, whether it could explain relationship quality across relationship types.

To answer the first question, we estimated, using hierarchical linear modeling (HLM), the degree of within-person variance in perceived conditional positive regard relative to the between-person variance. The results indicated that 57% of the variance in conditional positive regard was due to the within-person level, whereas 43% of the variance was due to the between-person level. To answer the second question, we constructed a relationship-level HLM equation that predicted relationship quality within each relationship from perceived conditional positive regard within that relationship, controlling for the effects of relationship type.

Results of the within-person HLM analyses indicated a significant effect of perceived conditional positive regard. Thus, perceived conditional positive regard predicted a decrease in (a) relationship satisfaction, (b) feelings of closeness, and (c) secure attachment to the relationship partner. These findings supported the SDT notion regarding the harmful consequences of perceived conditional positive regard and demonstrated that to some extent relationship quality is an inverse function of the amount of perceived conditional positive regard.

A limitation of this study was the exploration of the association between conditional positive regard and relationship quality without considering the potential effect of conditional negative regard. Thus, in a second study we examined the associations between both forms of conditional regard and relationship quality in daily life using a diary methodology. This method allowed us to capture day-to-day fluctuations in conditional regard and relationship satisfaction at the between- and within-person levels simultaneously. The analysis at the between-person level explored the qualities of conditional regard that vary among people, whereas the within-person or day-level analysis assessed fluctuations around a person's baseline.

Based on previous studies demonstrating the harmful effects of conditional negative regard on relationship quality, we expected that conditional negative regard would be associated with lower relationship satisfaction at both between- and within-person levels. However, because conditional positive regard is less harmful than conditional negative regard, we expected it to be a weaker predictor of relationship quality when controlling for conditional negative regard.

A sample of 50 undergraduate students completed questionnaires that included the trait-level measures of their partner's conditional positive and negative regard. During the following week, participants began completing a short online daily diary for 14 days, measuring partner's daily conditional positive and negative regard, as well as daily relationship satisfaction.

To examine the association between relationship conditional regard and satisfaction, we constructed a daily-level HLM equation that predicted relationship satisfaction each day from perceived conditional positive and negative regard that day while controlling for the effects of weekends and relationship satisfaction on the previous day. Weekends were controlled because several investigators have noted that people tend to engage in different relational activities on weekdays and weekends, which can affect relationship satisfaction (e.g., Reis, Sheldon, Gable, Roscoe, & Ryan, 2000). Relationship satisfaction on the previous day was controlled because of possible carryover effects. Between-person differences in relationship satisfaction were measured by aggregating daily reports and predicting them from trait-level measures of perceived conditional positive and negative regard.

Results from the between-person HLM analyses indicated significant unique effects on relationship satisfaction of both conditional negative and conditional positive regard. In line with Roth et al.'s (2009) findings, conditional negative and conditional positive regard both predicted relationship dissatisfaction.

The within-person HLM analyses yielded significant effects of perceived conditional negative regard. As expected, on days when greater conditional negative regard was experienced, relationship satisfaction was lower. However, conditional positive regard was positively related to relationship satisfaction. Thus, relationship satisfaction increased on days that conditional positive regard was above a person's baseline.

The unexpected positive effect of conditional positive regard on relationship quality at the within-person level suggests that receiving more affection from one's romantic partner as a result of complying with his or her requests or demands may temporarily contribute to relationship satisfaction, even if this affection is perceived as conditional. This finding is consistent with previous findings showing that conditional positive regard is less harmful than conditional negative regard, and that meeting external expectations may be accompanied by short-lived satisfaction (Assor et al., 2004; Assor, Vansteenkiste, & Kaplan, 2009; Roth et al., 2009). In the long run, however, this practice is harmful to relationship satisfaction, as indicated by the negative effect of conditional positive regard at the between-person level.

CONCLUDING REMARKS

Despite the findings reviewed here concerning the negative consequences of conditional regard, a number of parenting guidebooks and several psychologists still argue that parenting strategies involving conditional regard lead children to perform behaviors that parents and educators believe to be in the child's best interests (e.g., Frost, 2005; Gewirtz & Pelaez-Nogueras, 1991; Latham, 1994; McDowell, 1988; McGraw, 2004). It is notable that a recent *New York Times* article (Kohn, 2009) concerning the harmful consequences of parental conditional regard resulted in hundreds of negative reader responses.

What makes conditional regard so widely endorsed? It is possible that conditional regard may be a more convenient and less demanding socialization or persuasion technique than other alternatives. As noted by Roth et al. (2009), the alternative to conditional regard is autonomy support. When people use autonomy support for persuading another person, they first need to understand his or her perspective and feelings and convey understanding for this perspective and feelings even if they disagree with the acts those feelings may generate. People should also provide a meaningful rationale for the value or behavior they want the other person to internalize and enact. Moreover, they should allow the other people some choice in the way they will enact the valued behavior. Carrying out these autonomy-supportive acts requires more effort and self-control than conditional regard, and there is extensive research showing that people who are under pressure or have few available social or psychological resources are often unable to use autonomy-support means and prefer to rely on less demanding controlling means, such as conditional regard (e.g., Grolnick, 2003).

In addition, once people prefer to use less demanding controlling means, it may actually feel better to rely on conditional regard than on power-assertive strategies or physical punishment because conditional regard is less punitive and can lead others, especially children, to perform the valued behavior. There are emotional costs for conditional regard (e.g., Assor et al., 2004), but at least the behavior is enacted. Furthermore, conditional regard is likely to be more effective than power assertion or physical punishment (e.g., Hoffman, 1970).

It is important to note that the findings reviewed in this chapter do not mean that unconditional regard is the best approach to convey expectations and promote internalization of values. From this perspective, let us examine Albert Bandura's (1977) statement concerning unconditional regard:

> Some child-rearing authorities have popularized the view that healthy personality development is built on "unconditional love." If this principle were, in fact, unfailingly applied, parents would respond affectionately

regardless of how their children behaved—whether or not they mistreated others, stole whatever they wanted, disregarded the wishes and rights of others, or demand instant gratification. Unconditional love, were it possible, would make children directionless and quite unlovable. (p. 102)

It appears that Bandura confused unconditional regard for another person's inner state and feelings with unconditional regard for any behavior. We do not suggest that parents, educators, or partners should unconditionally accept and respond affectionately to any destructive or antisocial behavior. Rather, they may express their disapproval for such behaviors and at the same time overtly convey that they do not disapprove of the person as a whole or the feelings that might have promoted the negative behavior. In our view, it is this sentiment of unconditional regard that lies at the core of true and effective attempts to take others' perspectives and empathize with them even when disagreeing with their behavior. This view was elaborated long ago by Ginott (1969) and provided the basis for the research of Koestner, Ryan, Bernieri, and Holt (1984) on autonomy-supportive limiting setting.

Overall, although the use of conditional regard may be an effortless, relatively convenient, and seemingly effective socialization or persuasion technique, its negative psychological and relational consequences argue for the use of less controlling methods. However, one should take into account that most of the reviewed studies focused on conditional regard in parent–child relationships and relied on offspring's reports, although some studies examined conditional regard in more egalitarian romantic relationships. Unfortunately, we have no prospective longitudinal data that would allow us to make causal inferences more confidently. Future research should assess conditional regard using additional methods and use prospective longitudinal and experimental designs.

REFERENCES

Assor, A., Cohen-Melayev, M., Kaplan, A., & Friedman, D. (2005). Choosing to stay religious in a modern world: Socialization and exploration processes leading to an integrated internalization of religion among Israeli Jewish youth. In M. L. Maehr & S. Karabenick (Eds.), *Advances in motivation and achievement: Vol. 14. Religion and motivation* (pp. 105–150). Amsterdam, The Netherlands: Elsevier.

Assor, A., Kaplan, H., Kanat-Maymon, Y., & Roth, G. (2005). Directly controlling teacher behaviors as predictors of poor motivation and engagement in girls and boys: The role of anger and anxiety. *Learning and Instruction, 15,* 397–413. doi:10.1016/j.learninstruc.2005.07.008

Assor, A., & Roth, G. (2005). Conditional love as a socializing approach: Costs and alternatives. *Scientific Annals of the Psychological Society of Northern Greece, 7,* 17–34.

Assor, A., Roth, G., & Deci, E. L. (2004). The emotional costs of perceived parents' conditional regard: A self-determination theory analysis. *Journal of Personality, 72*, 47–88. doi:10.1111/j.0022-3506.2004.00256.x

Assor, A., & Tal, K. (in press). When parents' affection depends on child's achievement: Parental conditional positive regard, self-aggrandizement, shame, and coping in adolescents. *Journal of Adolescence.*

Assor, A., Vansteenkiste, M., & Kaplan, A. (2009). Identified versus introjected-approach and introjected-avoidance motivations in school and in sports: The limited benefits of self-worth strivings. *Journal of Educational Psychology, 101*, 482–497. doi:10.1037/a0014236

Barber, B. K., Stolz, H., & Olsen, J. (2005). Parental support, psychological control and behavioral control: assessing relevance across time, culture and method. *Monographs of the Society for Research in Child Development, 70*, 1–137.

Bandura, A. (1977). *Social learning theory*. Englewood Cliffs, NJ: Prentice-Hall.

Chapman, M., & Zahn-Waxler, C. (1982). Young children's compliance and noncompliance to parental discipline in a natural setting. *International Journal of Behavioral Development, 5*, 81–94.

Covington, M. (1992). *Making the grade: A self-worth perspective on motivation and school reform*. New York, NY: Cambridge University Press.

Deci, E. L., Koestner, R., & Ryan, R. M. (1999). A meta-analytic review of experiments examining the effects of extrinsic rewards on intrinsic motivation. *Psychological Bulletin, 125*, 627–668. doi:10.1037/0033-2909.125.6.627

Deci, E. L., & Ryan, R. M. (1985). *Intrinsic motivation and self-determination in human behavior*. New York, NY: Plenum Press.

Deci, E. L., & Ryan, R. M. (2000). The "what" and "why" of goal pursuits: Human needs and the self-determination of behavior. *Psychological Inquiry, 11*, 227–268. doi:10.1207/S15327965PLI1104_01

Eilot, K., Assor, A., & Roth, G. (2006). *Styles of negative emotion regulation: Processes and parental correlates*. Paper presented at the International Workshop on Autonomy Support across Cultures, Mitzpe Ramon, Israel.

Elliot, A. J., & Thrash, T. M. (2004). The intergenerational transmission of fear of failure. *Personality and Social Psychology Bulletin, 30*, 957–971. doi:10.1177/0146167203262024

Erikson, E. H. (1950). *Childhood and society*. New York, NY: Norton.

Fromm, E. (1941). *Escape from freedom*. New York, NY: Holt.

Frost, J. (2005). *Supernanny: How to get the best from your children*. New York, NY: Hyperion.

Gewirtz, J. L., & Pelaez-Nogueras, M. (1991). Proximal mechanisms underlying the acquisition of moral behavior patterns. In W. M. Kurtines, & J. L. Gewirtz (Eds.), *Handbook of moral behavior and development: Vol. 1. Theory* (pp. 153–182). Hillsdale, NJ: Erlbaum.

Ginott, H. (1969). *Between parent and child*. New York, NY: Avon Books.

Grolnick, W. S. (2003). *The psychology of parental control: How well-meant parenting backfires*. Mahwah, NJ: Erlbaum.

Hoffman, M. L. (1970). Moral development. In P. H. Mussen (Ed.), *Carmichael's manual of child psychology* (Vol. 2, pp. 261–360). New York, NY: Wiley.

Kanat-Maymon, Y., & Roth, R. (2011). [Parental conditional regard and stress in an academic achievement task]. Unpublished raw data.

Kanat-Maymon, Y., Roth, R., & Reizer, A. (2011). [Conditional regard in close relationships]. Unpublished raw data.

Kernis, M. H., & Paradise, A. W. (2002). Distinguishing between fragile and secure forms of high self-esteem. In E. L. Deci & R. M. Ryan (Eds.), *Handbook of self-determination research* (pp. 339–360). Rochester, NY: University of Rochester Press.

Koestner, R., Ryan, R. M., Bernieri, F., & Holt, K. (1984). Setting limits on children's behavior: The differential effects of controlling versus informational styles on children's intrinsic motivation and creativity. *Journal of Personality, 52*, 233–248. doi:10.1111/j.1467-6494.1984.tb00879.x

Kohn, A. (2009, September 14). When a Parent's 'I Love You' Means 'Do as I Say.' *The New York Times*. Retrieved from http://www.nytimes.com/2009/09/15/health/15mind.html

Latham, G. I. (1994). *The power of positive parenting: A wonderful way to raise children*. Logan, UT: P&T Ink.

McDowell, J. J. (1988). Matching theory in natural environments. *The Behavior Analyst, 11*, 95–109.

McGraw, P. (2004). *Family first*. New York, NY: Free Press.

Miller, A. (1981). *Prisoners of childhood*. New York, NY: Basic Books.

Reis, H. T., Sheldon, K. M., Gable, S. L., Roscoe, J., & Ryan, R. M. (2000). Daily well-being: The role of autonomy, competence, and relatedness. *Personality and Social Psychology Bulletin, 26*, 419–435. doi:10.1177/0146167200266002

Rogers, C. R. (1951). *Client-centered therapy*. Boston, MA: Houghton Mifflin.

Roth, G. (2008). Perceived parental conditional regard and autonomy support as predictors of young adults' self- versus other-oriented prosocial tendencies. *Journal of Personality, 76*, 513–534. doi:10.1111/j.1467-6494.2008.00494.x

Roth, G., & Assor, A. (2003, April). *Autonomy supporting and suppressing parental practices as predictors of flexible versus rigid emotion regulation in children*. Paper presented at the meeting of the Society for Research in Child Development, Tampa, FL.

Roth, G., & Assor, A. (2010). Parental conditional regard as a predictor of deficiencies in young children's capacities to respond to sad feelings. *Infant and Child Development, 19*, 465–477.

Roth, G., Assor, A., Niemiec, C. P., Ryan, R. M., & Deci, E. L. (2009). The negative emotional and behavioral consequences of parental conditional regard: Comparing positive conditional regard, negative conditional regard, and autonomy support as parenting practices. *Developmental Psychology, 45*, 1119–1142. doi:10.1037/a0015272

Ryan, R. M., & Connell, J. P. (1989). Perceived locus of causality and internalization: Examining reasons for acting in two domains. *Journal of Personality and Social Psychology, 57*, 749–761. doi:10.1037/0022-3514.57.5.749

Ryan, R. M., & Deci, E. L. (2000). Self-determination theory and the facilitation of intrinsic motivation, social development, and well-being. *American Psychologist, 55*, 68–78. doi:10.1037/0003-066X.55.1.68

Ryan, R. M., Deci, E. L., & Grolnick, W. S. (1995). Autonomy, relatedness, and the self: Their relation to development and psychopathology. In D. Cicchetti & D. J. Cohen (Eds.), *Developmental psychopathology: Theory and methods* (pp. 618–655). New York, NY: Wiley.

Sears, R. R., Maccoby, E., & Levin, H. (1957). *Patterns of child rearing.* Evanston, IL: Row, Peterson.

Shavit-Miller, A., & Assor, A. (2003). *The experience of conditional parental regard and its effects on development: A study of gender differences.* Paper presented at the Tenth Conference of the European Association for Research on Learning and Instruction, Padua, Italy.

14

REMOVING THE CONSTRAINTS ON OUR CHOICES: A PSYCHOBIOLOGICAL APPROACH TO THE EFFECTS OF MINDFULNESS-BASED TECHNIQUES

NAVA LEVIT BINNUN, RACHEL KAPLAN MILGRAM, AND JACOB RAZ

In Chapter 12 of this volume, Ryan, Legate, Niemiec, and Deci highlighted the basic human need for autonomy and summarize the copious research evidence concerning people's ability to act in accord with their own inner values and goals in a mindful and autonomous way. Kanat-Maymon, Roth, Assor, and Reizer, in Chapter 13, followed this line of thinking and presented a comprehensive review of evidence concerning the ways conditional regard can inhibit autonomous motivation, and the harmful effects of such inhibition on well-being and relationship quality. In the present chapter, we present a theoretical analysis and relevant empirical evidence showing that even the simplest sensory processing can constrain our actions and inhibit autonomy but that higher level cognitive processes can counteract these constraints, facilitate autonomous motivation, and increase our sense of personal freedom. Specifically, we focus on the practice of mindfulness as a powerful means for removing sensory constraints on one's choices and resisting defensive and externally controlled responding.

Mindfulness practice, developed more than 2,500 years ago as one of several Buddhist paths to liberation from suffering, is part of an enquiry into human existence that has much in common with existential themes. Jon Kabat-Zinn (1994), a contemporary expert on mindfulness, has defined it as "paying attention in a particular way, on purpose, in the present moment and nonjudgmentally" (p. 4). Nyanaponika Thera (1972), a Buddhist monk and scholar, called mindfulness "the clear and single-minded awareness of what actually happens to us and in us at the successive moments of perception" (p. 5). According to contemporary Buddhist scholars, mindfulness practice can move an individual toward freedom by encouraging him or her to let go of notions of permanent structures of self and reality (Beck, 2000; Kornfield, 2008; Rahula, 1959).

Mindfulness is part of many Buddhist practices. Currently, there is also a variety of Western mindfulness-based interventions that have been adapted from Buddhist contemplative traditions, ranging from stand-alone programs, such as the 8-week mindfulness-based stress reduction program (MBSR), to others that combine mindfulness with other kinds of psychological interventions, such as cognitive behavior therapy (for a review, see Chambers, Gullone, & Allen, 2009). For the purposes of this chapter, we use the term *mindfulness* broadly, not in relation to a specific program but in reference to a general "construct, mode of awareness, meditation practice, or psychological practice" (Chambers et al., 2009, p. 562).

Recently, psychologists and neuroscientists have taken an interest in mindfulness, and the number of published mindfulness studies has grown exponentially. Following mindfulness skill development, people report an increase in well-being and a reduction in stress, anxiety, and depression (Sahdra et al., 2011). In addition, accumulating empirical evidence suggests that people who possess higher natural levels of mindfulness—even without formal meditation practices—report feeling more joyful, inspired, grateful, hopeful, content, vital, and satisfied with life (for a review, see Greeson, 2009). According to first-person reports, the phenomenological experience of mindfulness is that of an increased sense of freedom and meaning (Pelled, 2007).

Although knowledge regarding the psychological and physiological effects of mindfulness practices is rapidly increasing, it is still not clear how these empirical findings translate to the first-person experience of an increased sense of freedom. In this chapter, we integrate wisdom from two fields that are not often reviewed together—occupational therapy and Buddhism—to explore how mindfulness may remove the constraints on basic biological systems, such as the sensory system, which in turn can lead to a greater phenomenological sense of freedom.

We begin with a review of research in the field of occupational therapy, which shows how differences in the "tuning" patterns of sensory systems and the ways in which they are "coupled" with other systems affect people's choices, decisions, and values and can restrict the sense of personal freedom. We then examine the Buddhist view, derived from contemplative Buddhist traditions, that also proposes that sensory experiences can put restrictive limits on the way the world is filtered and formulated into particular mental con-structions that guide choices. Finally, we show how these ideas are grounded in neuroscience findings and how bridging the gap between biological and phenomenological findings regarding mindfulness practice can lead to greater insight into ways to increase our sense of personal freedom and remove con-straints on our choices.

INSIGHTS FROM OCCUPATIONAL THERAPY

Disciplines such as occupational therapy are providing a wealth of infor-mation about how individuals differ in the processing of sensory information and how these processing methods guide their choices and behavior (Dunn, 2001; Engel-Yeger, 2008). At a basic level, humans are biological machines that create models of reality through input and output systems. Input from the world around us and from our bodies enters the brain through our *exteroceptive* sensory systems (visual, auditory, somatosensory, olfactory, and gustatory) and *interoceptive* systems (vestibular, proprioceptive, kinesthetic, and nociceptive).

People Differ in Their Sensory-Processing Patterns

In certain conditions, such as autism, schizophrenia, attention-deficit/hyperactivity disorder, and even normal fatigue, individuals often exhibit extreme patterns of sensory processing, such as being overreactive or under-reactive to incoming stimuli (for a review, see Dunn, 2001). Recently, these extreme patterns of sensory processing have recaptured scientists' attention because they may provide insight into these abnormal conditions. For instance, the rigid and inflexible behavior often observed in autism can be explained partly by oversensitivity to stimuli and the consequent overwhelming of sensory systems (Baranek, Foster, & Berkson, 1997; Markram, Rinaldi, & Markram, 2007).

A smaller but intriguing body of research focuses on the differences in sensory patterns in healthy people without disabilities. Distinct patterns of noticing and habituating to sensory information have been found in healthy preschoolers, for example (Engel-Yeger, 2008; McIntosh, Miller, Shyu, & Hagerman, 1999), and in healthy adults (Aron & Aron, 1997; Brown, Tollefson, Dunn, Cromwell, & Filion, 2001). These differences have been found using both self-report and physiological measures of autonomic (Brown et al., 2001; McIntosh et al., 1999) and central nervous system activity (Jagiellowicz et al., 2011).

Dunn (2001) found that people without disabilities can be situated on a continuum of neurological reactivity. People with low neurological thresholds notice sensory stimuli quite readily and experience more sensory events in daily life than others, whereas people with high neurological thresholds require more sensory input to generate reactions and responses.

Individual Differences in Sensory Processing Affect Choices and Values

Dunn (2001) suggested that one's threshold for incoming sensory stimuli can influence choices and, consequently, one's personal freedom and ability to live a satisfying life. Dunn demonstrated that a relation can be found between people's neurological thresholds and their behavior, temperament, and personality. For instance, people with a high neurological threshold (i.e., those who experience only salient sensory stimuli) are often *sensation seekers* who enjoy sensory experiences and find ways to enhance and extend sensory experiences in daily life (Dunn, 2001). Examples include wearing perfume, smelling flowers, feeling vibrations in stereo speakers, seeking crowded events, and pursuing active and often extreme physical activities (Brown et al., 2001; Dunn, 2001). Sensation seeking has been found to relate to dimensions of temperament such as openness, agreeableness, and extraversion (Levit Binnun, Stern-Ellran, & Engel-Yeger, 2011). Sensation seekers score relatively high on Sensory Profile Questionnaire items such as "I enjoy being close to people who wear perfume or cologne" and "I like to wear colorful clothing" (Brown et al., 2001). Therefore, a high neurological threshold tends to restrict our freedom or choices by leading us to seek sensations and avoid routines, rituals, and situations with little stimulation.

People with low neurological thresholds are *sensation avoiders*. They stay away from distracting settings and often leave a room if others are moving, talking, or bumping into them. They create rituals for daily routines, which may be an attempt to generate familiar and predictable sensory patterns for themselves. When these rituals are interrupted, such people become unhappy (Brown et al., 2001; Dunn, 2001). Not surprisingly, they are likely to score relatively high on negative affect and the temperament trait of neuroticism (Levit Binnun, Stern-Ellran, & Engel-Yeger, 2011). These individuals identify closely with such items on the Sensory Profile Questionnaire as "I choose to shop in smaller stores because I'm overwhelmed in large stores" and "I avoid standing in lines or standing close to other people because I don't like to get too close to others" (Brown et al., 2001). In this way, a low neurological threshold tends to restrict freedom of choice by leading people to avoid sensations and highly stimulating situations.

Interestingly, these sensory patterns correlate not only with temperament but also with personal values (Sverdlik & Levit Binnun, 2011) and attachment orientations (Levit Binnun, Szepsenwol, Stern-Ellran, & Engel-Yeger, 2011).

For example, sensation seeking correlates negatively with favoring conformity and tradition and with avoidant attachment (see Chapter 16, this volume, on avoidant attachment).

Introducing the Concept of Tuning

The human sensory systems are sensitive to a wide range of environmental signals. For example, the human ear is capable of detecting and discerning anything from a quiet murmur to the sounds of the loudest heavy metal rock concert. However, the fact that the sensory systems have such a wide detection range does not necessarily imply that people are all "tuned" similarly to the world. The information detected by the sensory receptors is modulated almost immediately by subcortical areas in charge of arousal and vigilance and by processes in charge of *habituation* (a decreased response to familiar stimuli) and *sensitization* (an increased response to stimuli of importance to the organism). These processes, based on an individual's genetic endowment and past experience, result in different neurological thresholds for incoming information—or, in our terminology, different *tuning patterns* of the sensory systems. Thus, although the biological systems responsible for sensation may have theoretically similar ranges of operation in most people, there are important individual differences in the tuning of these systems.

Individuals Differ Not Only in How Their Sensory Systems Are Tuned But Also in How Their Sensory Systems Are Coupled to Other Systems

At first glance, sensation avoiders and sensation seekers seem to be opposite sensory types, representing two extremes on a continuum. However, another glance reveals that they actually have something in common: In both sensory types, there seems to be an active regulatory process in charge of balancing the amount of incoming sensory stimuli. For example, sensation seekers will be attracted to crowded places, whereas sensation avoiders will be repelled by them. Although the behavioral outcome is different, in both cases a regulatory attempt is taking place, leading to an increase in sensations for the sensation seekers and a decrease in sensations for the sensation avoiders. It is notable that Dunn (2001) found that this regulatory process can itself be represented on a continuum, ranging from active regulation to passive regulation. That is, whereas individuals with high neurological thresholds and active regulatory processes would be termed *sensation seekers*, individuals with the same high neurological thresholds but with passive regulation may live their lives with many sensory events going unnoticed. Because they receive less sensory stimulation, they may not notice changes in the environment, such as when people enter the room, or changes related to their own bodies, such as when they have food or dirt on their face. These individuals identify with such items on the Sensory Profile Questionnaire as "I don't notice when people enter the room" (Brown et al., 2001).

However, people with low neurological thresholds who are passive with respect to sensory regulation may have trouble limiting the amount of incoming stimulation. These people are easily distracted by movements, sounds, or smells. They notice food textures, temperatures, and spices more rapidly than others and they often let things happen without moving away from them. These individuals will often score high on Sensory Profile Questionnaire items such as "I startle easily to unexpected or loud noises (e.g., vacuum cleaner, dog barking, telephone ring)" (Brown et al., 2001).

The two axes that Dunn (2001) discussed—*sensory reactivity* (neurological threshold) and *sensory regulation strategy* (balancing the amount of incoming information)—suggest that people differ not only in their tuning patterns (high or low neurological threshold) but also in the way their sensory systems are coupled to other basic systems, such as those in charge of regulating vigilance and alertness and those in charge of emotional valence and action systems. Here we use the term *coupling* to refer to the fact that activity in one system can increase the probability of activity in another system. The more strongly the two systems are coupled, the greater the causal connection between them. The fact that people can have similar neurological thresholds but different regulation strategies suggests that people also differ in the coupling between systems and that coupling strength can constrain freedom of choice.

Although the two axes do not entirely capture an individual's sensory complexity—people have multiple sensory channels, each of which may have a different neurological threshold—the four simplistic tuning patterns we have described show how particular sensory tuning and coupling patterns can influence choices and behavior.

INSIGHTS FROM BUDDHISM

Just as the view from occupational therapy emphasizes the role of individual sensory experiences in constraining behavior, so too does Buddhism place central importance on the role of sensation and perception in shaping human actions, choices, and understanding of the world. Buddhist texts organize human experience around the concept of suffering and propose that at the basis of our existence there is unease, restlessness, and sometimes even physical and mental suffering.

In Buddhism, Individual Sensory Processing Is Central to Perception of the World and Constrains Actions and Choices

Buddhism attempts to explain the origins of this restlessness or unease and claims that at the root of suffering lie ignorance, clinging, and aversion. We suffer because we are unable to see that what we experience as a permanent structure of self and reality is actually an ever-changing subjective construct. Furthermore, we cling to the desire that our experiences will play out according to our expectations, and when they do not, we feel distressed and unhappy. This ignorance, according to the Buddhist texts, begins with a basic unawareness of how our perception is constrained by our genetic makeup, past experience, and needs. In turn, our perceptions themselves constrain our feelings and motivations, which in turn constrain our actions and freedom. Thus, the Buddhist view, through a different framework and with slightly different definitions, emphasizes the strong link between sensory perception and freedom. Examining canonical Buddhist texts, which are based on the phenomenological experiences following meditative self-inquiry, can therefore shed light on the fine details of subjective sensory processing and how they relate to well-being.

Buddhism Emphasizes the Working of the Sensory Systems

In the *Paticca Samuppada*[1] (Bhikku, 1997), a canonical Buddhist text that presents a model of the causes of suffering (see Figure 14.1), half of these causes concern the ways in which people sense and perceive reality. The other half of the causes concern the ways in which we react to the world and create our self-identity and conception of reality. Importantly, the *Paticca Samuppada* represents all these causes in the form of a circular chain, with each link (each cause) being conditioned by the preceding link as well as actively conditioning the following link.

As described in the *Paticca Samuppada* (Bhikku, 1997), the sensory process can be broken down into several interrelated stages. We fail to see how the combination of our experiences and needs govern us (Link 1: "lack of self-awareness") and how this in turn influences the way our patterns and internal representations of the world are imprinted on us (Link 2: "internal representation, patterns"). These representations influence how we are able to discriminate and discern external and internal stimuli (Link 3: "discriminative consciousness"). These discrimination abilities constrain the

---

[1]*Paticca* means "because of" or "dependent on"; *samuppada* means "arising" or "origination." *Paticca Samuppada*, therefore, literally means "dependent arising" or "dependent origination," a central concept in Buddhist philosophy.

Figure 14.1. Paticca Samuppada Cycle. A circular model representing a chain of conditioned arising of suffering, each cause (each link) being conditioned by the preceding link as well as actively conditioning the following link. The links in Pali begin with "lack of self-awareness" and continue in clockwise order: *avijja, sankhara, vinnana, nama-rupa, salayatana, phassa, vedana, upadana, bhava, jati, jara-marana,* and *dukkha.*

way we organize both our experiences and our perceptions of the world by naming, labeling, and creating forms (Link 4: "forms and names"). With our minds already disposed to discern, shape, and label certain kinds of objects, our senses become attuned to detect the sensory data associated with such objects, and overlook others (Link 5: "attunement of senses"). These stages form filters that condition our contact with reality (Link 6: "contact"). As they occur, incoming sensory experiences are immediately tinted in shades of "pleasant," "unpleasant," or "natural" (Link 7: "sensations").

Thus, our past experience will dispose us to a different level of active sensing—such as listening, seeing, smelling—as we experience different situations. For example, when observing an object such as a leaf, an artist may notice its various shades, a botanist may be attuned to its shape, and a gardener may notice that it needs water. Thus, "an object of perception is designed by pre-knowledge, information, predispositions, needs and fears from the external object, which is allegedly the objective source [of] our sensations [of] it" (Aran, 1993, p. 38).

It is notable that the first half of the model provides a detailed description of filters and constrictions on the sensory processes that constrain our perception of reality. According to the model, these sensory processes directly condition our motives, feelings, clinging tendencies, actions, and development of self-concept, all of which are represented in the second half of the model (see Figure 14.1). Because the model is circular, these motives, feelings, clinging, and actions condition future sensory processes. The model therefore represents how human beings are trapped in a cycle that limits perceptions, actions, and freedom.

Buddhism Does Not Merely Identify Constraints; It Also Identifies Exit Points, or Paths to Liberation

Importantly, each of the links in the model can serve as a means to break free from the endless cycle. The *Paticca Samuppada* (Bhikku, 1997) contains not only the Buddha's teachings about the origins of suffering and conflict but also a practical guide to the various exit points to liberation. It suggests that we have a choice of either being locked into the same physical–mental patterns and constructions or of unlocking these constraints. Thus, by becoming aware of the factors that condition or constrain our reality, we can break free of them and increase our sense of freedom.

Although the "letting go" of craving and clinging (central links in the second half of the model) is a Buddhist idea familiar to Westerners (Mikulas, 2007; Pelled, 2007), the letting go of the constraints on our perceptions and senses (the first half of the model) is a less familiar notion. According to the Buddhist view, just as letting go of craving and clinging can lead to freedom, so too can awareness of the workings of the senses. Becoming aware of the working of our senses can increase our freedom in several ways. First, attending to sensory experiences, without projecting onto them past experiences or restricting them with labels, fears, and plans, expands them and enables new possibilities that have not been noticed before. Second, awareness of mental constrictions can loosen their restrictive power and enable us to let go of them, providing us with the possibility of choosing when they are indeed needed as restraints and when they are constraining and limiting us. Third, we can achieve a sense of freedom by cultivating the ability to hold a similar, unbiased attitude toward what is pleasant and what is unpleasant. This skill, called *equanimity* in Buddhism, enables one to be less manipulated and controlled by likes and dislikes concerning a certain sensory experience and to be able to choose more clearly the best actions and solutions.

Mindfully "Retuning" the Senses: Another Path to Liberation

How can we overcome ignorance of the links described in the *Paticca Samuppada* (Bhikku, 1997) and see these invisible patterns, constructions, and automatic actions that rule us? Buddhism suggests mindfulness practice as a form of mental training that can lead to an awakening from ignorance and lack of awareness. In the *Satipatthana Sutta*[2] (Thera, 1993), which contains one of the earliest instructions for mindfulness practice, the Buddha teaches his disciples about "mindfulness" and its uses: "How, monks, does a monk live contemplating mental objects in the mental objects of the six internal and the six[3] external sense-bases?" (para. 52).

The Buddha then teaches the monks how to cultivate mindful awareness, how to gain insight into the workings of the visual system, and how to notice the *fetters*, or the constraints and bonds on our sensory experience:

> Herein, monks, a monk knows the eye and visual forms [and the fetter that arises dependent on both (the eye and forms)]; he knows how the arising of the non-arisen fetter comes to be; he knows how the abandoning of the arisen fetter comes to be; and he knows how the non-arising in the future of the abandoned fetter comes to be. (Thera, 1993, para. 53)

The Buddha goes on to emphasize the importance of awareness to all of the senses, not just the visual sense:

> He knows the *ear* and *sounds* . . . the *nose* and *smells* . . . the *tongue* and *flavors* . . . the *body* and *tactual objects* . . . and the fetter that arises dependent on both; he knows how the arising of the non-arisen fetter comes to be; he knows how the abandoning of the arisen fetter comes to be; and he knows how the non-arising in the future of the abandoned fetter comes to be. (Thera, 1993, para. 54; emphasis in original)

---

[2]"Mindfulness" is the most common translation of the Pali word *sati*. The *Satipatthana Sutta*, or "the four foundations of mindfulness," is one of the earliest instructions for mindfulness practice, in which the Buddha teaches his disciples to be mindful and attentive to the activities of the body (*kaya*), the sensations or feelings (*vedana*), the activities of the mind (*citta*), and to ideas, thoughts, conceptions, and things (*dhamma*).
[3]The sixth "sense-base" here refers to thoughts, which are considered to be another domain of sensation in Buddhism.

Thus, according to this text, mindfulness practice facilitates the development of a skill by which one can become aware of fetters (or mental constrictions, described in the *Paticca Samuppada* model) and let them go when they arise. Most contemporary mindfulness practices also emphasize awareness of moment-to-moment sensory experiences. Mindful awareness of a sensory experience without labeling it (e.g., "itch," "knee pain") can develop not only sensitivity to the subtle details of our experiences but also an ability to stay with these experiences, suspend an immediate response, and create a space wherein a novel viewpoint and behavioral options may arise. Mindfulness practice can therefore have a profound effect on the filters and constrictions that limit our perception. By broadening our range of sensitivity, we are in essence "retuning" our senses. Thus, the Buddhist concept of mindfulness, like occupational therapy, discussed in the previous section, strongly relates sensory experiences to choices, actions, and therefore freedom.

AN INTEGRATIVE DISCUSSION

We have shown how two distinct fields of wisdom, occupational therapy and Buddhism, have realized, each in its own context and tradition of inquiry, how the working of our senses can influence our behavior and constrain our range of choices. Schwartz (Chapter 15, this volume) defined *choice* as "what enables each person to pursue precisely those objects and activities that best satisfy his or her own preferences within the limits of his or her resources" (p. 272). The empirical and phenomenological evidence provided by Buddhism and occupational therapy demonstrates that the way we are tuned to the world can greatly limit our preferences and resources. In this sense, the term *tuning* is advantageous in that it can translate across fields of wisdom. It is broadly relevant because both Buddhism and occupational therapy acknowledge and emphasize that at a basic level individuals differ in their fundamental patterns of sensory processing.

The Buddhist view goes a step further in offering a detailed description of the subtle stages of sensory processing that can constrain our perception of reality and subsequently our actions. These stages range from the internal representations that provide our model of the world, to the later tagging of a sensation as "pleasant," "unpleasant," or "neutral." From the Buddhist point of view, all of these stages, even the contact point of external stimuli with a sensory organ's receptors, are already imprinted by an individual's prior experience, survival patterns, and attentional priorities. Thus, one's range of choices is constrained by many constrictions that begin in the earliest stages of sensory processing.

Buddhism Suggests Mindfulness Practice as a Way of Retuning

If sensory tuning constrains our choices and sense of freedom, how can we remove these constraints? Buddhism suggests mindfulness practice as a form of perceptual therapy that deconditions normal human perception (Shulman, 2010). Thus, by focusing our attention and awareness nonjudgmentally on the subtle workings of the senses, we can let go of the effect that individual tuning patterns have on our choices and consequently increase our sense of freedom.

This chapter's title, "Removing the Constraints on Our Choices," has a deeper meaning in the Buddhist view, which does not consider the removal of a problem as the way to alleviate it. In fact, Buddhists view "problem" as a label that in itself imposes a constraint. Furthermore, a problem does not necessarily require a "solution." Rather, understanding the constraint and its nature—accepting it and letting go of the need to either grasp or reject it—is what enables changing the constraint to a restraint.[4] Thus, in keeping with the tuning framework described here, we can say that mindfulness practice actually "retunes" rather than "removes" constraints.

It is also important to note that occupational therapists suggest that understanding individual sensory tuning patterns can help inform people about the nature of their humanity. Dunn (2001) stated, "In *knowing* [our own] 'features' we might be *set free* to learn, evolve, and live a satisfying life. I believe that the essential gift of our sensory processing knowledge is in providing opportunities for *insight*" (p. 617; emphasis added). Although it is beyond the scope of this chapter to review the various occupational therapy techniques, it seems that retuning in occupational therapy occurs through the interaction between the therapist and the patient, and less through self-guided mental training.

Biological Correlates of the Retuning Process

What are the biological correlates of the retuning processes that occur through mindfulness training? Neuroscientific evidence regarding the anatomical and functional connectivity patterns in the brain is accumulating, and with it comes a deeper understanding of how various brain areas can modulate and influence each other through complex interconnections. The reactivity in each brain area arises from a delicate balance between local and global excitatory and inhibitory neuronal influences (Dani et al., 2005).

---

[4]An even deeper understanding in Buddhism is that the concept of a separate and constant self is illusionary. The letting go of the concept of self is the deepest practice in Buddhism, and also in mindfulness meditation. If not overcome, this construct of separateness will cause innumerable problems.

Highly connected areas in the brain, considered polymodal because of their integrative nature, receive a wide range of sensory, motor, and emotional input that enables them to modulate behavior through motor and visceral outputs and by direct modulation of the sensory systems (Honey, Kotter, Breakspear, & Sporns, 2007; Mesulam, 2008; Pessoa, 2008). Examples of such polymodal nodes are the orbitofrontal cortex, an area involved in emotion regulation and modification of reactions to aversive stimuli, and the insula, an area involved in interoception and awareness of bodily sensations (Kringelbach, 2005; Pessoa, 2008).

It is interesting that contemplative neuroscience, a rapidly growing field concerned with the effects of mindfulness practice on the brain, has found that these polymodal areas are among a number of brain regions affected by this form of training (Hölzel et al., 2008; Lazar et al., 2005; Luders et al., 2009). Other areas affected by mindfulness training include the frontal cortex (involved in integrating emotion and cognition) and sensory cortices (Lazar et al., 2005). In other words, key players in modulation processes that can affect the first stages of sensory processing have been found to respond to mindfulness training. Recently, Kilpatrick et al. (2011) demonstrated that an 8-week MBSR course induced changes in intrinsic connectivity networks comprising parts of the sensory cortices and parts of the insula. These findings may reflect the consistent attentional focus, enhanced sensory processing, and reflective awareness of sensory experience often found following MBSR training (Kilpatrick et al., 2011). In sum, both sensory cortices and areas involved in modulation of sensory processes are affected by mindfulness practices. Remarkably, these neuroscience findings support the Buddhist view, over 2,000 years old, regarding the relation of mindfulness to sensory processes.

The Term *Coupling* and Biological Correlates of Decoupling

The tuning of the sensory processes, as well as the way they are coupled to other processes, affects choices and behavior. From occupational therapy, we learn that individuals can differ in the strength of this coupling, as Dunn (2001) demonstrated by showing that people can have different thresholds for sensory stimuli and can also differ in the amount of regulation they apply to those stimuli. In Buddhism, this coupling is reflected in the *Paticca Samuppada* model, whereby each link is conditioned by the link before it and conditions the link after it. In a larger sense, the workings of the sensory systems (the first half of the model) condition our cravings, actions, and self-definition (the second half of the model), thus coupling them together. By paying mindful attention to the various types of conditioning, a *decoupling* or "loosening of coupling" can occur. For example, following such decoupling, the activation of the sensory process need not activate processes related to cravings, actions, and self-definition. In support of this view, a recent study showed that Zen mindfulness practitioners report lower levels of pain in response to a thermal pain stimulus (Grant, Courtemanche, & Rainville, 2011). The neuroscientific findings showed a functional decoupling between sensory brain areas and brain areas that play a role in cognitive evaluation of sensations. This decoupling was interpreted by the researchers as paralleling the mindfulness practitioners' reports that the practice enables them to adopt a more neutral view of painful sensory stimuli (Grant et al., 2011).

Expanding the Framework Beyond the Sensory System

Although this chapter has focused mainly on the sensory system, similar claims can be made regarding the effects of mindfulness on other basic neurological systems. For instance, emotional processes are described in the *Paticca Samuppada* and are considered a target for mindfulness practice in the *Satipatthana Sutta*. Indeed, emotion-related areas such as the amygdala have been found to display a range of reactivity patterns—and thus different tuning—for different individuals (Hariri, 2009). Moreover, mindfulness practice has been shown to affect emotion-regulation processes (Chambers et al., 2009). Although similar evidence can be brought forth for other brain processes (e.g., attention, action processes), a complete review is beyond the scope of this chapter.

In sum, we have attempted to understand the psychological and biological correlates of the first-person phenomenological experience of an increased sense of freedom following mindfulness practices. We used the terms *tuning* and *coupling* to integrate Buddhist phenomenological insights, observations from occupational therapy, and empirical evidence to show that individual tuning and coupling patterns impose limitations on an individual's range of choices and that these concepts are grounded in neurobiology findings. These limits can be retuned and decoupled by mindfulness practices, leading to loosened constraints and increased ranges of perception, choices, and action. We hope that our preliminary discussion of these issues will spur further research aimed at linking biology with our phenomenological sense of freedom.

REFERENCES

Aran, L. (1993). *Buddhism*. Tel Aviv, Israel: Dvir.

Aron, E.N., & Aron, A. (1997). Sensory-processing sensitivity and its relation to introversion and emotionality. *Journal of Personality and Social Psychology, 73*, 345–368. doi:10.1037/0022-3514.73.2.345

Baranek, G. T., Foster, L. G., & Berkson, G. (1997). Tactile defensiveness and stereotyped behaviors. *The American Journal of Occupational Therapy, 51*, 91–95. doi:10.5014/ajot.51.2.91

Beck, C. J. (2000). *Everyday Zen: Love and work*. New York, NY: HarperCollins.

Bhikku, T. (Trans.). (1997). *Paticca samuppada vibhanga sutta: Analysis of dependent co-arising*. Retrieved from http://www.accesstoinsight.org/tipitaka/sn/sn12/sn12.002.than.html

Brown, C., Tollefson, N., Dunn, W., Cromwell, R., & Filion, D. (2001). The Adult Sensory Profile: Measuring patterns of sensory processing. *American Journal of Occupational Therapy, 55*, 75–82. doi:10.5014/ajot.55.1.75

Chambers, R., Gullone, E., & Allen, N. B. (2009). Mindful emotion regulation: An integrative review. *Clinical Psychology Review, 29*, 560–572. doi:10.1016/j.cpr.2009.06.005

Dani, V. S., Chang, Q., Maffei, A., Turrigiano, G. G., Jaenisch, R., & Nelson, S. B. (2005). Reduced cortical activity due to a shift in the balance between excitation and inhibition in a mouse model of Rett syndrome. *PNAS Proceedings of the National Academy of Sciences of the United States of America, 102*, 12560–12565. doi:10.1073/pnas.0506071102

Dunn, W. (2001). The sensations of everyday life: Theoretical, conceptual, and pragmatic considerations. *American Journal of Occupational Therapy, 55*, 608–620. doi:10.5014/ajot.55.6.608

Engel-Yeger, B. (2008). Sensory processing patterns and daily activity preferences of Israeli children. *Canadian Journal of Occupational Therapy, 75*, 220–229.

Grant, J. A., Courtemanche, J., & Rainville, P. (2011). A non-elaborative mental stance and decoupling of executive and pain-related cortices predicts low pain sensitivity in Zen meditators. *Pain, 152*, 150–156. doi:10.1016/j.pain.2010.10.006

Greeson, J. M. (2009). Mindfulness research update: 2008. *Complementary Health Practice Review, 14*, 10–18. doi:10.1177/1533210108329862

Hariri, A. R. (2009). The neurobiology of individual differences in complex behavioral traits. *Annual Review of Neuroscience, 32*, 225–247. doi:10.1146/annurev.neuro.051508.135335

Hölzel, B. K., Ott, U., Gard, T., Hempel, H., Weygandt, M., Morgen, K., & Vaitl, D. (2008). Investigation of mindfulness meditation practitioners with voxel-based morphometry. *Social Cognitive and Affective Neuroscience, 3*, 55–61. doi:10.1093/scan/nsm038

Honey, C. J., Kotter, R., Breakspear, M., & Sporns, O. (2007). Network structure of cerebral cortex shapes functional connectivity on multiple time scales. *PNAS Proceedings of the National Academy of Sciences of the United States of America, 104*, 10240–10245. doi:10.1073/pnas.0701519104

Jagiellowicz, J., Xu, X., Aron, A., Aron, E., Cao, G., Feng, T., & Weng, X. (2011). The trait of sensory processing sensitivity and neural responses to changes in visual scenes. *Social Cognitive and Affective Neuroscience, 6,* 38–47. doi:10.1093/scan/nsq001

Kabat-Zinn, J. (1994). *Wherever you go, there you are: Mindfulness meditation in everyday life.* New York, NY: Hyperion.

Kilpatrick, L.A., Suyenobu, B. Y., Smith, S. R., Bueller, J. A., Goodman, T., Creswell, J. D. . . . Naliboff, B. D. (2011). Impact of mindfulness-based stress reduction training on intrinsic brain connectivity. *NeuroImage, 56,* 290<ens>298. doi:10.1016/j.neuroimage.2011.02.034

Kornfield, J. (2008). *The wise heart: A guide to the universal teachings of Buddhist psychology.* New York, NY: Bantam Books.

Kringelbach, M.L. (2005). The human orbitofrontal cortex: Linking reward to hedonic experience. *Nature Reviews Neuroscience, 6,* 691–702. doi:10.1038/nrn1747

Lazar, S.W., Kerr, C.E., Wasserman, R.H., Gray, J.R., Greve, D.N., Treadway, M.T., . . . Fischl, B. (2005). Meditation experience is associated with increased cortical thickness. *Neuroreport, 16,* 1893–1897. doi:10.1097/01.wnr.0000186598.66243.19

Levit Binnun, N., Stern-Ellran, K., & Engel-Yeger, B. (2011). *The relation between individual sensory profiles and temperament.* Manuscript in preparation.

Levit Binnun, N., Szepsenwol, O., Stern-Ellran, K., & Engel-Yeger, B. (2011). *The relationship between sensory processing patterns, attachment styles, and negative affective conditions in healthy adults.* Manuscript in preparation.

Luders, E., Toga, A. W., Lepore, N., & Gaser, C. (2009). The underlying anatomical correlates of long-term meditation: Larger hippocampal and frontal volumes of gray matter. *NeuroImage, 45,* 672–678. doi:10.1016/j.neuroimage.2008.12.061

Markram, H., Rinaldi, T., & Markram, K. (2007). The intense world syndrome: An alternative hypothesis for autism. *Frontiers in Neuroscience, 1,* 77–96. doi:10.3389/neuro.01.1.1.006.2007

McIntosh, D.N., Miller, L.J., Shyu, V., & Hagerman, R.J. (1999). Sensory-modulation disruption, electrodermal responses, and functional behaviors. *Developmental Medicine & Child Neurology, 41,* 608–615. doi:10.1017/S0012162299001267

Mesulam, M. (2008). Representation, inference, and transcendent encoding in neuro-cognitive networks of the human brain. *Annals of Neurology, 64,* 367–378. doi:10.1002/ana.21534

Mikulas, W.L. (2007). Buddhism and western psychology: Fundamentals of integration. *Journal of Consciousness Studies, 14,* 4–49.

Pelled, A. (2007). *Raising goodness all around: Buddhism, meditation, psychotherapy.* Tel Aviv, Israel: Resling.

Pessoa, L. (2008). On the relationship between emotion and cognition. *Nature Reviews Neuroscience, 9,* 148–158. doi:10.1038/nrn2317

Rahula, W. (1959). *What the Buddha taught.* New York, NY: Gove/Atlantic.

Sahdra, B. K., MacLean, K. A., Ferrer, E., Shaver, P. R., Rosenberg, E. L., Jacobs, T. L., . . . Saron, C. D. (2011). Enhanced response inhibition during intensive meditation training predicts improvements in self-reported adaptive socio-emotional functioning. *Emotion, 11*, 299–312. doi:10.1037/a0022764

Shulman, E. (2010). Mindful wisdom: The Satipatthana Sutta on mindfulness, memory and liberation. *History of Religions, 49*, 393–420.

Sverdlik, N., & Levit Binnun, N. (2011). *Can individual sensory profiles predict individual personal values?* Manuscript in preparation.

Thera, N. (1972). *The power of mindfulness.* San Francisco, CA: Unity Press.

Thera, N. (1986). *The power of mindfulness: An inquiry into the scope of bare attention and the principal sources of its strength.* Retrieved from http://www.accesstoinsight.org/lib/authors/nyanaponika/wheel121.html

Thera, N. (1993). *Satipatthana sutta: The foundations of mindfulness.* Retrieved from http://www.accesstoinsight.org/tipitaka/mn/mn.010.nysa.html

15

CHOICE, FREEDOM, AND AUTONOMY

BARRY SCHWARTZ

Security is more important than wealth.
—Jacob von Uexkull, *A Stroll Through the Worlds of Animals and Men*

In his master work, *Suicide* (1897/1951), the great sociologist Emile Durkheim attempted to determine the factors that affected the suicide rate in different European societies. What he found was that the more unconstrained people were—the fewer their ties to family, community, church, or nation—the higher the suicide rate. The more people depended only on themselves to make decisions and articulate rules of conduct, the more vulnerable they were. In short, people seemed to need obligations and constraints to give structure and meaning to their lives. Durkheim coined the term *anomie* to describe the normlessness that characterizes a society of autonomous, freely choosing individuals (see Haidt, 2006, for a discussion of the relevance of Durkheim's ideas to contemporary society). This theme was in many respects echoed years later by Erich Fromm (1941) in *Escape from Freedom*. Though Fromm celebrated human autonomy and rationality and urged resistance to values that were simply derived from authority, he also identified relatedness, rootedness, a need to see oneself as part of a social group, and a need to understand one's place in the world as central ingredients of well-being. Needs such as these led people to "escape from freedom." Similarly, Yalom (1980) discussed the paradoxes and tensions that could bring isolation and meaninglessness as consequences of freedom and responsibility. Both Fromm and Yalom were writing from a view of the world articulated by Sartre (1943/2001), who saw a kind of radical freedom of choice as the human condition. Though Sartre's arguments were largely ontological, both Fromm's and Yalom's were distinctly psychological.

In this chapter, I attempt to provide support for Durkheim's (1897/1951) observations by examining recent research on the relation between freedom of choice, autonomy, and well-being. To anticipate my conclusion, if Durkheim was correct in his observations of life at the turn of the 20th century, his conclusion is even more correct now.

Western societies are guided by a set of assumptions about well-being that is so deeply embedded in most of us that we do not realize either that we make these assumptions or that there is an alternative. The assumptions can be stated in the form of a rough syllogism:

> The more freedom and autonomy people have, the greater their well-being.
> The more choice people have, the greater their freedom and autonomy.
> Therefore, the more choice people have, the greater their well-being.

It is hard to quarrel—either logically or psychologically—with this syllogism. The moral importance of freedom and autonomy is built into this nation's founding documents, and the psychological importance of freedom and autonomy is now amply documented (e.g., Deci & Ryan, 2000, 2002; Ryan & Deci, 2000; Seligman, 1975; see also Chapters 12 and 13, this volume). There is also no denying that choice improves the quality of people's lives (see Chapters 14 and 21, this volume). It enables people to control their destinies and to come close to getting exactly what they want out of any situation. Choice is essential to autonomy, which is fundamental to well-being. Healthy people want and need to direct their own lives. And whereas many needs are universal (food, shelter, medical care, social support, education, and so on), much of what people need if they are to flourish is highly individualized. Choice is what enables each person to pursue precisely those objects and activities that best satisfy his or her own preferences within the limits of his or her resources. Any time choice is restricted in some way, there is bound to be someone, somewhere, who is deprived of the opportunity to pursue something of personal value.

As important as the instrumental value of choice may be, choice reflects another value that might be even more important. Freedom to choose has expressive value. Choice is what enables people to tell the world who they are and what they care about. Every choice people make is a testament to their autonomy. Almost every social, moral, or political philosopher in the Western tradition since Plato has placed a premium on such autonomy. It is difficult to imagine a single aspect of collective social life that would be recognizable if this commitment to autonomy were abandoned.

When people have no choice, as Fromm (1941) realized, life is almost unbearable. As the number of available choices increases, as it has in modern consumer culture, the autonomy, control, and liberation this variety brings is powerful. And because people are free to ignore choice possibilities when they do not want them, increasing the amount of choice people have seems to be what economists call a *Pareto-efficient move*: It will make some people (those who want increased choice) better off, but make no one worse off. Said another way, it seems reasonable to assume that the relation between choice and well-being is monotonic.

In this chapter, I argue that however reasonable the syllogism seems, and however consistent it may seem to be with past psychological research and theory, it is false. The relation between choice and well-being is nonmonotonic (Grant & Schwartz, 2011). There can be too much freedom, too much choice. And when there is, it induces paralysis or, when paralysis is overcome, dissatisfaction even with good choices. I review the empirical evidence that supports this view, almost all of it derived from studies of choice in the domain of goods and services. I then speculate that the same processes that seem to threaten well-being when people are completely free to choose what to buy also threaten well-being when people are completely free to choose how or who to be.

CHOICE OVERLOAD AND PARALYSIS

The first demonstration that too many choices can induce decision paralysis was provided by Iyengar and Lepper (2000). They reported a series of studies that showed how choice can be "demotivating." One study was set in a gourmet food store in which the researchers set up a display featuring a line of exotic, high-quality jams. Customers who came by could taste samples and then were given a coupon for a dollar off if they bought a jar. In one condition of the study, six varieties of the jam were available for tasting. In another, 24 varieties were available. In either case, the entire set of 24 varieties was available for purchase. The large array of jams attracted more people to the table than the small array, though in both cases people tasted about the same number of jams on average. When it came to buying, however, 30% of people exposed to the small array of jams actually bought a jar; only 3% of those exposed to the large array of jams did so.

In a second study, this time in the laboratory, college students were asked to evaluate a variety of gourmet chocolates (six for some participants and 30 for others). The students were then asked which chocolate—based on description and appearance—they would choose for themselves. They then tasted and rated that chocolate. Finally, in a different room, the students were offered a small box of the chocolates in lieu of cash as payment for their participation. The key results of this study were that the students faced with the small array were more satisfied with their tasting than those faced with the large array. In addition, they were 4 times as likely to choose chocolate rather than cash as compensation for their participation.

Since this initial demonstration, Iyengar, with various collaborators, has provided similar evidence from a wide variety of different domains, many of them far more consequential than jams or chocolates (e.g., Botti & Iyengar, 2004, 2006; Botti, Orfali, & Iyengar, 2009; Fisman et al., 2006; Iyengar & DeVoe, 2003; Iyengar, Jiang, & Huberman, 2004; Iyengar & Lepper, 1999, 2002). For example, adding mutual fund options to a 401(k) menu decreases rate of participation (Iyengar et al., 2004). Participation rate drops 2% for each 10 options, even though, by failing to participate, employees often pass up significant amounts of matching money from their employers. Though there are no doubt limits to the choice overload phenomenon that remain to be determined, and conditions under which it does not seem to hold (Chernev, 2003; Scheibehenne, Greifeneder, & Todd, 2009), it now seems clear that under a broad range of circumstances, people find a large number of options paralyzing rather than liberating.

CHOICE OVERLOAD AND SATISFACTION

When people overcome paralysis and choose, it is logical to expect that when the choice set is large, chances improve that people will choose well, simply because large choice sets are more likely to include a person's most desirable option. Though there is evidence that, at least sometimes, large choice sets will increase the chances of nonoptimal decisions (e.g., Hanoch & Rice, 2006; Hanoch, Rice, Cummings, & Wood, 2009; Iyengar et al., 2004; Tanius, Wood, Hanoch, & Rice, 2009), let us assume that large choice sets will, in general, enable people to do better objectively. The question is, how will people feel about how they do; that is, will better objective decisions produce better subjective results? I (Schwartz, 2004; see also Schwartz et al., 2002) have argued that large choice sets actually undermine satisfaction, even with good decisions. And I have identified several psychological processes, each of which reduces satisfaction with decisions and each of which is exacerbated when choice sets are large.

Regret

When a decision yields less than perfect results, people may regret having made the decision, convinced that an alternative would have worked out better. *Postdecision regret*, sometimes referred to as "buyer's remorse," induces second thoughts that rejected alternatives were actually better than the chosen one or that there were better alternatives that were not even explored.

The bitter taste of regret detracts from satisfaction, whether or not the regret is justified. The more options there are, the more easily one can imagine having done better, and thus the greater the likelihood of regret. *Anticipated regret* may contribute to paralysis in the face of a large number of options. If someone asks herself how it would feel to buy this house only to discover a better one next week, she probably will not buy this house. Both types of regret—anticipated and postdecision—will raise the emotional stakes of decisions (Bell, 1982; Loomes & Sugden, 1982). Anticipated regret will make decisions more difficult, and postdecision regret will make them harder to enjoy (see Gilovich & Medvec, 1995; Landman, 1993, for thoughtful discussions of the determinants and consequences of regret). Landman (1993) summed it up this way: "Regret may threaten decisions with multiple attractive alternatives more than decisions offering only one or a more limited set of alternatives. . . . Ironically, then, the greater the number of appealing choices, the greater the opportunity for regret" (p. 184).

Missed Opportunities

Related to regret, large choice sets make salient to people the opportunities they are foregoing in making their choice. Missed opportunities subtract from the satisfaction people get from what they actually choose, as confirmed by a study in which people were asked how much they would be willing to pay for subscriptions to popular magazines or to purchase videotapes of popular movies (Brenner, Rottenstreich, & Sood, 1999). Some were asked about individual magazines or videos. Others were asked about these same magazines or videos as part of a group with other magazines or videos. In almost every case, respondents placed a higher value on the magazine or the video when they were evaluating it in isolation than when they were evaluating it as part of a cluster. When magazines were evaluated as part of a group, missed opportunities associated with the other options reduced the value of each of them.

High Expectations

When people evaluate an experience, they are performing one or more of the following comparisons (see Michalos, 1980, 1986):

- comparing the experience with what they hoped it would be,
- comparing the experience with what they expected it to be,
- comparing the experience with other experiences they have had in the recent past, and/or
- comparing the experience with experiences that others have had.

As material and social circumstances improve, standards of comparison go up. As people have contact with items of high quality, they begin to suffer from "the curse of discernment." The lower quality items that used to be perfectly acceptable are no longer good enough. The hedonic zero point keeps rising, and expectations and aspirations rise with it. As a result, the rising quality of experience is met with rising expectations, and people are just running in place. As long as expectations keep pace with realizations, people may live better, but they will not feel better about how they live.

Large choice sets can have similar effects. If there are two or three styles of jeans to choose from, one's expectations about how well a pair of jeans will fit will be modest. The chosen pair may not fit that well, but what can one reasonably expect with such a small choice set? However, if there are dozens of styles to choose from, it seems inevitable that expectations about quality of fit will rise. Large choice sets will indeed enable people to find better fitting jeans than small choice sets, but if expectations have risen along with the size of the choice set, a good fit will bring no more satisfaction, and may bring less, than a mediocre fit.

Self-Blame

One more effect of large choice sets on satisfaction should be discussed. Suppose a person devotes a great deal of time and energy to making a decision, and then, because of some combination of regret, missed opportunities, and high expectations, ends up disappointed with the results. The questions this person might ask are "Why?" "What went wrong?" "Whose fault is it?" What are the likely answers to these questions? When the choice set is small, it seems natural and straightforward to blame the world for disappointing results. "They had only three styles of jeans. What could I do? I did the best I could." However, when the choice set is large, blaming the world is a much less plausible option. "With so many options available, success was out there to be had. I have only myself to blame for a disappointing result." In other words, self-blame for disappointing results becomes more likely as the choice set grows larger. Because large choice sets increase the chances of disappointing results (because of regret, missed opportunities, and raised expectations), self-blame becomes more common.

"FREEDOM," "CHOICE," "AUTONOMY," AND THE "SELF"

As I indicated earlier, virtually all of the empirical evidence on choice overload and its effects comes from contexts in which people are choosing goods. In consumer societies, the importance of contexts such as these should not be dismissed. Yet, they seem to pale to insignificance when compared with decisions involving core aspects of one's identity and mode of being in the world. "What should I buy?" does not amount to much when compared with "What should I do with my life?" or "Who should I be?" Moreover, it is in connection with these identity-shaping decisions that the benefits of freedom and autonomy (i.e., choice) loom largest. There is little doubt, as I have previously argued (Schwartz, 2000, 2004), that freedom of choice in these self-defining domains has expanded along with freedom of choice in the world of goods. Young people find themselves with relatively unconstrained choices when it comes to where they live, what they study, what kind of work they do, what religion they practice and how they practice it, what kind of intimate relations they will enter into, and what kind of family commitments they will make. People are free to decide matters of identity, of who they will be in the world. They are no longer stuck with identities they inherit from family and community. And having made the decision about who they are, people are also free to change it (see Gilbert & Ebert, 2002, for evidence that reversibility of decisions decreases people's satisfaction with them).

One plausible view of the modern explosion of choice is that although it does produce the negative effects I described earlier in regard to the world of goods, it also produces significant positive effects with respect to the things that really matter. No longer are people "stuck" with the identities and life paths that accidents of birth, or the views of others, have imposed on them (see Chapter 13, this volume, for a discussion of the concept of conditional regard). Self-invention and reinvention are now real options. Occasional paralysis in the cereal aisle of the supermarket is a small price to pay for this kind of liberation. As I say, this is a plausible view. Nonetheless, I think, as Durkheim (1897/1951) foresaw, it is mistaken. In the admittedly speculative discussion that follows, I try to justify this belief.

Philosopher Charles Taylor (1989, 1992a, 1992b) pointed out that over the past 500 years, self-understanding has been moving in a more or less straight line from "outside-in," through participation in larger entities (the divine order, the "great chain of being," nation, community, family, etc.) to "inside-out," with purpose discovered from within each individual, and the notion of "authentic" self-expression as the supreme aspiration. We in the West have seen this evolution as progress, each step enhancing freedom. Like fish that do not know they live in water, we find it hard to imagine thinking about our lives in any other way. But Markus and collaborators (e.g., Markus & Kitayama, 1991), in research on East Asian versus Western cultures, has shown that this movement from outside-in to inside-out is not universal: Most East Asians still define themselves in terms of their relations to others (and some of Markus's most recent research suggests that the inside-out view may be limited to the West's educated elite; see Schwartz, Markus, & Snibbe,

2006; Snibbe & Markus, 2005). Further, choice does not have the same significance for East or South Asians as it seems to have for Westerners (Iyengar & DeVoe, 2003; Iyengar & Lepper, 1999; Kitayama, Snibbe, Markus, & Suzuki, 2004; Savani, Markus, Naidu, Kumar, & Berlia, 2010; see also Markus & Schwartz, 2010). This research does not challenge the notion that within Western culture, more freedom—more inside-out—is better. Durkheim's (1897/1951) work does that. The Iyengar and Lepper (2000) "jam study" and its companions suggest that perhaps more inside-out is not better and that this is not just a matter of cultural preferences. East Asians may know something that Westerners have forgotten.

Consistent with this possibility, there is good evidence from recent research on well-being—again affirming both Durkheim (1897/1951) and Fromm (1941)—that the most significant determinant of our well-being is our network of close relationships with other people (e.g., Diener, 2000; Diener, Diener, & Diener, 1995; Diener & Suh, 2001; Diener, Suh, Lucas, & Smith, 1999; Lane, 2000; Myers, 2000; see also Chapter 16, this volume). The more connected we are, the better off we are. The thing to notice about close relationships, in connection with freedom, choice, and autonomy, is that close relationships generally constrain, they do not liberate. When people have responsibilities for and concerns about other people, they often cannot do many things they might otherwise choose to do. Until now, the thought has been that this constraint is perhaps just a price worth paying for rich social ties. What the choice overload research suggests is that in modern society, with overwhelming choice in every aspect of life, the constraints of close relationships may actually be part of the benefit of those relations rather than being a cost. And like close relationships with others, outside-in definitions of the self provide significant constraints on what is possible, constraints that, in modern Western societies, may be desperately needed (see Markus & Nurius, 1986; Schlenker, 1985, for a discussion of social and cultural constraints on self-definition found at other times and in other cultures).

What is the evidence that modern Westerners are suffering from this lack of constraint? As Durkheim (1897/1951) foresaw, first, there has been a significant rise in the incidence of clinical depression and suicide, both of which are befalling people at younger and younger ages (e.g., Angst, 1995; Eckersley, 2002; Eckersley & Dear, 2002; Klerman et al., 1985; Klerman & Weissman, 1989; Lane, 2000; Myers, 2000; Rosenhan & Seligman, 1995). Second, there is a substantial increase in the rate at which college students are flocking to counseling centers (Kadison & DiGeronimo, 2004). Third, there is a palpable unease in the reports of young college graduates, who seem to lack a clear idea of what they are meant to do in their lives (Robbins & Wilner, 2001). Finally, among upper class adolescents, whose family affluence makes anything possible, there are the same levels of drug abuse, anxiety disorder, and depression as there are in the children of the poor (Luthar & Latendresse, 2005). Further, there is reason to believe that whereas the poor take drugs "recreationally," the rich do so to self-medicate (Luthar & Latendresse, 2005).

SINCERITY AND AUTHENTICITY

More than 30 years ago, literary critic Lionel Trilling (1972) made a distinction that I think has greater resonance now than it had when he made it. The distinction is between *sincerity* and *authenticity*, two terms that many of us probably use interchangeably. Sincerity is about meaning what one says. Sincere people are honest—true to the cognitive and emotional content of their beliefs. Authentic people are honest as well, but they are also true to themselves. So not only do authentic people mean what they say but also what they say, and mean, is a deep reflection of who they are. Trilling suggested that the threat of modernity is that "the center will not hold," so that people increasingly have no self to be true to. They settle for sincerity—in themselves and in those close to them—because that is the best they can hope for.

In a world of uncertain, completely chosen, and easily altered selves, the distinction between sincerity and authenticity vanishes because the idea of authenticity is inapplicable. What can it mean to be "authentic" to a self that can turn on a dime? All it can mean is that one means what one says at the moment one says it. Others do not know what to expect from such a malleable self. Indeed, even the possessor of such a self does not know what to expect. "Where do you want to go today?" as the Microsoft ad asks, becomes "Who do you want to be today?"

The problems for self and others of this kind of malleability are, I think, quite significant. Others lose the ability to depend on such a malleable self. There is no assurance that such a person will wake up as the same person who went to sleep. Perhaps more troubling, the self starts to lose a grasp of who it is. In Hochschild's (1983) study of flight attendants, she observed that what competing airlines had to sell at that time was service quality, and what service quality often meant was the service provided by flight attendants. What mattered to that service was not how many drinks, snacks, and pillows attendants brought but rather how much they really "cared" about the passengers' welfare. In other words, what the flight attendants were "selling" was sincerity ("I really want you to be comfortable. I really want you to be able to relax and not be anxious. I'll be here for you if there are any problems"). The performance of their jobs required flight attendants to have training in what Hochschild called *deep acting*. After all, the best way to feign genuine concern is actually to feel genuine concern (as a famous disc jockey is reported to have said, "The secret to success in this business is sincerity. If you can fake that, you've got it made").

Flight attendants are skilled at deep acting. But what they reported to Hochschild (1983) was that they were experiencing real difficulty distinguishing the emotional attachments they displayed at work from their real emotional attachments to friends and loved ones at home. That is, it became increasingly difficult for flight attendants to discern what they "really felt." The price of all this sincerity was a loss of authenticity.

That was 30 years ago, when selves were not as malleable as they are now. It seems to me quite likely that the flight attendants' problem has become more acute because more people than ever earn a living providing services and because with a malleable, chosen self, people may not be anything other than what they are saying and feeling at the moment. "Who am I?" was never an easy question to answer. It may now be an impossible question to answer.

FREEDOM, CHOICE, AND WELL-BEING: A NONMONOTONIC RELATION

I acknowledged at the beginning of this chapter that freedom, autonomy, and choice are essential to well-being. I then devoted the remainder of the chapter to arguing that there can be too much of a good thing. The question I address now is how choice can be good and bad.

My answer is that choice has independent positive and negative effects. The positive effects—enabling people to get and do what they want and demonstrating to people the control and autonomy they possess—have diminishing marginal utility. Just as the 100th orange one procures provides much less utility than the first, so the 30th entrée on the menu provides less utility than the first. Thus, the curve relating the benefits of choice—material and psychological—to the amount of choice has an ever-decreasing slope as the choice set increases.

What about the negative effects—paralysis, regret, missed opportunities, raised expectations, and self-blame? These effects are minimal when the choice set is small, but as the choice set increases, the effects increase. Unlike the positive effects of choice, the negative effects escalate (see Coombs & Avrunin, 1977, for a rationale for this assumption that "bad things escalate").

How, then, does it feel to have a given amount of choice? The answer, I propose, is the algebraic sum of the positive and negative curves. And what the algebraic sum looks like is that, initially, adding options improves well-being. However, a point is reached when the magnitude of the negative effects is large enough that the curve changes direction. In other words, the relation between choice and well-being is nonmonotonic (Grant & Schwartz, 2011). It is a significant practical task to locate the "sweet spot," the point along the choice magnitude axis where the benefits outweigh the costs by the largest amount and well-being is highest. This is likely to vary from person to person and from situation to situation.

I think Fromm (1941) recognized the nonmonotonicity of freedom of choice when he wrote,

> There is only one possible, productive solution for the relationship of individualized man with the world: his active solidarity with all men and his spontaneous activity, love and work, which unite him again with the world, not by primary ties but as a free and independent individual. . . . However, if the economic, social and political conditions . . . do not offer a basis for the realization of individuality in the sense just mentioned, while at the same time people have lost those ties which gave them security, this lag makes freedom an unbearable burden. It then becomes identical with doubt, with a kind of life which lacks meaning and direction. Powerful tendencies arise to escape from this kind of freedom into submission or some kind of relationship to man and the world which promises relief from uncertainty, even if it deprives the individual of his freedom. (pp. 36–37)

When Fromm wrote those words in 1941, the specter of Nazism and fascism was casting a dark shadow on the world. Thus, his worry was about political regimes that deprived people of their essential autonomy. What the modern world teaches us is that this is not the only worry. Too much freedom can lead to insecurity and doubt just as too little freedom can.

CONCLUSION: FREEDOM FROM AND FREEDOM TO

I have tried to argue that whereas there is no denying that "choice is good," it is not always and only good. Further, the relation between choice and freedom is also complex. Though one cannot be free without choice, it is arguable that choice-induced paralysis is a sign of diminished rather than enhanced freedom. The scope and limits of the negative effects of choice remain to be determined. Virtually all of the research to date has involved consumer goods, and usually trivial ones at that. My effort to extend the conclusions of that research to significant nonconsumption domains, including the "choice" of a "self," is an exercise in speculation. Given the amount of dissatisfaction that choice overload seems to cause, and given the large-scale dissatisfaction in the midst of plenty that seems to characterize modern Western societies, the stakes are high. Empirical evidence on choice and well-being in nonmaterial areas of life needs to be collected.

Suppose this evidence is collected and bears out the arguments in this chapter. What then? What would be the implications of such results for public policy? It is difficult to come up with a straightforward answer to this question. First, for those committed to the moral and philosophical view that "freedom" is the highest good and that more choice always means more freedom, evidence that (some) people suffer from choice overload, although perhaps unfortunate, is irrelevant. A little bit of regret is a small price to pay for freedom. Nobody said being free was easy.

Second, and even more challenging, how, where, and by whom is freedom of choice to be restricted? Modern Western political culture is a battle between two ideologies, both of which are incoherent. Liberalism advocates freedom of choice in the domain of lifestyle and culture but regulation and control in the material world of market goods and services. Conservatism advocates unbridled freedom in the market but stringent regulation and control in lifestyle and culture. Conservatives are appalled by the "anything goes" attitude on college campuses, and liberals are appalled by the "casino capitalism" of our speculative financial markets. It is hard to see making much headway on the "choice problem" in an atmosphere as polarized as this one.

Third, and perhaps most challenging, if we were able to find a way to rein in choice, there is no avoiding the fact that some people would suffer—some people's lives would get worse. It is hard to convince someone who has just been deprived of lifestyle options that feel central to life as they want to live it that they have actually been made better off.

Because of these difficulties, it seems to me that the best route to eliminating some of the negative effects of choice overload without also eliminating the liberating effects of choice is not through public policy but through a change in awareness, sensibility, and aspiration on the part of individuals. If people can come to see that sometimes unfettered choice is paralyzing, whereas constrained choice may be liberating, they may seek and embrace constraints in their own lives instead of avoiding them. Helpful here, I think, is a classic distinction made many years ago by philosopher Isaiah Berlin (1958). He distinguished between what he called *negative* and *positive liberty*— freedom from and freedom to. The primary focus of the American embrace of freedom has been "freedom from." The Bill of Rights, the bible of American freedom, is all about freedom from, as it limits the power of the state to intrude in the lives of its citizens. With the meddling of the state kept at bay, "freedom to" is pretty much up to each of us. That is, there are no guarantees that the conditions needed for Americans to live rich, meaningful, and satisfying lives will be present.

What I have tried to suggest in this chapter is that if we pay more attention to "freedom to"—to the conditions that enable the living of good lives, it may turn out that there can be too much "freedom from." That is, a good life may require constraints, whether imposed by the state, by the family, by the school, or by religious institutions. Greater willingness on the part of psychologists to determine what the constituents of a good life are may embolden them to offer suggestions about which kinds of constraints are needed, and why.

I have suggested elsewhere that perhaps the best model we have for the importance of constraints for freedom comes from our understanding of human language abilities (Schwartz, 2000). The capacity to use language is perhaps the single most liberating characteristic of human beings. It frees people in significant ways from the temporal and material limitations that afflict other organisms. People can say anything about any thing, any time, or any place—even things, times, and places that have never existed. And they can be understood. Thus, language is probably as vivid an embodiment of human freedom and autonomy as anything. What decades of research on language ability has made clear is that the thing that makes the liberating features of language possible is that language is heavily constrained by rules. The reason people can say anything and be understood is that they cannot say anything in any way they want. It is linguistic constraint, in the form of these rules, that makes linguistic freedom possible. What I have suggested in this chapter is that exactly the same thing may be true in connection with the determination of the self. Unconstrained freedom leads to paralysis and becomes a kind of self-defeating tyranny. It is freedom of choice within significant constraints—within "rules" of some sort—that leads to well-being, to optimal functioning. A significant future task for psychology is to identify which constraints on self-determination are the crucial ones.

When Jacob von Uexkull (1938/1954) wrote the sentence with which this chapter began, that "security is more important than wealth," he was trying to understand how organisms of limited cognitive capacity could survive in a complex world. His answer was that although the forest was indeed a complex environment, it was not complex to the squirrel. The squirrel's limited perceptual sensitivities made most of what was happening in the forest invisible and inaudible to it. The squirrel saw and heard what it needed to see and hear. Thus, it survived. Evolution traded the richness of experience ("wealth") that the squirrel might enjoy if it had sensory systems such as human ones for the guarantee ("security") that the squirrel would notice what it had to. According to von Uexkull, this trade was not restricted to squirrels trying to negotiate forests; it was evolution's grand bargain. In largely freeing ourselves from the constraints of evolution, by developing culture and cultivating freedom of choice, we have rejected that bargain. This may turn out to have been a significant mistake.

REFERENCES

Angst, J. (1995). The epidemiology of depressive disorders. *European Neuropsycho-pharmacology*, *5*, 95–98. doi:10.1016/0924-977X(95)00025-K

Bell, D. E. (1982). Regret in decision making under uncertainty. *Operations Research*, *30*, 961–981. doi:10.1287/opre.30.5.961

Berlin, I. (1958). Two concepts of liberty. In I. Berlin (Ed.), *Four essays on liberty* (pp. 6–67). Oxford, England: Oxford University Press.

Botti, S., & Iyengar, S. S. (2004). The psychological pleasure and pain of choosing: When people prefer choosing at the cost of subsequent outcome satisfaction. *Journal of Personality and Social Psychology*, *87*, 312–326. doi:10.1037/0022-3514.87.3.312

Botti, S., & Iyengar, S. S. (2006). The dark side of choice: When choice impairs social welfare. *Journal of Public Policy & Marketing*, *25*, 24–38. doi:10.1509/jppm.25.1.24

Botti, S., Orfali, K., & Iyengar, S. S. (2009). Tragic choices: Autonomy and emotional response to medical decisions. *Journal of Consumer Research*, *36*, 337–352. doi:10.1086/598969

Brenner, L., Rottenstreich, Y., & Sood, S. (1999). Comparison, grouping, and preference. *Psychological Science*, *10*, 225–229. doi:10.1111/1467-9280.00141

Chernev, A. (2003). Product assortment and individual decision processes. *Journal of Personality and Social Psychology*, *85*, 151–162. doi:10.1037/0022-3514.85.1.151

Coombs, C. H., & Avrunin, G. S. (1977). Single-peaked functions and the theory of preference. *Psychological Review*, *84*, 216–230. doi:10.1037/0033-295X.84.2.216

Deci, E. L., & Ryan, R. M. (2000). The "what" and "why" of goal pursuits: Human needs and the self-determination of behavior. *Psychological Inquiry*, *11*, 227–268. doi:10.1207/S15327965PLI1104_01

Deci, E. L., & Ryan, R. M. (Eds.). (2002). *Handbook of self-determination research*. Rochester, NY: University of Rochester Press.

Diener, E. (2000). Subjective well-being: The science of happiness and a proposal for a national index. *American Psychologist*, *55*, 34–43. doi:10.1037/0003-066X.55.1.34

Diener, E., Diener, M., & Diener, C. (1995). Factors predicting the subjective well-being of nations. *Journal of Personality and Social Psychology*, *69*, 851–864. doi:10.1037/0022-3514.69.5.851

Diener, E., & Suh, E. M. (Eds.). (2001). *Subjective well-being across cultures*. Cambridge, MA: MIT Press.

Diener, E., Suh, E. M., Lucas, R. E., & Smith, H. L. (1999). Subjective well-being: Three decades of progress. *Psychological Bulletin*, *125*, 276–302. doi:10.1037/0033-2909.125.2.276

Durkheim, E. (1951). *Suicide* (J. A. Spalding & G. Simpson, Trans.). New York, NY: Free Press. (Original work published 1897)

Eckersley, R. (2002). Culture, health, and well-being. In R. Eckersley, J. Dixon, & B. Douglas (Eds.), *The social origins of health and well-being* (pp. 51–70). Cambridge, England: Cambridge University Press.

Eckersley, R., & Dear, K. (2002). Cultural correlates of youth suicide. *Social Science & Medicine, 55*, 1891–1904. doi:10.1016/S0277-9536(01)00319-7

Fisman, R., Iyengar, S. S., Kamenica, E., & Simonson, I. (2006). Gender differences in mate selection: Evidence from a speed dating experiment. *Quarterly Journal of Economics, 121*, 673–697. doi:10.1162/qjec.2006.121.2.673

Fromm, E. (1941). *Escape from freedom.* New York, NY: Rinehart.

Gilbert, D. T., & Ebert, J. E. J. (2002). Decisions and revisions: The affective forecasting of changeable outcomes. *Journal of Personality and Social Psychology, 82*, 503–514. doi:10.1037/0022-3514.82.4.503

Gilovich, T., & Medvec, V. H. (1995). The experience of regret: What, when, and why. *Psychological Review, 102*, 379–395. doi:10.1037/0033-295X.102.2.379

Grant, A. M., & Schwartz, B. (2011). Too much of a good thing: The challenge and opportunity of the inverted-U. *Perspectives on Psychological Science, 6*, 61–76. doi:10.1177/1745691610393523

Haidt, J. (2006). *The happiness hypothesis.* New York, NY: Basic Books.

Hanoch, Y., & Rice, T. (2006). Can limiting choice increase social welfare? The elderly and health insurance. *Milbank Quarterly, 84*, 37–73. doi:10.1111/j.1468-0009.2006.00438.x

Hanoch, Y., Rice, T., Cummings, J., & Wood, S. (2009). How much choice is too much? The case of the Medicare Prescription Drug Benefit. *Health Services Research, 44*, 1157–1168. doi:10.1111/j.1475-6773.2009.00981.x

Hochschild, A. (1983). *The managed heart: Commercialization of human feeling.* Berkeley, CA: University of California Press.

Iyengar, S. S., & DeVoe, S. E. (2003). Rethinking the value of choice: Considering cultural mediators of intrinsic motivation. In V. Murphy-Berman & J. Berman (Eds.), *Cross-cultural differences in perspectives on the self* (pp. 129–174). London, England: University of Nebraska Press.

Iyengar, S. S., Jiang, W., & Huberman, G. (2004). How much choice is too much: Determinants of individual contributions in 401K retirement plans. In O. S. Mitchell & S. Utkus (Eds.), *Pension design and structure: New lessons from behavioral finance* (pp. 83–95). Oxford, England: Oxford University Press.

Iyengar, S. S., & Lepper, M. (1999). Rethinking the value of choice: A cultural perspective on intrinsic motivation. *Journal of Personality and Social Psychology, 76*, 349–366. doi:10.1037/0022-3514.76.3.349

Iyengar, S. S., & Lepper, M. (2000). When choice is demotivating: Can one desire too much of a good thing? *Journal of Personality and Social Psychology, 79*, 995–1006. doi:10.1037/0022-3514.79.6.995

Iyengar, S. S., & Lepper, M. R. (2002). Choice and its consequences: On the costs and benefits of self-determination. In A. Tesser (Ed.), *Self and motivation: Emerging psychological perspectives* (pp. 71–96). Washington, DC: American Psychological Association. doi:10.1037/10448-003

Kadison, R.D., & DiGeronimo, T.F. (2004). *The college of the overwhelmed: The campus mental health crisis and what to do about it.* San Francisco, CA: Jossey-Bass.

Kitayama, S., Snibbe, A.C., Markus, H.R., & Suzuki, T. (2004). Is there any "free" choice? Self and dissonance in two cultures. *Psychological Science, 15,* 527–533. doi:10.1111/j.0956-7976.2004.00714.x

Klerman, G.L., Lavori, P.W., Rice, J., Reich, T., Endicott, J., Andreasen, N.C., . . . Hirschfeld, R.M.A. (1985). Birth cohort trends in rates of major depressive disorder among relatives of patients with affective disorder. *Archives of General Psychiatry, 42,* 689–693. doi:10.1001/archpsyc.1985.01790300057007

Klerman, G.L., & Weissman, M.M. (1989). Increasing rates of depression. *JAMA, 261,* 2229–2235. doi:10.1001/jama.1989.03420150079041

Landman, J. (1993). *Regret: The persistence of the possible.* New York, NY: Oxford University Press.

Lane, R. (2000). *The loss of happiness in market democracies.* New Haven, CT: Yale University Press.

Loomes, G., & Sugden, R. (1982). Regret theory: An alternative theory of rational choice under uncertainty. *The Economic Journal, 92,* 805–824. doi:10.2307/2232669

Luthar, S.S., & Latendresse, S.J. (2005). Children of the affluent: Challenges to well-being. *Current Directions in Psychological Science, 14,* 49–53. doi:10.1111/j.0963-7214.2005.00333.x

Markus, H.R., & Kitayama, S. (1991). Culture and the self: Implications for cognition, emotion, and motivation. *Psychological Review, 98,* 224–253. doi:10.1037/0033-295X.98.2.224

Markus, H., & Nurius, P. (1986). Possible selves. *American Psychologist, 41,* 954–969. doi:10.1037/0003-066X.41.9.954

Markus, H.R., & Schwartz, B. (2010). Does choice mean freedom and well-being? *Journal of Consumer Research, 37,* 344–355. doi:10.1086/651242

Michalos, A.C. (1980). Satisfaction and happiness. *Social Indicators Research, 8,* 385–422. doi:10.1007/BF00461152

Michalos, A.C. (1986). Job satisfaction, marital satisfaction, and the quality of life: A review and a preview. In F. M. Andrews (Ed.), *Research on the quality of life* (pp. 57–83). Ann Arbor, MI: Institute for Social Research, University of Michigan.

Myers, D. (2000). *The American paradox.* New Haven, CT: Yale University Press.

Robbins, A., & Wilner, A. (2001). *Quarterlife crisis: The unique challenges of life in your twenties.* New York, NY: Putnam.

Rosenhan, D.L., & Seligman, M.E.P. (1995). *Abnormal psychology.* New York, NY: Norton.

Ryan, R.M., & Deci, E.L. (2000). Self-determination theory and the facilitation of intrinsic motivation, social development, and well-being. *American Psychologist, 55,* 68–78. doi:10.1037/0003-066X.55.1.68

Sartre, J.-P. (2001). *Being and nothingness: An essay in phenomenological ontology*. New York, NY: Citadel Press. (Original work published 1943)

Savani, K., Markus, H. R., Naidu, N. V. R., Kumar, S., & Berlia, N. (2010). What counts as a choice? U.S. Americans are more likely than Indians to construe actions as choices. *Psychological Science, 21*, 391–398. doi:10.1177/0956797609359908

Scheibehenne, B., Greifeneder, R., & Todd, P. M. (2009). What moderates the too-much-choice effect? *Psychology and Marketing, 26*, 229–253. doi:10.1002/mar.20271

Schlenker, B. R. (1985). *The self and social life*. New York, NY: McGraw-Hill.

Schwartz, B. (2000). Self-determination: The tyranny of freedom. *American Psychologist, 55*, 79–88. doi:10.1037/0003-066X.55.1.79

Schwartz, B. (2004). *The paradox of choice: Why more is less*. New York, NY: Ecco Press.

Schwartz, B., Markus, H. R., & Snibbe, A. C. (2006, February 26). Is freedom just another word for many things to buy? *New York Times Magazine*, pp. 14–15.

Schwartz, B., Ward, A., Monterosso, J., Lyubomirsky, S., White, K., & Lehman, D. R. (2002). Maximizing versus satisficing: Happiness is a matter of choice. *Journal of Personality and Social Psychology, 83*, 1178–1197. doi:10.1037/0022-3514.83.5.1178

Seligman, M. E. P. (1975). *Helplessness: On depression, development, and death*. San Francisco, CA: Freeman.

Snibbe, A. C., & Markus, H. R. (2005). You can't always get what you want: Social class, agency, and choice. *Journal of Personality and Social Psychology, 88*, 703–720. doi:10.1037/0022-3514.88.4.703

Tanius, B., Wood, S., Hanoch, Y., & Rice, T. (2009). Aging and choice: Applications to Medicare Part D. *Judgment and Decision Making, 4*, 92–101.

Taylor, C. (1989). *Sources of the self*. Cambridge, MA: Harvard University Press.

Taylor, C. (1992a). *The ethics of authenticity*. Cambridge, MA: Harvard University Press.

Taylor, C. (1992b). *Multiculturalism and the "politics of recognition."* Princeton, NJ: Princeton University Press.

Trilling, L. (1972). *Sincerity and authenticity*. Cambridge, MA: Harvard University Press.

von Uexkull, J. (1938/1954). A stroll through the worlds of animals and men. In C. H. Schiller (Ed.), *Instinctive behavior* (pp. 3–59). New York, NY: International Universities Press.

Yalom, I. D. (1980). *Existential psychotherapy*. New York, NY: Basic Books.

IV

CONNECTION VERSUS ISOLATION AND LONELINESS

16

AN ATTACHMENT PERSPECTIVE ON COPING WITH EXISTENTIAL CONCERNS

PHILLIP R. SHAVER AND MARIO MIKULINCER

In recent years, attachment theory (e.g., Bowlby, 1973, 1980, 1982, 1988), which was originally formulated to describe and explain infant–parent emotional bonding, has been applied first to the study of adolescent and adult romantic relationships and then to the study of group dynamics and intergroup relationships. To distinguish this elaborated version of the theory, which now has hundreds of studies supporting it, from the original child-oriented theory, we use the term *adult attachment theory* (Mikulincer & Shaver, 2007a). In the present chapter, we extend the theory further to apply it to the ways in which people experience and cope with the existential concerns addressed in this volume: mortality, meaninglessness, isolation, and lack of freedom. Our main idea is that *attachment security*—a felt sense, rooted in one's history of close relationships, that the world is generally safe, other people are generally helpful when called on, and I, as a unique individual, am valuable and lovable, thanks to being valued and loved by others—provides a psychological foundation for easing existential anxieties and constructing an authentic sense of continuity, coherence, meaning, connectedness, and autonomy.

We begin by presenting an overview of attachment theory and our theoretical model of the activation and psychodynamics of the attachment behavioral system in adulthood (Mikulincer & Shaver, 2007a). We then apply this model to ways of coping with existential concerns. We show, on the basis of empirical studies, that a heightened awareness of existential concerns (worries about finitude, isolation, meaninglessness, or lack of freedom) automatically activates what Bowlby (e.g., 1973) called the *attachment system*. This in turn motivates what he called *proximity seeking*—moving toward actual others or mental representations of them to bolster feelings of safety and security and thereby reduce existential anxiety. We review studies showing that the availability of a loving and supportive external or internalized attachment figure and the resulting sense of security are effective antidotes to the four major existential threats. Along the way, we explain how individual differences in attachment-system functioning shape the ways in which people experience, think about, and cope with existential concerns.

OVERVIEW OF ADULT ATTACHMENT THEORY

The main construct in Bowlby's (1982) attachment theory is the *attachment behavioral system*, an innate psychobiological system that motivates people to seek proximity to supportive others (*attachment figures*) in times of need. Although the attachment system is most crucial in the early years of life, because of human infants' extreme immaturity and dependence on others, Bowlby (1988) claimed that it is active throughout life and is manifested in thoughts and behaviors related to proximity- and support-seeking and in the resulting sense of security. This idea has now been bolstered by neuropsychological research (summarized by Coan, 2008) indicating that the human brain evolved to function within the context of social relationships.

According to Bowlby (1973), whose ideas were operationalized in landmark studies by Ainsworth and her colleagues (Ainsworth, Blehar, Waters, & Wall, 1978), although all human beings are born with a capacity to seek proximity, safety, and help with the regulation of negative emotions in times of need, important individual differences arise in close relationships that affect psychological and social functioning. When attachment figures are reliably available if needed, are sensitive to one's attachment needs, and respond warmly to one's bids for proximity and support, a person feels generally secure and efficacious and can explore the physical and social environment curiously, learn diverse skills, develop cognitively and emotionally, and enjoy life's challenges, often with other people.

A history of security-enhancing interactions with close others results in the formation of positive expectations about others' availability and generosity, which Bowlby (1973) called *internal working models of self and others*.

Because a person who is treated well by attachment figures learns to deal effectively with challenges and stressors, he or she can generally marshal effective affect-regulation strategies throughout life (Mikulincer & Shaver, 2007a). However, when attachment figures are not reliably available and supportive, a sense of security is not attained, doubts about one's lovability and worries about others' motives and intentions are formed, and strategies of affect regulation other than confident proximity seeking and effective self-regulation are adopted.

In studies of adolescents and adults, tests of these propositions from attachment theory have focused on a person's *attachment orientation*—the systematic pattern of relational expectations, emotions, and behavior that results from a particular history of attachment experiences (Fraley & Shaver, 2000). Beginning with Ainsworth et al.'s (1978) studies of infant attachment, and followed by hundreds of studies of adult attachment, researchers have found that attachment orientations can be measured along two orthogonal dimensions of attachment-related anxiety and avoidance (Brennan, Clark, & Shaver, 1998). Attachment *anxiety* reflects the degree to which a person worries that relationship partners will not be available in times of need and is afraid of being rejected or abandoned. Attachment-related *avoidance* reflects the extent to which a person distrusts relationship partners' goodwill and strives to maintain independence and emotional distance from partners. People who score low on both dimensions are said to be secure, or secure with respect to attachment. The two dimensions can be measured with reliable and valid self-report scales and are associated in theoretically predictable ways with many aspects of personal well-being and relationship quality (see Mikulincer & Shaver, 2007a, for a review).

We have proposed that a person's location in the two-dimensional space defined by attachment anxiety and avoidance reflects both the person's sense of attachment security and the ways in which he or she deals with threats and stressors (Mikulincer & Shaver, 2007a). People who score low on these dimensions are generally secure and tend to use constructive and effective affect-regulation strategies. In contrast, people who score high on either attachment anxiety or avoidance, or both (a condition called *fearful avoidance*), suffer from attachment insecurities. Insecure people tend to use secondary attachment strategies that we, following Cassidy and Kobak (1988), characterize as hyperactivating or deactivating the attachment behavioral system in an effort to cope with threats.

People who score high on attachment anxiety rely on *hyperactivating* strategies—energetic attempts to achieve proximity, support, and love combined with a lack of confidence that these resources will be provided and with feelings of sadness or anger when they are in fact not provided. These reactions occur in relationships in which an attachment figure is sometimes responsive but unreliably so, placing the needy person on a partial reinforcement schedule that rewards exaggeration and persistence in proximity-seeking attempts because these efforts sometimes succeed (Ainsworth et al., 1978). In contrast, people who score high on avoidant attachment tend to use *deactivating* strategies: trying not to seek proximity to others when threatened, denying attachment needs, and avoiding closeness and interdependence in relationships. These strategies develop in relationships with attachment figures who disapprove of and punish frequent bids for closeness and expressions of need (Ainsworth et al., 1978).

In short, each attachment strategy has a major regulatory goal (insisting on proximity to an attachment figure or on self-reliance) that goes along with particular cognitive and affective processes that facilitate goal attainment. These strategies affect the formation and maintenance of close relationships as well as the experience, regulation, and expression of negative emotions, such as anxiety, anger, or sadness (Mikulincer & Shaver, 2007a). Moreover, the strategies affect the ways in which people experience and cope with threatening events, including existential threats—the focus of the following sections of this chapter.

ATTACHMENT ORIENTATIONS AND COPING WITH EXISTENTIAL CONCERNS

We propose that the attachment system was "designed," or selected, by evolution as a regulatory device for dealing with all kinds of stressors and threats, including existential concerns about annihilation or death, which Bowlby (1982) discussed in relation to the threat of predation in early humans' environment of adaptation. Because of the way the attachment system is constructed, external or internal (symbolic) threats to one's sense of continued existence, life's predictability and meaning, social connectedness, or freedom and autonomy automatically activate the goal of approaching an attachment figure and obtaining protection and support. If this strategy regularly evokes the desired responses from sensitive attachment figures, a person learns how to cope with existential threats and restore feelings of safety, continuity, meaning, relatedness, and autonomy. Unfortunately, unresponsive, unsupportive attachment figures and the attachment insecurities they arouse can leave a person vulnerable to anxieties about mortality, meaninglessness, isolation, and lack of freedom, causing him or her to adopt less constructive ways of coping with these existential concerns. In subsequent sections, we review studies of attachment-system activation and attachment-related individual differences in responses to each of the four major existential concerns.

Mortality Concerns

As reviewed in several other chapters in this volume (Chapters 1, 3, 4, 5, 6, and 10), awareness of one's mortality is a major cause of existential anxiety, one that automatically activates psychological defenses. According to attachment theory, making mortality salient also activates the attachment system and energizes a person's attempts to attain care, protection, and safety. This means that a sense of attachment security should be an effective terror management mechanism that restores a person's sense of value and continuity, rendering other symbolic defenses less necessary. In contrast, lack of available, responsive, and sensitive attachment figures may cause people to rely on other forms of defense against death anxiety.

Death Awareness and Attachment-System Activation

In a study of the mental accessibility of attachment-related representations, Mikulincer et al. (2000) found that even preconscious reminders of death can automatically activate the attachment system. They (Mikulincer et al., 2000, Study 3) subliminally exposed participants to the word *death* or a neutral word for 22 ms in each of several trials and found that words related to attachment security (e.g., love, hug, closeness) became more available for processing (as indicated by faster reaction times in a lexical decision task) following the death prime. The word *death* had no effect on the mental availability of attachment-unrelated positive or neutral words.

There is also evidence that conscious death reminders cause a person to think of seeking proximity to a close other (see Mikulincer, Florian, & Hirschberger, 2003, for a review). For example, experimentally heightened mortality salience is associated with greater psychological commitment to a romantic partner (Florian, Mikulincer, & Hirschberger, 2002), a heightened desire for emotional intimacy with a romantic partner (even if he or she has recently complained or been critical; Hirschberger, Florian, & Mikulincer, 2003), and a heightened preference for sitting near other people in a group discussion context, rather than sitting alone, even if this seating preference exposes one's worldviews to potential attack (Wisman & Koole, 2003), something people often avoid when mortality has been made salient (see Chapters 3 and 4, this volume).

Attachment-Related Differences in Managing Death Anxiety

Attachment-related individual differences are moderators of the effects of mortality salience. For example, Mikulincer and Florian (2000) and Mikulincer, Florian, and Tolmacz (1990) found that attachment security is associated with lower levels of death-related thoughts and fear of death measured by self-report scales, projective tests (narrative responses to The-matic Apperception Test [TAT] cards), and cognitive tasks (completion of death-related word fragments). In contrast, attachment anxiety is asso-ciated with heightened fear of death, as measured by both self-reports and TAT responses, and with greater accessibility of death-related thoughts even when no death reminder is present. Attachment-related avoidance is related to lower self-reported fear of death but with a higher level of death-related thoughts and anxiety in TAT responses. That is, avoidant individuals tend to suppress death concerns and exhibit dissociation between their conscious and unconscious thoughts about death.

Secure and insecure people differ in the way they manage concerns related to death. Although seeking support for one's cultural worldview has been considered the normative defense against existential threats (see Chapter 1, this volume), there is evidence that this response is more charac-teristic of insecure than of secure individuals. For example, experimentally induced death reminders produced more severe judgments and punishments of moral transgressors only among insecurely attached people, whether anxious or avoidant (Mikulincer & Florian, 2000). People scoring higher on secure attachment did not recommend harsher punishments for transgressors fol-lowing a mortality salience manipulation. In contrast, they reacted to mor-tality salience with heightened proximity seeking, a more intense desire for intimacy in close relationships (Mikulincer & Florian, 2000), and greater willingness to engage in social interactions (Taubman–Ben-Ari, Findler, & Mikulincer, 2002). These studies imply that even when mortality is made salient, secure individuals maintain their sense of security and engage in gen-erally prosocial activities, even if these are partially defensive in nature. In contrast, defensively hostile, reality-distorting reactions to mortality seem to result from recurrent failures of attachment figures to accomplish their protective, supportive, anxiety-buffering functions.

Concerns About Life's Meaning

The perception of coherence and meaning in life is crucial for maintain-ing emotional balance (see Chapters 7 and 8, this volume), and people often react defensively when their sense of meaning is threatened or is shattered by life circumstances (see Chapters 8, 10, and 11, this volume). From the standpoint of attachment theory, we would expect threats to one's sense of meaning, like any other serious threat to one's welfare, to trigger a search for comfort, love, and reassurance from attachment figures. As a result, the avail-ability of supportive attachment figures, in actuality or in one's mind, and the resulting sense of attachment security, should contribute to maintaining a solid sense of life's coherence, value, and meaning. In contrast, attachment insecurity should leave a person vulnerable to threats of meaninglessness and in need of alternative, less constructive ways of creating meaning.

Meaninglessness and Attachment-System Activation

Adult attachment researchers have not focused specifically on meaninglessness and its effects on attachment-system activation. We therefore conducted a study especially for this chapter to examine in a preliminary way the influence of meaninglessness on proximity seeking. Sixty Israeli undergraduates (66% women) were randomly assigned to one of three meaning-related conditions (a procedure based on King, Hicks, & Abdelkhalik, 2009, Study 3). Participants in a high-meaning condition ($n = 20$) and a low-meaning condition ($n = 20$) wrote a brief essay about how the statement "Human life is purposeful and meaningful" could be viewed as either true or untrue, respectively. Participants in the control condition ($n = 20$) wrote an essay on a neutral topic (shopping at a drugstore). Immediately after writing the essay, participants completed Sharabany's (1994) 32-item Intimacy Scale, assessing their desire for honesty, spontaneity, and closeness in relationships. We asked participants to focus on romantic relationships and to rate, on a 7-point scale ranging from 1 (*not at all*) to 7 (*very much*), the extent to which each item expressed their wishes in this kind of relationship. For each participant, we computed a total score by averaging the 32 items.

A one-way analysis of variance on the reported desire for intimacy was significant, $F(2, 57) = 6.54, p < .01$. Scheffé post hoc tests revealed that participants in the low-meaning condition reported a stronger desire for romantic intimacy ($M = 5.68, SD = 1.31$) than those in the high-meaning ($M = 4.86$, $SD = 0.83$) and control conditions ($M = 4.50, SD = 0.96$). No significant difference was found between the latter two conditions. Supporting our hypothesis, raising the specter of life's possible meaninglessness led to an increased wish for closeness and intimacy—the motivational signature of attachment-system activation. However, attachment-system activation was assessed only with a self-report measure rather than with an indicator of automatic, preconscious activation of the attachment system or observations of actual proximity-seeking behavior. Hence, more probing studies are still needed.

Attachment-Related Differences in the Perception of Life's Meaning

Unfortunately, adult attachment researchers have not yet examined systematically whether people differing in attachment security also differ in their perceptions of life's meaning and in ways of coping with the threat of meaninglessness. However, there is evidence that feelings of closeness and social support (which are aspects of felt security) are associated with a heightened sense of life's meaning (e.g., Hicks & King, 2009; Steger, Kashdan,

Sullivan, & Lorentz, 2008). Similarly, Lambert et al. (2010) reported that perceived closeness to family members and support from them was associated with greater meaning in life among young adults, even when self-esteem, feelings of autonomy and competence, and social desirability were statistically controlled. Moreover, implicit priming of relational closeness increased the perception of life's meaning when participants were in a bad mood (Hicks & King, 2009). In contrast, experimental manipulations of rejection, social exclusion, and loneliness (which are related to attachment insecurity) reduce people's sense that life is meaningful (e.g., Hicks, Schlegel, & King, 2010; Stillman et al., 2009; Williams, 2007).

Mikulincer and Shaver (2005) reported a preliminary study that examined the association between attachment insecurities and perception of life's meaning. Participants who had previously completed a self-report attachment measure were primed with representations of either a security provider (thinking about a supportive other) or a person who did not serve attachment functions. They then completed a self-report measure of the extent to which they perceived the world as understandable and life as "making sense" (Antonovsky, 1987). Lower scores on attachment anxiety and avoidance (i.e., greater attachment security) were associated with higher levels of meaning and coherence in life. Moreover, compared with neutral priming, security priming increased the sense of meaning and coherence even among dispositionally insecure participants.

More research is needed on the extent to which attachment security helps people find meaning in religious faith (see Chapter 8, this volume), engage in generative activities such as caring for offspring or teaching a new generation (Chapter 9), or enjoy moments of happiness (Chapter 7). Future research should determine whether attachment insecurity leaves people vulnerable to threats of meaninglessness; causes them to follow less constructive paths to meaning, such as political terrorism (Chapter 11) or disruptive religious fundamentalism (Chapter 8); or encourages self-destructive tendencies that may end in suicide (Chapter 18).

Isolation Concerns

Experiences of disapproval, criticism, rejection, betrayal, social exclusion, separation, loss of significant others, and loneliness can lead to aggression, social withdrawal, and even suicide (see Chapters 17 and 18, this volume). According to attachment theory, these kinds of experiences erode felt security and automatically activate the attachment system and attachment-related defenses. When sensitive and responsive attachment figures are available, felt security is heightened, one feels stably connected to others, and the threat of isolation is removed. In contrast, lack of security-enhancing attachment figures exacerbates isolation-related concerns, erodes the sense of relatedness, and leads insecurely attached people to search for other ways of coping with loneliness and isolation.

The Threat of Isolation and Attachment-System Activation

The idea that the threat of isolation (a relationship partner's unavailability, disapproval, criticism, rejection, or betrayal; separation from or the death of loved ones) is distressing and can activate the attachment system is one of the central tenets of attachment theory. Observations of infants who were separated from their mother (e.g., Heinicke & Westheimer, 1966) convinced Bowlby (1982) that this threat arouses anxiety, anger, protest, and yearning for proximity, love, and security. An infant, finding itself without an attentive caregiver, cries, thrashes, attempts to reestablish contact with the absent figure by calling and searching, and resists other people's well-intentioned efforts at soothing. Similar reactions are often observed among adolescents and adults following episodes of rejection, disapproval, or criticism by close relationship partners (e.g., J. Feeney, 2005) or the breakup of a romantic relationship (e.g., Sbarra & Emery, 2005). In a naturalistic study of behavioral reactions to separation from a romantic partner in the departure lounges of an airport, Fraley and Shaver (1998) found that couples who were separating were more likely than couples who were not separating to seek and maintain physical contact (e.g., by mutually gazing at each other's faces, talking intently, and touching).

Such activations of the attachment system can be detected even at an unconscious level. Mikulincer, Gillath, and Shaver (2002) found that, as compared with subliminal priming with neutral words, subliminal priming with the word *separation* produced (a) faster identification in a lexical decision task of names of people whom participants had identified as security-enhancing attachment figures and (b) slower reaction times for naming the colors in which attachment figures' names were presented in a Stroop (color-naming) task. In both cases, fast lexical decisions and slower color naming indicated heightened activation of mental representations of attachment figures in response to an implicit separation threat. Priming with the word *separation* had no effect on mental representations of people who did not serve attachment functions.

Attachment-Related Differences in Managing Isolation-Related Threats

Although isolation-related threats automatically activate the attachment system and motivate most people to restore their sense of security by seeking contact with attachment figures, attachment insecurities seem to distort this process and encourage other coping strategies. For example, whereas attachment-anxious individuals react to temporary separations from a romantic partner, or to divorce, with excessive rumination, catastrophizing, and distress, avoidant individuals emotionally, cognitively, and behaviorally distance themselves from their partner and suppress tendencies to vocalize their distress (e.g., Birnbaum, Orr, Mikulincer, & Florian, 1997; Davis, Shaver, & Vernon, 2003; J. Feeney, 1998). Similar findings have been obtained in studies in which mere thoughts of hypothetical or actual separation were aroused (e.g., Meyer, Olivier, & Roth, 2005).

The distortion of attachment-system activation produced by anxious attachment was observed by Mikulincer, Florian, Birnbaum, and Malishkevich (2002), who found that anxiously attached people mentally equated separation with death. Participants were asked to imagine being separated from a loved partner and then to perform a word completion task that measured accessibility of death-related thoughts. Those who scored higher on attachment anxiety reacted to separation reminders with more death-related thoughts. This may help to explain why anxious individuals tend to experience intense distress following separations.

A conceptually similar pattern of results was reported by Hart, Shaver, and Goldenberg (2005), who examined defensive reactions to separation and reminders of death. Undergraduates were asked to think about their own death, separation from a close relationship partner, or a control theme and then to report their attitudes toward the writer of a pro-American essay. People who scored relatively high on attachment anxiety rated the pro-American writer more favorably not only in the death condition—the typical defensive reaction to mortality salience (see Chapter 1, this volume)—but also in the separation condition. In other words, anxious individuals exhibited the same defensive reaction to reminders of death and separation.

In a pair of experimental studies, Fraley and Shaver (1997) asked participants to write about whatever thoughts and feelings they experienced while also trying not to think about their romantic partner leaving them for someone else. Anxious individuals were less able to suppress separation-related thoughts, as indicated by more frequent thoughts of loss following the suppression task and higher skin conductance during the task. In contrast, more avoidant people showed less frequent thoughts of loss following the suppression task and lower skin conductance during the task. Gillath, Bunge, Shaver, Wendelken, and Mikulincer (2005) documented related differences in patterns of brain activation (using functional magnetic resonance imaging) when people were thinking about breakups and losses or attempting to suppress such thoughts.

In a recent laboratory experiment, Cassidy, Shaver, Mikulincer, and Lavy (2009) examined the ways in which attachment insecurities shape cognitive and emotional reactions to episodes of rejection, criticism, or betrayal in close relationships and explored whether security priming could reduce these reactions. Participants wrote a description of an incident in which a close relationship partner criticized, disapproved, rejected, or ostracized them. They then completed a short computerized task in which they were repeatedly exposed subliminally (for 22 ms) to either a security-enhancing prime word (*love, secure, affection*) or a neutral prime (*lamp, staple, building*). Immediately after the priming trials, participants were asked to think again about the hurtful event they had described and to rate how they would react to such an event if it happened in the future: how rejected they would feel, how they would feel about themselves, and how they would react to these events.

In the neutral priming condition, the findings fit well with previous correlational studies of attachment-related differences in response to isolation-related threats. Avoidance was associated with less negative appraisals of the relational threat, less intense feelings of rejection, less crying, and more defensive or hostile reactions; attachment anxiety was associated with more intense feelings of rejection, more crying, and more negative emotions. These typical findings were dramatically reduced in size (most approached zero) in the security-priming condition. In other words, security priming reduced the tendency of avoidant people to dismiss relational threats and distance themselves from a hurtful partner and the tendency of anxious people to intensify distress and ruminate.

Concerns About Freedom and Autonomy

As with the other existential threats discussed so far, threats to freedom and autonomy should activate the attachment system, along with characteristic affect-regulation strategies related to different attachment orientations. According to attachment theory, the sense of attachment security allows people to tolerate necessary separations from attachment figures and to use them, when they are present or held warmly in mind, as secure bases from which to explore the world, acquire new skills, and eventually operate autonomously with confidence that support will be available if needed. In contrast, insecurity causes people to adopt either an overly cautious and dependent stance (in the case of anxiously attached people) or to compulsively pursue self-reliance (in the case of avoidant people).

Unfortunately, there is little research on attachment-system activation following actual or imagined threats to the sense of personal freedom and autonomy. However, research has shown that more secure people tend to engage in more relaxed and confident exploration and learning of new activities and ideas and that security priming supports exploration (e.g., Green & Campbell, 2000; Mikulincer, 1997). In the domain of career choice, it has been found that adolescents with more supportive parents or friends have more positive attitudes toward career-related exploration and a stronger sense of autonomy and mastery in choosing a career (e.g., Blustein et al., 2001; Schultheiss, Kress, Manzi, & Glasscock, 2001).

Studies of the extent to which a person's goals and plans are internally, autonomously regulated also point to the importance of other people's supportiveness (see Chapters 12 and 13, this volume). For example, Ryan, Stiller, and Lynch (1994) found that children who felt securely attached to parents and teachers displayed greater internal, autonomous regulation of school-related behaviors. In addition, some studies have established a link between attachment security and intrinsic motivation, the tendency to extend and exercise one's capacities and to enjoy exploration and learning (Elliot & Reis, 2003; Ryan & Deci, 2000). For example, Hazan and Shaver (1990) found that securely attached people were more likely than insecure ones to perceive work as an opportunity for learning, and Elliot and Reis (2003) found that self-reports of attachment security were associated with stronger endorsement of mastery goals in academic settings (goals focused on learning and on expanding one's capacities). Interestingly, Roth, Assor, Niemiec, Ryan, and Deci (2009) found that adolescents who perceived their parents as providing a more secure base for exploration and autonomy had a higher sense of personal freedom and reported more interest-focused academic engagement (see also Chapter 13, this volume).

This association between the availability of supportive attachment figures and the sense of autonomy has also been examined in romantic relationships. In a behavioral observation study, B. C. Feeney (2007) examined the extent to which one's partner's availability and supportiveness affects the other partner's independent pursuit of personal goals. B. C. Feeney found that reports of a partner's availability and supportiveness were associated with a person's perceived independence and self-efficacy, engagement in independent exploration, and ability to achieve independent goals. In addition, one partner's availability and supportiveness during a videotaped discussion of personal goals for the future was associated with the other partner's autonomous functioning (e.g., confident exploration of independent goals). Finally, participants whose partners were available and supportive (as observed at one point in time) experienced increases in independent functioning over 6 months, and were more likely to achieve an important independent goal by the end of the 6-month period.

CONCLUDING REMARKS

Although existential threats are obviously real and of great consequence, it would be a mistake to conclude that human beings are insufficiently equipped to deal with them or cannot do so without erecting psychologically distorting and socially damaging defenses. A host of studies have shown that people who have developed dispositional attachment security deal effectively with the fact of mortality, the need for meaning, and the challenges of freedom and independence. Moreover, they deal with these threats while remaining relatively open, optimistic, internally integrated, and well-connected socially. We had space here to focus on only a few examples, but there are other relevant and important studies of attachment security and honesty, authenticity, and creativity (e.g., Gillath, Sesko, Shaver, & Chun, 2010; Mikulincer, Shaver, & Rom, 2011). Overall, a coherent body of research indicates that people who are treated well by others, beginning early in life, find life engaging, enjoyable, and meaningful.

Because research on adult attachment has grown up under the strong influence of prior research on infant–parent attachment, existential concerns that emerge later in development have not been systematically tackled by attachment researchers. There are many indications, however, that if we consider adult attachment research in the context of theories and bodies of research regarding existential concerns, the two lines of research are compatible and have a great deal to offer each other. For scientists as well as nonscientists, realizing that there is more to explore, more to learn, and numerous engaging and supportive companions with whom to share these activities goes a long way toward fending off existential anxieties and providing life with enriched meaning.

REFERENCES

Ainsworth, M. D. S., Blehar, M. C., Waters, E., & Wall, S. (1978). *Patterns of attachment: Assessed in the Strange Situation and at home*. Hillsdale, NJ: Erlbaum.

Antonovsky, A. (1987). The salutogenic perspective: Toward a new view of health and illness. *Advances, 4*, 47–55.

Birnbaum, G. E., Orr, I., Mikulincer, M., & Florian, V. (1997). When marriage breaks up: Does attachment style contribute to coping and mental health? *Journal of Social and Personal Relationships, 14*, 643–654. doi:10.1177/0265407597145004

Blustein, D. L., Fama, L. D., White, S. F., Ketterson, T. U., Schaefer, B. M., Schwam, M. F., . . . Skau, M. (2001). A qualitative analysis of counseling case material: Listening to our clients. *The Counseling Psychologist, 29*, 242–260. doi:10.1177/0011000001292004

Bowlby, J. (1973). *Attachment and loss: Vol. 2. Separation: Anxiety and anger*. New York, NY: Basic Books.

Bowlby, J. (1980). *Attachment and loss: Vol. 3. Sadness and depression*. New York, NY: Basic Books.

Bowlby, J. (1982). *Attachment and loss: Vol. 1. Attachment* (2nd ed.). New York, NY: Basic Books.

Bowlby, J. (1988). *A secure base: Clinical applications of attachment theory*. London, England: Routledge.

Brennan, K. A., Clark, C. L., & Shaver, P. R. (1998). Self-report measurement of adult attachment: An integrative overview. In J. A. Simpson & W. S. Rholes (Eds.), *Attachment theory and close relationships* (pp. 46–76). New York, NY: Guilford Press.

Cassidy, J., & Kobak, R. R. (1988). Avoidance and its relationship with other defensive processes. In J. Belsky & T. Nezworski (Eds.), *Clinical implications of attachment* (pp. 300–323). Hillsdale, NJ: Erlbaum.

Cassidy, J., Shaver, P. R., Mikulincer, M., & Lavy, S. (2009). Experimentally induced security influences responses to psychological pain. *Journal of Social and Clinical Psychology, 28*, 463–478. doi:10.1521/jscp.2009.28.4.463

Coan, J. A. (2008). Toward a neuroscience of attachment. In J. Cassidy & P. R. Shaver (Eds.), *Handbook of attachment: Theory, research, and clinical applications* (2nd ed., pp. 241–265). New York, NY: Guilford Press.

Davis, D., Shaver, P. R., & Vernon, M. L. (2003). Physical, emotional, and behavioral reactions to breaking up: The roles of gender, age, emotional involvement, and attachment style. *Personality and Social Psychology Bulletin, 29*, 871–884. doi:10.1177/0146167203029007006

Elliot, A. J., & Reis, H. T. (2003). Attachment and exploration in adulthood. *Journal of Personality and Social Psychology, 85*, 317–331. doi:10.1037/0022-3514.85.2.317

Feeney, B. C. (2007). The dependency paradox in close relationships: Accepting dependence promotes independence. *Journal of Personality and Social Psychology, 92*, 268–285. doi:10.1037/0022-3514.92.2.268

Feeney, J. A. (1998). Adult attachment and relationship-centered anxiety: Responses to physical and emotional distancing. In J. A. Simpson & W. S. Rholes (Eds.), *Attachment theory and close relationships* (pp. 189–218). New York, NY: Guilford Press.

Feeney, J. A. (2005). Hurt feelings in couple relationships: Exploring the role of attachment and perceptions of personal injury. *Personal Relationships, 12*, 253–271. doi:10.1111/j.1350-4126.2005.00114.x

Florian, V., Mikulincer, M., & Hirschberger, G. (2002). The anxiety buffering function of close relationships: Evidence that relationship commitment acts as a terror management mechanism. *Journal of Personality and Social Psychology, 82*, 527–542. doi:10.1037/0022-3514.82.4.527

Fraley, R. C., & Shaver, P. R. (1997). Adult attachment and the suppression of unwanted thoughts. *Journal of Personality and Social Psychology, 73*, 1080–1091. doi:10.1037/0022-3514.73.5.1080

Fraley, R. C., & Shaver, P. R. (1998). Airport separations: A naturalistic study of adult attachment dynamics in separating couples. *Journal of Personality and Social Psychology, 75*, 1198–1212. doi:10.1037/0022-3514.75.5.1198

Fraley, R.C., & Shaver, P.R. (2000). Adult romantic attachment: Theoretical developments, emerging controversies, and unanswered questions. *Review of General Psychology, 4*, 132–154. doi:10.1037/1089-2680.4.2.132

Gillath, O., Bunge, S.A., Shaver, P.R., Wendelken, C., & Mikulincer, M. (2005). Attachment-style differences in the ability to suppress negative thoughts: Exploring the neural correlates. *NeuroImage, 28*, 835–847. doi:10.1016/j.neuroimage.2005.06.048

Gillath, O., Sesko, A.K., Shaver, P.R., & Chun, D.S. (2010). Attachment, authenticity, and honesty: Dispositional and experimentally induced security can reduce self- and other-deception. *Journal of Personality and Social Psychology, 98*, 841–855. doi:10.1037/a0019206

Green, J.D., & Campbell, W. (2000). Attachment and exploration in adults: Chronic and contextual accessibility. *Personality and Social Psychology Bulletin, 26*, 452–461. doi:10.1177/0146167200266004

Hart, J., Shaver, P.R., & Goldenberg, J.L. (2005). Attachment, self-esteem, worldviews, and terror management: Evidence for a tripartite security system. *Journal of Personality and Social Psychology, 88*, 999–1013. doi:10.1037/0022-3514.88.6.999

Hazan, C., & Shaver, P.R. (1990). Love and work: An attachment-theoretical perspective. *Journal of Personality and Social Psychology, 59*, 270–280. doi:10.1037/0022-3514.59.2.270

Heinicke, C., & Westheimer, I. (1966). *Brief separations*. New York, NY: International Universities Press.

Hicks, J.A., & King, L.A. (2009). Positive mood and social relatedness as information about meaning in life. *The Journal of Positive Psychology, 4*, 471–482. doi:10.1080/17439760903271108

Hicks, J.A., Schlegel, R.J., & King, L.A. (2010). Social threats, happiness, and the dynamics of meaning in life judgments. *Personality and Social Psychology Bulletin, 36*, 1305–1317. doi:10.1177/0146167210381650

Hirschberger, G., Florian, V., & Mikulincer, M. (2003). Strivings for romantic intimacy following partner complaint or partner criticism: A terror management perspective. *Journal of Social and Personal Relationships, 20*, 675–687. doi:10.1177/02654075030205006

King, L.A., Hicks, J.A., & Abdelkhalik, J. (2009). Death, life, scarcity, and value: An alternative perspective on the meaning of death. *Psychological Science, 20*, 1459–1462. doi:10.1111/j.1467-9280.2009.02466.x

Lambert, N.M., Stillman, T.F., Baumeister, R.F., Fincham, F.D., Hicks, J.A., & Graham, S.M. (2010). Family as a salient source of meaning in young adulthood. *The Journal of Positive Psychology, 5*, 367–376. doi:10.1080/17439760.2010.516616

Meyer, B., Olivier, L., & Roth, D.A. (2005). Please don't leave me! BIS/BAS, attachment styles, and responses to a relationship threat. *Personality and Individual Differences, 38*, 151–162. doi:10.1016/j.paid.2004.03.016

Mikulincer, M. (1997). Adult attachment style and information processing: Individual differences in curiosity and cognitive closure. *Journal of Personality and Social Psychology, 72*, 1217–1230. doi:10.1037/0022-3514.72.5.1217

Mikulincer, M., Birnbaum, G., Woddis, D., & Nachmias, O. (2000). Stress and accessibility of proximity-related thoughts: Exploring the normative and intra-individual components of attachment theory. *Journal of Personality and Social Psychology, 78*, 509–523. doi:10.1037/0022-3514.78.3.509

Mikulincer, M., & Florian, V. (2000). Exploring individual differences in reactions to mortality salience: Does attachment style regulate terror management mechanisms? *Journal of Personality and Social Psychology, 79*, 260–273. doi:10.1037/0022-3514.79.2.260

Mikulincer, M., Florian, V., Birnbaum, G., & Malishkevich, S. (2002). The death-anxiety buffering function of close relationships: Exploring the effects of separation reminders on death-thought accessibility. *Personality and Social Psychology Bulletin, 28*, 287–299. doi:10.1177/0146167202286001

Mikulincer, M., Florian, V., & Hirschberger, G. (2003). The existential function of close relationships: Introducing death into the science of love. *Personality and Social Psychology Review, 7*, 20–40. doi:10.1207/S15327957PSPR0701_2

Mikulincer, M., Florian, V., & Tolmacz, R. (1990). Attachment styles and fear of personal death: A case study of affect regulation. *Journal of Personality and Social Psychology, 58*, 273–280. doi:10.1037/0022-3514.58.2.273

Mikulincer, M., Gillath, O., & Shaver, P. R. (2002). Activation of the attachment system in adulthood: Threat-related primes increase the accessibility of mental representations of attachment figures. *Journal of Personality and Social Psychology, 83*, 881–895. doi:10.1037/0022-3514.83.4.881

Mikulincer, M., & Shaver, P. R. (2005). Mental representations of attachment security: Theoretical foundation for a positive social psychology. In M. W. Baldwin (Ed.), *Interpersonal cognition* (pp. 233–266). New York, NY: Guilford Press.

Mikulincer, M., & Shaver, P. R. (2007). *Attachment in adulthood: Structure, dynamics, and change*. New York, NY: Guilford Press.

Mikulincer, M., Shaver, P. R., & Rom, E. (2011). The effects of implicit and explicit security priming on creative problem solving. *Cognition and Emotion, 25*, 519–531. doi:10.1080/02699931.2010.540110

Roth, G., Assor, A., Niemiec, C. P., Ryan, R. M., & Deci, E. L. (2009). The emotional and academic consequences of parental conditional regard: Comparing conditional positive regard, conditional negative regard, and autonomy support as parenting practices. *Developmental Psychology, 45*, 1119–1142. doi:10.1037/a0015272

Ryan, R. M., & Deci, E. L. (2000). Self-determination theory and the facilitation of intrinsic motivation, social development, and well-being. *American Psychologist, 55*, 68–78. doi:10.1037/0003-066X.55.1.68

Ryan, R. M., Stiller, J., & Lynch, J. H. (1994). Representations of relationships with teachers, parents, and friends as predictors of academic motivation and self-esteem. *The Journal of Early Adolescence, 14*, 226–249. doi:10.1177/027243169401400207

Sbarra, D. A., & Emery, R. E. (2005). The emotional sequelae of nonmarital relationship dissolution: Analysis of change and intraindividual variability over time. *Personal Relationships, 12,* 213–232. doi:10.1111/j.1350-4126.2005.00112.x

Schultheiss, D. E. P., Kress, H. M., Manzi, A. J., & Glasscock, J. M. J. (2001). Relational influences in career development: A qualitative inquiry. *The Counseling Psychologist, 29,* 216–241. doi:10.1177/0011000001292003

Sharabany, R. (1994). Intimacy friendship scale: Conceptual underpinnings, psychometric properties, and construct validity. *Journal of Social and Personal Relationships, 11,* 449–469. doi:10.1177/0265407594113010

Steger, M. F., Kashdan, T. B., Sullivan, B. A., & Lorentz, D. (2008). Understanding the search for meaning in life: Personality, cognitive style, and the dynamic between seeking and experiencing meaning. *Journal of Research in Personality, 42,* 660–678. doi:10.1016/j.jrp.2007.09.003

Stillman, T. F., Baumeister, R. F., Lambert, N. M., Crescioni, A. W., DeWall, C. N., & Fincham, F. D. (2009). Alone and without purpose: Life loses meaning following social exclusion. *Journal of Experimental Social Psychology, 45,* 686–694. doi:10.1016/j.jesp.2009.03.007

Taubman – Ben-Ari, O., Findler, L., & Mikulincer, M. (2002). The effects of mortality salience on relationship strivings and beliefs: The moderating role of attachment style. *British Journal of Social Psychology, 41,* 419–441. doi:10.1348/014466602760344296

Williams, K. D. (2007). Ostracism. *Annual Review of Psychology, 58,* 425–452. doi:10.1146/annurev.psych.58.110405.085641

Wisman, A., & Koole, S. L. (2003). Hiding in the crowd: Can mortality salience promote affiliation with others who oppose one's worldview. *Journal of Personality and Social Psychology, 84,* 511–526. doi:10.1037/0022-3514.84.3.511

17

OSTRACISM: THE IMPACT OF BEING RENDERED MEANINGLESS

KIPLING D. WILLIAMS

In what turns out to be a most prescient observation, William James (1890/1950) wrote,

> If not one turned round when we entered, answered when we spoke, or minded what we did, but if every person we met "cut us dead," and acted as if we were nonexisting things, a kind of rage and impotent despair would ere long well up in us, from which the cruelest bodily tortures would be a relief; for these would make us feel that, however bad might be our plight, we had not sunk to such a depth as to be unworthy of attention at all. (pp. 293–294)

In one eloquent sentence, James captured the essence of being ostracized by one's mates. Being ignored and excluded by others is like being dead, like not existing at all, like having no meaning or value (e.g., Pinel, Long, Landau, & Pyszczynski, 2004; Yalom, 1989; see also Chapter 16, this volume).

In this chapter, I present my theory of ostracism and the relevant research that pertains particularly to feelings of meaninglessness. I argue that being ostracized, even in brief and innocuous episodes, quickly and powerfully envelopes an individual in a cloak of invisibility, along with the sick and painful feeling of, at least momentarily, having no purpose, no meaning, no worth. Before presenting the formal aspect of my theory, let me begin with a personal example.

THE SCARLET LETTER O

In 1996, I was about to leave the University of Toledo to take a new job at the University of New South Wales, in Sydney, Australia. During the last week of my final semester at Toledo, my colleagues agreed to participate in a 5-day-long immersive role-play study on ostracism (Williams, Bernieri, Faulkner, Grahe, & Gada-Jain, 2000). There were five of us, two professors and three graduate students, and on each day of the week, one of us would be randomly selected as the target of ostracism by the others. That meant that one of us would arrive in the morning to see a scarlet letter O fixed to our office door. The others would see this too and know that their task for the entire day was to ignore and exclude the O person. Thus, over a 5-day period, each of us was ostracized for a full day and each engaged in collaborative ostracism for 4 days.

We agreed to keep a diary during the week, entering any thoughts, feelings, or behaviors we experienced or engaged in that we believed were relevant to either ostracizing or being ostracized. Our other colleagues in the department thought our activity was a waste of time, that it would yield nothing because we had all agreed to participate and knew the ostracism was not being delivered because of anger or dislike or disgust. Because we knew why we were being ostracized, they argued, it would have no impact on us. We acknowledged that this was certainly a possibility, but a prior experience suggested otherwise.

We were developing an ostracism paradigm that used ball tossing among three individuals—two confederates and one participant. In the inclusion condition, the participant received the ball on one third of the throws (Williams & Sommer, 1997). In the ostracism condition, they were to receive the ball about three to four times at the beginning but then never again for the remainder of the 5-minute period. I had to train our confederates not to throw a ball to a participant but only to each other during the 5-minute ball toss game that presumably emerged spontaneously while participants waited for the return of the experimenter. Thus, playing the role of the participant, I instructed the confederates not to throw the ball to me, not to look at me, and to engage in eye gaze and ball tossing only with each other. One would think that being ignored and excluded when one instructed the others to do so would have no impact on me. Yet, for reasons I could not fathom at the time, I nevertheless felt a sinking feeling that got worse over the course of the

5 minutes. It was a visceral feeling, certainly not a rational one, and it made me feel alone, helpless, invisible, and meaningless.

Thus, it did not seem entirely implausible that a collaboratively planned ostracism role-play exercise could have an important and revealing effect on my colleagues and me. So, what happened? We got more than we bargained for. It would be an understatement to say that we were not productive that week. We were so consumed by the ostracism (both giving and getting), that none of us were able to do much else. It was not that we were not going through the motions of a typical productive week—we met about research, we presented and discussed ideas frequently—but in our diary reports we could not recall the content of our meetings. The ostracizers appeared to be devoting so much time and effort to ostracizing that they were unable to remember what they were talking about in their meetings. The ostracized individuals were consumed with an existential dread such that they were unable to think about much else.

The night before I was ostracized, I actually dreamt about being ostracized by my colleagues and even my wife. On the day I was ostracized, we had a group research meeting. One of the others was presenting a research idea. I frequently contributed, and the fact that I was apparently invisible (and inaudible) to others did not stop me, at first. I would interject, give my two cents worth, and wait for the others' reactions. However, no reaction was forthcoming. Often, they would talk right over me. Sometimes, one of them would contribute the same idea I had just offered, and that individual got all the credit and attention. It was a surreal experience, and incredibly unpleasant. How did I deal with this? I cared nothing about being liked or fitting in; I cared completely about being noticed, favorably or unfavorably, it did not matter. So, I wrote the letter O on a piece of paper and pasted it on my forehead during the meeting. That was sufficient to irritate one of my colleagues, and that brief expression of irritation was so rewarding—I did exist! I also honked my horn at one of my colleagues as I drove back to my office. By habit, he waved, but then when he saw it was I who had honked, he quickly pulled his hand down in disgust. Again, I felt vindicated. I was not concerned with his disgust, only with his recognition. Finally, later that day during a departmental colloquium in which my colleague was the presenter, I raised my hand several times during and after his talk. He glanced around the room, pointing to others who raised their hands, but never acknowledged me. Words cannot express the rage, then helplessness, I felt being ostracized not only in front of the other four who were in on the plan but also in front of about 100 others in the room.

What had I learned from this experience? First, even though we planned the exercise, it had a powerful effect on all of us. Second, and most pertinent to the theme of this book, I felt meaningless and unimportant. I was not concerned about feeling disliked; I was concerned only about feeling invisible to others. I felt nonexistent and meaningless. If I could feel such strong existential threat when I was one of the chief planners of the role-play exercise, imagine the impact that being ostracized has on someone who is not asking for it.

OSTRACISM THEORY

My theory of ostracism, first presented in 1997 and revised most recently in 2009, asserts the following temporal sequence:

1. We detect any hint of ostracism quickly, yet crudely.
2. Our first reaction to ostracism, no matter how irrational, is to feel pain and a threat to desires for belonging, self-esteem, control, and meaningful existence.
3. We then reflect and appraise the ostracism episode to determine its importance and accuracy.
4. We attempt to cope with the pain and threat by either diminishing the episode's importance, or by engaging in thoughts or behaviors that elevate belonging, self-esteem, control, and/or meaningful existence; if the ostracism persists over time, our ability and resources to cope will diminish.
5. This results in an internalization and passive acceptance of our plight, the consequences of which are feelings of alienation, depression, helplessness, and worthlessness (Williams, 1997, 2009).

Athenians coined the term *ostracism* (from the word *ostraca*, which were shards of clay on which the names of individuals to be exiled could be written), but the phenomenon itself appears to have evolved along with the development of social animals, including humans (for a review of the animal literature, see Gruter & Masters, 1986; for humans, see Fry, 2007). Being ostracized is to be excluded and ignored. In some ways of thinking, this is a *nonbehavior*, defined as the absence of attention and inclusion but signaled often by lack of eye contact, responsiveness, and recognition by others. Perhaps because we overestimate the consequences of actions and underestimate the consequences of inactions (Kahneman & Miller, 1986), ostracism was virtually ignored by social scientists until the end of the 20th century.

The experience of long-term ostracism is strong and devastating. Structured interviews with individuals who were ostracized by their church, workmates, classmates, or family members indicated a breakdown of psychological motivation and functioning, including suicidal ideation or attempts, eating disorders, depression, and helplessness (Williams & Zadro, 2001). Books written by individuals who were ostracized (e.g., Davis, 1991) reveal dark, cold, and painful periods that required superhuman efforts to recover from.

From the perspective of evolutionary theory, ostracism is adaptive for the groups that employ it, because it strengthens the group by either removing or rehabilitating burdensome members (Goodall, 1986; Gruter & Masters, 1986). I (and others) have argued that detection of ostracism is also adaptive and that it is quickly signaled within a person as psychological pain (Eisenberger, Lieberman, & Williams, 2003), which alerts the person to the danger of social exclusion (Eisenberger & Lieberman, 2004; Kerr & Levine, 2008; MacDonald & Leary, 2005; Spoor & Williams, 2007).

Without the ability to quickly detect signs of ostracism, individuals could lose their social bonds and become vulnerable to psychological and physical dysfunction (Baumeister & Leary, 1995). Thus, even brief and seemingly innocuous episodes of ostracism are painful and distressing, and they threaten the satisfaction of important psychological needs. Because detection is quick, it is necessarily crude. The trade-off for quick detection of ostracism is a false-alarm bias: Ostracism is initially distressing even when individuals are playing a virtual ball toss game with strangers (Williams, Cheung, & Choi, 2000), computer players (Zadro et al., 2004), and despised others (Gonsalkorale & Williams, 2007), and when playing by rules that make ostracism financially advantageous (Van Beest & Williams, 2006).

Perhaps because people are particularly sensitive to minimal signs of ostracism, they are often able to adjust their interpersonal behavior to be reincluded in the group or attractive to other groups. Thus, most people are unlikely to experience prolonged or long-term ostracism; instead, they learn to cope effectively with a variety of relatively brief ostracism episodes that occur in everyday life. Daily event-contingent diary research indicates, in fact, that people experience about one ostracism episode a day (Nezlek, Wesselmann, Wheeler, & Williams, in press). Despite the seeming triviality of some of these episodes (e.g., being ignored by one's seatmate on a bus), research shows that being ignored by an elevator rider causes a momentary downturn in mood (Zuckerman, Miserandino, & Bernieri, 1983).

Attempts to improve one's social inclusion in response to ostracism seem to be the rule, but there are exceptions. Certain circumstances and individual differences encourage a more antisocial response to ostracism. When ostracism seems inevitable and unalterable, attempts to reconnect give way to aggression (Twenge, Baumeister, Tice, & Stucke, 2001; Warburton, Williams, & Cairns, 2006). Similarly, highly angered individuals or those with narcissistic traits may be predisposed to respond aggressively (Chow, Tiedens, & Govan, 2008; Twenge & Campbell, 2003).

The research findings obtained to date are consistent with predictions derived from my theory (Williams, 2009). There are three stages of response to ostracism: Stage 1—reflexive, Stage 2—reflective, and Stage 3—resigned.

Stage 1

The *reflexive* response is triggered by pain (Eisenberger et al., 2003), psychological threat to four fundamental needs (Williams, 2009), and negative affect. This alarm system directs the individual's attention to the episode, which is then interpreted and appraised in terms of its meaning and importance. Emotional responses to a brief ostracism episode are dynamic. Within only 100 seconds, an array of emotions is aroused, from humor, to anger, to sadness. This cluster of immediate reactions has shown to be remarkably resistant to moderation by either individual differences or situational factors (Williams, 2009).

Stage 2

The *reflection* stage involves directing one's attention to and appraising the meaning, cause, and reasons for the ostracism, and motivates cognitions and actions aimed at fortifying the threatened need or needs (see Jamieson, Harkins, & Williams, 2010). Studies show that individuals are more likely to conform, comply, obey, mimic, work harder collectively, detect genuine smiles, remember social information, and show more emotional intelligence following ostracism (this research is reviewed in Williams, 2009). All of these behaviors serve to increase one's sense of belonging and self-esteem. Thwarting control and meaningful existence, however, especially when social reconnection seems difficult or impossible, can lead to need-fortifying behaviors that reclaim control or force others toward the ostracized individual. Thus, research shows that when control is strongly threatened, ostracized individuals are more likely to be provocative, antisocial, and aggressive (see, e.g., Warburton et al., 2006).

Stage 3

The *resignation* stage applies to individuals who experience long-term ostracism. They eventually exhaust their coping resources and experience alienation, depression, helplessness, and existential angst. My laboratory work has provided substantial support for the first two stages, whereas our qualitative interviews with long-term targets of ostracism (work conducted with Lisa Zadro) provide anecdotal support for Stage 3 (see Williams, 2001; Williams & Zadro, 2001). As one example, a young woman in her 20s told us,

In high school, the other students thought me weird and never spoke to me. I tell you in all honesty that at one stage they refused to speak to me for 153 days, not one word at all, doctor. That was a very low point for me in my life and on the 153rd day, I swallowed 29 Valium pills. My brother found me and called an ambulance. When I returned to school, the kids had heard the whole story and for a few days they were falling over themselves to be my friend. Sadly, it didn't last. They stopped talking to me again and I was devastated. I stopped talking myself then. I figured that it was useless to have a voice if no one listened.

Over the past few years, I have received about two e-mails a month in my clinical practice that illustrate the devastating effects of long-term ostracism. Yesterday's e-mail was similar to most:

> Hello Kip, I am an outcast. My family has forbidden me access to my grandchildren. I am finding it very difficult to "hang on." This isn't the first time I have experienced being shun [sic], rejected, excluded etc., etc. Different yet similar situations in the past made me a depressive from an early age. This is the worst ostracism I have endured and I need help. I will go anywhere in order to get the help I need.

The impact of ostracism on meaninglessness, therefore, is likely to be most pronounced for those who experience ostracism repeatedly over a relatively long period of time. For these individuals, meaningless is internalized; they have no more regard for their own worth than they perceive that others have for them. If they are able to consider coping, it is only in the form of asking for help; they seem unwilling or unable to do things on their own that will substantiate their purpose and significance in daily life. Although these effects stem from long-term ostracism, recent experiments suggest that even brief episodes of ostracism may result in a temporary loss of meaning. I now review these studies.

RESEARCH FOCUSED ON MEANINGLESSNESS

Let me begin again with an anecdote from one of our early studies in which we used a conversation paradigm to manipulate ostracism. Participants were asked to discuss a topic in groups of three. Two of the participants were instructed to totally disregard, exclude, and ignore the third participant after 1 minute of discussion. I vividly recall one participant standing, looking around as if she were in a *Twilight Zone* episode, and then pinching her arm. Apparently, she was trying to assure herself that she existed. She then sat down and said nothing further. It was clear to me that at least for some, a few minutes of ostracism was sufficient to induce a sense of invisibility and, possibly, loss of meaning.

As reviewed by Case and Williams (2004), ostracism can be considered a "metaphor for death"—that is, being ostracized evokes a feeling that this is what others would act like if the ostracized individual were, in fact, dead or nonexistent. A few examples suggest that some people can use this sense of invisibility to their advantage. In Ralph Ellison's (1952) *Invisible Man*, the Black male protagonist (whose name we never learn) uses his invisibility to infiltrate and disrupt those who persecute him. Similarly, Muzafir Sherif posed as a janitor in the famous "Robbers Cave" experiments (Sherif & Sherif, 1953), so that he could be in the social presence of the boys under study while not inhibiting their conversations and behaviors. He reasoned that as a janitor, he would be ignored.

For most individuals who are ostracized, however, it is likely that the perception of invisibility and meaninglessness is extremely unpleasant. As suggested by the James quotation that opens this chapter, feeling unworthy of attention at all is worse than bodily tortures. Do we have empirical evidence that ostracism leads to loss of meaning?

The first study I summarize hints at this possibility, if we allow that loss of meaning is related to feelings of disconnection with others. Certainly, Baumeister and Leary (1995) and more recently Cacioppo and Patrick (2008) have made this argument. Loss of a feeling of connection with others is physically and psychologically debilitating. It leads not only to depression and suicidal ideation but also to eating and sexual disorders and to vulnerability to disease and illness. How much is needed to feel disconnected from others?

We tested this idea last summer in a field study (Wesselmann, Cardoso, Slater, & Williams, in press). One experimenter would walk past a pedestrian on campus. She would either glance quickly at the passerby, giving a nominal nod and minimal smile that signaled acknowledgment of the other person, or she would look in the same direction, but not at the passerby, as though the individual was not there. A trailing experimenter would stop the pedestrian and ask if he or she would be willing to answer a quick question for a class project: To what extent do they feel disconnected from others? The results showed that despite noting in a pilot study that over half of all passersby were observed not to look at other passersby, not receiving that brief glance of acknowledgement from a stranger was sufficient to significantly lower a person's perception of being socially connected with others.

If not receiving that glance of acknowledgement from a stranger who is walking by is sufficient to reduce one's feeling of social connection, how does a 2-minute episode of ostracism affect the individual in a laboratory setting?

In a study conducted a few years ago by Schefske for her honors thesis, we examined whether being ostracized in a Cyberball game by three others was worse than by two others, and whether having a co-target of ostracism diffused the distress experienced when one was the sole target (Wirth, Schefske, & Williams, 2011). Contrary to predictions based on Latané's (1981) social impact theory, the immediate pain and distress of ostracism did not increase with more sources of ostracism, nor did having a co-target diffuse it. One of our measures was a "Life is Meaningless" scale (Kunzendorf & McGuire, 1994), which consisted of 25 items, such as "The likelihood that I shall be remembered by no one in two hundred years makes my current life seem unimportant" and "There is no sense in feeling hopeful about the future because, in the end, death robs life of all meaning." Clearly, these are more easily viewed as enduring philosophical beliefs that are unlikely to be affected by a 2-minute experience with on online ball game. Nevertheless, just 2 minutes of ostracism, with or without a co-target, was sufficient to significantly increase participants' endorsement of these items. Apparently, even a brief episode of ostracism is enough to make individuals ponder and consider views espoused by existentialists and nihilists.

In addition, in a nice set of four studies by Stillman et al. (2009), participants were excluded either by a confederate who refused to work with them or in a Cyberball game. Compared with those who were included, ostracized individuals perceived life to be less meaningful as measured either by Kunzendorf and McGuire's Life is Meaningless scale or by a subscale of the Daily Meaning Scale (Steger, Kashdan, & Oishi, 2008). Loss of meaning was also highly related to self-reported loneliness, and the authors contended, as did Cacioppo and Patrick (2008), that loneliness is virtually synonymous with social exclusion. Finally, in their fourth study, they found that the association between ostracism and feelings of meaninglessness was moderated by self-reports of purpose, value, and positive self-worth.

These two separate investigations provide converging evidence that brief episodes of ostracism (or exclusion) are sufficient for individuals to doubt life's meaning. This is particularly impressive (although disconcerting), given that such views are considered to be enduring beliefs rather than views easily subject to situational manipulation.

The perception of coldness is often semantically linked with loneliness and social exclusion. Either being left "out in the cold" or receiving the "cold shoulder," an ostracized individual experiences not only pain and a threat to fundamental needs but also an embodied perception of coldness. Zhong and Leonardelli (2008) found, in two studies, that either recalling exclusion or being ostracized in Cyberball caused individuals to estimate colder ambient temperature or to prefer a warm drink. Whereas the authors contend that this perception is based on a metaphor, we have recently found that ostracized participants' finger temperature dropped significantly compared with included participants' finger temperature (Ijzerman et al., 2011). Apparently, the subjective feeling of coldness is based on an objective perception. This research, although not directly involving meaninglessness, does suggest a powerful link between coldness, exclusion, and perhaps even death (e.g., a cold body signifies death). Because death and meaninglessness are both associated with primary fears that result in terror (see Chapters 1, 2, and 8, this volume), it seems that research into temperature (both perceived and actual) may prove fruitful.

Two recent lines of research examined other links between death and ostracism. First, if ostracism triggers automatic pain responses because of its adaptive value, suppose an individual was ostracized from an activity that related to death. At a literal level, suppose two friends who were playing Russian roulette ostracized you? Would you feel relieved because you avoided death, or would you still feel the pain of ostracism? Van Beest, Williams, and van Dijk (2011) manipulated whether participants played either Cyberball or Cyberbomb. In Cyberbomb, their online characters were throwing a bomb with a lit fuse and were told it could blow up at any time and would kill the character that was holding it. The results indicated that when these two adaptive fears, death and ostracism, were pitted against each other, participants still felt the pain and psychological threats associated with ostracism but to a lesser extent than those simply playing Cyberball. Furthermore, in Study 2, participants first read evidence in favor of or against the existence of an afterlife before playing either Cyberball or Cyberbomb. In addition, they could be overincluded in these games, receiving the ball (or bomb) more often than their fair share. Although the afterlife manipulation did not affect the "reflexive" measures of discomfort and threat, it did affect coping: Those who read evidence against an afterlife were most aggressive (using hot sauce allocation), and reading about an afterlife reduced aggression. Finally, being overincluded in Cyberbomb (a form of bullying, perhaps?) was more distressing than being included in Cyberbomb, but it was less distressing than being ostracized in Cyberball. Overall, this research speaks to the intimate relation between ostracism and survival that has been proposed in theories of belonging.

For some people, believing that there is no afterlife, or no entry to heaven, is the ultimate form of meaninglessness, because to them life has meaning only in terms of what happens after one's death. Given this view, how would individuals who had especially strong beliefs in God and heaven react when primed with Bible passages that espoused exclusion rather than inclusion? Across two studies, Van Beest and Williams (2011) found that the prospect of being excluded by God threatened satisfaction with the fundamental needs for belonging, self-esteem, control, and a meaningful existence; it also decreased well-being and prosocial behavior. This was especially true for individuals who were most intrinsically involved in their faith. Finally, this difference in prosocial behavior was mediated by a loss of perceived control and not by other indices of well-being.

Finally, Wesselmann et al. (in press) recently conducted a field experiment in which individual pedestrians were passed by an experimenter who either briefly made eye contact with the pedestrian, made eye contact with a smile, or "looked through the person, as though they were air." There was also a control group of pedestrians for whom the first experimenter was absent. Pedestrians were then asked by a second experimenter, "How socially disconnected do you feel?" Participants who received eye contact (with or without the smile) reported less social disconnection than pedestrians in the control condition, whereas those "looked at as though air" felt significantly more socially disconnected. Thus, even in a "noisy" field environment lacking the advantages of experimental control, individuals are sensitive to feeling invisible.

SUMMARY

This review of qualitative and empirical research provides evidence that ostracism—being ignored and excluded—has important consequences for individuals' feelings of meaning and existence, and is associated with perceptions of death. My temporal need-threat model describes three stages of responses to the detection of the onset of ostracism. In the first stage, individuals appear to respond reflexively to minimal cues of ostracism with pain, negative affect, and threats to their senses of belonging, self-esteem, control, and meaningful existence. In the second stage, individuals reflect on the context and significance of the ostracism episode to assess its importance and meaning and to direct coping responses that might satisfy thwarted needs. For those who experience long-term or prolonged ostracism, fortification efforts become depleted and give way to resignation, alienation, helplessness, depression, and feelings of worthlessness. Unlike other aversive interpersonal behaviors, ostracism can uniquely threaten existential needs related to being recognized as existing and being worthy of attention. Feelings of invisibility and meaninglessness prompt people to demote desires to be liked in favor of provoking others to attend to, recognize, and reckon with them as individuals who are worthy of attention and consideration.

These findings converge with other theories and research presented in this volume, particularly terror management theory, proposed by Greenberg (Chapter 1), Pyszczynski and Kesebir (Chapter 4), and Solomon (Chapter 22) and in several other chapters in this volume, and Kruglanski, Gelfand, and Gunaratna's analysis of the quest for significance (Chapter 11), as well as with other existentialistic writings (e.g., Yalom, 1980). If people feel ostracized by important others, whether members of their family, church, work group, or society at large, then the loss of personal meaning and worth can be so devastating as to push some toward extreme worldviews or to accept the overtures of extreme groups that promise to provide a sense of meaning (Hogg, 2007, 2012) or personal significance (Chapter 11, this volume). Research on groups that are ostracized suggests that they are even more inclined to react with aggressive responses (Van Beest, Carter-Sowell, van Dijk, & Williams, 2011), making this an important focus for future investigation.

REFERENCES

Baumeister, R. F., & Leary, M. R. (1995). The need to belong: Desire for interpersonal attachments as a fundamental human motivation. *Psychological Bulletin*, *117*, 497–529. doi:10.1037/0033-2909.117.3.497

Cacioppo, J. T., & Patrick, B. (2008). *Loneliness: Human nature and the need for social connection.* New York, NY: Norton.

Case, T. I., & Williams, K. D. (2004). Ostracism: A metaphor for death. In J. Greenberg, S. L. Koole, & T. Pyszczynski (Eds.), *Handbook of experimental existential psychology* (pp. 336–351). New York, NY: Guilford Press.

Chow, R. M., Tiedens, L. Z., & Govan, C. L. (2008). Excluded emotions: The role of anger in antisocial responses to ostracism. *Journal of Experimental Social Psychology*, *44*, 896–903. doi:10.1016/j.jesp.2007.09.004

Davis, B. O. (1991). *Benjamin O. Davis, Jr., American: An autobiography.* Washington, DC: Smithsonian Institution Press.

Eisenberger, N. I., & Lieberman, M. D. (2004). Why rejection hurts: A common neural alarm system for physical and social pain. *Trends in Cognitive Sciences*, *8*, 294–300. doi:10.1016/j.tics.2004.05.010

Eisenberger, N. I., Lieberman, M. D., & Williams, K. D. (2003, October). Does rejection hurt? An fMRI study of social exclusion. *Science*, *302*, 290–292. doi:10.1126/science.1089134

Ellison, R. (1952). *Invisible man.* New York, NY: Random House.

Fry, D. P. (2007). *Beyond war: The human potential for peace.* New York, NY: Oxford University Press.

Gonsalkorale, K., & Williams, K. D. (2007). The KKK won't let me play: Ostracism even by a despised outgroup hurts. *European Journal of Social Psychology*, *37*, 1176–1185. doi:10.1002/ejsp.392

Goodall, J. (1986). Social rejection, exclusion, and shunning among the Gombe chimpanzees. *Ethology and Sociobiology*, *7*, 227–236.

Gruter, M., & Masters, R. D. (Eds.). (1986). Ostracism: A social and biological phenomenon. *Special Issue of Ethology and Sociobiology*, *7*, 149–395.

Hogg, M. A. (2007). Uncertainty-identity theory. In M. P. Zanna (Ed.), *Advances in experimental social psychology* (Vol. 39, pp. 69–126). San Diego, CA: Academic Press.

Hogg, M. A. (2012). Uncertainty-identity theory. In P. A. M. Van Lange, A. W. Kruglanski, & E. T. Higgins (Eds.), *Handbook of theories of social psychology* (Vol. 2, pp. 62–80). Thousand Oaks, CA: Sage.

Ijzerman, H., Gallucci, M., Pouw, W. T. J. L., Weissgerber, C. S., Van Doesum, N. J., Vetrova, M., & Williams, K. D. (2011). *Biological markers for close relations: Social exclusion leads to lower skin temperatures.* Manuscript submitted for publication.

James, W. (1950). *Principles of psychology* (Vol. 1). New York, NY: Dover. (Original work published 1890)

Jamieson, J., Harkins, S. G., & Williams, K. D. (2010). Need threat can motivate performance after ostracism. *Personality and Social Psychology Bulletin, 36,* 690–702. doi:10.1177/0146167209358882

Kahneman, D., & Miller, D. T. (1986). Norm theory: Comparing reality to its alternatives. *Psychological Review, 93,* 136–153. doi:10.1037/0033-295X.93.2.136

Kerr, N. L., & Levine, J. M. (2008). The detection of social exclusion: Evolution and beyond. *Group Dynamics: Theory, Research, and Practice, 12,* 39–52. doi:10.1037/1089-2699.12.1.39

Kunzendorf, R. G., & McGuire, D. (1994). *Depression: The reality of "no meaning" versus the delusion of "negative meaning."* Unpublished manuscript.

Latané, B. (1981). The psychology of social impact. *American Psychologist, 36,* 343–356. doi:10.1037/0003-066X.36.4.343

MacDonald, G., & Leary, M. R. (2005). Why does social exclusion hurt? The relationship between social and physical pain. *Psychological Bulletin, 131,* 202–223. doi:10.1037/0033-2909.131.2.202

Nezlek, J. B., Wesselmann, E., Wheeler, L., & Williams, K. D. (in press). Ostracism in everyday life. *Group Dynamics: Theory, Research, and Practice.*

Pinel, E. C., Long, A. E., Landau, M. J., & Pyszczynski, T. (2004). I-Sharing, the problem of existential isolation, and their implications for interpersonal and intergroup phenomena. In J. Greenberg, S. L. Koole, L. Sander, & T. Pyszczynski (Eds.), *Handbook of experimental existential psychology* (pp. 352–368). New York, NY: Guilford Press.

Sherif, M., & Sherif, C. W. (1953). *Groups in harmony and tension: An integration of studies on intergroup relations.* Oxford, England: Harper & Brothers.

Spoor, J., & Williams, K. D. (2007). The evolution of an ostracism detection system. In J. P. Forgas, M. Haselton, & W. von Hippel (Eds.), *The evolution of the social mind: Evolutionary psychology and social cognition* (pp. 279–292). New York, NY: Psychology Press.

Steger, M. F., Kashdan, T. B., & Oishi, S. (2008). Being good by doing good: Daily eudaimonic activity and well-being. *Journal of Research in Personality, 42,* 22–42. doi:10.1016/j.jrp.2007.03.004

Stillman, T. F., Baumeister, R. F., Lambert, N. M., Crescioni, A. W., DeWall, C. N., & Fincham, F. D. (2009). Alone and without purpose: Life loses meaning following social exclusion. *Journal of Experimental Social Psychology, 45,* 686–694. doi:10.1016/j.jesp.2009.03.007

Twenge, J. M., Baumeister, R. F., Tice, D. M., & Stucke, T. S. (2001). If you can't join them, beat them: Effects of social exclusion on aggressive behaviors. *Journal of Personality and Social Psychology, 81,* 1058–1069. doi:10.1037/0022-3514.81.6.1058

Twenge, J. M., & Campbell, W. K. (2003). "Isn't it fun to get the respect that we're going to deserve?" Narcissism, social rejection, and aggression. *Personality and Social Psychology Bulletin, 29,* 261–272. doi:10.1177/0146167202239051

Van Beest, I., Carter-Sowell, A. R., van Dijk, E., & Williams, K. D. (2011). *Groups being ostracized by groups: Is the pain shared, is recovery quicker, and are groups more likely to be aggressive?* Manuscript submitted for publication.

Van Beest, I., & Williams, K. D. (2011). "Why hast thou forsaken me?" The effect of thinking about being ostracized by God on well-being and prosocial behavior. *Social Psychology and Personality Science, 2,* 379–386.

Van Beest, I., Williams, K. D., & van Dijk, E. (2011). Cyberbomb: Effects of being ostracized from a death game. *Group Processes and Intergroup Relations, 14,* 581–596.

Warburton, W. A., Williams, K. D., & Cairns, D. R. (2006). When ostracism leads to aggression: The moderating effects of control deprivation. *Journal of Experimental Social Psychology, 42,* 213–220. doi:10.1016/j.jesp.2005.03.005

Wesselmann, E. D., Cardoso, F., Slater, S., & Williams, K. D. (in press). "To be looked at as though air": Civil attention matters. *Psychological Science.* doi:10.1177/0956797611427921

Williams, K. D. (1997). Social ostracism. In R. M. Kowalski (Ed.), *Aversive interpersonal behaviors* (pp. 133–170). New York, NY: Plenum Press.

Williams, K. D. (2007). Ostracism. *Annual Review of Psychology, 58,* 425–452. doi:10.1146/annurev.psych.58.110405.085641

Williams, K. D. (2009). Ostracism: A temporal need-threat model. In M. Zanna (Ed.), *Advances in experimental social psychology* (Vol. 41, pp. 279–314). New York, NY: Academic Press.

Williams, K. D., Bernieri, F., Faulkner, S., Grahe, J., & Gada-Jain, N. (2000). The Scarlet Letter Study: Five days of social ostracism. *Journal of Personal and Interpersonal Loss, 5,* 19–63. doi:10.1080/10811440008407846

Williams, K. D., Cheung, C., & Choi, W. (2000). Cyberostracism: Effects of being ignored over the Internet. *Journal of Personality and Social Psychology, 79,* 748–762. doi:10.1037/0022-3514.79.5.748

Williams, K. D., & Sommer, K. L. (1997). Social ostracism by one's coworkers: Does rejection lead to loafing or compensation? *Personality and Social Psychology Bulletin, 23,* 693–706. doi:10.1177/0146167297237003

Williams, K. D., & Zadro, L. (2001). Ostracism: On being ignored, excluded, and rejected. In M. R. Leary (Ed.), *Interpersonal rejection* (pp. 21–53). New York, NY: Oxford University Press.

Wirth, J. H., Schefske, E. M., & Williams, K. D. (2011). *Does company reduce misery? Immediate distress of ostracism not predicted by social impact factors.* Manuscript submitted for publication.

Yalom, I. D. (1980). *Existential psychotherapy.* New York, NY: Basic Books.

Yalom, I. D. (1989). *Love's executioner.* New York, NY: HarperPerennial.

Zadro, L., Williams, K. D., & Richardson, R. (2004). How low can you go? Ostracism by a computer lowers belonging, control, self-esteem, and meaningful existence. *Journal of Experimental Social Psychology, 40,* 560–567. doi:10.1016/j.jesp.2003.11.006

Zhong, C. B., & Leonardelli, G. J. (2008). Cold and lonely: Does social exclusion literally feel cold? *Psychological Science, 19,* 838–842. doi:10.1111/j.1467-9280.2008.02165.x

Zuckerman, M., Miserandino, M., & Bernieri, F. (1983). Civil inattention exists in elevators. *Personality and Social Psychology Bulletin, 9,* 578–586. doi:10.1177/0146167283094007

18

WHY PEOPLE DIE BY SUICIDE: FURTHER DEVELOPMENT AND TESTS OF THE INTERPERSONAL-PSYCHOLOGICAL THEORY OF SUICIDAL BEHAVIOR

THOMAS E. JOINER JR. AND CAROLINE SILVA

Finding meaning or value in life has been framed by philosophers and scientists alike as the most essential need for living. As social creatures, our connection and value with others are intimately tied to this pursuit. Existential writers have suggested that meaninglessness, arising from the inability to resolve basic existential concerns, may lead to the desire for death. Death, however, is inherently a fearsome prospect, so fearsome that it is thought to motivate a great number of human behaviors (Becker, 1973). The dilemma of who will develop a desire for death and who will go on to die by suicide may be better understood through the frustration of our basic needs to belong and contribute, as well as our ability to learn fearlessness.

The *interpersonal-psychological theory* of suicidal behavior (Joiner, 2005, 2010; Van Orden et al., 2010) posits that the fundamental constituents of suicidal ideation—as distinct from suicidal behavior—are the perceptions that

This research was supported, in part, by a grant awarded to Florida State University by the Department of Defense. The Department of Defense had no further role in the study design; in the collection, analysis, and interpretation of data; in the writing of the report; or in the decision to submit the paper for publication. The views and opinions expressed do not represent those of the Department of Defense or the United States Government.

one is alienated from others and that one is simultaneously a burden on others. These two perceptions—"I am hopelessly alienated" and "My death will be worth more than my life to others"—according to the theory, characterize the suicidal mind. Thwarted needs to belong and perceived burdensomeness are subcategories of more general states of emotional pain and hopelessness; low belonging and high burdensomeness are theorized to explain why the parent categories sometimes produce suicidal ideation. Put differently, the theory asserts that mental states such as hopelessness and emotional pain will not eventuate in suicidal ideation unless they involve feelings of alienation and burden.

Suicidal ideation is relatively common, certainly in clinical settings, but also more broadly. However, even among those with severe forms of suicidal ideation, suicide attempts are, relatively speaking, not common, and death by suicide, far less so. Among people with severe suicidal ideation, what differentiates those who attempt or die by suicide from those who do not? The theory's answer involves fearlessness about physical pain, physical injury, and death itself. Death is inherently fearsome and daunting, and it thus takes considerable resolve, intent, and fearlessness to attempt suicide. This does not make it laudable, but it does make it difficult.

The following sections take each of the theory's three constructs in turn, and for each, adds more conceptual detail and summarizes recent research. It should be emphasized, however, that the theory does not predict a main effect of each of the three constructs on suicidal ideation (although these effects often emerge in empirical work, particularly with regard to low belonging and high burden predicting suicidal ideation). Rather, with regard to the emergence of suicidal ideation, the theory hypothesizes a two-way interaction between (low) belonging and (high) burdensomeness; with regard to suicide attempts and death by suicide, the theory predicts a three-way interaction between (low) belonging, (high) burdensomeness, and (high) fearlessness about physical threat. Among those who attempt suicide, lethality is proposed to correspond to fearlessness about physical threat. After the sections on these three constructs, we close with a discussion of future directions for conceptual and empirical work on the theory.

LEARNED FEARLESSNESS: THE ACQUIRED CAPABILITY FOR DEATH BY SUICIDE

A woman in Israel has decided on death by suicide at the railway tracks. Security cameras record her as she approaches the track and kneels before an oncoming train, with her head slightly bowed. As the roar of the train grows louder, she looks up, and an instant thereafter a remarkable thing occurs: She throws herself backward just before the train hits her. On the security cameras, a few seconds tick away as the train rushes by, and once it finally passes, the woman stands up and walks away, unharmed.

A woman in the United States has also decided on her death and ingests a full bottle of a powerful household cleaner that contains a 35% solution of hydrochloric acid. Within seconds of ingesting the fluid, she wishes strongly to survive and calls 911. She is rushed to the hospital, where, a few hours later, she dies from internal injuries caused by the cleaner.

Two women, both so intent on suicide that they do harrowing things to enact it, nevertheless flinch in one way or another in the final moments. They flinch because their bodies, like those of creatures the earth over, are designed to flinch in the face of danger. And flinching can save lives (as in the case of the woman at the tracks) or at least give a chance for survival (as in the case of the woman who ingested the cleaner). That people flinch under conditions such as these is not surprising; what is surprising is that some people do not flinch under such conditions. These individuals have learned fearlessness of mortal danger, a fearlessness that the interpersonal-psychological theory asserts is a necessary precondition for death by suicide.

Death is inherently fearsome and daunting (see Chapters 1–4, this volume); to enact it therefore requires an undoing of the natural fear we have of physical pain, physical injury, and death itself. This occurs through a process of habituation and the engagement of opponent processes in response to repeated and escalating exposure to actual or potential physical threat. Specifically, opponent-process theory posits that observed affective responses are due to two underlying, oppositely valenced processes. Importantly, with repeated exposure, an affective stimulus loses its ability to elicit the original response and, instead, the opposite response is amplified (e.g., the primary effect of painful and provocative stimuli is fear and pain, whereas the opponent process is relief and analgesia; Solomon, 1980). As we will see, encounters with painful and provocative experiences can come in many guises.

The involvement of fearlessness in suicide sheds light on many disparate phenomena that are otherwise difficult to explain. For example, why, despite the involvement of depression in suicidal behavior, are suicide decedents virtually never described as down and sluggish in the moments before their deaths but are frequently described as agitated and keyed up? A possible answer is that the fear of death is too difficult to overcome unless one is highly activated and aroused. Similarly, why do deaths by suicide occur more frequently on Mondays and Tuesdays than on other days (e.g., MacMahon, 1983; Massing & Angermeyer, 1985)? Possibly because the Monday–Tuesday period is a time of activation following a time of rest. On this logic, suicide rates should peak in the May–June period in the Northern hemisphere and the November–December period in the Southern hemisphere because those time frames occur in the respective hemispheres' spring, and spring is activating. This is indeed the case (e.g., Chew & McCleary, 1995; Massing & Angermeyer, 1985).

Several strands of empirical evidence corroborate the theory's view of the acquired fearlessness construct and its basis in habituation and opponent processes. Self-report measures of the construct correlate in expected ways with gender (males, on average, score higher), age (it tends to heighten with age), occupation (e.g., it is higher in military populations), various indices of laboratory-assessed pain tolerance (those with higher tolerance report greater fearlessness), and a laboratory self-aggression paradigm (those who report greater fearlessness self-administer higher shock levels; Bender, Gordon, Bresin, & Joiner, 2011; Bryan, Morrow, Anestis, & Joiner, 2010; Teale, 2010; Van Orden, Witte, Gordon, Bender, & Joiner, 2008). An important piece of discriminant validity is that self-reports of fearlessness do not correlate with suicidal ideation (Bender, 2009; Van Orden et al., 2008); this is as expected because the theory predicts a role for acquired fearlessness only under conditions of low belonging and high burdensomeness and only then a role in suicidal behavior (not ideation). Joiner et al. (2009) affirmed this role, showing that the three-way interaction of fearlessness, low belonging, and high burdensomeness did indeed predict suicide attempts.

THWARTED BELONGINGNESS AND PERCEIVED BURDENSOMENESS

Mental states such as sadness, depression, emotional pain, and hopelessness are often invoked as explanations of suicidal ideation and behavior (e.g., Beck, Brown, Berchick, & Stewart, 1990; Shneidman, 1996), and indeed virtually every seriously suicidal person displays one or more of these states. A problem, however, is that the majority of people who display one or more of these states do not experience suicidal ideation or exhibit suicidal behavior. In other words, explanations based on general risk factors such as emotional pain and hopelessness face a severe specificity problem. One preoccupation of our own work over the past 20 years has been to propose solutions to this problem.

The concepts of perceived burdensomeness and perceived social alienation, discussed earlier, have several advantages, including that each is more delimited than concepts such as emotional pain and hopelessness. The conjunction between burdensomeness and alienation, which the interpersonal-psychological theory proposes is the fundamental cause of serious suicidal ideation, is (assuming that alienation and burdensomeness are not perfectly correlated, an assumption borne out by empirical work), by definition, more delimited still. Empirical studies have affirmed the connection of these concepts to suicide-related outcomes; in such studies, when the concepts of burden-someness and alienation are pitted against emotional pain and hopelessness in their ability to predict suicide-related outcomes, the former concepts win out (Joiner et al., 2009; Van Orden et al., 2008).

Further still, the reach of the concepts of burdensomeness and alien-ation outpaces that of emotional pain and hopelessness (Joiner et al., 2002). By *reach*, we mean the scope of suicide-related phenomena, both core and peripheral, which the concepts can illuminate. Consider suicidal ideation as an example of a core phenomenon. The following description by a person with a long history of suicidal behavior, including a near-lethal attempt, is characteristic of suicidal patients:

> I felt my mind slip back into the same pattern of thinking I'd had when I was 14 [when he first attempted suicide]. I hate myself. I'm terrible. I'm not good at anything. *There's no point in me hanging around here ruining other people's lives* [emphasis added]. I've got to get out of here. I've got to figure out a way to get out of my life.

The progression of thought contained in these words is not, in our opin-ion, coincidental. It begins with negative self-views (e.g., "I'm terrible"), but instead of stopping there, the progression goes on to an expression of perceived burdensomeness ("There's no point in me hanging around here ruining other people's lives"). Immediately after perceived burdensomeness is expressed, so is suicidal ideation. One implication of this anecdote—one that has been corroborated by empirical studies—is that general expressions of distress (e.g., emotional pain, hopelessness) do not eventuate in suicidal ideation or behavior unless they produce perceptions of burdensomeness (as in the anecdote) or of social disconnection (e.g., Jahn, Cukrowicz, Linton, & Prabhu, 2011). Burdensomeness and alienation represent the final com-mon pathway through which general risk factors affect core suicide-related phenomena, such as suicidal ideation.

Whereas the role of hopelessness or emotional pain in self-initiated death is quite hard to discern in any species other than humans, "death worth more than life" calculations are seen across nature, as are connec-tions between social connectedness and death, including self-initiated death. Researchers studying ants infected with a certain fungus stated,

> Leaving one's group to die in seclusion might be an efficient way of mini-mizing the risk of infecting kin. Anecdotal observations of moribund individuals deserting from their groups exist for several species, includ-ing humans, but have rarely been substantiated by quantitative analysis. (Heinze & Walter, 2010, p. 249)

The report showed that worker ants of the species *Temnothorax unifasciatus* self-sacrifice under conditions of lethal fungal infection. When ants were infected (and thus not only their survival but also that of their nestmates—and their genes in their nestmates—was threatened), they left the nest hours or days before death. For an ant, there could be no more certain way to ensure death. This remarkable ant behavior is reflective of the roles of both social alienation and burdensomeness in self-caused death.

It is not just in ants (or in the many other nonhuman species for which these kinds of behaviors have been documented) that this occurs; much the same processes precede death by suicide in humans. A growing number of empirical reports document the involvement of these two processes in human suicidal behavior (e.g., Conner, Britton, Sworts, & Joiner, 2007; Van Orden, Lynam, Hollar, & Joiner, 2006); some of these studies directly tested and corroborated the interpersonal-psychological theory's predictions that the two processes would interact to predict suicidal ideation (e.g., Van Orden et al., 2008) and that the two would be involved in a three-way interaction with fearlessness of physical threat to predict suicide attempt (Joiner et al., 2009).

FUTURE DIRECTIONS

The interpersonal-psychological theory of suicidal behavior provides a viable framework for enhancing our understanding of death by suicide. The following sections of this chapter delineate future directions for conceptual and empirical work on the theory, including research on causal claims, experiences of burdensomeness, mechanisms of recovery, and processes of habituation versus sensitization.

Interrelations of the Theory Constructs

Notice that in the study of ants described previously, the sequencing suggested a specific causal chain in which perceptions of burdensomeness led to isolation behaviors which in turn led to death. Might this same chain apply to death by suicide in people?

The following description of experiences with alcoholism and suicidal behavior suggests possibly so: "The reason [for suicide] is the conviction that you deserve your loneliness, that no one needs to be cast out more than you do" (Martin, 2011, p. 38). This possible sequencing would be of more than just theoretical interest; if it were the case that the chain ran from perceived burdensomeness to social isolation to suicidal ideation, the emergence of perceived burdensomeness could be viewed clinically as a kind of early warning system, analogous to a tornado watch. By the same logic, extreme states of social isolation could be viewed as clinically ominous, analogous to a tornado warning.

The possible causal interrelations between the fearlessness aspect of the theory, on the one hand, and burdensomeness and alienation experiences, on the other hand, are also a promising avenue for future research. For instance, there is some evidence that social isolation can increase pain tolerance (an important aspect of the fearlessness substrate postulated as key in suicidal behavior by the interpersonal-psychological theory; Coudereau, Monier, Bourre, & Frances, 1997; Puglisi-Allegra & Oliverio, 1983). As another example, might stoicism—a psychological dimension of the fearlessness substrate according to the theory—make judgments of one's burdensomeness harsher?

Final Common Pathway Claim

The interpersonal-psychological theory of suicidal behavior makes the ambitious claim that all documented risk factors for suicidal behavior—and they are legion, ranging from the molecular level to the cultural level—exert influence on suicidal outcomes because they exert influence on fearlessness of physical threat, perceived burdensomeness, and/or thwarted belongingness. Evidence to date suggests that this is likely the case regarding general factors such as emotional pain, but future research would benefit from testing the theory against rival accounts with a similar level of specificity as the interpersonal-psychological theory. Currently, the best candidate in this regard is a model that emphasizes feelings of entrapment as a causal mechanism in suicidal behavior (Baumeister, 1990). The model is complex, but it poses psychological processes such as suboptimal coping abilities leading to an individual feeling that he or she has no options and no way to escape from painful situations; to escape these feelings of entrapment, the individual resorts to suicidal behavior. Chatard and Selimbegović (2011), for example, found that realization of failure to attain an important standard resulted in increased accessibility of suicide-related thoughts, especially when associated with high levels of self-consciousness, escapist motivations, and a large discrepancy between self and a standard. Chatard and Selimbegović interpreted these findings as reflecting motivations to escape from negative self-awareness, considering that increased suicide-thought accessibility was associated with simultaneous increases in desire for an altered state of consciousness and accessibility of general escape-related concepts.

Feelings of entrapment may be a general factor, much like hopelessness and emotional pain, that does not culminate in suicidal thinking unless the entrapment is characterized by themes of burdensomeness and social alienation. Alternatively, entrapment may fit as an additional node in the causal sequence involving burdensomeness and alienation. These possibilities would be compatible with the interpersonal-psychological theory of suicidal behavior.

Of course, it is possible, contrary to the latter theory, that burdensomeness and social alienation will fall away as predictors of suicidal ideation once entrapment is accounted for. Work is in the preliminary stages to empirically arbitrate these questions.

Is It Worse to Be a Burden on Others or on Oneself?

The interpersonal-psychological theory was developed with burdensomeness on others as the focus. This was based in part on clinical experience but also on evidence from other species in which self-sacrifice is made on the basis of inclusive fitness calculations along the lines of "My death will be worth more than my life to my genes" (Andrade, 1996; McAllister, Roitberg, & Weldon, 1990; O'Connor, 1978; Poulin, 1992). However, based in part on sociometer theory (which views self-esteem as a gauge for social standing; Leary, Tambor, Terdal, & Downs, 1995), we have pondered whether burden on self may be as much as or more fundamental in leading to suicidal thought than burden on others. The jury is out on this question, but we do have mounting data from multiple studies that suggest the importance of being a burden to oneself.

Enhanced Connectedness and Reduced Burdensomeness as Mechanisms of Recovery

The interpersonal-psychological theory predicts that as suicidal crises resolve, they do so largely as a function of increasing connection to others as well as an improved sense of meaningful contribution to others (viewed as the opposite of perceived burdensomeness). An interesting possibility in this regard involves the "Hope Box," which is literally a box (e.g., a shoe box) in which the patient collects mementos, objects, photos, letters, and the like, all of which, at times of crisis, remind the patient of reasons for living and for hope. (Work is underway on the "Virtual Hope Box," a version for smartphone platforms). As the name implies, the proposed mechanism of action for this approach is the restoration of hope. Given this, it would be substantial evidence in favor of the theory if enhanced connection and contribution accounted for the mediational effects of restored hope.

The Continuum of Habituators That Facilitate Acquisition of Fearlessness

In talks we give to general audiences on this theory and its relevance to suicide prevention, the following question almost always comes up: "Can exposure to violent video games and movies and the like significantly increase someone's fearlessness about suicide?" Our usual way of answering this question is to imagine a scale that runs from 0 to 10, with 10 being the strongest habituator of all. At 10 would reside a recent past suicide attempt in which intent was high, lethality considerable, and relief at surviving minimal. At 9 would be a less serious attempt; at 8, nonsuicidal self-injury; at 7, injuries sustained in an accident or as part of work duties (e.g., as a police officer); and so on. With regard to the effects of media violence, we then reply that we believe their effects are above 0 and probably less than 5, but we await future research to determine where exactly to locate those effects on the continuum.

There is accruing evidence that this continuum contains a diverse array of experiences. For example, Bryan and Anestis (2011) found that the mental reexperiencing of combat trauma was predictive of fearlessness about suicidal behavior in military traumatic brain injury patients, and this relationship was not statistically accounted for by general mental health. Thus, even just the mental rehearsal of painful and provocative events, as opposed to continually encountering the event over and over, may increase acquired capability. As another and quite different example, we have evidence that (a) anorexia nervosa is highly associated with death by suicide (as distinct from death caused by self-starvation, which occurs as well but more rarely than suicide), (b) one of the reasons for this association is that people with anorexia have taught themselves fearlessness of bodily travail through self-starvation, and (c) some of this fearlessness is also learned through extremely hard bouts of exercise.

Delineating the range of habituators, as well as their relative power, is an important part of the research agenda for the future. In addition, as described in the next section, differentiating experiences that serve to habituate, versus those that instill fear, represents a potentially intriguing future direction.

Why Does Exposure to Suicide Sensitize Some and Habituate Others?

A psychiatrist who worked in inner city and prison settings observed:

> Many of my patients explain their bad behavior, for example their violence to women, by the fact that they had witnessed such behavior at home from the earliest age; others recoiled in horror from the very idea of violence to women for precisely the same reason. (Dalrymple, 2007, p. 94)

Much the same observation can be made about those close to a suicide decedent (though we think it can be problematic to equate "bad behavior" with suicidal behavior). Some are sensitized by the event and resolve never to go through such an ordeal themselves and never to put their friends and families through it. Others are desensitized by the same kind of event, as may occur in suicide clusters. It is likely that such reactions are determined in part by genetically based temperamental factors, but this does not explain all outcomes. More research is needed to determine who becomes sensitized versus habituated in response to exposure to suicide and whether aspects of the incident (e.g., closeness to the decedent, whether the person discovered the decedent's body) are systematically predictive of response type.

Conclusion

Mounting evidence from diverse perspectives corroborates the claims of the interpersonal-psychological theory of suicidal behavior. It has survived "risky tests," but more such tests are welcome (including those that specifically pit rival claims against the theory). One criterion for a vibrant research paradigm is that it is advancing by creating new frontiers of inquiry (as opposed to reacting and changing its claims in response to criticism; cf. Lakatos, 1970). Such frontiers include the nature of habituators, mechanisms of recovery, and the like, and extend to topics not covered here, such as the neurobiology of the fearlessness dimension emphasized by the theory. Further articulations and tests of these conceptual frontiers will, it is hoped, point to advances in intervention and prevention. In addition, given that suicide is by definition a life-or-death topic, this research should illuminate aspects of human nature, such as the will to live and reasons for living. Such reasons include contributing (rather than being a burden) and connecting (rather than being isolated and alienated).

REFERENCES

Andrade, M.C.B. (1996, January 5). Sexual selection for male sacrifice in the Australian redback spider. *Science*, *271*, 70–72. doi:10.1126/science.271.5245.70

Baumeister, R.F. (1990). Suicide as an escape from self. *Psychological Review*, *97*, 90–113. doi:10.1037/0033-295X.97.1.90

Beck, A.T., Brown, G., Berchick, R.J., & Stewart, B.L. (1990). Relationship between hopelessness and ultimate suicide: A replication with psychiatric outpatients. *The American Journal of Psychiatry*, *147*, 190–195.

Becker, E. (1973). *The denial of death*. New York, NY: Simon & Schuster.

Bender, T.W. (2009). *Suicidality and impulsivity: A test of the mediating role of painful experiences* (Master's thesis). Retrieved from http://etd.lib.fsu.edu/theses/available/etd-04122009-180947/unrestricted/BenderTthesis.pdf

Bender, T.W., Gordon, K.H., Bresin, K., & Joiner, T.E. (2011). Impulsivity and suicidality: The mediating role of painful and provocative experiences. *Journal of Affective Disorders*, *129*, 301–307. doi:10.1016/j.jad.2010.07.023

Bryan, C.J., & Anestis, M.D. (2011). Reexperiencing symptoms and the interpersonal-psychological theory of suicidal behavior among deployed service members evaluated for traumatic brain injury. *Journal of Clinical Psychology, 67*, 856–865. doi:10.1002/jclp.20808

Bryan, C. J., Morrow, C. E., Anestis, M. D., & Joiner, T. E. (2010). A preliminary test of the interpersonal-psychological theory of suicidal behavior in a military sample. *Personality and Individual Differences, 48*, 347–350. doi:10.1016/j.paid.2009.10.023

Chatard, A., & Selimbegović, L. (2011). When self-destructive thoughts flash through the mind: Failure to meet standards affects the accessibility of suicide-related thoughts. *Journal of Personality and Social Psychology, 100*, 587–605. doi:10.1037/a0022461

Chew, K. S. Y., & McCleary, R. (1995). The spring peak in suicides: A cross-national analysis. *Social Science & Medicine, 40*, 223–230. doi:10.1016/0277-9536(94)E0070-9

Conner, K. R., Britton, P. C., Sworts, L. M., & Joiner, T. E. (2007). Suicide attempts among individuals with opiate dependence: The critical role of belonging. *Addictive Behaviors, 32*, 1395–1404. doi:10.1016/j.addbeh.2006.09.012

Coudereau, J. P., Monier, C., Bourre, J. M., & Frances, H. (1997). Effect of isolation on pain threshold and on different effects of morphine. *Progress in Neuro-Psychopharmacology & Biological Psychiatry, 21*, 997–1018. doi:10.1016/S0278-5846(97)00094-8

Dalrymple, T. (2007). *In praise of prejudice*. New York, NY: Encounter Books.

Heinze, J., & Walter, B. (2010). Moribund ants leave their nests to die in social isolation. *Current Biology, 20*, 249–252. doi:10.1016/j.cub.2009.12.031

Jahn, D. R., Cukrowicz, K. C., Linton, K., & Prabhu, F. (2011). The mediating effect of perceived burdensomeness on the relation between depressive symptoms and suicide ideation in a community sample of older adults. *Aging & Mental Health, 15*, 214–220. doi:10.1080/13607863.2010.501064

Joiner, T. E. (2005). *Why people die by suicide*. Cambridge, MA: Harvard University Press.

Joiner, T. E. (2010). *Myths about suicide*. Cambridge, MA: Harvard University Press.

Joiner, T. E., Pettit, J. W., Walker, R. L., Voelz, Z. R., Cruz, J., Rudd, M. D., & Lester, D. (2002). Perceived burdensomeness and suicidality: Two studies on the suicide notes of those attempting and those completing suicide. *Journal of Social and Clinical Psychology, 21*, 531–545. doi:10.1521/jscp.21.5.531.22624

Joiner, T. E., Van Orden, K. A., Witte, T. K., Selby, E. A., Ribeiro, J. D., Lewis, R., & Rudd, M. D. (2009). Main predications of the interpersonal-psychological theory of suicidal behavior: Empirical tests in two samples of young adults. *Journal of Abnormal Psychology, 118*, 634–646. doi:10.1037/a0016500

Lakatos, I. (1970). Falsification and the methodology of scientific research programmes. In I. Lakatos & A. Musgrave (Eds.), *Criticism and the growth of knowledge* (pp. 91–95). Cambridge, England: Cambridge University Press.

Leary, M. R., Tambor, E. S., Terdal, S. K., & Downs, D. L. (1995). Self-esteem as an interpersonal monitor: The sociometer hypothesis. *Journal of Personality and Social Psychology, 68*, 518–530. doi:10.1037/0022-3514.68.3.518

MacMahon, K. (1983). Short-term temporal cycles in the frequency of suicide, United States, 1972–1978. *American Journal of Epidemiology, 117*, 744–750.

Martin, C. (2011, January). The drunk's club: A.A., the cult that cures. *Harper's Magazine*, 28–38.

Massing, W., & Angermeyer, M. C. (1985). The monthly and weekly distribution of suicide. *Social Science & Medicine, 21*, 433–441. doi:10.1016/0277-9536 (85)90223-0

McAllister, M. K., Roitberg, B. D., & Weldon, K. L. (1990). Adaptive suicide in pea aphids: Decisions are cost sensitive. *Animal Behaviour, 40*, 167–175. doi:10.1016/S0003-3472(05)80676-1

O'Connor, R. J. (1978). Brood reduction in birds: Selection for fratricide, infanticide and suicide? *Animal Behaviour, 26*, 79–96. doi:10.1016/0003-3472(78)90008-8

Poulin, R. (1992). Altered behavior in parasitized bumblebees: Parasite manipulation or adaptive suicide? *Animal Behaviour, 44*, 174–176. doi:10.1016/S0003-3472(05)80769-9

Puglisi-Allegra, S., & Oliverio, A. (1983). Social isolation: Effects on pain threshold and stress-induced analgesia. *Pharmacology, Biochemistry, and Behavior, 19*, 679–681. doi:10.1016/0091-3057(83)90344-1

Shneidman, E. S. (1996). *The suicidal mind.* New York, NY: Oxford University Press.

Solomon, R. L. (1980). The opponent-process theory of acquired motivation: The costs of pleasure and the benefits of pain. *American Psychologist, 35*, 691–712. doi:10.1037/0003-066X.35.8.691

Teale, N. E. (2010). *Self-verification and self-aggressive behavior: The negative consequences of receiving positive feedback* (Doctoral dissertation, Florida State University). Retrieved from http://etd.lib.fsu.edu/theses_1/available/etd-10112006-105405/unrestricted/NET_Thesis.pdf

Van Orden, K. A., Lynam, M. E., Hollar, D., & Joiner, T. E. (2006). Perceived burdensomeness as an indicator of suicidal symptoms. *Cognitive Therapy and Research, 30*, 457–467. doi:10.1007/s10608-006-9057-2

Van Orden, K. A., Witte, T. K., Cukrowicz, K. C., Braithwaite, S. R., Selby, E. A., & Joiner, T. E. (2010). The interpersonal theory of suicide. *Psychological Review, 117*, 575–600. doi:10.1037/a0018697

Van Orden, K. A., Witte, T. K., Gordon, K. H., Bender, T. W., & Joiner, T. E. (2008). Suicidal desire and the capability for suicide: Tests of the interpersonal-psychological theory of suicidal behavior among adults. *Journal of Consulting and Clinical Psychology, 76*, 72–83. doi:10.1037/0022-006X.76.1.72

V

OVERCOMING EXISTENTIAL THREATS AND CHALLENGES

19

THE CASE OF ALLISON: AN EXISTENTIAL-INTEGRATIVE INQUIRY INTO DEATH ANXIETY, GROUNDLESSNESS, AND THE QUEST FOR MEANING AND AWE

KIRK J. SCHNEIDER

The aim of this chapter is to introduce an existential-integrative approach to death anxiety, groundlessness, and the quest for meaning and awe. Drawing from a variety of sources, I illustrate how an *existential-integrative approach*, a comprehensive model of personality based on a constrictive–expansive continuum of conscious and subconscious functioning, can complement the recent social psychological literature summarized in this book concerning death anxiety and its personal and interpersonal effects. In the first part of the chapter, I discuss parallels between the existential-integrative perspective on personality and recent social psychological findings concerning death anxiety.

In the next part of the chapter, I show how an existential-integrative case study—"The Case of Allison"—can be used to elaborate on and deepen the social psychological findings concerning death anxiety while simultaneously illuminating some avenues for the transformation of that anxiety into constructive functioning. One such avenue is the encounter with the sense of groundlessness that is purported to underlie perceptions of death anxiety. This encounter is illustrated by Allison's ability to stay present with her most turbulent fears and to discover as a result a renewed ability to find meaning and even awe—or humility and wonder—in her life.

In the final part of the chapter, I consider the implications of Allison's transformation for the potential transformation of others who struggle with similar issues. I conclude that social psychology in particular, and psychology as a whole, could benefit from an existential-integrative perspective on death anxiety, groundlessness, and the cultivation of meaning and awe.

DEATH ANXIETY AND THE GROUNDLESSNESS OF EXISTENCE

Most of our troubles as human beings are traceable to one overriding problem: our suspension in the groundlessness of existence. Clinical experience, coupled with recent empirical studies, has convinced me that Søren Kierkegaard (1849/1954) had it right when he wrote that the "self is . . . a synthesis of infinitude and finitude, which relates itself to itself, whose task is to become itself" (p. 162). Kierkegaard's basic thesis was that by our very nature, human beings are confronted by three core existential challenges—necessity and possibility, finitude and infinitude, and temporality and eternality—all of which point to the same basic problem: our suspension in a vast, indefinite expanse. We have a tremendous capacity to enlarge ourselves, Kierkegaard explained (e.g., through our imaginations, time, and space), but we also have inescapable limits to these abilities (e.g., because of our finite life spans; see Chapter 1, this volume). The challenge for us is how best to manage these ostensibly contrary tendencies and to cope with what happens when our management falters (Becker, 1973; May, 1981; Schneider, 1999). Kierkegaard speculated (and I have elaborated on his thoughts) that such faltering can be understood in terms of two basic positions: a terror of expansion due to the death anxiety or groundlessness associated with endless self-extension (e.g., uncontrollable disarray, chaos) and a terror of constriction due to the death anxiety or groundlessness associated with endless self-contraction (e.g., uncontrollable decay, dissolution). Put another way, people fear infinity of the small as well as infinity of the large—the common thread between these infinities is *groundlessness,* or the indefinite spectrum of consciousness.

The result of these dynamics is that people experience a wide array of psychological disturbances in the face of their terrors, from disorders of hyperconstriction (e.g., depression, withdrawal, obsessive–compulsiveness) in the face of harrowing self-expanse (e.g., risk taking), to disorders of hyperexpansion (e.g., sociopathy, narcissism, megalomania) in the face of withering self-constraint (e.g., helplessness; Becker, 1973; Schneider, 1999, 2008a). Another way to state these axioms is that people will do everything they can—including becoming extreme themselves—to avoid the doom associated with their chaotic or obliterating histories (Becker, 1973; Laing, 1969; Schneider, 1999; see also Chapter 11, this volume).

Pyszczynski, Solomon, and Greenberg (2003) added empirical heft to these postulates with their studies of the impact of the 9/11 attack on people's social, political, and religious ideologies (see also Greenberg, Koole, & Pyszczynski, 2004; Chapter 4, this volume). Consistent with Kierkegaard's original thesis, and Becker's (1973) later update of that thesis, they found that the more people experienced the 9/11 attacks as a mortal threat, the greater their tendency to identify with hyperconstrictive or hyperexpansive ideologies. These hyperconstrictive or hyperexpansive ideologies were understood by the authors as manifestations of proximal defenses (e.g., "flight" reactions) and distal defenses (e.g., "fight" reactions). Whereas proximal defenses dispose people toward patterns of self-contraction (e.g., conservatism), distal defenses dispose people toward patterns of self-inflation (e.g., militarism); and whereas proximal defenses highlight areas of evasion, distal defenses highlight areas of retaliation. For example, the more people tended to feel mortally threatened by 9/11, the more they also tended to identify with right-wing and militaristic political agendas, thus exhibiting a combination of both proximal and distal defensive reactions. These reactions could be seen in the participants' tendencies toward nationalism and xenophobia as well as aggressive, "black and white" thinking regarding people they considered foreign or "other." The reactions could also be seen, finally, in participants' tendency to identify more strongly with those of similar religious beliefs and to become less tolerant toward people with dissimilar religious beliefs (Greenberg et al., 2004; Pyszczynski et al., 2003; see also Chapter 4, this volume).

Analogous findings were obtained in a controlled study of voting preferences in the 2004 presidential election. When study participants were primed with evocative depictions of their own and others' deaths, they tended to vote predominantly for the militarily inclined, flagrantly conservative George Bush and not the more dovish, liberally inclined John Kerry. This finding, according to the researchers, suggested "that President Bush's reelection may have been facilitated by nonconscious concerns about mortality in the aftermath of September 11, 2001" (Cohen, Ogilvie, Solomon, Greenberg, & Pyszczynski, 2005, p. 177).

Studies such as these are reminiscent of the classic obedience studies of the early 1960s, in which fear of humiliation (also a correlate of death anxiety; e.g., see Miller, 2009) appeared to play a greater role than the desire to be just (Milgram, 1974, p. 209).[1] In these experiments, participants who were instructed by highly authoritative experimenters to purportedly shock helpless

---

[1]Psychodynamic theorists such as Miller (2009), Laing (1969), and Kohut (1977) have shown that death anxiety (or what Kohut, 1977, pp. 102–104, aptly termed *disintegration anxiety*) can be triggered by many developmental stressors including physical and emotional abuse, neglect, abandonment, humiliation, shaming, and depersonalization. Given the pervasiveness of this problem, therefore, it would not be surprising if some, or even many, of the participants in the Milgram and terror management studies had a history of such stressors, and that their behavior in the experiments reflected that history.

victims tended to conform to the experimenters' instructions, despite the perceived harm they were doing to the "victims" (Milgram, 1974). What all of these studies have in common is that people tend to become either constrictively or expansively extreme in the face of perceived (constrictive or expansive) threats and that the more such threats are associated with survival, or desperate, uncontrollable anxiety, the more they are likely to become extreme.

Although the social psychology experiments point to the salience of death anxiety and the groundlessness of existence as key factors in psychological polarization, they do not, it seems to me, illuminate the subtleties of that polarization—how it forms over time, how it is experienced by participants, or what it potentially implies for a richer or fuller life. To elucidate these details, we need to turn to the moment-by-moment experiences of individuals who are traumatized. The clinical setting—particularly if it involves in-depth and existentially informed practices—provides an ideal investigative portal (Bugental, 1976; May, 1969, 1983; Schneider, 1998, 2008a; Schneider & Krug, 2010; Stolorow, 2007; Yalom, 1980).

Let us turn, then, to a clinical case that I recorded for the American Psychological Association, for a DVD series called *Existential–Humanistic Psychotherapy Over Time* (2009). This case concerns a six-session intervention with a woman named "Allison".[2] Here, I first discuss the theoretical basis for this case study. Next, I review the major challenges posed by the case. Finally, I consider some implications of the case for psychological well-being, not just of the client but also of our Western industrialized culture as a whole.

The chief and pervasive question for an existential-integrative therapy is how one is willing to live, in this remarkable moment, with this exceptional opportunity to explore one's life. Depending on a client's desire and capacity for change, there are many modalities, such as nutritional, medical, and cognitive–behavioral, through which such a question can be approached. In my existential-integrative approach (Schneider, 2008a; Schneider & Krug, 2010), I try to stay open to any of a variety of these recognized modalities but always within a context of finely attuned presence and the opportunity for the client to be present.

THE CASE OF ALLISON

Allison was a 40-year-old White working class woman with a history of severe emotional and sexual abuse. Her father was an inveterate alcoholic with an explosive temper, and her uncle sexually molested her when she

---

[2]It is important to note that the client's name and other identifying information have been changed here to protect her confidentiality. The reader who watches the DVD may notice some discrepancies.

was approximately 7 years old. When Allison was 4, she was regularly left alone with a "schizophrenic" aunt. These visits terrified her, but apparently, there was no parental recognition of this sentiment. When Allison was 6, her mother suddenly died, leaving Allison with her volatile alcoholic father, her rapacious uncle, and her psychotic aunt. As if that earlier background was not enough, Allison struggled in her adulthood with two failed marriages, one in which she was physically abused; raising a son who reportedly shirked his scholastic and later vocational responsibilities; and a brother whose drinking and scrapes with the law culminated in his death just prior to our third therapy appointment. According to Allison, her brother was shot and killed by the police for public drunkenness while wielding a knife.

How Allison even partially emerged from these circumstances is a testament to her resilience as well as the support systems that both she and others helped to mobilize. One of these was her involvement in Alcoholics Anonymous (AA) following an intense period of drinking in her youth. This involvement, according to Allison, led to 16 years of sobriety and many supportive contacts. She also reported several delimited but helpful therapeutic contacts over the years, which bolstered her stabilization.

As Allison and I greeted each other for our first of six allotted sessions, I was struck by her composure and her bright, articulate style. Although Allison ostensibly came to therapy because of her lack of assertiveness with men, I sensed—and in her tacit way, she conveyed—that the assertiveness issue was not her ultimate concern.

At first I worked with Allison to help her build confidence when she confronted men. I invited her to engage in role plays with me where I would stand in for the menacing fellow (e.g., her curmudgeonly boss or problematic 20-year-old son) and she would play herself in a particular dilemma. I also worked with Allison to restructure her thinking about how these men perceived her. Would she really be seen as a "bitch" if she clarified her needs to them, I would ask. And even if she was seen that way, would that make her a "bitch"? As we deepened and rehearsed these scenarios, Allison was gradually able to develop new skills that helped her confront and successfully assert herself with the aforementioned men.

At the same time that she was working on these cognitive and behavioral restructuring skills, however, something else began to happen: Allison began to acknowledge, and I encouraged her to stay present to, fears that went beyond feeling intimidated by men. These fears related to a sense of being intimidated by life.

In this context, she began to share powerful dreams with me, such as a recent dream of feeling like a tree with its limbs severed. In time, I took the risk of inviting Allison, not just to "talk about" such dreams and fantasies but also to experience them "here and now" with me. I invited her, in other words, to become more present to how she felt, sensed, and pictured these dreams and fantasies. I also invited her to share her responses about what it was like to interact with me, and to experience the difficult sides of herself— such as shame or weakness—in my presence. This brought the work alive between Allison and me and significantly deepened our bond. It also enabled her to plumb depths only hinted at during our cognitive restructuring exercises. Finally, it moved Allison to realize how her suffering stemmed not just from her relationships with men (and sometimes women) but also from her relationship with life's uncertainties and from the need for courage in facing them. This courage became evident to both of us when she confided in me that she had been able to really "let go" and cry at her AA meeting following our second session—and that it was the "first time" that she had been able to fully cry with another person.

After her brother was killed by the police and during our third session, Allison's focus on existential or ontological themes seemed to intensify. She began to allude to a completely new language in our work together, a language that emphasized her concerns about existence, not just specific aspects of existence. For example, she started speaking about being "terrified" of a "dark spot" or "black hole." She further articulated this condition as equivalent to the Bermuda Triangle (where according to legend, airplanes have been lost or destroyed). She indicated feeling "held back" by these sensibilities and stifled in her life because of them.

At the same time, however, she also began to experience some remarkable healing images along with these terrors. As I invited Allison to stay present to her fear of the dark spot, for example, she reported feeling herself growing—like the Jolly Green Giant—and gradually, towering above it. When I asked her what she really wanted in her life, she said she would love to feel "free," but that she was not quite sure what she was afraid of. She also said she had kept a diary as a child and that freedom was a core focus in it. She noted writing about being like a bird so that she could fly and be totally free to move about the world, and she equated that feeling with some of the experiences she was having on her motorcycle at the time.

Then, seemingly out of the blue, she began to speak about her identification with American Indians. She wished she could live on a reservation, or better yet, live at a time when American Indians roamed free and subsisted entirely off the land. She described her passionate desire to help Indians and to support their philosophy of nature. She also complimented me for being open to and asking about her interest in Indians—she said, "Nobody has asked me that before," and she lit up while being immersed in the topic. American Indians, it appeared, had become an extraordinarily important touchstone for Allison—a touchstone pointing to a free and dignified life.

In my experience, such ranges of resonance are not extraordinary in depth-existential therapy. As people feel safer to explore, they begin to unveil the parts of themselves that both torment them and, potentially, set them free. These parts are not necessarily Freudian in nature. That is, they do not necessarily evoke sexual or aggressive conflict or frustrated parental attachments, but they do in my experience stir primordial undercurrents, only aspects of which may be sexual, aggressive, or interpersonal. To put it succinctly, these undercurrents strike me and others who witness them as emphatically existential in nature—pertaining not just to turbulent sexual–aggressive drives or attachments to parental figures but also to fears and desires concerning the uncontrollability of existence itself (see Chapter 2, this volume). For example, behind the fear (and sometimes attraction) of aggression can be an even deeper anxiety about imminent disarray, uncontrollability, and ultimately, chaos. Beneath the terror of parental devaluation can be the thornier challenge of one's significance in the grand scheme of existence.

These were precisely the mooring points I faced with Allison on a fateful afternoon some seven weeks following our initial session. She was on the brink of a breakthrough, and we both knew it. But she also grappled with great fears and the need to come to terms with them. My dilemma was this: Given that we had arrived at our sixth and final meeting together, should I invite and, to some extent, challenge Allison to engage more fully the profound issues we had awoken within her, or should I cut our losses, deescalate our interchange, and help her transition back to what would likely be a slightly improved but static life of manageable constraint? My concern on the one hand was that if we worked more intensively in this final session, we risked the possibility that it might exceed her capacity to absorb it. On the other hand, I was concerned that given her resources and mind-set, an opportunity of this nature might never come again. Would it not be better to give her a "taste" of what optimal self-integration could offer, rather than bypass the opportunity altogether? After much reflection, I opted for the latter option, taking a risk that her desire and strengths would redeem the experience.

I invited Allison to engage in what I (Schneider, 2008a) call *embodied meditation*, and she agreed to try it. I have found embodied meditation to be a powerful way of helping clients become concertedly present to their concerns and, as a result of this, become more fully present and integrated within themselves.

Because Allison seemed ready, I invited her to simply close her eyes and become aware of her breathing. I then invited her to become aware of any tension she was experiencing in her body—any areas that felt tight or blocked and that she was willing to describe. She began by identifying a tension in her neck area, which loosened as she stayed present to it. Then she experienced a flash of anger. When I asked what the anger was about, she replied that it was because she felt held back in some way, stifled. Then, gradually, she began to overcome the anger and perceive an image. It was an image of a "tiny" little girl surrounded by whiteness, except for the central core, which was dark. She equated the feeling with a fetus-like child holed up in a closet (although later in the session she likened the feeling to being swallowed by a black hole). Slowly, methodically, she began to perceive a "big light" headed to the core enveloping the little girl—it was "like rays from the sun, warming rays." Allison felt the little girl could not trust the rays at first; she remained in a "tight ball," as if in a "womb." Then she suddenly experienced an upwelling of emotion: "I almost feel like stepping into the room [with the little girl] and holding her," Allison confided. "Can you picture that?" I replied. After a few moments, Allison conveyed that she was close to tears (and began actually tearing). "I feel like I'm holding her," Allison said, "and I feel like I'm crying with her." The tears began to stream from Allison's eyes as she described patting the little girl's head and kissing her face. She then assured her, "It's OK, it's really OK," and it felt clear to me that Allison genuinely experienced that sentiment. For that fleeting flash of time at least, it felt like Allison was genuinely able to venture into one of the core domains of her terror. Possibly for the first time, she was able to reclaim herself and to reclaim the possibility of being more than her broken image of herself. She discovered a new alignment with being, an alignment that could include a broken creature in a dark void but that was not reducible to a creature in a void.

With this simple yet profound development, Allison acquired a glimpse of a remarkable self-transformation. She moved from a position of abject terror (hyperconstriction) to one of wonder to one of love. Through embracing the little girl, Allison at the same time embraced the chasm in which the little girl (as well as her adult self) had languished for years; now she found solace there and a chance for self-renewal.

I won't say that this moment completely changed Allison's life, but it seemed to go a long way toward freeing her and relieving her panic. Although the specifics of Allison's life—for example, her long-time employment and her involvement with her family—may not dramatically change on the basis of this final exercise, what she brings to those specifics has a significant chance of being different from what she experienced before. At the close of the session, Allison and I spoke frankly about what she gained and what struggles remained for her as she returned to her routine life. She said she felt a renewed excitement about being closer with her family, especially her boyfriend's little girls. She felt like she embraced them as she embraced her "tiny" self, and she experienced a deep feeling of warmth toward them. She also expressed that "it would be so awesome to be totally free" in her life going forward. This feeling spurred her to recommit to writing in her journal and staying in touch with the sensibilities that moved her so deeply during the session, such as her feelings about American Indians, her dream life, her connection to the little girl in her imagination, and her need for "quietness." Finally, she made a curious yet revealing statement about how she wants to live going forward. She needs, she remarked, to "focus on being scared but not being afraid," and with that intriguing yet courageous quip, our work came to a close.

In the end, Allison learned much more than assertiveness skills or an ability to think more "rationally." She did acquire important skills, which appeared to help her with problematic relationships, but she also learned something much more—to be present to her life—and this presence enabled her to more fully experience her life.

THE EXISTENTIAL-CLINICAL IMPLICATIONS FOR PSYCHOSOCIAL WELL-BEING

The case of Allison illustrates how anguish, but also transformation, is traceable to our suspension in the groundlessness of existence. Could it be that all or most forms of struggle—whether personal or collective—can also be characterized in that way? Let us consider the following.

When a loved one dies or we are attacked or we fall ill, it often feels like the bottom has dropped out and there is nothing left to hold us up. Like the astronaut who is cut from his tether, or like Allison who was stripped of her safety, we suddenly come face to face not just with our particular difficulty but also with the difficulty of existence itself.

This "difficulty" is traumatic. It strips our culturally sanctioned frame and ruptures our culturally agreed-on security systems—for example, our jobs, our cherished values, and our identities. We feel eviscerated in this state, rootless. We also feel what the existential psychiatrist R. D. Laing (1969) aptly termed *ontological insecurity* (p. 39). To be ontologically insecure, according to Laing, is not just to be insecure with a given person or situation but also to be insecure with (or lack a sense of comfort in) "being" itself. The ontologically insecure person, according to Laing, is "precariously differentiated from the rest of the world. . . . His identity and autonomy are always in question. . . . [and he may lack a sense] that the stuff he's made of is good, genuine, [and] valuable" (p. 42). As a result of this condition, and depending on people's traumatic past, ontological insecurity tends to jar them in either of two directions: toward expansive grandiosity to overcompensate for the fragility they feel or toward constrictive withdrawal to overcompensate for the unsustainability of their grandiose expansion. Yet, either way, people are imprisoned by these extremes, and both sabotage their growth (Becker, 1973; Laing, 1969; Schneider, 1999).

The goal is not so much to "get rid of" a condition that is inherently human but, as with Allison, to develop a new relationship to that condition. As clinicians, we need to help people face and gradually realign themselves with respect to the groundlessness of their existence. We need to help them move, in the words of Laing (1969), from a position of "precariousness" toward one of greater alignment or coexistence. What would such a realignment look like? It would look like something that existentially oriented practitioners see in their consulting rooms every day: an improved ability to be present to one's sense of groundlessness, an enhanced ability to stay centered or deliberative within that sense of groundlessness, and an enhanced ability to respond meaningfully to, rather than simply react against, its ferocity (Yalom, 1980).

TOWARD AN AWE-BASED REFORMATION

Undeniably, the ability to respond meaningfully to the groundlessness of existence is a critical task of individual and collective humanity. Although cases such as Allison's provide glimpses into the potential fruit of such an undertaking, I believe we need to stretch ourselves much further. Given the state of despair and abject strife in our world, it is incumbent on existential psychology to look beyond the consulting room and apply its findings to society at large.

One of the ways I have pursued this large goal is to develop what I call *awe-based psychology* (Schneider, 2004, 2009b), which begins with humility and wonder, or a sense of adventure, concerning all that exists. Put another way, awe-based psychology cultivates the ability to coexist with, and consciously appreciate, the groundlessness of being. This means, first, to be present, cultivate a capacity to attune to the maximal ranges of human experience. It also means to cultivate freedom, the capacity for choice (see Chapter 21, this volume, for a similar analysis). Allison evolved both of these capacities within the constraints of our time together and her particular resources. Her newfound capacity to cry, for example, illustrated her increased ability to stay present with herself. Accordingly, her increasing willingness to acknowledge deep yearnings within herself exemplified her cultivation of freedom. Finally, the coexistence with, and appreciation of, the groundlessness of being enables one to foster a sense of awe—the humility and wonder, or sense of adventure, regarding living itself. Allison experienced glimpses of this sensibility when she spoke about freedom and her love of American Indian culture.

How do we translate these awe-based insights into the larger social world? What can dimensions of presence, freedom, and awe contribute to the understanding and remediation of our many social ills? I now offer a few thoughts about this.

There is clearly a self-esteem problem in our culture and in many of the cultures with which we interact. The levels of despair, prejudice, and violence in our and in many other cultures are unacceptably high, and they are at least partly a result of neglectful or abusive childrearing practices (Erikson, 1963; Miller, 2009; Stephenson, 1998). However, what if a different scenario were to prevail? Consider, for example, an awe-based child-rearing approach that from the outset stressed coexistence with, and appreciation of, the groundlessness of being (see Chapters 12, 13, and 20, this volume, for similar analyses). Consider how this could be encouraged early through parental appreciation of a child not merely as an achiever of developmental milestones but also as a being who, in Tillich's (1952) terms, has been "accepted" by the universe (see also Chapter 13, this volume). "Accepting acceptance," wrote Tillich, "is the paradoxical act by which one is accepted by that which infinitely transcends one's individual self" (p. 165), and by implication, that validates one's individual self. To give a child a sense that simply by existing he or she has been "chosen" by something much greater than the observable world is to instill in the child that he or she is part of something amazing and is worthy of partaking in that amazement. This inspiring sentiment, moreover—which can be adaptively humbling as well as exhilarating—can then be transmitted to all that the child discovers, grapples with, and acquires.

In sum, there is likely to be a significant difference between the way a parent is perceived who simply "goes through motions" with a child or who focuses strictly on skill acquisition and a parent who revels in the experience of being with his or her child. There is a significant difference in the respective effects on the child's ability to be with himself or herself as well (Winnicott, 1971).

At the same time, none of this should be construed as advocating lax or indulgent parenting. To the contrary, the awe-based style can coexist with firmness, discipline, and limits, as those are warranted. For example, it is readily compatible with what has elsewhere been called an *authoritative* as distinct from a *permissive* or *authoritarian* parenting style (e.g., Baumrind, 1971). That said, however, the awe-based style provides a continually replenishing base on which a child can draw—a sense that his or her existence is accepted for itself (Tillich, 1952).

This sense of acceptance can (and in my view, should) provide ballast for many adults in their struggle to evolve as well. In previous writings (e.g., Schneider, 2004, 2005, 2008b, 2009a, 2009b), I speculated briefly about ways in which this sense of acceptance might be further cultivated. These encompass awe-based reformations of the educational system, the work setting, and the general conduct of democratic life.

CODA

Psychologists today can talk until the point of exhaustion about pat formulas and programmatic treatments. They can cite chemical imbalances in the brain, for example, or the lack of ability to regulate emotions or the irrationality of conditioned thoughts as the bases for our disorders. However, until psychologists get down to the fundamental problem that appears to fuel these secondary conditions—our precariousness as creatures—they will be operating at a restrictive level (e.g., see Wampold, 2008). The work I did with Allison had elements of this restrictive level (e.g., behavioral rehearsal)— and that was important work to accomplish. However, we constantly need to ask ourselves whether helping a person to change behavior patterns and recondition thoughts is enough. Or do we owe it to that person to make available to him or her a deeper dimension of self-exploration? Do we owe it to that person to enable him or her to discover what really matters about his or her life, wherever that may lead? I believe that Allison and many others in our society would answer those questions in the affirmative and that our culture as a whole would benefit immensely from its exploration.

In this chapter, I have proposed that our suspension in the groundlessness of being is a key basis for both our misery and our vitality as human beings. To the extent that we can grapple with this condition, we may discover how to thrive within, rather than simply blunt, its embrace.

REFERENCES

American Psychological Association. (Producer). (2009). *Existential–humanistic therapy over time* [DVD]. Available from http://www.apa.org/pubs/videos/4310867.aspx

Baumrind, D. (1971). Current patterns of parental authority. *Developmental Psychology Monograph*, *4*, 1–103. doi:10.1037/h0030372

Becker, E. (1973). *Denial of death*. New York, NY: Free Press.

Bugental, J. F. T. (1976). *The search for existential identity: Patient–therapist dialogues in humanistic psychotherapy*. San Francisco, CA: Jossey-Bass.

Cohen, F., Ogilvie, D. M., Solomon, S., Greenberg, J., & Pyszczynski, T. (2005). American roulette: The effect of reminders of death on support for George W. Bush in the 2004 presidential election. *Analyses of Social Issues and Public Policy (ASAP)*, *5*, 177–187. doi:10.1111/j.1530-2415.2005.00063.x

Erikson, E. (1963). *Childhood and society*. New York, NY: Norton.

Greenberg, J., Koole, S. L., & Pyszczynski, T. (Eds.). (2004). *Handbook of experimental existential psychology*. New York, NY: Guilford Press.

Kierkegaard, S. (1954). *Fear and trembling and the sickness unto death*. (W. Lowrie, Trans.). Princeton, NJ: Princeton University Press. (Original works published in 1843 and 1849)

Kohut, H. (1977). *The restoration of the self*. New York, NY: International Universities Press.

Laing, R. D. (1969). *The divided self: An existential study in sanity and madness*. Middlesex, England: Penguin.

May, R. (1969). *Love and will*. New York, NY: Norton.

May, R. (1981). *Freedom and destiny*. New York, NY: Norton.

May, R. (1983). *The discovery of being*. New York, NY: Norton.

Milgram, S. (1974). *Obedience to authority: An experimental view*. New York, NY: HarperCollins.

Miller, A. (2009). *Breaking down the wall of silence: The liberating experience of facing the painful truth*. New York, NY: Basic Books.

Pyszczynski, T., Solomon, S., & Greenberg, J. (2003). *In the wake of 9/11: The psychology of terror*. Washington, DC: American Psychological Association. doi:10.1037/10478-000

Schneider, K. J. (1998). Toward a science of the heart: Romanticism and the revival of psychology. *American Psychologist, 53*, 277–289. doi:10.1037//0003-066X.53.3.277

Schneider, K. J. (1999). *The paradoxical self: Toward an understanding of our contradictory nature* (2nd ed.). Amherst, NY: Humanity Books.

Schneider, K. J. (2004). *Rediscovery of awe: Splendor, mystery, and the fluid center of life*. St. Paul, MN: Paragon House.

Schneider, K. J. (2005). Biology and awe: Psychology's critical juncture. *The Humanistic Psychologist, 33*, 167–173. doi:10.1207/s15473333thp3302_6

Schneider, K. J. (2008a). *Existential-integrative psychotherapy: Guideposts to the core of practice*. New York, NY: Routledge.

Schneider, K. J. (2008b). Rediscovering awe: A new front in humanistic psychology, psychotherapy, and society. *Canadian Journal of Counselling, 42*, 67–74.

Schneider, K. J. (2009a, April). Applying therapeutic methods to legislative deliberations: A proposal. *Psychologists for Social Responsibility Blog*. Retrieved from http://psysr.wordpress.com/2009/04/02/applying-therapeutic-methods-to-legislative-deliberations-a-proposal/

Schneider, K. J. (2009b). *Awakening to awe: Personal stories of profound transformation*. Lanham, MD: Aronson.

Schneider, K. J., & Krug, O. T. (2010). *Existential–humanistic therapy*. Washington, DC: American Psychological Association.

Stephenson, J. (1998). *Poisonous power: Childhood roots of tyranny*. New York, NY: Diemer, Smith.

Stolorow, R. D. (2007). *Trauma and existence: Autobiographical, psychoanalytic, and philosophical reflections*. New York, NY: Analytic Press.

Tillich, P. (1952). *The courage to be*. New Haven, CT: Yale University Press.

Wampold, B. (2008). Existential-integrative psychotherapy comes of age. [Review of the book *Existential-integrative psychotherapy: Guideposts to the core of practice* by K. J. Schneider]. *PsycCritiques, 53*, Release 6, Article 1.

Winnicott, D. W. (1971). *Playing and reality*. New York, NY: Basic Books.

Yalom, I. (1980). *Existential psychotherapy*. New York, NY: Basic Books.

20

SEPARATION THEORY AND VOICE THERAPY METHODOLOGY

ROBERT W. FIRESTONE AND LISA FIRESTONE

Our life is what our thoughts make it.

—Marcus Aurelius, *Meditations*

This chapter explains *separation theory*, a comprehensive system of concepts and hypotheses that integrates psychoanalytic principles and existential thought. The theory explains how early interpersonal pain and separation anxiety lead to the formation of defenses and how these defenses become more elaborate and entrenched in the personality as a developing child becomes aware of his or her personal mortality. Thereafter, existential concerns and the associated defenses continue to have a profound impact, usually negative, on individuals throughout their lives, especially in relation to generating self-protective, maladaptive behavioral responses. To avoid the full realization of death, people tend to retreat to an inward, self-protective posture, narrow their life experience, and, to varying degrees, cut off feeling for themselves and others (see Chapter 1, this volume, for a review on symbolic defenses against death awareness). In their withdrawal from life, they are able to maintain an unconscious imagination of immortality. In embracing life, one automatically embraces death; as Paul Tillich (1952) once asserted, "One avoids being so as to avoid nonbeing" (p. 66).

Separation theory is a departure from classical Freudian psychoanalytic theory and is akin to the theories of Rank (1936/1972), Sullivan (1953), Fairbairn (1952), Guntrip (1969), and, to an extent, Kohut (1977). The theory focuses on the polarity within a person between self-affirming, goal-directed tendencies, on the one hand, and defensive, self-defeating processes on the other (R. W. Firestone, 1997a; see also Chapter 12, this volume, for a related analysis of this polarity). The developmental aspect of the theory provides an understanding of how events and experiences in early childhood influence the ways in which individuals cope with interpersonal pain and death anxiety throughout their lifetime (see Chapter 16, this volume, for a related developmental analysis). In an attempt to defend themselves against both kinds of pain, children develop an illusory connection or *fantasy bond* with their mother or primary caregiver, thereby achieving a modicum of security and a sense of safety. As they merge with the parent in their imagination, children and the adults they develop into become at once parent and child, a self-sufficient system in which they both nurture and punish themselves in much the same manner that they were treated. In this regard, they develop a split in their personality that reflects their parents' ambivalent feelings. We conceptualize this internal division as the *self system* and the *anti-self system* (see Figure 20.1).

Defenses formed early in life in response to emotional pain are reinforced as a child faces the dawning awareness of death's inevitability. He or she then employs these early defenses to repress or deny the reality of death and to maintain an unconscious illusion of immortality. However, maintaining defensive illusions comes with a price: It leads to maladaptation and deterioration in quality of life (see Chapters 1, 3, and 4, this volume, for related analyses of these prices). Although many people say they do not fear death, they unconsciously guide their lives and personal interactions to avoid arousing remnants of their original death anxiety. Separation anxiety and death anxiety, and the subsequent defensive reactions to them, are at the core of resistance to developing a differentiated identity characterized by individuation, personal autonomy, and fulfillment.

Voice therapy is a cognitive, affective, and behavioral methodology developed by the first author (R. W. Firestone) to help individuals access, identify, and challenge fantasy bonds, as well as associated destructive thoughts or critical inner voices. This form of therapy leads to significant insights into the sources of negative thinking as well as to an understanding of how the alien elements of the anti-self system influence one's behavior. The therapeutic methodology enables people to free themselves from harmful developmental influences and strengthen their real self, and to pursue priorities and goals that are more rewarding.

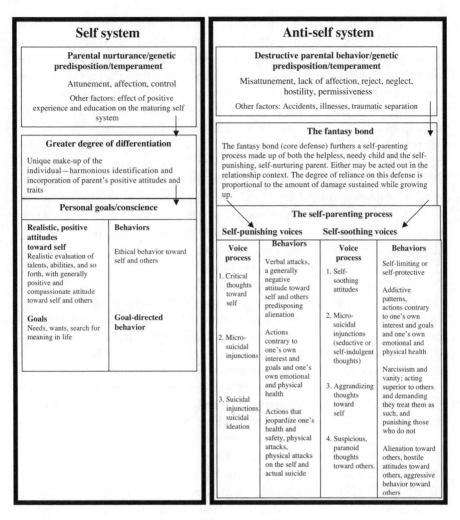

Figure 20.1. Division of the mind.

THE FANTASY BOND

> The wish for fusion and merger denies the reality of separation and, thus, the reality of death.
> —James B. McCarthy, *Death Anxiety: The Loss of the Self*

The fantasy bond is a defensive adaptation that relies on an illusion of connection, originally formed as an imaginary fusion with the mother or primary caregiver. It is the core defense—a way of parenting oneself—that arises in response to emotional deprivation, frustration, and/or separation trauma in early childhood. Children develop a psychological equilibrium and use fantasy processes and self-nurturing, self-soothing behaviors in an attempt to relieve their anxiety and to compensate for what is lacking in the environment. The degree to which they come to rely on the fantasy bond or self-parenting process is proportional to the damage they sustained in their formative years. In an extensive study, the Adverse Childhood Experiences (ACE) study, Felitti et al. (1998) showed that the cumulative number of aversive childhood incidents (e.g., neglect, abuse, witnessing violence, poverty) experienced by children was directly proportional to the severity of their physical and mental health problems as adults: "We found a strong graded relationship between the breadth of exposure to abuse or household dysfunction during childhood and multiple risk factors for several of the leading causes of death in adults" (p. 245). The researchers also identified self-nurturing, addictive behaviors, including smoking, alcoholism, and drug abuse, as mediating factors operating between the aversive childhood experiences and elevated rates of early mortality. Bessel van der Kolk (2005) referred to the ACE study when describing his research demonstrating that cumulative or "chronic trauma interferes with neurobiological development . . . and the capacity to integrate sensory, emotional and cognitive information into a cohesive whole" (p. 402).

Attachment theorists have observed that children make the best adaptation possible by developing specific strategies to maintain proximity to the parent for the purposes of safety and survival. Children are born with an evolutionarily based behavioral system that is designed to achieve this goal (Bowlby, 1973). The mother's or caregiver's capacity to fully feel the pain of her early years and to make sense of her childhood experiences, together with the sensitivity and ability to attune her responses to her infant's nonverbal and bodily cues, will determine which pattern of attachment the infant develops with her: a secure attachment or an anxious/insecure, avoidant/insecure, or disorganized pattern (Siegel & Hartzell, 2004).

The Fantasy Bond as Manifested in Adult Relationships

The defenses that people originally developed in an attempt to heal the fracture caused by early interpersonal experiences become limiting and dysfunctional factors in their adult lives. The original fantasy bond is reinstated with one's romantic partners, authority figures, or other parental substitutes. When this type of relating begins to occur, there is a decline in the genuine companionship, affection, passion, and sexual attraction that usually characterize the initial phases of a relationship. Over time, each partner tends to revert to a more self-protective, defended posture. Real feelings of love are gradually replaced by a fantasy of love. The increased reliance on the fantasy bond strengthens the illusion of connection and leads to a further deterioration within the relationship, with each partner retreating to the safety of the imagined union and giving up the real substance of the relationship.

Adults establish a fantasy bond or illusion of fusion in their intimate relationships by recreating negative aspects of their early attachment to parents, such as forms of insecure (anxious, avoidant, or disorganized) attachment. (See Shaver and Mikulincer, 2002, for a review of measures used in investigating the linkages between early attachment patterns and styles of relating in adult romantic attachments.) In explaining the dynamics involved in the replication of defensive behaviors developed in relation to one's parent or parents, Lorna Smith Benjamin (2003) contended that these

> problem patterns are linked to learning with important early loved ones
> via one or more of three copy processes: (1) Be like him or her; (2) Act
> as if he or she will still be there and in control; and (3) Treat yourself as
> he or she treated you. (p. vii)

Recapitulating the Past Through Selection, Distortion, and Provocation

This repetition is achieved through selection, distortion, and provocation. First, adults can unconsciously *select* as a partner someone who is similar in behavior and/or defenses to a parent. They are naturally attracted to someone whose style of relating feels comfortable and familiar, whose defenses mesh with their own. Second, they can also *distort* a partner by exaggerating his or her positive or negative qualities to make the person more closely approximate their parent. For example, in observing how distortion operates in the relationships of insecure or preoccupied individuals, Mikulincer and Shaver (2007) noted that they have strong desires "for close proximity to and fusion with relationship partners . . . [leading them] to project their negative self-views onto relationship partners, thereby creating an illusory sense of similarity and union" (p. 171). Third, insecure individuals may use *provocation* to manipulate a partner to respond to them in the same manner as their parent did. They often provoke angry, critical, or harsh reactions from their mate by unconsciously holding back the behavior, personal communication, affection, kindness, and sexuality that one's partner originally valued.

THE VOICE PROCESS

What we call the *voice* is the language of the defense system; it supports the fantasy bond and the self-parenting process. It is a well-integrated system of thoughts and attitudes, antithetical to the self and cynical about others that is at the core of an individual's maladaptive or self-destructive behavior. Voice attacks are directed inward toward the self and outward toward others; both predispose alienation in relationships. Voice attacks are sometimes experienced consciously, but more often than not, they are only partially conscious or even unconscious. They are not auditory hallucinations but can be conceptualized as a way of talking to or "coaching" oneself as though from an external point of view (R. W. Firestone, 1988). The specific subject matter, content, and sources of voices as they exist within the personality are composed of (a) the internalization of parents' (and other significant figures in the child's early environment, e.g., siblings, relatives, teachers, peers) destructive attitudes toward self and others, (b) an imitation of one or both parents' maladaptive defenses and views about life (e.g., social relationships, religious beliefs, political ideologies), and (c) a defensive outlook and approach to life based on emotional pain suffered in the developmental years.

We conceptualize the voice as a dynamic representation of what attachment theorists have referred to as *internal working models*. Attachment researchers (e.g., Shaver & Clark, 1996; see also Chapter 16, this volume) have hypothesized that internal working models mediate people's attachment patterns and influence how adults interact in close relationships. Similarly, the voice process helps to reestablish the original parent–child attachment in a new relationship by supporting the same self-image and point of view that developed within the first attachment relationship. In a 30-year longitudinal study of a unique psychological laboratory composed of three generations of individuals and families, we were able to study the dynamics of the voice process (R. W. Firestone, Firestone, & Catlett, 2003). We observed that destructive thoughts or voices contribute to a person's negative self-concept and feelings of low self-esteem and promote distrust of others and an inward, isolated lifestyle. These voices support illusions of connection and self-nurturing habit patterns that are emotionally and physically deadening and endorse a victimized orientation toward life that blames others for one's own failures. In addition, voices advise a person to be secretive about self-nurturing, indulgent, or self-destructive habit patterns, thereby contributing to a paranoid, suspicious view of other people. Self-aggrandizing voices distort reality and set a person up to feel slighted by others, leading to a sense of demoralization, self-hatred, and feelings of failure.

As participants in the group we studied verbalized their destructive thoughts, we noted that the content of their self-attacks and hostile attitudes toward others corresponded to our observations of their behavior. Because we observed multiple generations, we were able to notice the intergenerational transmission of these destructive thoughts and defensive behavior patterns (R. W. Firestone, 1990a; R. W. Firestone & Catlett, 1999). As children matured, we witnessed them soothing and punishing themselves in the same ways that they had been parented. The intergenerational repetition was obvious in the hostile attitudes they developed toward themselves. We also observed the selection process operating in young people as they became romantically involved. Again, our observations tended to validate the findings of Shaver and Clark (1996), who suggested that children who have a negative internal model of the attachment relationship with a parent often distrust relationship partners and expect them to "be cruel, neglectful, or unpredictable . . . and feel unworthy of anyone's love" (p. 34).

Voices oppose vulnerability and discourage wanting and are therefore anti-body, anti-pleasure, and distorting of sexuality. Identifying the contents of the destructive thought process helps explain seemingly irrational negative behaviors that contradict people's stated goals. In general, operating on the basis of internalized voices and not challenging their prohibitions and self-protective directives negatively affect a person's overall adjustment, sense of independence, and feeling of personal worth. The concepts of the fantasy bond and the voice help to explain the resistance to a better life. People tenaciously hold on to fantasized connections that are a fundamental part of their defense system, because they offer a false sense of safety and security. Because fantasy bonds support an illusion of merged identity and permanence, they also serve as a buffer against death anxiety.

THE FORMATION OF THE SELF SYSTEM AND THE ANTI-SELF SYSTEM

The newborn does not develop a self system, or personal identity, in a vacuum; the self emerges only in relation to another person or persons (Siegel, 1999, 2007; Stern, 1985). Positive life experiences favor the evolution of the self system, whereas negative experiences support the formation of the anti-self system. Developmental psychologists and neuroscientists emphasize that the development of the neonate's brain and personality is environment dependent; that is, the growth and development of the brain are dependent on inputs from the environment, specifically those provided by other human beings (Schore, 2003; Siegel, 1999, 2007; Siegel & Hartzell, 2004). In an optimal setting, infants tend to encounter attuned responses from caring adults that promote feelings of safety, which in turn facilitate learning and further development. When early interactions with parents are nurturing, they provide a child with a secure base from which to explore his or her environment (Ainsworth, Blehar, Waters, & Wall, 1978; Bowlby, 1973; see also Chapter 16, this volume).

Unfortunately, even in a relatively benign environment, a certain amount of damage occurs because of the unusual sensitivity of the infant to sensory inputs (Stern, 1985). Indeed, the prolonged dependence of the human infant on parents for physical and psychological survival provides the first condition for the formation of the self and the anti-self systems. According to Guntrip (1961), the infant's need for "reliable maternal support" is so absolute, and failure to provide it so nearly universal, that "varying degrees of neurotic instability . . . are the rule rather than the exception" (p. 385).

Every child needs warmth, affection, direction, and control from adults who would ideally possess the ability as well as the desire to provide satisfaction of the child's basic needs. However, all parents have a fundamental ambivalence toward themselves, and they automatically extend the same ambivalence to their products (i.e., their children). It manifests itself in their positive traits and in their compassion, concern, and desire to love and nurture their children, while at the same time it is also reflected in their negative attitudes toward themselves and in their anger, resentment, and feelings of emotional hunger toward their children.

Parents' anxieties are aroused when their child goes through phases in development that parallel exceptionally painful and unpleasant experiences in their own lives, and at those times they tend to insulate themselves emotionally and create for the child the same circumstances they faced as children. The degree to which parents have failed to resolve or work through their own trauma is proportional to the degree to which they will be dysfunctional and misattuned in relation to their own children (Cassidy & Mohr, 2001; Main & Hesse, 1990).

Because negative, hostile feelings toward children are considered socially unacceptable, parents are often resistant to acknowledging their aggressive feelings toward their offspring, and they attempt to deny or suppress them. Nevertheless, the destructive part of parents' ambivalence is expressed through critical, hostile attitudes and behaviors that contribute to the formation of defenses in their children and lead to an essential division in the children's personality between the self system and the anti-self system. Parents' nurturance and their positive attitudes contribute to the positive development of the individual, whereas their destructive attitudes, both overt and covert, contribute to a person's tendency to live a more inward, self-protective, or self-destructive lifestyle.

The Self System

The self system is composed of the child's unique physiological and genetic make-up as well as his or her harmonious assimilation of the parents' positive attitudes and traits (see Figure 20.1). Parents' positive inputs, as well as their ability to repair misattunements, support the development of vital functions of the prefrontal cortex in the child's brain: body regulation, attunement, emotional balance, response flexibility, empathy, self-knowing awareness (insight), fear modulation, intuition, and morality (Siegel, 2007, 2010).

The effects of ongoing psychological development, further education, and imitation of other positive role models throughout a person's life continue to contribute to the evolution of the self system.

People's personal goals—their basic needs for food, water, safety, and sex; their desire for social affiliation, achievement, and activity; their expression of love, compassion, generosity, and so forth; and their transcendent goals related to seeking meaning in life—are all aspects of the self system. Positive environmental influences enable the mature individual to formulate his or her own value system, develop integrity, and live according to chosen morals and principles.

The Anti-Self System

The anti-self system develops as a defensive response to the destructive side of the parents' ambivalence: their hostility, rejection, and neglect (see Figure 20.1). In addition, parents' emotional hunger, overprotectiveness, ignorance, and lack of understanding of a child's nature negatively affect a child's development. Often, parents attempt to dispose of traits they dislike in themselves by projecting them onto their children, and their children absorb these into their self-concept. The anti-self system is also affected by other negative environmental influences, including birth trauma, accidents, illnesses, traumatic separations, and the actual loss of a parent or sibling.

Because of their pressing need for love and their utter helplessness during the formative years, children are frightened to recognize their parents' inadequacies or weaknesses and must therefore see their caregivers as adequate, nurturing, and good, and themselves as being at fault, worthless, or bad (e.g., Bloch, 1978; R. W. Firestone, 1985). Similarly, rather than perceiving their parents as incapable of loving them, children come to see themselves as unlovable. This idealization of parents at the child's expense is a fundamental part of the anti-self system.

In situations in which there are serious deficiencies and neglect in the parental environment or in which parents are punitive or abusive, the child attempts to escape from experiencing him- or herself as a helpless victim at the mercy of an angry, out-of-control parent by identifying with the aggressor (Ferenczi, 1933/1955; A. Freud, 1966). This maneuver of splitting from the self and joining with the threatening parent partially alleviates the child's terror and provides a sense of relief. However, in the process, the child takes on the aggression the parent is directing toward him or her, as well as the parent's guilt and fear associated with the aggressive behavior (R. W. Firestone, 1997a). At the same time that children incorporate these destructive parental attitudes, they also project their parents' negative characteristics onto the world at large, damaging their personal relationships and distorting their overall experience because of their heightened sense of suspicion and threat.

Fonagy, Gergely, Jurist, and Target (2002) explained how failures in parents' attunement or *affect mirroring* lead to the formation of an "alien self" within the child. They asserted that

> the alien self is present in all of us, because transient neglect is part of ordinary caregiving; it is pernicious when later experiences of trauma in the family or the peer group force the child to dissociate from pain by using the alien self to identify with the aggressor. Hence the vacuous self comes to be colonized by the image of the aggressor, and the child comes to experience himself as evil and monstrous. . . . [Later, there is a] vital dependence on the physical presence of the other as a vehicle for externalization [projective identification]. (p. 198)

The sources of self-soothing, self-nurturing voices can be found in parents' treatment of their children, both in their build-up of the child to compensate for their lack of love and in their attempts to live through their child's achievements. Often parents inadvertently train their children to adopt addictive behaviors by excessive coddling and babying or by unduly comforting them with food, toys, or pacifiers—in essence, by not allowing the children to feel their actual pain and frustration. Children also model themselves after their parents' defenses and habit patterns, especially addictions to food, alcohol, and other forms of substance abuse. They also mimic other maladaptive behaviors, such as their parents' victimized orientation and hostile or prejudicial attitudes toward other people.

The anti-self system supports an inward, self-destructive lifestyle. Under stressful conditions people tend to regress and fragment into either the parent or child aspect of the fantasy bond. In the child state, the person is overly dependent, clingy, and/or victimized, whereas in the parental state, he or she acts superior, all-knowing, critical, and/or judgmental. Both parental and childish elements of the personality contribute to dysfunctional styles of relating and do not reflect the state of mind or behavior of an emotionally mature, differentiated adult.

There are two aspects of the anti-self: a self-punishing side and a self-protective, self-nurturing side. Both are composed of voices mediating the individual's self-defeating, self-destructive behavior and/or destructive behavior toward others. On the self-punishing side, self-attacking thoughts range from self-critical thinking ("You're worthless," "You don't fit in") to more self-destructive thoughts and ultimately to suicidal ideology and injunctions to commit bodily harm ("Go ahead, hurt yourself!" "Just end it; you don't deserve to live"). Similarly, self-destructive behaviors based on destructive voices exist on a continuum ranging from self-denial and self-defeating behaviors (actions contrary to one's goals) to accident proneness, substance abuse, and actual suicide.

The self-nurturing and self-protective side of the anti-self system is ostensibly friendly; seductive voices urge the individual to be both self-indulgent ("Go ahead, have a drink; you've had a hard day") and self-aggrandizing ("You're so great. You're better than those other people"). These voices support a victimized orientation that can develop into suspicious, paranoid thoughts toward others ("They don't appreciate you. You better watch out. They'll take advantage of you"). At their worst, these cynical and paranoid attitudes can lead to violence.

THE IMPACT OF THE CHILD'S EVOLVING KNOWLEDGE OF DEATH

> Such awareness may be our uniquely human legacy, emerging from our cortical capacity to represent the future and be aware of the movement of time and our limited place in its passage. Within this challenge to live with eyes and heart wide open rests the ultimate goal: of how to be fully human.
>
> —Daniel Siegel, in a Foreword to R. W. Firestone,
> L. A. Firestone, and J. Catlett's *Creating a Life of Meaning
> and Compassion: The Wisdom of Psychotherapy*

As noted earlier, the defenses and fantasy bonds that a child forms early in life in response to stress and deprivation are strongly reinforced, becoming crystallized in the personality as children's understanding of death evolves, usually between the ages of 3 and 7. First, children become aware that their parents will die. They tend to feel fear and sadness at the possible loss of their parents but retain a modicum of security. Later, they come to realize that they themselves will die (Anthony, 1971/1973). This terrifying discovery destroys their illusion of self-sufficiency or omnipotence. The world that they believed to be permanent is turned upside down by their realization that all people, even they, must die. On an unconscious level, they deny the reality of their personal death by regressing to a previous stage of development and intensifying the self-parenting process or fantasy bond (R. W. Firestone, 1994; R. W. Firestone & Catlett, 2009a).

At a critical point, they tend to resolve their conflict between fantasy and reality by choosing denial rather than facing the existential crisis (see also Chapter 1, this volume, for a similar analysis). Clearly, they are not making a philosophical decision in which they meticulously weigh the pros and cons of the two choices. This conflict is faced and resolved in the midst of turmoil and emotional upheaval that is torturous for the vulnerable child. As Ernest Becker (1973/1997) observed in *The Denial of Death*:

> There can be no clear-cut victory or straightforward solution to the existential dilemma he is in. It is his problem almost right from the beginning almost all of his life, yet he is only a child to handle it. . . . To grow up at all is to conceal the mass of internal scar tissue that throbs in our dreams. (pp. 28–29)

Research suggests that children who are raised in a more nurturing, benevolent environment appear to be better equipped to cope with this crisis, are more likely to develop a positive outlook on life, and tend to be less driven to adopt mechanisms of denial (Mikulincer & Florian, 2000; see also Chapter 16, this volume).

Throughout the life span, defenses against death anxiety continue to exert an insidious influence. In attempting to elude unconscious fears of death, most people tend to ration their aliveness and spontaneity, carefully doling out or restricting pleasant or enriching experiences. They often become indifferent to significant events that impinge on their lives and numb themselves by attending instead to life's trivialities (see Chapter 19, this volume). Nevertheless, when an individual experiences an increase in death salience or an indirect reminder of death, the primitive fear reaction tends to resurface, and the person regresses to a greater reliance on fantasy and/or other defenses. This regression takes many forms: For example, some people increase their drinking or turn to drugs whereas others attempt to lose themselves through compulsive work habits or routines that are distractions and give an illusion of permanence (R. W. Firestone & Catlett, 2009a). Research based on terror management theory (Solomon, Greenberg, & Pyszczynski, 2004; see also Chapters 1, 2, 3, and 4, this volume) has clearly shown that when faced with death awareness, people often tend to become more conventional, more moralistic and punitive, and more identified with their ingroup and opposed to outsiders. However, there are notable exceptions to this general tendency. Some people respond to a heightened awareness of death by appreciating life more, by taking pleasure in meaningful activities, and by valuing the people they love (see Chapter 16, this volume).

In our work with our multigenerational reference group, we used voice therapy procedures to help individuals cope more directly with death anxiety. We provided a forum for the expression of deep feelings of anger, grief, and sadness at the prospect of their eventual demise. Many participants rose to the challenge and were able to release intense feelings. In essence, they were mourning their own death, and as a result, they became far less defensive, more vulnerable, open, and "feelingful," and more accepting and empathic toward others. Rather than defensively retreating from life-affirming activity, they were more likely to use their heightened awareness of personal mortality to make their lives more meaningful and fulfilling.

VOICE THERAPY

> No treatment could do any good until I understood the voice and saw that it was running me, that I was an automaton. . . . I feel as if I've been reprieved from a lifelong sentence.
> —From a patient's journal in James Masterson's *The Real Self*

> The voice is a continuous, although not always conscious, process that is carried inside one's head but usually not open to external interpretation because it remains unspoken. Voice therapy is the process by which people can expose and come face to face with the demons they carry.
> —Pamela Cantor in a Foreword to R. W. Firestone's
> *Suicide and the Inner Voice: Risk Assessment,*
> *Treatment, and Case Management*

Voice therapy involves breaking away from negative parental introjects that support the self-parenting system and learning to live as a separate, unique, differentiated individual. In voice therapy sessions, internalized destructive thought processes are brought to the surface along with the accompanying affect. This procedure allows clients to confront alien components of their personality and understand the source of these components.

Voice therapy is a process of giving spoken words to thoughts and attitudes at the core of an individual's self-limiting, self-defeating behavior. In our early investigations, which took place in a group setting, one participant started by saying her self-critical thoughts as "I" statements: "I'm stupid," "I'm a failure." At this point, we encouraged her to express the same thoughts in the second person, "you," as though someone else were talking to her, for example, "You're stupid," "You're a failure" (R. W. Firestone, 1997b). We observed that when individuals verbalized their self-criticisms in this format, they began by speaking softly, but then their tone often became angry and they expressed malicious statements toward themselves in powerful language. Later, we encouraged others in the group to adopt this format when expressing their voice attacks. We were impressed by the intensity of the aggression that accompanied these outbursts. The marked hostility that participants expressed was uncharacteristic of their normal composure or their way of thinking of themselves and others. In addition, we observed notable changes in the physical appearance and expression of individuals as they verbalized their voice attacks. Frequently, they took on the speech patterns, colloquialisms, and regional accents of their parents, often the parent of the same sex. It was as though the negative side of the parental figure was living inside the person and could be accessed by this method.

Initially, we used the techniques of voice therapy to understand and expand the first author's theoretical framework. Later, we recognized its value as a therapeutic methodology. We observed that when the voice predominated over rational thinking, participants tended to be more cut off or removed from their feelings and were more likely to act out or externalize aversive traits and behaviors in their social interactions, especially with the people closest to them. They were two very different people depending on which mode of experience was dominant: the self system or the anti-self system. When the anti-self system was ascendant, individuals viewed events and situations from a negative perspective and responded more critically, cynically, and aggressively to others.

We observed that as people verbalized their self-attacks, they gained clarity and insight, made significant connections between their destructive voices and harmful behaviors, and were better able to control the tendency to act out negative behavior. In expressing the feelings associated with their destructive thoughts and attitudes, they overcame their distorted self-critical views, which enabled them to feel greater compassion for themselves (R. W. Firestone, 1997a).

Last, we conducted an empirical research project to test the validity of the voice concept in relation to its potential for determining self-destructive, suicidal, and violent behavior. This led to the development of four assessment scales: the Firestone Assessment of Self-Destructive Thoughts (FAST), the Firestone Assessment of Suicide Intent (FASI; R. W. Firestone & Firestone, 2006), the Firestone Assessment of Violent Thoughts (FAVT; R. W. Firestone & Firestone, 2008b), and the Firestone Assessment of Violent Thoughts Adolescent Version (FAVT-A; R. W. Firestone & Firestone, 2008a). The items selected for the scales were obtained directly from voice statements gathered during pilot studies. Reliability and validity studies were conducted using subjects from diverse populations, including psychotherapy inpatients, outpatients, prison inmates, individuals on probation, participants in court-mandated anger management groups, and also normal and comparison groups. Results of reliability and validation studies showed that the FAST and FAVT effectively discriminated between suicidal and nonsuicidal subjects and between violent and nonviolent subjects at a high level of significance. The findings supported the hypothesis that an individual's voices are directly related to self-destructive and violent behavior.

Specifically in relation to self-destructive behavior and suicide, the results tended to validate our hypotheses regarding the concept of the voice: "Self-destructive thoughts exist on a continuum from mildly self-critical to suicidal; [and] . . . there is a corresponding continuum of self-destructive behaviors that are strongly influenced or controlled by these destructive thoughts, or 'voices'" (L. Firestone, 2006, p. 120). Participants in early clinical studies identified their voices as parental statements or as representative of overall attitudes they perceived as directed toward them in their early years. The fact that these statements were able to distinguish those at risk for suicide more accurately than other instruments lends support to the hypothesis that destructive voices associated with self-destructive acts may well represent introjected parental attitudes (L. Firestone, 2006).

Steps in the Voice Therapy Process

1. *Verbalizing voice attacks.* Clients are instructed to articulate their self-attacks in a second-person format, using "you" statements rather than first person "I" statements. Often a client will spontaneously adopt the second-person format when prompted by a question from the therapist: "What do you think you are telling yourself in the situation?" For example, instead of saying, "I'm unattractive," the person would say, "You're unattractive!" as though talking to oneself from another person's perspective. They also verbalize their hostile, cynical attitudes toward others as though someone were imparting bad information to them about the other person, being a kind of malicious counsel or coach: "He doesn't really love you," "She's deceiving you."

When clients speak these voices, they are encouraged to fully express the accompanying feelings, and there is usually a considerable release of feeling. Our emphasis on the importance of gaining access to clients' emotions is supported by a number of other clinicians, including Greenberg, Rice, and Elliott (1993) and Watson, Goldman, and Greenberg (2007) in the practice of emotion-focused therapy (EFT). This approach focuses primarily on eliciting emotion by directing the client to amplify his or her self-critical statements.

For example, if the client says "you're worthless" or sneers while criticizing, direct the client to "do this again . . . " "do this some more . . . "; "put some words to this . . ." This operation will intensify the client's affective arousal and help access core criticisms. (Greenberg et al., 1993, p. 205)

Cognitive therapist Judith Beck (1995) has also underscored the necessity for eliciting clients' *hot cognitions*, "important automatic thoughts and images that arise in the therapy session itself and are associated with a change or increase in emotion. . . . Generally, these affect-laden thoughts are most important to work with" (p. 80).

2. *Identifying the source of voices.* When clients express their destructive thoughts and release accompanying feelings of anger and sadness, they often recall specific family interactions in which they internalized their parents' critical or hateful attitudes toward them. They make the connection between what their parents and other significant figures in their childhood environment, such as siblings, relatives, teachers, and peers, thought of them and the destructive points of view expressed in their internal voice attacks. If the client does not make the connection, the therapist might ask, "Where do you think these thoughts come from?" This is not a form of psychotherapy in which we make interpretations to clients about the sources of their voices; rather, clients come to their own realizations, which we have found to be much more powerful.

3. *Answering back to voice attacks.* Clients take their own side and answer back to the attacks of the voice. This is often an angry, cathartic experience. Afterward, they answer the attacks more rationally and objectively appraise themselves from an adult point of view. The process allows them to become more realistic about their lives and to have a more accurate perspective. Watson et al. (2007) provided a descriptive account of the step in EFT that focuses on encouraging the client to answer back to his or her voice attacks: In one case, a client "Gayle . . . identified how crippling the critical voice was and how tired it made her feel. She asked the critic to go away. She was angry that her inner critic was inducing fear and worry" (p. 80).

4. *Developing insight about how voices influence present-day behavior.* Coming to understand why they act out negative behavior in everyday interactions provides the impetus for clients to alter their negative traits at the behavioral level (R. W. Firestone & Catlett, 2009b). In this process, they develop a coherent narrative about what happened to them and an awareness of how developmental issues are affecting their lives.

5. *Collaborating with the therapist to institute corrective suggestions.* Clients work with the therapist to plan behavioral changes that challenge the dictates of the voice and are in accord with the client's personal motivation. These plans fall into two categories: (a) corrective suggestions that involve stopping the self-

defeating, self-destructive behaviors encouraged by the voice (e.g., self-nurturing habit patterns, compulsive routines) and (b) corrective suggestions that involve initiating constructive behaviors that run counter to the dictates of the voice. Both types of suggestions facilitate moving away from passivity and fantasy gratification in the direction of an active pursuit of satisfying clients' needs in the real world. This process involves changing from an inward, self-protective, self-attacking orientation to one of interacting authentically with others and reaching out to life.

We and our associates have found that voice therapy techniques work well in a group-therapy setting. When participants listen to a person expressing his or her voice attacks, the hostile attitudes and powerful release of feelings resonate with their own self-attacks. Within a particular culture, there is a commonality in voices, so in the group setting, people benefit and expand their own understanding.

Voice therapy is similar in certain respects to Aaron Beck's (A. T. Beck, Rush, Shaw, & Emery, 1979) and Judith Beck's (1995) cognitive therapy (CT). For example, both therapeutic approaches attempt to access destructive voices or "automatic thoughts" that influence maladaptive behavior. Treatment outcome studies (A. T. Beck, 2005; Butler, Chapman, Forman, & Beck, 2006; Forman, Herbert, Moitra, Yeomans, & Geller, 2007) have demonstrated the effectiveness of CT and cognitive behavior therapy (CBT). Butler et al. (2006) noted, "Large effect sizes were found for CBT for unipolar depression, generalized anxiety disorder, panic disorder . . . social phobia, post traumatic stress disorder, and childhood depressive and anxiety disorders" (p. 17). According to A. T. Beck (2005), extensive research has shown CT and CBT to be more successful than drug treatment in reducing anxiety: "Meta-analyses indicate that CT/CBT protocols are more effective in reducing panic and anxiety symptoms than pharmacological treatments" (p. 956).

In voice therapy, the technique of verbalizing the voice in the second-person format not only elicits strong affect but also appears to access core negative beliefs or schema more quickly than other methods. In addition, we found that using this format "facilitates the process of *separating* the client's own point of view from hostile thought patterns that make up an alien point of view toward self" (R. W. Firestone, 1988, p. 205). The combination of identifying automatic thoughts or self-attacks, which is the focus of CT and CBT, and verbalizing these thoughts in the second person, which is a key component of voice therapy, shifts clients' point of view in a positive direction and leads to enduring changes in their behavior.

Voice Therapy for Couples

Voice therapy techniques are effective in couple therapy, where partners express their critical thoughts in the voice format. As they work on themselves, individuals experience their own and their partner's personal psychotherapy. Partners develop empathy for one another and come to know and appreciate each other on a deep level. In recognizing that their voice attacks are the primary source of misery in their lives and their relationship, they take back their projections and stop blaming each other; the pressure is taken off the relationship (R. W. Firestone & Catlett, 1999).

In addition, partners challenge the false security of the fantasy bond by learning to be direct and honest in their communication with each other and to be nondefensive and open to feedback. Through corrective suggestions, they are encouraged to change their withholding behaviors, refrain from acting out polarized child and parent roles, break patterns of dominance and submission, increase respect for each other's goals and priorities, and strive to establish equality in the relationship.

In our work with couples, we became increasingly aware that through the process of projective identification, people incorporate voices on the basis of critical attitudes their partners have toward them. These attacks may not necessarily be verbalized but they are conveyed through expressive gestures and the nuances of personal interactions. The new voices often resonate with old voice attacks from childhood, but when they do not, they can create an entirely new set of voice attacks.

Relationship partners either support each other's real self by offering acceptance, affection, and understanding, or they support their partner's anti-self and destructive voice process. When they harbor hostility or are intolerant of love or acceptance from the other, they provoke anger and distance. When partners are truly themselves, they are inclined to be loving and supportive, but when these feelings are rejected, they become angry and bitter. This not only forces them to lose their good feelings but also tends to turn them against themselves. In that sense, one's partner can become an intimate enemy. To achieve differentiation, partners must learn to identify, sort out, and separate from negative attitudes they internalized in their primary relationship with parents.

In its application to couples, voice therapy has some elements in common with emotionally focused couples therapy as described by Johnson (2004). For example, in delineating Steps 5 and 6 in emotionally focused couples therapy, Johnson emphasized that these steps "also involve the accessing of core self-concepts or models, which are associated with the intense emotions that arise here" (p. 164). In one session, a client verbalized the self-attacks he experiences in a sexual situation with his partner using the second person format: "So I say to myself, *what do you expect? You're not good at this love stuff*. I feel about this big. (Making a small space between thumb and forefinger). I can't even ask her anymore" (p. 164).

Johnson, Hunsley, Greenberg, and Schindler (1999) reported the following:

> A pilot study is planned on the use of EFT when one partner suffers from posttraumatic stress disorder. The work with traumatized couples is particularly interesting in that initial indications are that EFT interventions appear to not only improve the couple's relationship but to create a healing environment that allows the trauma survivor to deal more constructively with trauma symptoms such as flashbacks and emotional numbing. (p. 76)

Johnson and Denton (2002) cited results indicating "that 70–75% of couples see their relationships as no longer distressed after 10–12 sessions of EFT, and these results appear to be less susceptible to relapse than in other approaches" (p. 226).

Voice therapy techniques challenge basic defenses and in so doing facilitate the process of differentiation. This process helps people develop a unique perspective in relation to themselves and to the world, and it frees them to formulate their own goals and values (R. W. Firestone, 1997a; R. W. Firestone & Catlett, 1999). It offers a means by which one can resist the false security of the fantasy bond. Overall, by disrupting illusions of connection and breaking down defensive patterns, individuals can move on to new levels of vulnerability and personal freedom.

CONCLUSION

Separation theory focuses on breaking with destructive parental introjects and moving toward individuation. This theoretical position represents the ultimate challenge to one's defense system. Psychological defenses are maladaptive because they cut deeply into an individual's life; anything that fragments or denies the reality of an individual's experience or deprives him or her of that experience is, in our opinion, clearly destructive.

The techniques of voice therapy help people identify and separate from a destructive thought process that influences the acting out of aversive behavior toward self and others. The choice to break away from fantasy bonds and deadening habit patterns is partially an ethical one, not only because of the inherent damage caused by defenses that effectively limit a person's capacity for living and feeling but also because of the corresponding damage to loved ones. Voice therapy, by "counteracting the dictates of the voice and disrupting fantasies of connection, offers people a unique opportunity to fulfill their human potential, thereby giving life its special meaning" (R. W. Firestone, 1990b, p. 73).

Although separation theory is a psychodynamically based system of concepts that explains the formation of psychological defenses in response to emotional trauma, it also has powerful philosophical implications. It entails an inherent morality based on sound mental health principles. Through understanding how people are hurt in their interactions with others, these destructive behaviors can be minimized or eliminated (R. W. Firestone & Catlett, 2009b).

Fantasy bonds that are formed in the family constellation are externalized to include one's ingroup, one's religious beliefs, and one's nationalism. In that sense, society and social systems represent a pooling of individual defenses, particularly in relation to death anxiety. Like Ernest Becker (1975), we challenge the concept of cultural relativity. Cultures, much like families, vary considerably in relation to their ability to meet their members' core needs for basic satisfaction in life and the maintenance of each individual's feelings of self-worth.

Separation theory synthesizes psychodynamic concepts and existential issues of aloneness, sickness, aging, and death. Human beings as a species are uniquely cursed with a conscious awareness of their own mortality. Fantasy bonds represent a desperate attempt to cope not only with separation anxiety but also with the despair and horror of facing a life that unfolds under the shadow of an ultimate death sentence. One resolution to this dilemma is to develop fantasy processes of immortality and an imagination of a life after death. Aware that the body dies and decays, the defense is to postulate a soul, but the price is to turn against the body and sexuality (see Chapter 5, this volume). In this sense, people turn against themselves. Faced with a death sentence, they know that they must have done something wrong, that they must be bad or sinful. Therefore, they must purify themselves and make some form of atonement. As people defend against death anxiety, their tendency is to align themselves with death and, to varying degrees, limit or give up life-affirming activities.

Ironically, the fantasy bond offers people a sense of safety, but at the same time, sadly, it polarizes people against one another. If the beliefs of another person or group differ from one's own, it challenges one's defensive solution and threatens one's security. Those others must be "processed," assimilated, or destroyed. We believe this is the psychological basis of ethnic cleansing and religious warfare. To cope with this core dilemma and its tragic consequences, it is essential to understand the fantasy bond and the formation of the anti-self system.

In attempting to make sense of man's destructiveness throughout history, Sigmund Freud (1925/1959) postulated the concept of the *death instinct*, a basic aggressive or destructive predilection. In subsequent years, this concept has come under criticism for lack of empirical evidence. The first author's point of view denies the contention that human beings are hostile but understands that aggressive attitudes and behavior are based on the frustration, emotional pain, and fear people experienced in their developmental years.

In summary, separation theory explains the process of how, under painful conditions and stress, children incorporate cynical, hostile attitudes toward self and others that are manifested in an alien part of their personalities that we refer to as the anti-self system. In voice therapy, these internalized attitudes are identified and individuals learn to understand and overcome their destructive programming. In our long-term observational study, we found that when people were more themselves and were not possessed by these alien elements, they had more feeling, empathy, and compassion and were kinder and more generous toward others (Firestone & Catlett, 2009b).

When people spoke about the inevitability of their impending death in group sessions and fully experienced the depth of their fear and sadness, they had a greater appreciation and respect for other people and their struggles. Experiencing death as the great leveler favors a one-world view and gives value and respect to people of different backgrounds and belief systems. Accepting the reality of death without illusion and thereby maintaining reverence for life, one is unlikely to take up arms against others.

Voice therapy is not restricted to helping neurotic or disturbed individuals; it is valuable for any person who wishes to identify and eliminate impediments to his or her autonomy and individuality. Confronting one's critical and hostile internalized thought processes and having the courage to challenge one's negative and dysfunctional behaviors offer the maximum opportunity to lead one's own authentic life.

REFERENCES

Ainsworth, M. D. S., Blehar, M. C., Waters, E., & Wall, S. (1978). *Patterns of attachment: A psychological study of the Strange Situation.* Hillsdale, NJ: Erlbaum.

Anthony, S. (1973). *The discovery of death in childhood and after.* Harmondsworth, England: Penguin. (Original work published 1971)

Beck, A. T. (2005). The current state of cognitive therapy: A 40-year retrospective. *Archives of General Psychiatry, 62,* 953–959. doi:10.1001/archpsyc.62.9.953

Beck, A. T., Rush, A. J., Shaw, B. F., & Emery, G. (1979). *Cognitive therapy of depression.* New York, NY: Guilford Press.

Beck, J. S. (1995). *Cognitive therapy: Basics and beyond.* New York, NY: Guilford Press.

Becker, E. (1975). *Escape from evil.* New York, NY: Free Press.

Becker, E. (1997). *The denial of death*. New York, NY: Free Press. (Original work published 1973)

Benjamin, L.S. (2003). *Interpersonal reconstructive therapy: Promoting change in non-responders*. New York, NY: Guilford Press.

Bloch, D. (1978). *"So the witch won't eat me" Fantasy and the child's fear of infanticide*. New York, NY: Grove Press.

Bowlby, J. (1973). *Attachment and loss: Vol. II. Separation: Anxiety and anger*. New York, NY: Basic Books.

Butler, A.C., Chapman, J.E., Forman, E.M., & Beck, A.T. (2006). The empirical status of cognitive–behavioral therapy: A review of meta-analyses. *Clinical Psychology Review, 26*, 17–31. doi:10.1016/j.cpr.2005.07.003

Cantor, P.C. (1997). Foreword. In R. W. Firestone (Ed.), *Suicide and the inner voice: Risk assessment, treatment and case management* (pp. xi–xv). Thousand Oaks, CA: Sage.

Cassidy, J., & Mohr, J.J. (2001). Unresolvable fear, trauma, and psychopathology: Theory, research, and clinical considerations related to disorganized attachment across the life span. *Clinical Psychology: Science and Practice, 8*, 275–298. doi:10.1093/clipsy.8.3.275

Fairbairn, W.R.D. (1952). A revised psychopathology of the psychoses and psychoneuroses. In W.R.D. Fairbairn (Ed.), *Psychoanalytic studies of the personality* (pp. 28–58). London, England: Routledge & Kegan Paul.

Felitti, V.J., Anda, R.F., Nordenberg, D., Williamson, D.F., Spitz, A.M., Edwards, V., . . . Marks, J.S. (1998). Relationship of childhood abuse and household dysfunction to many of the leading causes of death in adults: The Adverse Childhood Experiences (ACE) study. *American Journal of Preventive Medicine, 14*, 245–258. doi:10.1016/S0749-3797(98)00017-8

Ferenczi, S. (1955). Confusion of tongues between adults and the child (E. Mosbacher, Trans.). In M. Balint (Ed.), *Final contributions to the problems and methods of psychoanalysis* (pp. 156–167). New York, NY: Basic Books. (Original work published 1933)

Firestone, L. (2006). Suicide and the inner voice. In T. Ellis (Ed.), *Cognition and suicide: Theory, research and practice* (pp. 119–147). Washington, DC: American Psychological Association. doi:10.1037/11377-006

Firestone, R.W. (1985). *The fantasy bond: Structure of psychological defenses*. Santa Barbara, CA: Glendon Association.

Firestone, R.W. (1988). *Voice therapy: A psychotherapeutic approach to self-destructive behavior*. Santa Barbara, CA: Glendon Association.

Firestone, R.W. (1990a). *Compassionate child-rearing: An in-depth approach to optimal parenting*. Santa Barbara, CA: Glendon Association.

Firestone, R.W. (1990b). Voice therapy. In J. Zeig & W. Munion (Eds.), *What is psychotherapy? Contemporary perspectives* (pp. 68–74). San Francisco, CA: Jossey-Bass.

Firestone, R. W. (1994). Psychological defenses against death anxiety. In R. A. Neimeyer (Ed.), *Death anxiety handbook: Research, instrumentation, and application* (pp. 217–241). Washington, DC: Taylor & Francis.

Firestone, R. W. (1997a). *Combating destructive thought processes: Voice therapy and separation theory.* Thousand Oaks, CA: Sage.

Firestone, R. W. (1997b). *Suicide and the inner voice: Risk assessment, treatment, and case management.* Thousand Oaks, CA: Sage.

Firestone, R. W., & Catlett, J. (1999). *Fear of intimacy.* Washington, DC: American Psychological Association.

Firestone, R. W., & Catlett, J. (2009a). *Beyond death anxiety: Achieving life-affirming death awareness.* New York, NY: Springer.

Firestone, R. W., & Catlett, J. (2009b). *The ethics of interpersonal relationships.* London, England: Karnac Books.

Firestone, R. W., & Firestone, L. (2006). *Firestone Assessment of Self-Destructive Thoughts (FAST)/Firestone Suicidal Intent (FASI) professional manual.* Lutz, FL: Psychological Assessment Resources.

Firestone, R. W., & Firestone, L. (2008a). *Firestone Assessment of Violent Thoughts— Adolescent (FAVT-A) manual.* Lutz, FL: Psychological Assessment Resources.

Firestone, R. W., & Firestone, L. (2008b). *Firestone Assessment of Violent Thoughts (FAVT) manual.* Lutz, FL: Psychological Assessment Resources.

Firestone, R. W., Firestone, L. A., & Catlett, J. (2003). *Creating a life of meaning and compassion: The wisdom of psychotherapy.* Washington, DC: American Psychological Association. doi:10.1037/10611-000

Fonagy, P., Gergely, G., Jurist, E., & Target, M. (2002). *Affect regulation, mentalization, and the development of the self.* New York, NY: Other Press.

Forman, E. M., Herbert, J. D., Moitra, E., Yeomans, P. D., & Geller, P. A. (2007). A randomized controlled effectiveness trial of acceptance and commitment therapy and cognitive therapy for anxiety and depression. *Behavior Modification, 31,* 772–799. doi:10.1177/0145445507302202

Freud, A. (1966). *The ego and the mechanisms of defense* (rev. ed.). Madison, CT: International Universities Press.

Freud, S. (1959). An autobiographical study. In J. Strachey (Ed. & Trans.), *The standard edition of the complete psychological works of Sigmund Freud* (Vol. 20, pp. 7–75). London, England: Hogarth Press. (Original work published 1925)

Greenberg, L. S., Rice, L. N., & Elliott, R. (1993). *Facilitating emotional change: The moment-by-moment process.* New York, NY: Guilford Press.

Guntrip, H. (1961). *Personality structure and human interaction: The developing synthesis of psychodynamic theory.* New York, NY: International Universities Press.

Guntrip, H. (1969). *Schizoid phenomena object-relations and the self.* New York, NY: International Universities Press.

Johnson, S. M. (2004). *The practice of emotionally focused couple therapy: Creating connection* (2nd ed.). New York, NY: Brunner-Routledge.

Johnson, S. M., & Denton, W. (2002). Emotionally focused couple therapy: Creating secure connections. In A. S. Gurman & N. S. Jacobson (Eds.), *Clinical handbook of couple therapy* (3rd ed., pp. 221–250). New York, NY: Guilford Press.

Johnson, S. S., Hunsley, J., Greenberg, L., & Schindler, W. (1999). Emotionally focused couples therapy: Status and challenges. *Clinical Psychology: Science and Practice, 6,* 67–79. doi:10.1093/clipsy.6.1.67

Kohut, H. (1977). *The restoration of the self.* New York, NY: International Universities Press.

Main, M., & Hesse, E. (1990). Parents' unresolved traumatic experiences are related to infant disorganized attachment status: Is frightened and/or frightening parental behavior the linking mechanism? In M. T. Greenberg, D. Cicchetti, & E. M. Cummings (Eds.), *Attachment in the preschool years: Theory, research, and intervention* (pp. 161–182). Chicago, IL: University of Chicago Press.

Masterson, J. F. (1985). *The real self: A developmental, self, and object relations approach.* New York, NY: Brunner/Mazel.

McCarthy, J. B. (1980). *Death anxiety: The loss of the self.* New York, NY: Gardner Press.

Mikulincer, M., & Florian, V. (2000). Exploring individual differences in reactions to mortality salience: Does attachment style regulate terror management mechanisms? *Journal of Personality and Social Psychology, 79,* 260–273. doi:10.1037/0022-3514.79.2.260

Mikulincer, M., & Shaver, P. R. (2007). *Attachment in adulthood: Structure, dynamics, and change.* New York, NY: Guilford Press.

Rank, O. (1972). *Will therapy and truth and reality* (J. Taft, Trans.). New York, NY: Knopf. (Original work published 1936)

Schore, A. N. (2003). *Affect regulation and the repair of the self.* New York, NY: Norton.

Shaver, P. R., & Clark, C. L. (1996). Forms of adult romantic attachment and their cognitive and emotional underpinnings. In G. G. Noam & K. W. Fischer (Eds.), *Development and vulnerability in close relationships* (pp. 29–58). Mahwah, NJ: Erlbaum.

Shaver, P. R., & Mikulincer, M. (2002). Attachment-related psychodynamics. *Attachment & Human Development, 4,* 133–161. doi:10.1080/14616730210154171

Siegel, D. J. (1999). *The developing mind: Toward a neurobiology of interpersonal experience.* New York, NY: Guilford Press.

Siegel, D. J. (2003). Foreword. In R. W. Firestone, L. A. Firestone, & J. Catlett (Eds.), *Creating a life of meaning and compassion: The wisdom of psychotherapy* (pp. ix–x). Washington, DC: American Psychological Association.

Siegel, D. J. (2007). *The mindful brain: Reflection and attunement in the cultivation of well-being.* New York, NY: Norton.

Siegel, D. J. (2010). *The mindful therapist: A clinician's guide to mindsight and neural integration.* New York, NY: Norton.

Siegel, D. J., & Hartzell, M. (2004). *Parenting from the inside out.* Los Angeles, CA: Tarcher.

Solomon, S., Greenberg, J., & Pyszczynski, T. (2004). The cultural animal: Twenty years of terror management theory and research. In J. Greenberg, S. L. Koole, & T. Pyszczynski (Eds.), *Handbook of experimental existential psychology* (pp. 13–34). New York, NY: Guilford Press.

Stern, D. N. (1985). *The interpersonal world of the infant: A view from psychoanalysis and developmental psychology.* New York, NY: Basic Books.

Sullivan, H. S. (1953). *The interpersonal theory of psychiatry.* New York, NY: Norton.

Tillich, P. (1952). *The courage to be.* New Haven, CT: Yale University Press.

van der Kolk, B. A. (2005). Developmental trauma disorder: Toward a rational diagnosis for children with complex trauma histories. *Psychiatric Annals, 35,* 401–408.

Watson, J. C. Goldman, R. N., & Greenberg, L. S. (2007). *Case studies in emotion-focused treatment of depression.* Washington, DC: American Psychological Association.

21

ACCEPTANCE AND COMMITMENT TO CHOSEN VALUES IN COGNITIVE BEHAVIOR THERAPY

IFTAH YOVEL AND NOA BIGMAN

The past 2 decades have witnessed the rapid rise of several different acceptance-based cognitive behavior therapies (CBTs). Examples of this generation of "third wave" treatments include dialectical behavior therapy for borderline personality disorder (Linehan, 1993), mindfulness-based cognitive therapy (Segal, Williams, & Teasdale, 2002), and behavioral activation for depression (Martell, Addis, & Jacobson, 2001), among several others. This chapter focuses on the most comprehensive and probably most influential third wave clinical approach: acceptance and commitment therapy (ACT; Hayes, Strosahl, & Wilson, 1999).

In many ways, ACT is similar to earlier CBTs. Treatment in ACT focuses for the most part on behaviors and cognitions, and it is collaborative, active, practical, and goal directed. Moreover, many of the interventions used in ACT (but not all) are essentially similar to the ones used in "traditional" CBT. Most important, ACT is an evidence-based clinical approach that is grounded in basic science. A rapidly growing body of published studies supports basic theoretical principles underlying ACT (e.g., Feldner, Zvolensky, Eifert & Spira, 2003; Hofmann, Heering, Sawyer, & Asnaani, 2009; Masuda, Hayes, Sackett, & Twohig, 2004; Najmi, Riemann, & Wegner, 2009) and demonstrates the efficacy of ACT-based treatments for a wide array of problems, ranging from chronic pain (Vowles & McCracken, 2008), management of diabetes (Gregg, Callaghan, Hayes, & Glenn-Lawson, 2007), and smoking cessation (Gifford et al., 2004) to a variety of mental disorders, such as generalized anxiety disorder (Roemer, Orsillo, & Salters-Pedneault, 2008), obsessive–compulsive disorder (OCD; Twohig et al., 2010), and schizophrenia (Bach & Hayes, 2002).

Despite the similarities, some of the essential foundations of ACT distinguish this broad therapeutic perspective from earlier forms of CBT. These foundations may be usefully conceptualized in terms of two themes in the present volume: *choice* and *meaning*. Unlike most clinical approaches, and in contrast to the intuitive and natural coping strategies people typically use, ACT does not directly target changes in the form, content, or frequency of psychological events (e.g., thoughts, emotions, urges, physical sensations), even if these are perceived as aversive, dysfunctional, or in any way "distorted." Instead, ACT focuses on changing the function of these events and the way individuals relate to them (e.g., believing they causally affect behavior). Thus, ACT highlights a basic choice one can make: Rather than having to "fight" troubling internal events, "solve" them, or act on them in ways that are self-damaging, one can accept their occurrence. It is important that *acceptance* in ACT is an active process based on willful awareness, and it refers mostly to internal events, not to things that are generally amenable to willful control (e.g., behaviors or certain environmental aspects).

The theory behind ACT and the clinical interventions it includes, some of which are influenced by Eastern philosophies, is consistent with the focus on choice. In terms of broad treatment objectives, ACT does not target the alleviation of disturbing symptoms. Instead, it aims to create flexible and effective psychological repertoires that help clients pursue their goals and chosen values. Moreover, similar to existential and humanistic therapies, ACT encourages clients to actively choose their own values and goals, thus providing themselves a sense of direction and meaning. The use of the word *choice* is of importance. Choices, as opposed to decisions, are verbally undefended selections among alternatives, that is, selections one does not rationalize logically. In ACT, it is argued that one cannot verbally justify a value or a life goal and that such an effort would unavoidably lead to an unfruitful logical entanglement (Hayes & Wilson, 1993). In other words, individuals do not logically discover the objective meaning of their lives in treatment, but rather choose it actively. This echoes the existential claim that existence precedes essence (Sartre, 1995).

In what follows, we provide a concise account of the theoretical foundations of ACT. We then present the basic therapeutic processes of this clinical approach while focusing especially on the treatment elements in ACT that address values and meaning. In each section, we describe recent studies from our laboratory that provide evidence of the efficacy of ACT interventions.

CONCEPTUALIZATION OF PSYCHOPATHOLOGY IN ACT

Most medical and psychological approaches to therapy assume that psychological suffering is the result of psychopathological processes. Different perspectives assume that these processes are associated with different kinds of abnormalities, such as morphological or chemical abnormalities in the central nervous system, abnormal learning histories, or unresolved internal conflicts. In ACT, however, it is assumed that psychological pain is ubiquitous because it is the inevitable result of normal psychological processes. These processes may prevent other phenomena that are indeed abnormal (e.g., hallucinations). However, more often, faulty attempts aimed to eliminate inevitable mental pain inadvertently increase this pain and turn it into more serious suffering, which then may be classified as psychopathological. The theoretical roots of this claim are briefly discussed next.

The Unique Abilities of the Human Mind

In ACT, it is assumed that the unique strength of the human mind is its ability to derive limitless arbitrary connections among stimuli. Consider, for example, a young child who learns that a certain animal is called *cat*, thus forming the arbitrary connection between the furry animal and the sound of the word *cat* (Hayes et al., 1999). Suppose that this child is later scratched while playing with a cat. After that incident, he may feel anxious, cry, and run away if he hears his father saying, "Look, Danny, a cat!" Many organisms are able to learn formal connections between stimuli (e.g., between the presence of a cat or any other stimulus such as a certain sound and the feelings of pain and anxiety). However, the child's strong reaction occurs despite the fact that he has never experienced physical pain in the presence of the actual sound *cat*, because his mind was able to bring these two stimuli together by using derived relations between them. That is, the change in status of one component of this simple relational frame (the actual animal, which is now associated with mental pain) has changed, without any additional training or exposure, the status of the other component (the sound *cat*). No other organism is able to do that (Ramnerö & Törneke, 2008).

The human mind is unique in its ability to derive complex arbitrary relations and use them in different contexts. As suggested by other theoretical perspectives (e.g., construal level theory; Liberman & Trope, 2008), humans can easily consider and manipulate events and contingencies that are temporally or physically remote or are of low probability, including ones that are experienced by other people. These abilities enable us to evaluate and respond effectively to an extremely wide range of situations. However, according to the ACT perspective on psychopathology, these extraordinary abilities are also the source of a great deal of pain and suffering (Hayes, Barnes-Holmes, & Roche, 2001).

Psychological Pain Is Ubiquitous and Unavoidable

Because of the abilities of the human mind, all kinds of external and internal events can become "present" at any given time if their mental representations are activated (Törneke, 2010). Internal events may have a strong psychological impact if they are perceived as relevant to the well-being of the person experiencing them. Most organisms are biased toward attending and responding to stimuli or events they perceive as dangerous or aversive. For humans, who have minds that can easily make any stimuli psychologically present, the availability of aversive stimuli—in the form of mental representations—is greatly enhanced. Thus, humans often feel distressed because of things that are not happening at the moment. People may worry about events that may happen in the future, regardless of how distant this future is or how likely it is to actually come about. They can also compare themselves, their partner, or the current situation with any kind of frightening alternative or desirable ideal. For example, a socially anxious person may think, "I will be anxious and miserable if I go to the party, so I'd better stay home." To take a more extreme but unfortunately common example, a depressed individual may say to herself, "I feel sad and hopeless now. If I kill myself I will not feel anything at all, which is better" (Hayes et al., 1999). Moreover, because of the great capacity of the mind to generate arbitrary relations, any person, object, or stimulus can be connected to any negative emotion, irrespective of the original or formal value of the stimulus (e.g., "This party depresses me because it reminds me of the times before the trauma when I could really enjoy things").

In sum, the unique ability of the human mind to generate countless arbitrary connections and to easily "travel" in time, space, probability, and social dimensions (cf. Liberman & Trope, 2008) is highly advantageous, but it also brings about a great deal of unavoidable pain. Representations and relations generated by the human mind greatly increase the reach of aversive stimuli, thus making mental pain common and intense.

Verbal Processes Often Intensify Suffering

Because of the efficiency of human language, verbal formulations and evaluative rules generated by the mind often dominate other potential sources of information, including the person's own direct experience. The term *cognitive fusion* is used in ACT to label this phenomenon (Hayes et al., 1999). For example, the typical behavior of phobic individuals is characterized by fear and rigid avoidance resulting from the way objects or events are conceptualized and by refusal to examine the actual attributes of these avoided external stimuli (e.g., a cockroach) or internal experiences (e.g., the pain associated with getting an injection). Similarly, many people refuse even to taste foods they "don't like."

Being overengaged with one's internal verbal relations can be detrimental in itself. Repetitive and unfruitful attempts to evaluate, find reasons for, or consider the consequences of negative thoughts may increase the complexity and availability of these problematic verbal relations and networks, a process that is called *cognitive entanglement* in ACT. Indeed, a large body of research documents the harmful effects of rumination—repetitive and passive engagement in self-focused, negatively valenced evaluative thinking (e.g., Nolen-Hoeksema, Wisco, & Lyubomirsky, 2008). ACT also highlights the indirect effects of cognitive entanglement, pointing out that such ruminative processes are particularly detrimental because they often come at the expense of other, more useful activities.

It is also important to acknowledge the futility of efforts directed at breaking or modifying verbal relations. Such attempts often lead to more entanglement because complex and highly interrelated cognitive networks tend to be stable and resistant to change and are efficient at maintaining and preserving themselves. For example, in agreement with self-verification theory (e.g., Kwang & Swann, 2010), it is assumed in ACT that the tendency to verify, validate, and confirm one's self-views, negative as these may be, often overrides the desire for positive evaluations. Therefore, people's perceptions of reality tend to be systematically skewed, causing them to dismiss any information that challenges their beliefs, regardless of how negative and self-damaging these beliefs are. Indeed, studies have shown that individuals with negative self-views seek unfavorable information from others, selectively remember feedback only if it is perceived as congruent with their beliefs, and become anxious if they receive positive self-discrepant feedback that they cannot easily dismiss (see Kwang & Swann, 2010, for a review). To use ACT terms, regardless of what the price is, the human mind "loves to be right" (Hayes & Strosahl, 2004).

Experiential Avoidance and Psychopathology

The power of verbal rules generated by the human mind may lead to *experiential avoidance* (Hayes, Wilson, Gifford, Follette, & Strosahl, 1996), which occurs when a person is unwilling to experience negatively evaluated private experiences such as feelings, thoughts, urges, memories, or bodily sensations, and therefore attempts to modify these experiences or their frequency of occurrence, even when such attempts are clearly inconsistent with well-being. Many mental disorders (e.g., OCD; posttraumatic stress disorder

[PTSD]) and pathological behaviors (e.g., suicide, substance abuse) can be usefully conceptualized as effects of particularly problematic methods of experiential avoidance (Hayes et al., 1996).

Why would experiential avoidance be so detrimental? As discussed earlier, humans use their minds, often quite successfully, to achieve desired goals and avoid stimuli or situations they deem aversive or dangerous. However, for a variety of reasons, success rates of such actions drop dramatically when the target stimuli people try to avoid are internal. It is a rather difficult task to "calm down" when feeling anxious, to "think positive" when worrying about something, or to willfully ignore physical sensations. Indeed, numerous studies have demonstrated the futility of attempts aimed at suppressing cognitions (e.g., Wegner, Schneider, Carter, & White, 1987). Moreover, such attempts paradoxically produce the opposite outcome, as deliberate thought suppression is typically followed by a period of increased frequency of the unwanted cognition (Wegner et al., 1987). This happens primarily because the regulatory process associated with avoiding an item necessarily includes that actual item (Hayes et al., 1996). Moreover, the inevitable failure of such experiential avoidance attempts may lead to increased stress and feelings of frustration, which create additional aversive experiences, which, in turn, may intensify the avoidance strategies, thus creating a vicious cycle. Indeed, failed thought suppression is etiologically related to several psychopathological syndromes, including OCD, depression, and PTSD (for a review, see Purdon, 1999). Thus, the human mind that generates much of the psychological pain we experience is, unfortunately, rather ineffective in dealing with it (see Chapter 3, this volume, for a similar analysis of suppression of death-related thoughts).

Experiential avoidance, especially when it is relatively isolated and time limited, is not always harmful. It is problematic, however, when it is persistent, chronic, and rigidly maintained. Management of inner experiences is particularly detrimental when it adversely affects other aspects of life and stands in the way of achieving one's goals. As acknowledged by many other forms of CBT, avoidance is strongly reinforced by the short-term relief it often provides. Therefore, it can be particularly difficult to deal with, even when it is associated with much distress and dysfunction.

Cognitive fusion, which results from the ability of the mind to make connections and associations, can turn any thought, memory, feeling, urge, or sensation into a target of avoidance. Any object or cognition associated with a trauma may be avoided in PTSD, and many individuals with panic disorder refrain from being sexually aroused because they associate these feelings with somatic anxiety. Thus, in many cases, cognitive fusion leads to narrow and rigid behavioral repertoires. These do not serve the person's interests because they are excessively governed by verbally generated relations, at the expense of being in contact with the actual contingencies of the internal and external environment. This general state is referred to in ACT as *psychological inflexibility*. People may devote enormous amounts of time and effort to managing their aversive inner experiences, to the extent that most other goals are "put on hold" (Hayes & Strosahl, 2004). They may then tell themselves that once they "get over" their problems, they will be able to go on with their lives. One of the main goals in ACT is to make clients realize that the former is not a necessary condition for the latter.

FEATURES OF ACT

Treatment in ACT is directly and explicitly based on the theory outlined earlier. Early in the therapeutic process, clients learn that the experience of psychological pain is unavoidable and that the use of strategies such as experiential avoidance to deal with this pain is natural and understandable but often leads to more suffering. This learning is accomplished by examining clients' typically long histories of ineffective struggle with their problems and by using a variety of metaphors and experiential exercises. It is important for clients to realize that the problem does not lie primarily with what they consider to be their difficulties (e.g., anxiety, obsessions, low self-esteem) but rather with the futile and endless fight against them. They also learn that there is another option, which is to stop fighting problems or attempting to solve them. In essence, they learn that they can simply "quit the war" (Hayes et al., 1999).

Many forms of pharmacotherapy and psychotherapy attempt to replace aversive inner experiences with more desirable or adaptive ones. For example, most treatments are aimed at changing certain emotions (e.g., anxiety) because they are perceived as aversive and because they are associated with problematic action tendencies (e.g., escape and avoidance; see, e.g., Roseman, Wiest, & Swartz, 1994). In contrast, ACT does not aim to modify the form, content, or frequency of unwanted feelings, cognitions, urges, or physical sensations. Instead, it is assumed that whether these unwanted events are problematic depends not on their own qualities but on the context in which they occur. That is, psychological events become harmful only when they need to be explained, believed, or disbelieved (thus leading to cognitive entanglement), controlled (thus leading to experiential avoidance), or acted on (thus causing adverse outcomes). For example, rather than targeting the content of certain cognitions or emotions, ACT aims at changing the way they are perceived (e.g., the importance attached to them) or the regulatory power they have on behavior.

The general goal in ACT is to increase *psychological flexibility*, defined as the ability to consciously and mindfully attend to the variety of internal and external experiences existing at the present moment and behave in ways that serve one's valued goals (for a recent review of this construct, see Kashdan & Rottenberg, 2010). This is achieved through several overlapping and inter-related core processes described briefly as follows.

Choice in ACT: Dealing With Aversive Internal Events

As a fundamental alternative to experiential avoidance, ACT encourages *acceptance*, or the conscious and active experience of unwanted private events, without attempting to alter their form, content, or frequency, particularly when these attempts cause adverse consequences. Such active acceptance is conditioned on the individual's willingness to be mindful of the present moment (see Chapter 14, this volume). Thus, ACT also emphasizes the state of *being present*, or the nonjudgmental, mindful experience of both internal and external events. This is done by a variety of mindfulness exercises in which language is used as a tool to describe rather than evaluate events, with the goal of increasing the previously limited repertoire of responses to such events (e.g., fear, avoidance).

Similarly, in contrast to many other forms of treatment, including earlier forms of cognitive therapy (CT), ACT practitioners do not attempt to modify problematic cognitions directly, mainly because it is assumed that relational networks are numerous and elaborated structures that tend to maintain and preserve themselves. Instead of focusing on the content (e.g., the validity) of troubling cognitions, treatment is aimed at changing the way people interact with their thoughts. Specifically, the goal is to modify the problematic function (rather than content) of unwanted thoughts by decreasing the tendency to relate to them as what they refer to (e.g., "She hates me") instead of what they really are (e.g., the thought "She hates me"). This is done using a variety of *cognitive defusion* techniques, in which clients are asked to distance themselves from the literal quality of negative thoughts in various ways, for example, by treating them as external and observable events, by repeating them out loud many times, or by labeling the actual process of thinking (e.g., "I am having a thought that . . . ").

Empirical Evidence

A rapidly growing body of research provides support for discrete components and processes associated with ACT (e.g., Forman, Herbert, Moitra, Yeomans, & Geller, 2007; Hofmann et al., 2009; Najmi et al., 2009). For example, Feldner et al. (2003) demonstrated the effectiveness of acceptance techniques in relation to tolerance of carbon dioxide-enriched air. Participants were instructed to observe their feelings and to not struggle with them during exposure to carbon dioxide-enriched air or to suppress their feelings during carbon dioxide inhalation. In the suppression condition, but not the acceptance condition, individuals who reported high levels of experiential avoidance showed greater levels of anxiety relative to those with low experiential avoidance. Another study examined the effects of a cognitive defusion technique on negative self-referential thoughts (Masuda et al., 2004), in which thoughts are rapidly repeated aloud until they lose their meaning. This technique was found to reduce discomfort and believability in the thoughts compared with several control conditions, such as distraction or positive thinking induction.

In a yet unpublished study recently conducted in our laboratory, we attempted to examine, in well-controlled experimental settings, the processes associated with cognitive restructuring and cognitive defusion, the core cognitive components of traditional CT and ACT, respectively (Yovel, Mor, & Shakarov, 2012). To do so, we used a three-phase procedure specifically designed for the study of therapeutic interventions that target troubling cognitions.

The aim of the tasks administered in Phase 1 of this procedure was to elicit an emotionally hot cognition (cf. Metcalfe & Mischel, 1999). Participants (136 college students) completed a paper-and-pencil task in which they were instructed to describe in writing an unpleasant event they had experienced that at times still disturbs and saddens them. Several general examples of such events were provided (e.g., "Has it ever happened that you failed at something that was important to you, and at times it still troubles you?"). In addition, they were asked to write a saddening thought about themselves that was triggered by the event and continues to be triggered by its recollection (e.g., "When Adam failed a test, he thought, 'I don't understand any of the material; there's no way I'll ever finish my degree'").

Subsequently, a focused rumination task was administered in which participants were requested to contemplate the thought they had selected by following the instructions displayed on a computer screen (12 items, each of which remained on the screen for 25 seconds). This task was based on Nolen-Hoeksema and Morrow's (1993) general rumination induction, but items were worded to refer to a particular cognition (e.g., "Consider the content of your thought; what does it reveal about you?" "Think what ramifications this event may have for your future"). The focused rumination task was designed to enable participants to conceptually and emotionally reexperience the saddening event and the negative thought and immerse themselves in it, thus facilitating the creation of an emotionally hot cognition that would be the target of the brief intervention.

Treatment-based interventions that targeted participants' idiosyncratic cognitions were administered in Phase 2. Participants were randomly assigned to one of four experimental conditions: ACT-based intervention (cognitive defusion), CT-based intervention (cognitive restructuring), and two control conditions. Each intervention commenced with a brief clinical rationale that explained the logic underlying the techniques to be used. The overall aim of the ACT-related task was to facilitate cognitive distancing from the literal meaning of the emotion-laden cognition (Hayes et al., 1999). It included a variety of cognitive defusion techniques in which participants were asked to write their thoughts in various ways (e.g., by using the nondominant hand, in upper case letters), label the process of thinking in writing ("The thought crossed my mind that . . . "), watch a cartoon character portrayed as thinking the thought, or visualize it from different vantage points (e.g., written on a bus moving away from them).

The CT intervention was designed to resemble cognitive restructuring or reappraisal procedures in which clients are asked to critically examine the validity of their aversive cognitions. It was based on CT techniques (adapted from Beck, 1995) that had been modified to suit the experimental framework. Participants were asked to designate the degree to which they believed the thought was correct, examine whether it was influenced by several common cognitive distortions (e.g., black-or-white thinking), and provide evidence supporting and disputing the validity of the thought. They then generated an alternative, more balanced thought and designated the degree to which they believed this new thought was accurate. Finally, they rated the accuracy of their original thought for a second time on the basis of the tasks they had just completed.

The two additional interventions, active distraction and written rumination, were used in the control conditions. The tasks that were used in the active distraction condition were essentially a combination of the tasks used in the two treatment-based interventions, but rather than participants' own distressing thoughts, the target was a nondistressing sentence provided by us. In contrast, in the written rumination condition, participants focused on their distressing thought by answering in writing questions that were essentially similar to the items of the focused rumination task (e.g., explore the causes of the thought). The nondistractive written rumination condition was designed to control for immediate effects of the intervention-based conditions (measured in Phase 2), and the active distraction condition was used to control for the protective effects against a reactivation of the distressing thought, assessed later in Phase 3.

The main goal of Phase 3 was to examine the protective or buffering effects of the two treatment-based interventions against a relevant emotional challenge compared with the active distraction control condition. To do that, a second focused rumination task was administered. This 5-minute task was similar to the task administered in Phase 1, but to avoid repetition, different items were used.

A computerized mood assessment was used to assess state negative affect throughout the experiment. This instrument included eight depression-related Positive and Negative Affect Schedule items (e.g., sadness, disappointment; Watson, Clark, & Tellegen, 1988), each measured by a visual analogue scale. Findings showed that the Phase 1 tasks reliably produced hot cognitions: Reported levels of negative affect at the end of this phase were considerably higher across all conditions compared with baseline ($ds > 1.0$). More important, a repeated measures analysis of covariance (ANCOVA), in which we controlled for baseline mood and for the subjective significance of the selected personal material (measured by several postexperiment items), indicated that both ACT- and CT-based intervention conditions resulted in greater reduction of negative mood, compared with the relevant nondistractive control condition.

The clinical significance of these interventions, which did not differ from each other, was further supported by the large effect sizes of the negative mood reduction in both conditions ($ds > 0.80$). Clinical significance was also indicated by the larger proportion of "greatly improved" participants in these conditions relative to the nondistractive control condition, identified by Jacobson's reliable change index (RCI) analysis (Jacobson, Roberts, Berns, & McGlinchey, 1999). It is notable that mood improvement in both treatment-based conditions (but not in the control conditions) correlated with theoretically relevant measures of metacognitive beliefs. In the CT condition, mood reduction correlated with a scale that included items such as "I think I need to correct my thought," whereas in the ACT condition, improvement was associated with statements such as "I believe that the very existence of this thought prevents me from living my life the way I want to" (reversed).

In terms of protective effects, both cognitive restructuring and cognitive defusion moderated the negative mood increase caused by the second focused rumination task (administered in Phase 3) better than the active distraction control task. The two treatment-based conditions did not differ from each other in terms of average performance. However, on the basis of Jacobson's RCI analysis, only the ACT-based condition produced better outcomes than the control condition (in terms of the proportion of individual participants who "survived the emotional challenge" and did not experience a significant mood increase).

In sum, these findings suggest that cognitive defusion, which encourages the acceptance of distressing cognitions without directly addressing their verbal content, is at least as efficacious as cognitive reappraisal and that improvement due to both kinds of interventions is specifically associated with theoretically relevant metacognitive beliefs. At the end of the experiment, participants rated the extent to which they believed the intervention was helpful, and it is interesting to note that this face validity measure was associated with mood improvement only in the CT-based condition, not in the ACT condition. This finding, which replicates similar findings in both field studies (Lappalainen et al., 2007) and laboratory settings (Hofmann et al., 2009), indicates that, compared with the strategies commonly used in CBT (e.g., reappraisal), those used in ACT (e.g., acceptance) are less straightforward and clear, despite their efficacy.

Meaning: Commitment to Chosen Values in ACT

ACT aims to increase psychological flexibility, not reduce psychological pain, and treatment goals are not defined in terms of symptom reduction per se. Thus, for example, acceptance-based techniques taught in therapy are not conceptualized as new ways of avoiding psychopathology but as positive psychological skills aimed at promoting valued living. Clients are encouraged in therapy to identify *values*, or consistent life directions that are meaningful to them in various domains (e.g., family, career). It is important that these values are not influenced by problematic processes such as experiential avoidance or social compliance. ACT also fosters the development of continuous *committed action*, or meaningful patterns of behavior aimed at achieving specific and concrete goals consistent with one's chosen values. This is typically done by using well-known behavioral techniques such as goal setting, problem solving, and exposure to feared objects and situations.

Arch and Craske (2008) identified the focus on values as a central component that distinguishes ACT from other forms of CBT. Although most types of psychotherapy view the facilitation of a fulfilling life as an important result of therapy, they differ in how directly and clearly valued living, as an alternative to symptom reduction, is addressed in treatment. ACT explicitly focuses on the former, whereas other forms of CBT typically focus on the latter. Promoting valued living and avoiding the experience of negative symptoms can both be conceptualized as broad and general motivators in psychotherapy. Indeed, theorists have long identified approaching desirable outcomes and avoiding undesirable states or events as two primary and distinct bases of human motivation (e.g., Elliot, 1999). For example, Higgins (1997) identified approach and prevention as two types of regulatory focus that lead to different desired end states: Promotion focus is associated with accomplishments and desired gains; prevention focus is associated with safety and security.

Focusing on Values in Therapy: Empirical Evidence

Although a great deal of research supports most core processes in ACT (Hayes, Luoma, Bond, Masuda, & Lillis, 2006; Ruiz, 2010), empirical support for interventions associated with the values component, which may function as a positive reinforcement in treatment (Wilson & Murrell, 2004), is relatively small. Basic research on regulatory focus has shown that promotion focus leads to greater action initiation and persistence, whereas prevention focus leads to earlier withdrawal (e.g., Crowe & Higgins, 1997; Roney, Higgins, & Shah, 1995). Support that is more specific comes from several recent studies that examined the efficacy of values-based interventions in dealing with the experience of physical pain (e.g., in a cold pressor task; see Ruiz, 2010). Findings from these studies suggest that focusing on one's values improves the ability to cope with pain and discomfort (Branstetter-Rost, Cushing, & Douleh, 2009) and may strengthen the efficacy of acceptance-based techniques in this regard (Páez-Blarrina et al., 2008).

In a study we recently conducted (Catane & Yovel, 2012), we attempted to examine in laboratory settings whether focusing on chosen personal values leads to greater motivation to undergo difficult tasks in therapy. The first part of the experiment, which was designed to create simulated therapeutic conditions, was identical to Phase 1 of the three-phase procedure described earlier. Participants (112 college students) recalled and wrote about an unpleasant event they had experienced, extracted a relevant negative thought, and performed a focused rumination task, with the aim of creating a distressing, emotion-laden idiosyncratic cognition. They were then randomly assigned to four experimental conditions.

Participants in the values condition were asked to identify personal values and goals by following procedures typically used in ACT (Hayes & Strosahl, 2004). For example, they rated the subjective importance of certain general value domains (e.g., intimacy, career, family), and identified personal goals they have not been able to achieve because of issues associated with the negative thought they had identified in the preceding task. They were then asked to write several sentences such as, "If the thought [thought] weren't such a problem for me, I would have [personal goal]." Participants in the symptom reduction experimental group performed similar tasks, but rather than emphasizing personal values, symptom reduction was emphasized. For example, participants rated the subjective importance of certain negative emotions and complete sentences, for example, "If the thought [thought] was not such a problem for me, I would feel less [negative emotion]." A control group performed distraction tasks that did not focus on distressing cognitions (e.g., they rated the extent to which they like certain colors), thus controlling for time and for the potential distraction effect from the negative thought caused by the manipulation. Because distraction has been shown to decrease negative affect (e.g., Fennell & Teasdale, 1984), a second control group did not perform any manipulation task, thus maintaining negative affect and controlling for mood. Similar to the experiment described earlier, negative mood was assessed several times using a computerized visual analogue scale instrument.

Subsequently, participants in all groups were asked to follow the instructions displayed on the computer screen and perform several tasks they were told would help them cope with their distressing thoughts. These tasks were all based on cognitive defusion techniques adapted from Hayes and Smith (2005).

Two different dependent measures indicated that participants in the values group showed particularly high levels of motivation when performing the therapeutic tasks. First, in one of the tasks they performed they were asked to imagine a certain scenario. An ANCOVA, in which negative mood and reading speed (measured by the time spent on reading instructions prior to the manipulation) were used as controls, showed that participants in the value condition spent significantly more time (measured by the computer) on this task, compared with all other groups (which did not differ significantly from each other). In addition, after performing several tasks, participants were presented with the option of completing additional therapeutic tasks or of doing a task unrelated to their distressing thought (rating a nature video clip), which was ostensibly needed for a different experiment. Of the participants who indicated in a postexperimental questionnaire that the therapeutic interventions were relevant to what they wrote about in the manipulation tasks (achieving values and goals or symptom reduction), a significantly larger proportion of the values group (80%) chose to continue doing therapeutic tasks, compared with only 38% in the symptom reduction group. Thus, in contrast to those who focused on their values, most participants who focused on the alleviation of their negative symptoms preferred to "quit therapy" and rate the video clip. Importantly, the groups did not differ in terms of negative mood levels, which remained high following the manipulations, except for the expected significant reduction observed in the active distraction control group. Thus, the findings cannot be attributed to any direct effect that focusing on personal values versus symptom reduction had on participants' mood. Taken together, these results suggest that focusing on one's chosen values rather than on the alleviation of disturbing symptoms may increase motivation in therapy, thus providing a rare support for the values component of ACT.

CONCLUDING REMARKS

ACT is a broad behavioral clinical approach based on a comprehensive theory of human language (Hayes et al., 1999). Unlike many kinds of psychological and psychiatric therapy, ACT does not focus directly on symptom reduction. Similar to other recently developed CBTs, ACT is influenced by Eastern philosophies in that it fosters acceptance and mindfulness where pain is inevitable. In terms of broad treatment objectives, ACT is similar to existential perspectives in encouraging the identification of personal values in therapy and strongly encouraging value-committed action where change is possible (see Chapter 19, this volume).

In ACT, clients are introduced to the fundamental choice they can make and may never have considered: to accept the unavoidable presence of unwanted experiences without attempting to prevent their occurrence, change their form, or act on them. They are further encouraged to behave in ways that are consistent with their chosen values. Many traditional CBT interventions (e.g., exposure, behavioral analysis) are frequently used in ACT treatments. However, ACT promotes the acceptance of unwanted private events, and therefore behavioral interventions (e.g., relaxation) or cognitive interventions (e.g., cognitive restructuring) that specifically target the change of such experiences are not compatible with this approach. Because ACT does not focus on the alleviation of narrowly defined symptoms, this approach expands the focus of change compared with earlier forms of CBT, and it may consequently suit a broader range of human difficulties.

Theories and research on issues such as psychological distance (Liberman & Trope, 2008), thought suppression (Wegner et al., 1987), rumination (Nolen-Hoeksema et al., 2008), self-verification (Kwang & Swann, 2010), and regulatory focus (Higgins, 1997) are consistent with central aspects of ACT theory and practice, and a rapidly growing body of literature provides support for the efficacy of treatments derived from ACT for a wide variety of difficulties and mental disorders (Ruiz, 2010). Here, we described two recently conducted laboratory examinations of core treatment processes in ACT. The findings demonstrate the efficacy of the unique methods used in ACT for dealing with aversive cognitions, as well as the superiority of considering one's chosen values versus symptom reduction while engaging in therapeutic tasks. Thus, the values-based treatment objectives of ACT, which greatly expand the focus of change in CBTs, may be useful motivators in therapy.

REFERENCES

Arch, J. J., & Craske, M. G. (2008). Acceptance and commitment therapy and cognitive behavioral therapy for anxiety disorders: Different treatments, similar mechanisms? *Clinical Psychology: Science and Practice, 15,* 263–279. doi:10.1111/j.1468-2850.2008.00137.x

Bach, P., & Hayes, S. C. (2002). The use of acceptance and commitment therapy to prevent the rehospitalization of psychotic patients: A randomized controlled trial. *Journal of Consulting and Clinical Psychology, 70,* 1129–1139. doi:10.1037/0022-006X.70.5.1129

Beck, J. (1995). *Cognitive therapy: Basics and beyond.* New York, NY: Guilford Press.

Branstetter-Rost, A., Cushing, C., & Douleh, T. (2009). Personal values and pain tolerance: Does a values intervention add to acceptance? *The Journal of Pain, 10*, 887–892. doi:10.1016/j.jpain.2009.01.001

Catane, S., & Yovel, I. (2012). *Focusing on personal values versus symptom reduction as motivating factors in therapy*. Manuscript in preparation.

Crowe, E., & Higgins, E. T. (1997). Regulatory focus and strategic inclinations: Promotion and prevention in decision-making. *Organizational Behavior and Human Decision Processes, 69*, 117–132. doi:10.1006/obhd.1996.2675

Elliot, A. J. (1999). Approach and avoidance motivation and achievement goals. *Educational Psychologist, 34*, 169–189. doi:10.1207/s15326985ep3403_3

Feldner, M. T., Zvolensky, M. J., Eifert, G. H., & Spira, A. P. (2003). Emotional avoidance: An experimental test of individual differences and response suppression using biological challenge. *Behaviour Research and Therapy, 41*, 403–411. doi:10.1016/S0005-7967(02)00020-7

Fennell, M. J. V., & Teasdale, J. D. (1984). Effects of distraction on thinking and affect in depressed-patients. *British Journal of Clinical Psychology, 23*, 65–66. doi:10.1111/j.2044-8260.1984.tb00628.x

Forman, E. M., Herbert, J. D., Moitra, E., Yeomans, P. D., & Geller, P. A. (2007). A randomized controlled effectiveness trial of acceptance and commitment therapy and cognitive therapy for anxiety and depression. *Behavior Modification, 31*, 772–799. doi:10.1177/0145445507302202

Gifford, E. V., Kohlenberg, B. S., Hayes, S. C., Antonuccio, D. O., Piasecki, M. M., Rasmussen-Hall, M. L., & Palm, K. M. (2004). Acceptance-based treatment for smoking cessation. *Behavior Therapy, 35*, 689–705. doi:10.1016/S0005-7894(04)80015-7

Gregg, J. A., Callaghan, G. A., Hayes, S. C., & Glenn-Lawson, J. L. (2007). Improving diabetes self-management through acceptance, mindfulness, and values: A randomized controlled trial. *Journal of Consulting and Clinical Psychology, 75*, 336–343. doi:10.1037/0022-006X.75.2.336

Hayes, S. C., Barnes-Holmes, D., & Roche, B. (2001). *Relational frame theory: A post-Skinnerian account of human language and cognition*. New York, NY: Kluwer Academic/Plenum.

Hayes, S. C., Luoma, J. B., Bond, F. W., Masuda, A., & Lillis, J. (2006). Acceptance and commitment therapy: Model, processes and outcomes. *Behaviour Research and Therapy, 44*, 1–25. doi:10.1016/j.brat.2005.06.006

Hayes, C., & Smith, S. (2005). *Get out of your mind & into your life: The new acceptance & commitment therapy*. Oakland, CA: New Harbinger.

Hayes, S. C., & Strosahl, K. D. (2004). *A practical guide to acceptance and commitment therapy*. New York, NY: Springer.

Hayes, S. C., Strosahl, K., & Wilson, K. G. (1999). *Acceptance and commitment therapy: An experiential approach to behavior change*. New York, NY: Guilford Press.

Hayes, S. C., & Wilson, K. G. (1993). Some applied implications of a contemporary analytic account of verbal events. *The Behavior Analyst, 16,* 283–301.

Hayes, S. C., Wilson, K. G., Gifford, E. V., Follette, V. M., & Strosahl, K. (1996). Experiential avoidance and behavioral disorders: A functional dimensional approach to diagnosis and treatment. *Journal of Consulting and Clinical Psychology, 64,* 1152–1168. doi:10.1037/0022-006X.64.6.1152

Higgins, E. T. (1997). Beyond pleasure and pain. *American Psychologist, 52,* 1280–1300. doi:10.1037/0003-066X.52.12.1280

Hofmann, S. G., Heering, S., Sawyer, A. T., & Asnaani, A. (2009). How to handle anxiety: The effects of reappraisal, acceptance, and suppression strategies on anxious arousal. *Behaviour Research and Therapy, 47,* 389–394. doi:10.1016/j.brat.2009.02.010

Jacobson, N. S., Roberts, L. J., Berns, S. B., & McGlinchey, J. B. (1999). Methods for defining and determining the clinical significance of treatment effects: Description, application, and alternatives. *Journal of Consulting and Clinical Psychology, 67,* 300–307. doi:10.1037/0022-006X.67.3.300

Kashdan, T. B., & Rottenberg, J. (2010). Psychological flexibility as a fundamental aspect of health. *Clinical Psychology Review, 30,* 865–878. doi:10.1016/j.cpr.2010.03.001

Kwang, T., & Swann, W. B., Jr. (2010). Do people embrace praise even when they feel unworthy? A review of critical tests of self-enhancement versus self-verification. *Personality and Social Psychology Review, 14,* 263–280. doi:10.1177/1088868310365876

Lappalainen, R., Lehtonen, T., Skarp, E., Taubert, E., Ojanen, M., & Hayes, S. C. (2007). The impact of CBT and ACT models using psychology trainee therapists: A preliminary controlled effectiveness trial. *Behavior Modification, 31,* 488–511. doi:10.1177/0145445506298436

Liberman, N., & Trope, Y. (2008, November 21). The psychology of transcending the here and now. *Science, 322,* 1201–1205. doi:10.1126/science.1161958

Linehan, M. (1993). *Cognitive–behavioral treatment of borderline personality disorder.* New York, NY: Guilford Press.

Martell, C. R., Addis, M. E., & Jacobson, N. S. (2001). *Depression in context: Strategies for guided action.* New York, NY: Norton.

Masuda, A., Hayes, S. C., Sackett, C. F., & Twohig, M. P. (2004). Cognitive defusion and self-relevant negative thoughts: Examining the impact of a ninety year old technique. *Behaviour Research and Therapy, 42,* 477–485. doi:10.1016/j.brat.2003.10.008

Metcalfe, J., & Mischel, W. (1999). A hot/cool-system analysis of delay of gratification: Dynamics of willpower. *Psychological Review, 106,* 3–19. doi:10.1037/0033-295X.106.1.3

Najmi, S., Riemann, B. C., & Wegner, D. M. (2009). Managing unwanted intrusive thoughts in obsessive-compulsive disorder: Relative effectiveness of suppression, focused distraction, and acceptance. *Behaviour Research and Therapy, 47*, 494–503. doi:10.1016/j.brat.2009.02.015

Nolen-Hoeksema, S., & Morrow, J. (1993). Effects of rumination and distraction on naturally occurring depressed mood. *Cognition and Emotion, 7*, 561–570. doi:10.1080/02699939308409206

Nolen-Hoeksema, S., Wisco, B. E., & Lyubomirsky, S. (2008). Rethinking rumination. *Perspectives on Psychological Science, 3*, 400–424. doi:10.1111/j.1745-6924.2008.00088.x

Páez-Blarrina, M., Luciano, C., Gutierrez-Martinez, O., Valdivia, S., Ortega, J., & Rodriguez-Valverde, M. (2008). The role of values with personal examples in altering the functions of pain: Comparison between acceptance-based and cognitive-control-based protocols. *Behaviour Research and Therapy, 46*, 84–97. doi:10.1016/j.brat.2007.10.008

Purdon, C. (1999). Thought suppression and psychopathology. *Behaviour Research and Therapy, 37*, 1029–1054. doi:10.1016/S0005-7967(98)00200-9

Ramnerö, J., & Törneke, N. (2008). *The ABCs of human behavior: Behavioral principles for the practicing clinician.* Oakland, CA: New Harbinger.

Roemer, L., Orsillo, S. M., & Salters-Pedneault, K. (2008). Efficacy of an acceptance-based behavior therapy for generalized anxiety disorder: Evaluation in a randomized controlled trial. *Journal of Consulting and Clinical Psychology, 76*, 1083–1089. doi:10.1037/a0012720

Roney, C. J. R., Higgins, E. T., & Shah, J. (1995). Goals and framing: How outcome focus influences motivation and emotion. *Personality and Social Psychology Bulletin, 21*, 1151–1160. doi:10.1177/01461672952111003

Roseman, I. J., Wiest, C., & Swartz, T. S. (1994). Phenomenology, behaviors, and goals differentiate discrete emotions. *Journal of Personality and Social Psychology, 67*, 206–221. doi:10.1037/0022-3514.67.2.206

Ruiz, J. R. (2010). A review of acceptance and commitment therapy (ACT) empirical evidence: Correlational, experimental psychopathology, component and outcome studies. *International Journal of Psychology & Psychological Therapy, 10*, 125–162.

Sartre, J.-P. (1995). *Existentialism and human emotions.* New York, NY: Carol.

Segal, Z. V., Williams, J. M. G., & Teasdale, J. D. (2002). *Mindfulness-based cognitive therapy for depression: A new approach to preventing relapse.* New York, NY: Guilford Press.

Törneke, N. (2010). *Learning RFT: An introduction to relational frame theory and its clinical application.* Oakland, CA: Context Press/New Harbinger.

Twohig, M. P., Hayes, S. C., Plumb, J. C., Pruitt, L. D., Collins, A. B., Hazlett-Stevens, H., & Woidneck, M. R. (2010). A randomized clinical trial of acceptance and commitment therapy versus progressive relaxation training for obsessive–compulsive disorder. *Journal of Consulting and Clinical Psychology, 78*, 705–716. doi:10.1037/a0020508

Vowles, K.E., & McCracken, L.M. (2008). Acceptance and values-based action in chronic pain: A study of treatment effectiveness and process. *Journal of Consulting and Clinical Psychology, 76*, 397–407. doi:10.1037/0022-006X.76.3.397

Watson, D., Clark, L.A., & Tellegen, A. (1988). Development and validation of brief measures of positive and negative affect: The PANAS scales. *Journal of Personality and Social Psychology, 54*, 1063–1070. doi:10.1037/0022-3514.54.6.1063

Wegner, D.M., Schneider, D.J., Carter, S.R., & White, T.L. (1987). Paradoxical effects of thought suppression. *Journal of Personality and Social Psychology, 53*, 5–13. doi:10.1037/0022-3514.53.1.5

Wilson, K.G., & Murrell, A.R. (2004). Values work in acceptance and commitment therapy. In S.C. Hayes, V.M. Follette, & M.M. Linehan (Eds.), *Mindfulness and acceptance: Expanding the cognitive–behavioral tradition* (pp. 120–151). New York, NY: Guilford Press.

Yovel, I., Mor, N., Shakarov, H. (2012). *Different routes leading to the same destination? A laboratory-based investigation of the core cognitive components of cognitive therapy and acceptance and commitment therapy.* Manuscript in preparation.

VI

SYNTHESIS

22

THE SOCIAL PSYCHOLOGY OF MEANING, MORTALITY, AND CHOICE: AN INTEGRATIVE PERSPECTIVE ON EXISTENTIAL CONCERNS

SHELDON SOLOMON

The Fourth Herzliya Symposium on Personality and Social Psychology was a spirited gathering of an eclectic group of experimental and clinical (including experimental clinical) psychologists, held at the Interdisciplinary Center in April 2011. The participants came to Herzliya for several days to exchange ideas about "The Social Psychology of Meaning, Mortality, and Choice." In accord with the title of the symposium, there was a general consensus that meaning making is a fundamentally social process (i.e., meanings are constructed with and for others), instigated and sustained by psychological motives that include uniquely human existential concerns, resulting—depending on individual dispositions and specific circumstances and experiences—in varying degrees of personal well-being and social harmony.

THE MEANING OF *MEANING*

The central concept of a human psychology is meaning and the processes and transactions involved in the construction of meanings.
—Jerome Bruner, *Acts of Meaning*

In *The Birth and Death of Meaning*, cultural anthropologist Ernest Becker (1971) proposed a distinction between reactive information processing, common to all forms of life, and the uniquely human proclivity for meaning making. To stay alive and reproduce successfully, organisms must systematically respond to the vagaries of their surroundings, given their sensory capacities and the relevant features of their environments (see Gibson's, 1979, analysis of environmental "affordances"). The cell membranes of amoebas, without brains and nervous systems, detect the proximal presence of nutritious or noxious stimuli; bats emit high-pitched sounds for navigation and locating prey; eagles rely on their visual acuity; dogs depend on their olfactory prowess. These are reactive forms of adaptation, which humans also use—using their senses, fortified by adaptive mental modules that solve evolutionarily significant physical, natural, technical, and social problems (Tooby & Cosmides, 1992; see also King, Chapter 7, this volume)—to detect and respond to environmental patterns that foster survival and enhance reproductive fitness.

Humans are unique, however, in their capacity for symbols, which enables them, in addition to extracting information from their surroundings, to construct and impose meaning on their environment and experiences (Donald, 1991). Other creatures use signs to communicate. Bees do a figure-eight-shaped waggle dance that conveys information to their hive mates about the location of, and distance to, food. Yet, bees cannot dance to discuss the weather or order a pizza, and their waggle dances always signify the location of food at the moment; they cannot represent where food was yesterday or might be tomorrow. Symbols are far more flexible because there is no necessary connection between a symbol and what it symbolizes. Symbols can refer to the remote past and the distant future. This liberation from the natural confines of space and time is what makes human imagination and creativity possible. With symbols, humans can conceive of themselves, as well as things not immediately present or previously existent, and then alter themselves and their surroundings in accord with their desires. Symbolization makes elaborate meaning making possible.

SELF-CONSCIOUSNESS, MORTALITY, AND MEANING

Yes.

—James Joyce, *Ulysses*

It has always seemed to me that the only painless death must be that which takes the intelligence by violent surprise and from the rear so to speak since if death be anything at all beyond a brief and peculiar emotional state of the bereaved it must be a brief and likewise peculiar state of the subject as well and if aught can be more painful to any intelligence above that of a child or an idiot than a slow and gradual confronting with that which over a long period of bewilderment and dread it has been taught to regard as an irrevocable and unplumbable finality, I do not know it.

—William Faulkner, *Absalom, Absalom*

According to the great 19th century Danish existentialist philosopher Søren Kierkegaard, only humans are sufficiently cognitively complex to be fully self-conscious—that is, to render themselves objects of their own subjective inquiry—which is both awesome and dreadful. To be alive and know it is exhilarating and liberating: Self-consciousness confers freedom of choice in the present and infinite possibilities in the future. In accord with this view, evidence derived from self-determination theory (SDT; Ryan, Legate, Niemiec, & Deci, Chapter 12, this volume) has demonstrated that "existential exertion of autonomy" (through personal dispositions or alterations in situational conditions) increases success at personal and collective goals, enhances connections to others, and reduces anxiety and defensiveness; undermining autonomy by making positive regard conditional in relationships undermines goal attainment, strains relationships, and increases anxiety and defensiveness (Kanat-Maymon, Roth, Assor, & Reizer, Chapter 13).

However, to be alive and to know it also gives rise to potentially debilitating dread and despair through the recognition that humans are finite creatures, perpetually vulnerable to a host of lethal encounters, necessarily culminating in their ultimate and irrevocable demise. Terror management theory (TMT; Greenberg, Chapter 1), originally derived from Becker's (1973) insights, posits that one of the most important functions of symbolic cultural worldviews is to "manage" existential terror through maintaining a meaningful conception of reality (Pyszczynski & Kesebir, Chapter 4) and the belief that one is meeting the standards of value prescribed by that worldview (i.e., self-esteem). This allows people to feel, much of the time, secure in the present and eligible for literal (via the heavens, afterlives, and reincarnations promised by most religions) or symbolic (through connection to one's nation, accumulation of vast resources or memorable accomplishments) immortality in the future.

Self-esteem and cultural worldviews acquire anxiety-buffering and death-denying properties in the context of forming psychological attachments to primary caretakers during socialization. According to John Bowlby (1982), because human infants are exceptionally immature and helplessly dependent at birth, they are prone to tremendous anxiety in times of need, which impels them to seek proximity (physically and eventually psychologically) to supportive others. Secure attachment gives infants a sense of safety and security that fosters self-efficacy, curiosity, and the development of cognitive, emotional, and interpersonal skills. In addition, Bowlby hypothesized that internal representations of secure relationships (i.e., working models of self and others) acquired in childhood are retained throughout the life span, are activated in response to threatening or stressful circumstances, and serve the same palliative functions as in infancy (see Shaver & Mikulincer, Chapter 16 for empirical corroboration of these claims).

Securely attached infants are the beneficiaries of unconditional positive regard from their primary caretakers for the first year or more of life, until their behavior comes under the influence of cultural dictates ("No spitting on Grandma") or to keep them alive ("Get away from the campfire"). Because socialization must commence before children are mature enough to understand rational explanations for proper behavior, parental approbation becomes contingent on "doing the right thing." Children are praised and rewarded for good conduct and belittled, punished, or ignored for inappropriate behavior (which inevitably occurs). Being a "good" boy or girl consequently engenders feelings of safety and security on the basis of remaining in parents' good graces, whereas being a "bad" boy or girl engenders feelings of anxiety, insecurity, and terror at the prospect of being abandoned. In this fashion, self-esteem becomes a potent anxiety buffer.

Then, as children mature, they become aware of, and distressed by, the prospect of their parents' and their own death (Yalom, 1980). At this point, their psychological allegiance is extended beyond their parents to their culture as a primary bulwark against existential terror. Now self-esteem and the resultant sense of psychological equanimity are derived from maintaining (in addition to a sense of security rooted in close relationships) faith in the culture and perceiving that one is meeting or exceeding the standards of value associated with the social role one inhabits in the context of that worldview. Although both religious and secular worldviews have "sacred" death-denying components (e.g., the "almighty dollar"), religious worldviews are especially well-suited for terror management because they likely evolved to foster social cohesion and coordination (the word *religion* is etymologically derived from "to bind together"). They emerged historically and are encountered now by individuals, prior to the development of explicit self-awareness with concomitant existential concerns about death. They are readily available for use in denying the inevitability of death. All religions rely on supernatural entities with death-defying powers to provide comprehensive accounts of all aspects of life, including an account of the origin and the ultimate fate of the universe. They offer explanations for unexpected and tragic events that are not subject to empirical disconfirmation (see Rappaport, 1999; Pyszczynski & Kesebir, Chapter 4; and Park & Edmondson, Chapter 8, for extended discussions of the role of religion in making meaning to be used in the service of mitigating existential terror).

Convergent empirical support for TMT is provided by studies demonstrating that self-esteem buffers anxiety in general and death-anxiety in particular (Arndt, Chapter 3), that reminding people of their mortality (mortality salience) instigates efforts to fortify faith in their cultural worldviews and augment their self-esteem, and that threats to basic terror management structures (e.g., cultural worldviews, self-esteem, close relationships) increase the accessibility of implicit death thoughts. For example, death thoughts come more readily to mind when devout Christians are confronted with inconsistencies in the Bible, when people are reminded of their inadequacies, or when they are asked to ponder the dissolution of a close relationship (see Hayes, Schimel, Arndt, & Faucher, 2010, for a comprehensive theoretical and empirical review of the role of death-thought accessibility (DTA) in terror management processes).

In sum, self-conscious symbolizing allows humans to make and share meanings in order to render coordinated social behavior possible (the Tower of Babel story in the Bible is an allegorical account of the chaos that ensues in the absence of shared meanings), to transform the awe and sense of mystery engendered by being alive and being able to think about it into bearable and shareable forms, and to dampen existential dread. Some theorists have argued that humans are not uniquely concerned about death per se; rather, they are fundamentally motivated to make meaning for its own sake (the meaning maintenance model; Heine, Proulx, & Vohs, 2006), to reduce uncertainty (the uncertainty management model; van den Bos & Miedema, 2000), or to increase perceived or actual control (Fritsche, Jonas, & Fankhänel, 2008). From these perspectives, death is problematic only to the extent that it undermines meaning, increases uncertainty, or diminishes perceived or actual control. At the symposium, each of these views was found wanting on theoretical, empirical, and epistemological grounds.

Pyszcznski and Kesebir (Chapter 4) proposed that in a world without death, the concept of meaning would be meaningless because all actions would be equally inconsequential given their lack of fatal consequences. Greenberg (Chapter 1) observed that if people were primarily motivated to reduce uncertainty, then a death row inmate given precise details about his upcoming electrocution—including the exact time he would die, the likelihood of severe external burning, exploding of his penis, defecation and urination, drooling and vomiting, intense muscle spasms and contractions, and odors resulting from the burning of the skin and the body—should be a paragon of psychological equanimity, given the total lack of uncertainty regarding his impending doom (see Hirschberger & Shaham, Chapter 6, for a description of empirical findings that are inexplicable from an uncertainty management perspective). And the claim that death reminders are problematic because they undermine perceptions of control is contradicted by Arndt and Solomon's (2003) finding that participants high in neuroticism, when reminded of their mortality, reported lower desire for personal control.

Finally, Greenberg (Chapter 1) emphasized that although TMT was originally developed to elucidate the psychological functions of self-esteem and cultural worldviews, most contemporary theoretical challenges to TMT are primarily efforts to generate alternative accounts of mortality salience effects rather than explaining self-esteem and cultural worldviews. Even in this regard, however, there are no existing theoretical alternatives to TMT that can account for the wide range of MS effects obtained from hypotheses derived from TMT (including studies in which MS inductions produced different effects than reminders of meaninglessness and uncertainty). There are no alternative theories that can explain Pyszczynski, Greenberg, and Solomon's (1999) dual process model of how conscious and unconscious death thoughts produce qualitatively different defensive reactions (proximal and distal, respectively) that unfold in an orderly sequence over time. There is no other theory that delineates the cognitive and affective processes that underlie MS effects independent of increased DTA.

THE THREAT OF MEANINGLESSNESS

> People die and murder, nurture and protect, go to any extreme, in behalf of their conception of the real. . . . They live out the details of their daily lives in terms of what they conceive to be real. . . . This is the domain of meaning making, without which human beings in every culture fall into terror.
> —Jerome Bruner, in a Foreword to Bradd Shore's
> *Culture in Mind: Cognition, Culture, and the Problem of Meaning*

Because human meaning-making consists primarily of shared symbolic constructions imposed on the environment (rather than specific information extracted from it), it is unlikely—indeed, it is impossible—that any specific cultural conception of reality is literally true or self-evidently and unequivocally superior to a wide range of previous, current, or future alternatives. Consequently, humans go to great lengths to preserve inherently fragile meaning systems by modifying their physical surroundings to accord with cultural constructs (e.g., majestic temples, churches, and mosques as tangible manifestations of religious beliefs), to maintain close physical and psychological contact with others who share their beliefs because even the most sublimely ridiculous notions remain credible when everyone around you subscribes to them, and to treat people who adhere to different belief systems with hostility and disdain. A plethora of empirical work provides convergent evidence that meaning maintenance is an arduous multidimensional enterprise motivated by existential concerns.

Death

Routledge et al. (2010) found that death reminders decrease feelings of vitality, decrease people's sense that life has meaning and purpose, impede exploratory activities, and increase negative affectivity and social withdrawal in participants who had dispositional or experimentally induced low self-esteem. Additional studies have found a negative correlation between DTA and perceptions of meaning (i.e., high DTA was associated with lower self-reported meaning and purpose). Mikulincer and Shaver (Chapter 2) proposed that such effects occur because death poses a unique threat to meaning by engendering the same sense of helplessness and powerlessness that infants experience in threatening circumstances and serves as the psychological impetus for the formation of secure psychological attachments that fosters instrumentally effective behaviors. Consistent with this view, Mikulincer and Shaver demonstrated in three experiments that MS increases perceptions of helplessness and impedes task performance.

Creatureliness

Although death is the ultimate challenge to humanly constructed meanings, it is by no means the only one. Culture, art, religion, and science (to name just a few) are potent and durable symbolic fruits of human minds, but these minds are inextricably entrenched in corporeal containers that break, bleed, breed, defecate, decline, and decay. The physical body and its associated biological functions is thus a glaring psychological affront, a perpetual reminder that humans, like all creatures, are animals destined to die (Goldenberg, Chapter 5). People in all cultures consequently go to great lengths to deny their affinity with other animals by wearing clothes, cosmetically altering their bodies (e.g., with hairstyles, make-up, piercings, and tattoos) and attempting to retard or obscure signs of aging. They wrap sexual reproduction in cultural prescriptions that transform animal lust into romantic love and often objectify women (who are vivid reminders of animality by virtue of giving birth, menstruating, lactating, and eliciting, even when not soliciting, lustful reactions from males). Research confirms that following reminders of death, people denigrate essays emphasizing similarities between humans and animals, report greater disgust reactions to bodily emissions, and (at least those high in neuroticism) find the physical aspects of sex less appealing. In addition, people reminded of their creatureliness find the physical aspects of sex less appealing and are subject to an increase in implicit reminders of death. Finally, studies show that male and female participants denigrate and (in some cases) physically distance themselves from pregnant, breast-feeding, or apparently menstruating women (i.e., a female confederate who "accidentally" drops a tampon).

Change

Change is another potent threat to meaning (Hirschberger & Shaham, Chapter 6). Although the most compelling meanings confer a sense that the universe is stable, orderly, and permanent (e.g., the classic Beatles tune "Strawberry Fields Forever"), reality is constantly in flux. Consequently, the prospect of change can undermine meaning and arouse existential concerns. In Wallace Stevens's poem "Sunday Morning," a woman who is enjoying a lovely day notices the changing seasons and says, "But in contentment I still feel the need of some imperishable bliss" (lines 61–62). That the prospect of change provokes existential concerns is empirically established by studies demonstrating that students high in need for cognitive closure (Webster & Kruglanski, 1994) and thus particularly likely to be unsettled by change have higher levels of DTA after reading about an alteration of their academic requirements or (in another study) the possibility of Israel signing a peace agreement with Syria and the Palestinians (relative to no change control conditions in both studies). Single participants high in attachment insecurity have increased levels of DTA after pondering the prospect of marriage (i.e., a change in their relationship status).[1]

Ostracism and Alienation

One extreme form of change that can jeopardize a sense of meaning and value is ostracism (Williams, Chapter 17). Social exclusion occurs in primates as well as humans. From an evolutionary perspective, expulsion of recalcitrant and overly exploitative individuals is necessary to maintain coordination and cohesion among social animals, who can survive only as members of groups.[2] Ostracized primates are unlikely to survive unless they

---

[1]People with a low need for cognitive closure or a low level of attachment insecurity were either unfazed or uplifted by the prospect of change; see Hirschberger and Shaham (Chapter 6) for an extended discussion of conditions in which change is existentially problematic versus psychologically fortifying; and see Taubman – Ben-Ari (Chapter 9) for an account of how changes associated with becoming a parent or grandparent can foster or undermine meaning and personal growth depending on individual differences in conjunction with specific environmental conditions.

[2]One need not subscribe to a group selection view of evolution to adhere to this view. From a neo-Darwinian perspective, individuals pursuing their own (or more precisely, their genes') interests are often best served by living in groups.

are able to join another group. Although ostracized humans fare a bit better physically, they pay a terrible psychological toll in that individuals shunned by others (even those they would not normally like or associate with) report feeling alone, invisible, and meaningless. In other words, ostracism "is like being dead, like not existing at all" (Williams, Chapter 17). Accordingly, people who are ostracized respond similarly to those reminded of their mortality: They engage in thoughts and behaviors that increase a sense of belonging and boost self-esteem, become more attracted to charismatic leaders, and are more derogatory and hostile toward members of outgroups. In addition, social exclusion, or a more general sense of cultural estrangement (Cozzarelli & Karafa, 1998), can under certain conditions increase the likelihood of suicidal behavior. Specifically, clinical and empirical evidence suggests that suicide-related phenomena occur most frequently when a thwarted sense of belonging is coincident with a sense of being burdensome to others (Joiner & Silva, Chapter 18).[3]

Enemies, Scapegoats, and Terrorism

Although cultures vary considerably, they share in common the same defensive psychological function: to afford meaning and significance (i.e., self-esteem) and in so doing to bestow psychological equanimity in the face of death. Problems arise, however, when people encounter others with different beliefs, because acknowledging the validity of an alternative conception of reality undermines confidence in the veracity of one's own cultural worldview, which can unleash the existential terror that such beliefs mitigate. In addition, because no symbolic cultural construction can actually overcome the physical reality of death, residual anxiety is unconsciously projected onto other group(s) of individuals as scapegoats, who are designated all-encompassing repositories of evil. People then typically respond to others with different beliefs—scapegoats—by berating them, trying to convert them to their own system of beliefs, or annihilating them to purify the world by eradicating evil. As Becker (1975) starkly put it, the "natural and inevitable urge to deny mortality and achieve a heroic self-image are the root causes of human evil" (p. xvii).

The claim that prejudice and ethnic strife are inflamed by existential concerns is empirically substantiated by studies (reviewed in Greenberg, Solomon, & Arndt, 2008) demonstrating that reminders of death (or threats to cherished beliefs or self-regard that in turn heighten DTA) increase ingroup favoritism and outgroup derogation; physical distancing from foreigners;

---

[3]Joiner and Silva (Chapter 18) proposed that whereas the combination of alienation and burdensomeness predicts suicidal ideation, actual (especially successful) suicide attempts also require a high degree of fearlessness to overcome human beings' natural fear of pain, injury, and death.

physical hostility toward others with dissimilar beliefs; support for preemptive nuclear, chemical, and biological attacks against countries deemed as evil (even if they pose no immediate threat); and willingness to die for one's country (through martyrdom or in warfare). In a particularly ominous study, Hayes, Schimel, and Williams (2008) had devoutly Christian participants read an article titled "Islam Poised to Swallow Jesus' Boyhood Home," concocted from actual news reports and designed to be threatening to Christians. Half of the participants also read an additional paragraph describing hundreds of Muslims perishing in a plane crash. Everyone then completed a measure of DTA. Not surprisingly, the Christians who had just read "Islam Poised to Swallow Jesus' Boyhood Home" exhibited much higher levels of DTA than those in a benign control condition. However, those who also read that Muslims had died in a plane crash had the same low level of death thoughts as control participants. The death of "evildoers" eliminated the mortal terror that existential threats otherwise elicit.

In the aftermath of the September 11, 2001, attacks on the Pentagon and the World Trade Center, Pyszczynski, Solomon, and Greenberg (2003) proposed that Islamic terrorists are motivated (at least in part) to restore their honor and self-esteem in response to a deep sense of humiliation and (perceived and actual) injustice perpetrated on their people by Western powers. In addition, for (some) Islamic fundamentalists, the United States and Israel (and Jews in general) serve as evil-incarnate targets of hatred, which provide a tangible outlet (i.e., a scapegoat) for their own repressed death anxiety. Indeed, Karen Armstrong (in *The Battle for God*, 2000), argued that, historically, fear of annihilation and efforts to restore honor in response to humiliation have motivated most Jewish, Christian, and Islamic terrorism. Kruglanski, Gelfand, and Gunaratna (Chapter 11) proposed, and presented supporting evidence, that such causes of terrorism (i.e., restoring honor, redressing humiliation, and avenging injustice) can be integrated into a more general motivational "quest for significance" aroused by an actual loss of significance (e.g., prior humiliation), the threat of losing significance (e.g., by disappointing significant others by declining to engage in acts of terrorism), or the prospect of gaining significance (e.g., anticipating heavenly approbation and community accolades by committing heroic acts of violence in societies in which such acts are encouraged or condoned).

Superficially, it may seem that annihilating a despised outgroup (e.g., the victims of the atomic bombings at Hiroshima and Nagasaki) or obliterating an evil person (e.g., the 2011 eradication of Osama bin Laden) should provide enduring psychological equanimity by eliminating the archenemies of specific cultures. This is not, however, the case, because the removal of a tangible focus of death anxiety offers only temporary relief from perpetual existential dread. After the initial euphoria of killing the evildoers subsides, new psychological lightning rods of death anxiety must be hoisted to avoid sinking into a collective uneasiness of diffuse and inchoate—and thus psychologically unbearable—apprehension, anger, and despair.

To the extent that this is true, people ironically require enemies and scapegoats to buffer the threat of meaninglessness by providing tangible and thus controllable outlets for mortal terror (Landau, Sullivan, Rothschild, & Keefer, Chapter 10). Moreover, ambiguously powerful enemies (as opposed to enemies with specific capabilities) are more effective for terror management purposes because they afford a more comprehensive sense of meaning (i.e., "We're not like those bastards; no matter who or what they are") and can be perceived as responsible for a broader assortment of otherwise seemingly random and unpredictable misfortunes (e.g., long-standing blame of Jews for problems ranging from plagues to global economic instability). In support of this view, Landau et al. (Chapter 10) demonstrated that framing a specific threat to chaotic, uncontrollable forces increases attribution of responsibility for that event to a scapegoat and greater power and influence to enemies when uncontrollable hazards are made salient, even when such hazards are clearly unrelated to the enemies' powers. Moreover, being exposed to multiple hazards in the environment and then exposed to an ambiguously powerful enemy causes people to report a heightened sense of personal control (presumably because there is a tangible locus of blame for all the potential dangers).

Rationality as a Potential Enemy of Meaning

Contemporary psychologists generally subscribe to dual process models of information processing (e.g., cognitive experiential self theory; Epstein, 1994), which include a preconscious *experiential* system that is rapid, heuristic, intuitive, and driven by emotion, and a conscious *rational* system that is slower, more effortful, analytical, and driven by reason.[4] Although both information processing systems are adaptive and generally operate in a dynamic and integrated fashion, there are times when experiential and rational thinking can be mutually antagonistic. Humans have, for example, yearned to fly since antiquity, but efforts based on intuitive and emotional faculties to do so (e.g., donning wings like Icarus and jumping off cliffs while flapping vigorously) surely led to numerous fatalities and no progress toward actually flying. In contrast, the Wright Brothers' rational and painstaking studies of aerodynamics in a wind tunnel made flight possible and allowed it to develop

---

[4]Cognitive experiential self-theory is based on Freud's distinction between primary and secondary mental processes, which was in turn derived from Plato's allegorical description (in Phaedrus) of the soul (i.e., psyche) as a charioteer driving two horses, one representing passion and the other representing reason. Metaphorically, a skillful charioteer able to effectively marshal the energies of both horses in a harmonious fashion attains enlightenment.

to the point where flying is safer than walking across the street in midtown Manhattan. In this case, the slow, plodding force of reason trumped the fast, intuitive emotional leaps of (lethal) faith.

However, the grand mythical and narrative constructions (religious and secular) that humans rely on to provide a sense of meaning and significance are primarily products of the experiential system, and they generally do not fare well when subjected to protracted "rational" scrutiny (e.g., "How could the rotund Santa Claus possibly have slithered down the 6-inch-wide chimney at our house?"). Excessive rationality undermines the credibility of the meaning systems that humans have relied on for most of their evolutionary history (King, Chapter 7), and this is particularly the case in Western cultures since the Enlightenment, with the ensuing scientific, industrial, commercial, and information revolutions characteristic of modernity. In this case, rationality fosters disenchantment and disillusionment: "Things and events must be stripped of their previous mythic significances before they can be subjected to . . . 'objective' theoretical analysis. In fact, the meaning of 'objectivity' is precisely this: a process of demythologization" (Donald, 1991, p. 275).

OVERCOMING EXISTENTIAL THREATS AND CHALLENGES

Until psychologists get down to the fundamental problem . . . —our precariousness as creatures—they will be operating at a very restrictive level . . . the groundlessness of being is a key basis for both our misery and our vitality as human beings. To the extent that we can grapple with this condition, we may discover how to thrive within, rather than simply blunt, its embrace.

—Kirk Schneider (Chapter 19, p. 350)

For if I cannot live without depending on externalities—status symbols, trinkets, money—then all my development was for naught. Hopefully, there will come a time when each individual would do what I aim to do each day . . . ENJOY LIFE!

—Pat Stevens (personal communication to Sheldon Solomon)[5]

Humans are fundamentally social symbolizing creatures who want to feel they are persons of worth in a cultural world of meaning. They need to construct security supports in response to the awe, wonder, and terror engendered by their unique cognitive capacities (i.e., self-awareness and awareness of mortality). Maximizing psychological well-being and social harmony (within and between

---

[5]Written at the conclusion of a therapeutic intervention in response to a florid schizophrenic episode.

cultures) consequently requires addressing existential concerns and threats to meaning, both as individuals and as members of society.

From a social perspective, Becker (1971) proposed that cultural worldviews can be judged by the extent to which they provide for the material needs of their members within the confines of existing technology and resources, afford social roles with associated standards of desirable conduct that make self-esteem attainable for most citizens (at least in principle), and satisfy these material and psychological needs without undue harm to people in other cultures and damage to the natural environment. When cultures (inevitably) fall short of these standards, attention should be devoted to modifying cultural worldviews and the religious, economic, and political institutions derived from them. This should be done while accepting (with humility and determination rather than cynicism and despair; Niebuhr, 1932) that the threats can never be entirely eliminated (see Schneider, Chapter 19; and Erich Fromm's *The Sane Society*, 1955, for specific suggestions regarding childrearing, education, work, and democracy).

From an individual perspective, existentially based therapies address (in various fashions) the trauma of *ontological insecurity* (Laing, 1969)— apprehension about current circumstances in addition to deep-seated trepidation about life in general resulting from childhood anxieties (especially as aroused in the context of relationships with primary caretakers) and the eventual awareness of the inevitability of death. Reactions to these anxieties range from compensatory reactions of expansive grandiosity all the way to constrictive resignation. The common and primary goal of such therapies is "not so much to 'get rid of' a condition that is inherently human but . . . to help people to develop a new relationship to that condition" (Schneider, Chapter 19); that is, to gain a fuller experience of life while keeping existential terror at bay.

Toward this end, acceptance and commitment therapy (ACT; Hayes, Strosahl, & Wilson, 1999; Yovel & Bigman, Chapter 21) uses interventions similar to cognitive behavior therapy (CBT) but with an existential twist. Rather than typical CBT efforts to change thoughts, emotions, and desires, ACT recognizes the inevitability of human suffering and aims to enhance psychological and behavioral flexibility and efficacy by emphasizing freedom of choice. It acknowledges the importance of clarifying personal meanings and values and then acting in accordance with them by promoting acceptance and a state of being present derived from "the nonjudgmental, mindful experience of both internal and external events" (Yovel & Bigman, Chapter 21, p. 386). See also Levit Binnun, Kaplan Milgram, and Raz (Chapter 14) for a description of Buddhist mindfulness practices and a psychobiological account of how Buddhist and Western-based mindfulness programs reduce stress, anxiety, and depression and increase a sense of freedom and meaning.

Voice therapy (Firestone & Firestone, Chapter 20), derived from R. W. Firestone's (1997) separation theory (an integration of attachment theory and existential thought) involves recognizing and disposing of maladaptive aspects of one's mental self-talk and related behaviors rooted in childhood efforts to deny vulnerability and, ultimately, mortality. The goal is to identify critical, demoralizing, self-destructive inner "voices" by saying them out loud from a second person perspective, for example, "You are the lazy and ugly one—the one who should never have been born," rather than "I am lazy and ugly and should never have been born." A client in this kind of therapy usually recognizes where these attacks on self come from: They originally came out of the mouths of adults or other close relationship partners. Externalizing the attacks, understanding their origins, and discussing alternatives with a therapist allows a person to challenge them and eventually replace them with more directly experienced aspects of selfhood, increased self-compassion, and realistic self-regard. This kind of therapy acknowledges mortality but moves a person toward rewarding pursuits and relationships that make a finite lifetime worthwhile.

Awe-based psychology (Schneider, 2004; Chapter 19) also acknowledges the mystery and challenge of a finite life span but emphasizes the depth and mystery, the wonder, of existence. It cultivates being fully present in the moment (as does Buddhism), promotes humility and wonder, freedom and awe. Presence is similar to one of the Big Five personality traits, Openness to Experience (Costa & McCrae, 1992), facets of which include active imagination, aesthetic sensitivity, attentiveness to inner feelings, preference for variety, and intellectual curiosity. Freedom is the capacity for choice—recognizing and relishing the fact that one has choices, realizing that paralyzing indecision in light of one's options ("choking on choices"; see Schwartz, Chapter 15, for an account of how too much choice leads to behavioral paralysis, dissatisfaction with choices, and poor decision-making) is itself a choice (i.e., choosing not to choose), and accepting responsibility for one's choices. Awe is the exhilaration, wonder, humility, and sense of adventure—the ultimate joy of living that each of us experiences, and is sublimely appreciative of, in our finer moments.

CONCLUSION

> Science at its highest level is ultimately the organization of, the systematic pursuit of, and the enjoyment of wonder, awe and mystery. . . . Science can be the religion of the nonreligious, the poetry of the nonpoet, the art of the man who cannot paint, the humor of the serious man, and the lovemaking of the inhibited and shy man. Not only does science begin in wonder; it also ends in wonder.
>
> —Abraham Maslow, *The Psychology of* Science[6]

[6]Thanks to Jonathan Beyrak-Lev at the Interdisciplinary Center Herzliya for drawing my attention to this quotation.

The Fourth Herzliya Symposium on Personality and Social Psychology was a stimulating, productive collective cogitation on the social psychology of meaning, mortality, and choice. Thanks to Mario Mikulincer and Phil Shaver for assembling such a brilliant, lively, and diverse group of researchers and clinicians and for their thoughtful organization of the conference proceedings. Thanks also to the Psychology School and students at the Interdisciplinary Center Herzliya for their tactical support and enthusiastic engagement throughout the conference. It was a wonderful experience.

REFERENCES

Armstrong, K. (2000). *The battle for God: Fundamentalism in Judaism, Christianity, and Islam*. New York, NY: Knopf.

Arndt, J., & Solomon, S. (2003). The control of death and the death of control: The effects of mortality salience, neuroticism, and worldview threat on the desire for control. *Journal of Research in Personality, 37*, 1–22. doi:10.1016/S0092-6566(02)00530-5

Becker, E. (1971). *The birth and death of meaning; An interdisciplinary perspective on the problem of man* (2nd ed.). New York, NY: Free Press.

Becker, E. (1973). *The denial of death*. New York, NY: Free Press.

Becker, E. (1975). *Escape from evil*. New York, NY: Free Press.

Bowlby, J. (1982). *Attachment and loss: Vol. 1. Attachment* (2nd ed.). New York, NY: Basic Books.

Bruner, J. (1990). *Acts of meaning*. Cambridge, MA: Harvard University Press.

Costa, P. T., & McCrae, R. R. (1992). *NEO Personality Inventory professional manual*. Odessa, FL: Psychological Assessment Resources.

Cozzarelli, C., & Karafa, J. (1998). Cultural estrangement and terror management theory. *Personality and Social Psychology Bulletin, 24*, 253–267. doi:10.1177/0146167298243003

Donald, M. (1991). *Origins of the modern mind: Three stages in the evolution of culture and cognition*. Cambridge, MA: Harvard University Press.

Epstein, S. (1994). Integration of the cognitive and the psychodynamic unconscious. *American Psychologist, 49*, 709–724. doi:10.1037/0003-066X.49.8.709

Faulkner, W. (1936). *Absalom, Absalom*. New York, NY: Random House.

Firestone, R. W. (1997). *Combating destructive thought processes: Voice therapy and separation theory*. Thousand Oaks, CA: Sage.

Fritsche, I., Jonas, E., & Fankhänel, T. (2008). The role of control motivation in mortality salience effects on ingroup support and defense. *Journal of Personality and Social Psychology, 95*, 524–541. doi:10.1037/a0012666

Fromm, E. (1955). *The sane society*. New York, NY: Holt.

Gibson, J. J. (1979). *The ecological approach to visual perception*. Boston, MA: Houghton Mifflin.

Greenberg, J., Solomon, S., & Arndt, J. (2008). A basic but uniquely human motivation: Terror management. In J. Y. Shah & W. L. Gardner (Eds.), *Handbook of motivation science* (pp. 114–134). New York, NY: Guilford Press.

Hayes, J., Schimel, J., Arndt, J., & Faucher, E. H. (2010). A theoretical and empirical review of the death-thought accessibility concept in terror management research. *Psychological Bulletin, 136,* 699–739. doi:10.1037/a0020524

Hayes, J., Schimel, J., & Williams, T. J. (2008). Fighting death with death: The buffering effects of learning that worldview violators have died. *Psychological Science, 19,* 501–507. doi:10.1111/j.1467-9280.2008.02115.x

Hayes, S. C., Strosahl, K., & Wilson, K. G. (1999). *Acceptance and commitment therapy: An experiential approach to behavior change*. New York, NY: Guilford Press.

Heine, S. J., Proulx, T., & Vohs, K. D. (2006). The meaning maintenance model: On the coherence of social motivations. *Personality and Social Psychology Review, 10,* 88–110. doi:10.1207/s15327957pspr1002_1

Joyce, J. (1922). *Ulysses*. New York, NY: Penguin Books.

Laing, R. D. (1969). *The divided self: An existential study in sanity and madness*. Middlesex, England: Penguin.

Maslow, A. (1966). *Psychology of science: A reconnaissance*. New York, NY: Harper & Row.

Niebuhr, R. (1932). *Moral man and immoral society: A study of ethics and politics*. New York, NY: Scribner.

Pyszczynski, T., Greenberg, J., & Solomon, S. (1999). A dual-process model of defense against conscious and unconscious death-related thoughts: An extension of terror management theory. *Psychological Review, 106,* 835–845. doi:10.1037/0033-295X.106.4.835

Pyszczynski, T., Solomon, S., & Greenberg, J. (2003). *In the wake of 9/11: The psychology of terror*. Washington, DC: American Psychological Association. doi:10.1037/10478-000

Rappaport, R. A. (1999). *Ritual and religion in the making of humanity*. New York, NY: Cambridge University Press.

Routledge, C., Ostafin, B., Juhl, J., Sedikides, C., Cathey, C., & Liao, J. (2010). Adjusting to death: The effects of mortality salience and self-esteem on psychological well-being, growth motivation, and maladaptive behavior. *Journal of Personality and Social Psychology, 99,* 897–916. doi:10.1037/a0021431

Schneider, K. J. (2004). *Rediscovery of awe: Splendor, mystery, and the fluid center of life*. St. Paul, MN: Paragon House.

Stevens, W. (1923). Sunday morning. In W. Stevens, *Harmonium*. New York, NY: Knopf.

Tooby, J., & Cosmides, L. (1992). The psychological foundations of culture. In J. H. Barkow, L. Cosmides, & J. Tooby (Eds.), *The adapted mind: Evolutionary psychology and the generation of culture* (pp. 19–136). New York, NY: Oxford University Press.

van den Bos, K., & Miedema, J. (2000). Toward understanding why fairness matters: The influence of mortality salience on reactions to procedural fairness. *Journal of Personality and Social Psychology, 79,* 355–366. doi:10.1037/0022-3514.79.3.355

Webster, D. M., & Kruglanski, A. W. (1994). Individual differences in need for cognitive closure. *Journal of Personality and Social Psychology, 67,* 1049–1062. doi:10.1037/0022-3514.67.6.1049

Yalom, I. D. (1980). *Existential psychotherapy.* New York, NY: Basic Books.

INDEX

Attachment orientation, *continued*
  and mortality meanings, 40
  and personal growth with mother-
      hood, 172–173
Attachment security
  in adult attachment theory, 291–294
  in integrative perspective, 403–404
  in terror management theory, 21–22
  threats to, 49–50
Attachment-system activation
  and autonomy, 301–302
  and death awareness, 295
  and freedom, 301–302
  and meaninglessness, 297
  and threat of isolation, 299
Attachment theory, 291–303
  for adults, 292–294
  existential concerns in, 294–302
  and fantasy bond, 356
  internal working models in, 358
Attributions, causal, 153
Authenticity, 279–280
Authoritarian parenting style, 349
Authoritative parenting style, 349
Autonomy, 215–229
  and attachment orientation,
      301–302
  and choice, 276–279
  and defenses, 226–227
  and defensiveness, 227–228
  experimental bias, 228–229
  as functional form of willing,
      221–222
  in humanistic perspectives, 235
  and illusion of free will, 218–221
  and motivation, 224–225
  relative continuum of, 223–224
  in social psychology, 216–218
  and suicide, 271–273
Autonomy-supportive contexts,
    224–225
Aversion, risk, 113
Aversive experiences, 356, 385
Aversive internal events, 385–386
Avoidance
  attachment, 40, 118–119
  experiential, 383–385
  fearful, 293
  motivation for, 86–87
  of sensation, 256, 257–258

Awareness
  of constraints, 261–262
  of death, 75–78, 295, 404
  as motivation, 40–42
  of physical body, 94–95
  self-esteem as protection from, 59
Awe-based psychology, 348–350
Ayers, S., 168

Baillargeon, R., 131–132
Bandura, A., 247–248
Bardo, 43
Bargh, J. A., 216, 218–219
Bartholow, B. D., 23
Basler, R. P., 122
The Battle for God (K. Armstrong), 410
Bauman, C. W., 78
Baumeister, R. F., 84, 316
BCI (brain–computer interface), 103
Beautification, 105–106
Beck, A. T., 369
Beck, Glenn, 183
Beck, J. S., 367–369
Becker, Ernest, 18, 28, 31, 55, 56, 68,
      93, 94, 114–115, 184, 186–187,
      194, 199, 341, 364, 372, 402,
      403, 409, 413
Behavior
  as externally regulated, 222
  and free will, 221
  healthy vs. unhealthy, 62–63
  and nonbehavior, 312
  prosocial, 242–243
  sexual, 95–96
  suicidal, 325–326
  and voice attacks, 368
Being present, 386
Beliefs, global, 149–151
Belongingness, 328–330
Benjamin, L. S., 357
Ben Shlomo, S., 176
Berlin, I., 282
Bernieri, F., 248
Bhikku, T., 259–262
Bibi, A., 205
Big Five personality traits, 414
Bin Laden, Osama, 196
Biology, 264–266
Birnbaum, G., 49, 300

Developmental experiences. *See also*
    Child development
    patterns of, 176
    with self and anti-self systems,
        359–360
    self-esteem in, 56–58
    in separation theory, 353–354
Devlin, J. T., 220
Diamant, I., 205
Diminished well-being, 243
Direct controlling contexts, 236
Disabilities, people with, 255
Discrepancies, 153–154, 157
Disintegration anxiety, 341n1
Disorders, psychological, 383–385
Dissociation, 27–28
Distal approach, 204–205, 208–209
Distortion, 357
Distress, 153–154
Douglas, M., 188, 200
Down syndrome (DS), 135–136
Dreams, 343–344
DTA. *See* Death-thought accessibility
Dual-defense model, 21
Dualism, mind–body, 102–103
Dual process approaches
    autonomy in, 226–227
    to information processing, 136–138
    self-esteem thriving in, 62–63
Dunn, W., 256–258, 264
Durkheim, E., 271, 272, 277, 278

East Asian culture, 277–278
Edmondson, D., 145
EFT. *See* Emotion-focused therapy
Ego involvement, 222
Eilot, K., 242
Ein-Dor, T., 81, 115
Elliott, A. J., 226, 302
Elliott, R., 367
Ellison, R., 316
Embodied meditation, 345–346
Embodiment, 97–98
Emotion-focused therapy (EFT)
    for couples, 370–371
    and voice therapy, 367, 368
Emotion regulation, 241–242
Enemies. *See* Scapegoats and enemies
Engagement, 241

Entanglement, cognitive, 383
Entrapment, 331–332
Environment, 173, 204–205
Equanimity, 262
ERPs (event-related potentials), 23
Error-related negativity (ERN), 23–24
Escape from Evil (E. Becker), 18
Escape from Freedom (E. Fromm), 235,
    271
Eternal body, 102–103
Event-related potentials (ERPs), 23
Evilness, 186–187
Evolutionary theory
    group selection view of, 408n2
    mammalian females in, 98
    ostracism in, 313
Exclusion. *See* Ostracism
Excrement, 96–97
Existential concerns. *See also specific*
        headings
    in attachment theory, 294–302
    in case example, 344
    finitude, 38
    illusions of human existence as, 17
    in integrative perspective, 412–414
    and motivation, 83
    and resistance to change, 114–116
    and status quo justifications, 80–82
    in terror management theory, 217
Existential defense, 65–68
Existential–Humanistic Psychotherapy
        Over Time (film), 342
Existential-integrative approach,
        339–350
    awe-based reformation in, 348–350
    in case example, 342–347
    groundlessness in, 340–342
    and psychosocial well-being,
        347–348
Existentialism, 4–5
Existential motivation, 83
Expectancy, 134–135
Expectations, high, 275–276
Experiences. *See also* Developmental
        experiences
    aversive, 356
    coincidences in, 135–136
    nonsensory, 130–131
    from past, 259–261

424   INDEX

Motivation, *continued*
    for scapegoating, 186–188, 194–195
    self-esteem as, 61–65
    for terrorism, 206–208
Motives
    implicit vs. explicit, 226–227
    psychological, 30–31
Motyl, M., 97
MS. *See* Mortality salience
Multidimensional conceptualizations,
        38–40
Murphy, C., 38
Murray, S. L., 66

Narratives, 135–136
Narrow overstriving, 241
Nash, K., 86–87
Need for cognitive closure (NFC),
        117–119
Negative affect, 243
Negative conditional regard, 237–241,
        244–246
Negative liberty, 282
Negative self-views, 329
Networks, 206–209
Neurological systems, 266
Neurological thresholds, 255–258
Neuroscience, contemplative, 264–265
Neuroticism, 95, 98
NFC (need for cognitive closure),
        117–119
Niemiec, C. P., 228, 302
9/11 attacks. *See* September 11 attacks
Nolen-Hoeksema, S., 387
Nonbehavior, 312
Nonconscious thoughts, 62–63
Nonmonotonicity, 280–281
Nonsensory experiences, 130–131
Nonviable scapegoats, 188

Obama, Barack, 28, 183, 191, 196
Obedience, 341–342
Objectification
    beautification vs., 105–106
    as dehumanization, 100–102
    of women's bodies, 98
Obsessive–compulsive disorder (OCD),
        383–384
Occupational therapy, 255–258
Ogilvie, D., 48

Ogilvie, D. M., 60
Older people, 28–29
Ontological insecurity, 347–348, 413
"On Transience" (S. Freud), 114
Opponent-process theory, 327–328
Opportunities, missed, 275
Optical illusions, 219–220
Ostracism, 309–320
    in integrative perspective, 408–409
    and meaninglessness, 309–310,
        315–319
    role-play study of, 310–312
    theory of, 312–315
Other-oriented prosocial helping, 242
Others, internal working models of,
        292–293
Overload of choice
    and constraint, 278
    negative effects of, 282–283
    paralysis with, 273–276
Overstriving, 240, 241

PA (positive affect), 136–140
Pain, psychological, 382
Palin, Sarah, 102
Paltrow, Gwyneth, 100
Paralysis, decision, 273–274
Parental regard
    for academic achievement, 241
    and child well-being, 243
    conditional, 238–240
    and emotion regulation, 241–242
    negative conditional, 244
    and prosocial behavior, 242–243
    unconditional, 247–248, 404
Parents. *See also* Grandparents
    approval from, 240
    authoritarian or authoritative, 349
    factors enabling personal growth in,
        169–175
    in formation of child's anti-self sys-
        tem, 361–363
    in formation of child's self system,
        360–361
    permissive, 349
    personal growth of, 165–168
    and self-esteem, 56
    transition to parenthood by,
        163–168, 171

ABOUT THE EDITORS

Phillip R. Shaver, PhD, a social and personality psychologist, is Distinguished Professor of Psychology at the University of California, Davis. Before moving there, he served on the faculties of Columbia University, New York University, University of Denver, and State University of New York at Buffalo. He has coauthored and coedited numerous books and has published over 200 scholarly journal articles and book chapters. Dr. Shaver's research focuses on attachment, human motivation and emotion, close relationships, personality development, and the effects of meditation on behavior and the brain. He is a member of the editorial boards of *Attachment and Human Development, Personal Relationships,* the *Journal of Personality and Social Psychology,* and *Emotion,* and he has served on grant review panels for the National Institutes of Health and the National Science Foundation. Dr. Shaver received a Distinguished Career Award and a Mentoring Award from the International Association for Relationship Research and has served as president of that organization.

Mario Mikulincer, PhD, is professor of psychology and dean of the New School of Psychology at the Interdisciplinary Center in Herzliya, Israel. He has published five books and over 280 scholarly journal articles and book chapters. Dr. Mikulincer's main research interests are attachment theory, terror management theory, personality processes in interpersonal relationships, coping with stress and trauma, grief-related processes, and prosocial motives and behavior. He is a member of the editorial boards of several scientific journals, including the *Journal of Personality and Social Psychology*, *Psychological Inquiry*, and *Personality and Social Psychology Review*, and he has served as associate editor of two journals, the *Journal of Personality and Social Psychology* and *Personal Relationships*. Recently, he was elected to serve as chief editor of the *Journal of Social and Personal Relationships*. He received the EMET Prize in Social Science for his contributions to psychology and the Berscheid-Hatfield Award for Distinguished Mid-Career Achievement from the International Association for Relationship Research.